MY LIFE, OUR TIMES

GORDON BROWN

My Life, Our Times

THE BODLEY HEAD
LONDON

1 3 5 7 9 10 8 6 4 2

The Bodley Head, an imprint of Vintage,
20 Vauxhall Bridge Road,
London SW1V 2SA

The Bodley Head is part of the Penguin Random House group of companies
whose addresses can be found at global.penguinrandomhouse.com.

First published by The Bodley Head in 2017

Extract from 'The Road Not Taken' from *The Poetry of Robert Frost* by Robert Frost published
by Jonathan Cape. Reproduced by permission of The Random House Group Ltd.

Extract from 'The Ted Williams Villanelle' from *If I Don't Know* by
Wendy Cope (© Wendy Cope, 2001). Reproduced by permission of Faber and Faber Ltd
and by permission of United Agents (www.unitedagents.co.uk) on behalf of Wendy Cope.

www.penguin.co.uk/vintage

A CIP catalogue record for this book is available from the British Library

Hardback ISBN 9781847924971
Trade paperback ISBN 9781847924988

Printed and bound by Clays Ltd, St Ives plc

Penguin Random House is committed to a sustainable future for our
business, our readers and our planet. This book is made
from Forest Stewardship Council® certified paper.

For John and Fraser
and in memory of Jennifer

All Gordon Brown's proceeds from this book will go to the Jennifer Brown Research Laboratory and Theirworld children's charity.

CONTENTS

PREFACE: MY LIFE

Twenty years on from when I became Chancellor of the Exchequer, and ten from when I became prime minister, I feel the time has come now to look back and take stock: of what I was trying to do, and of what I got wrong as well as what I got right.

I started out in politics as an idealist with a strong, perhaps naïve, conviction of what needed to change in Britain.

Politics, I thought, was more than the art of the possible; it was about making the desirable possible.

Of course, there is always a tension between idealism and pragmatism. Over five decades I have learned that leaders need a command of substance, mastery of detail, problem-solving skills and an ability to see the big picture. But that is not enough: above all else, leaders need to communicate a positive vision of the future that can inspire and motivate people and mobilise their enthusiasm for progress and change.

I was fortunate to meet the greatest leader of our generation, Nelson Mandela, and then to get to know him quite well over his later years. He told me candidly that he himself was no master of detail. But he had developed in his years in prison a clear vision of a democratic, multiracial South Africa – a vision soon realised under his presidency, an achievement that astonished the whole world.

The night before he left prison in 1990, he assembled African National Congress comrades to tell them that the oppression they had suffered under apartheid and the violence inflicted on their communities, including torture and state-sponsored murder, might be seen as justifying acts of revenge. Then he was measured and blunt: if they retaliated, South Africa would descend into a bloodbath and peace would forever be impossible. Only by showing no bitterness and by championing reconciliation could they avert such a tragedy, and for the rest of his life he exemplified the ideal of peace without recrimination, most memorably in the way he, as South Africa's president, embraced the nation's predominantly white World Cup-winning rugby team, the Springboks.

Ideas as big as Mandela's are, of course, few and far between, but lesser ideas can still move the dial, shift the pace, often via incremental, unsensational steps, and transform our view of what is possible. Importantly, they can do so to best effect if they create hope for a better future.

I had long since read Barack Obama's book, *The Audacity of Hope*, before he first came to London as the newly elected president of the United States in April 2009. I was aware that a painting entitled *Hope* by the British artist George Frederic Watts had inspired the theme of his book, and I was able to offer it to him as an official loan from the Government Art Collection. It shows a lone blindfolded girl sitting on a globe and trying to play a lyre whose strings are broken. That painting reflects something he had written about, and which I deeply believe – that even in the most hopeless of situations we can, and must, seek grounds for hope.

We often depict hope, or rather its death, in the most dramatic terms – a refugee boat capsized at sea or a food convoy unable to enter a besieged town. But hope can die in very ordinary, and seemingly unspectacular, ways as well: young people denied the opportunities their parents' generation enjoyed and deciding there is nothing worth striving for; unemployed men and women feeling rejected and losing all sense of self-worth; older people alone, fearful, their health and mobility needs mounting and feeling no one seems to care.

Progressive political parties exist to deliver a message of hope. For without a foundation built on hope, parties may survive without distinction in the short-term, but are destined to fail with time.

Perhaps it took me too long to understand fully another essential dimension of leadership: that any idea, big or small, is of little significance until it can be communicated compellingly and in clear terms. I had the privilege of meeting Anthony Burgess at the Edinburgh Festival in the early 1980s. His novel *A Clockwork Orange* was released to critical acclaim in the UK in 1962, and his publisher sold the rights to the US. Then the American publisher decided to release the novel without the twenty-first and final chapter, and it was this attenuated version of the text that became the basis for Stanley Kubrick's 1971 film. From the moment he agreed to the US deal, Burgess anguished over the deletion of the final chapter. Chapters 1 to 20 told a tale of never-ending violence. But Chapter 21 was about redemption, about a young man who had gone off the rails suddenly finding, as he was about to become a father himself, that there was a better way to live. To his lasting regret, Burgess's vision of a more optimistic future never reached a wider audience.

In politics, you not only have to do what is right, but you have to convince the wider audience. In this book, I write of the greatest test that I faced as prime minister: the gravest financial crisis of our lifetime, and one which could have rapidly gone critical in the form of a sweeping global depression. That did not happen – and, through unprecedented cooperation worldwide in a plan for recovery, growth quickly returned, unemployment started to fall and people's savings were secured. But I wish that in the midst of all that I was doing to forestall a depression, I had been able to do more to lift confidence and to convey hope. And I regret to this day being unable to convince the British people that we had to finish the work of recovery by rebuilding our still unreformed and risk-laden financial system. That crisis and the response to it, in the form of the innovative G20 meeting in London in April 2009, are matters I will deal with in detail in some of the following chapters.

As I reflect on these events, I realise that leadership is not just about what to do but when to act: to see when history is turning and to know when to move and when to wait on events. Robert Frost's 1916 poem 'The Road Not Taken' is both familiar and haunting:

> Two roads diverged in a wood, and I –
> I took the one less traveled by,
> And that has made all the difference.

Frost later commented that the poem should not be taken as one about destiny; but his close friend the poet Edward Thomas, having read the poem, was inspired to volunteer for service in the British Army. Thomas died in the trenches after only two weeks in France. He had concluded that life brings momentous choices which, once taken, define your whole future.

In politics, you can never assume that the old ways will do. There are turning points when one course of action has reached its end, and when a new course must be charted. It requires judgement. Sometimes what is reported as good judgement is, in fact, simply good fortune. But, at other times, the opposite is true: it was said of Abraham Lincoln that, with his party sometimes a fragile coalition, and in the rapidly fluctuating political and military complexities as the Civil War raged and moved towards its climax, 'he never took a step too early or too late'.

Like most politicians, I cannot claim to have always seen the writing on the wall, good or bad. In my thirteen years in government there were many turning points, some fundamental, others less important. In the chapters that follow I write about times when it was right to act – from making the Bank of England independent in our first days in government in 1997; introducing tax credits to address child and pensioner poverty in 1999; refinancing the NHS with the biggest single tax rise in our history in 2002; and ushering in the biggest peacetime fiscal stimulus in 2009. And I write about times when it was right to step back, as when in 2003 we rejected the euro and in 2007 decided to exit Iraq.

I will also set out what I have learned about myself, and the kind of challenges that will face anyone on assuming leadership in today's world. The year 2007 may prove to have been the last year in which a Scot became prime minister of the United Kingdom; but I suspect that beyond that, in one respect at least, I may have been a politician out of season.

Politics is, in fact, surprisingly physical. A life in politics is one of thousands upon thousands of handshakes, one at a time, with eye contact often more important than words. I love campaigning. I love meeting people. I love not just the big rallies but the face-to-face encounters. I feel drawn to people – hearing their stories, listening to their ideas, putting myself in their shoes and learning from their comments and criticisms. I miss the local advice surgeries I held for constituents in ten different locations in towns and villages across my constituency. And I was as grateful for the kindness shown to me as I was for the occasional extreme frankness of fiercely egalitarian Fifers.

All this matters, because it is the ability to connect that influences whether or not people decide to believe in what you are trying to do and support you. Getting it wrong can be damaging, and getting it wrong on camera – or on tape – immensely damaging. President George H. W. Bush was caught on camera glancing at his watch in a 1992 town-hall debate with Bill Clinton, just as a citizen was asking how the economic downturn had affected him personally. It conveyed a vivid impression that he could hardly wait to get out of there.

But in recent years 'connecting' seems to increasingly include the public display of emotion, with the latter – authentic or not – seen as evidence of a sincerity required for political success. In a more touchy-feely era, our leaders speak of public issues in intensely personal ways, and assume they can win votes by telling their electors that they 'feel their pain'. For me, being conspicuously demonstrative is uncomfortable – to the point that it has taken me years, despite the urging of friends, to turn to writing this book.

I can look back on a time about half a century ago when leaders were deemed self-absorbed and even out of touch if they were constantly self-referential in public. And when I was asked why I was reluctant to talk about myself while other political leaders freely broadcast what they claimed to be their deepest feelings, I was always tempted to reply: why don't you ask them why they are always speaking about themselves? What mattered, I thought, was how others might benefit from what I did for them as an active politician – not what I claimed to feel. If in my political career I was backward in coming forward, my failure was not so much a resistance to letting the public in – I never shrank from that – it was resisting the pressure to cultivate an image that made the personal constantly public. Reticence was the rule.

All this came home to me at a time of unspeakable tragedy in our lives, when our daughter Jennifer died just days after her birth, and when, for the first time, my private emotions were thrust front and centre into the public arena. Sarah and I were hit by tragedy and I had never even thought of talking in public about such a private matter. But in that terrible moment, I learned a lot. I reflected on how I had been brought up: to contain, even suppress, my inner feelings in public, and to view the expression of them as self-indulgence.

That kind of self-restraint may now be a barrier in politics.

Today there are few leaders – Angela Merkel, notably, is one – whose claim to office is grounded primarily in an undemonstrative command of detail – unlike, say, Donald J. Trump. But while the German chancellor would criticise those who put spin over substance, even she has, perhaps unintentionally, created a nationally appealing image that is about more than hard work and sound decision-making. Her nickname is 'Mutti' – German for 'mummy'.

I fully understand that in a media-conscious age every politician has to lighten up to get a message across and I accept that, in the second decade of the twenty-first century, a sense of personal reserve can limit the appeal and rapport of a leader. Although some politicians thrust their children into the limelight – think of the unfortunate child filmed eating a beefburger to reassure the public at the height of the BSE drama – Sarah and I were determined to let our sons, John and Fraser, grow up so far as possible as normal children, not especially privileged. We agreed to publish only one photograph after each was born, and generally I am grateful to the newspapers for allowing them their privacy. Interestingly, after we left Downing Street some people wrote to me saying that they had not known I had any children until they saw the footage of our family leaving together – and the warmth they saw between us revealed something about me of which they had also been unaware.

I am not, I hope, remote, offhand or uncommunicative. But if I wasn't an ideal fit for an age when the personal side of politics had come to the fore, I hope people will come to understand from these pages that this was not an aloofness or detachment or, I hope, insensitivity or a lack of emotional intelligence on my part, but an inner sense that what mattered was not what I said about myself, but what our government could do for our country.

A new age of social media elevates public displays of private emotions even further. We can now see on our phones and laptops – and talk instantaneously with – countless people in all corners of the world whom we will never meet. And communication like this represents a huge advance for free speech and human rights: regimes may censor and even silence opponents, but not for ever – ultimately the truth will get out.

The three years that I was prime minister were at the cusp of the transition from the TV age to the Internet age. Now no politician can succeed without mastering social media – and yet, in it, the prime minister becomes one among millions of voices competing to be heard.

The Internet often functions like a shouting match without an umpire. Trying to persuade people through social media seems to matter less than finding an echo chamber that reinforces one's own point of view. Too often, all we are hearing is the sound of voices like our own. The turnaround is so instantaneous that, for the luxury of sounding off, we often forgo the duty to sit and think. And because differentiation is the name of the political game – showing what divides you from your opponent, not what you have in common – achieving a consensus in a wilderness of silos is difficult, if not impossible.

As we found, first during the Scottish referendum of 2014 and more recently in the European referendum of 2016, a rational, civil and objective dialogue can give way to a battle of taunts, slogans and ideologies. Worse, objective facts are lost in the escalation of division, culminating in the absurdities of post-truth politics.

I was born about forty years before the World Wide Web, and arrived in Parliament twenty years before the advent of Twitter. During my time as an MP I never mastered the capacity to leave a good impression or sculpt my public image in 140 characters. It is impossible to imagine Clement Attlee – notoriously terse and unforthcoming, yet the power behind Labour's transformation of Britain in the years 1945 to 1951 – remotely fitting in as a politician in our Internet age. Nor perhaps Margaret Thatcher, whose appeal was based on her determination and her ideology. Despite her strategists' best efforts to present her as the housewife balancing the nation's family budget, her stock-in-trade was her near-dogmatic certainty that she was right. I met Lady Thatcher on a number of occasions, and the very idea that she could contain her thoughts to 140 characters is preposterous. The Lady was not for tweeting. But I should have been.

Today's social-media focus on the 'me' and the 'now' may be obscuring a vital truth and another lesson I discuss in the pages that follow: that a leader succeeds only if he or she creates a talented and effective team. No matter the spin, leaders cannot succeed as a one-man – or one-woman – band, and they will fail unless those around them are convinced that they are working in a worthwhile cause.

One of the memorabilia in No. 10 is a piece of moon rock gifted by the Americans, and when I spoke to my staff I often highlighted John F. Kennedy's visit to what is now called the Kennedy Space Center in Florida, where he asked everyone there what they did. He talked to an engineer, a research scientist, a manager and several astronauts. Then he came to a lady who happened to be the cleaner. He asked her what she did. 'I'm helping put a man on the moon,' she proudly replied. She had been captivated by a strong sense of what a group of people could achieve by working together. And where I succeeded, I did so – and did so only – thanks to a loyal, dedicated and hard-working team, and the team spirit and sense of common purpose that we built.

My purpose in politics was getting things done. I start in the pages that follow with a description of an ordinary day in the life of a prime minister in office, and a scene-setting account of the forces at work that necessitated, challenged and complicated the work that we did.

In the subsequent chapters, I discuss how, during our time in government, we tried to reach for what Sarah called 'the high-hanging fruit' – tax credits to eradicate family poverty; Sure Start and Child Trust Funds to give every child the right to the best start in life; the New Deal on jobs to renew the idea of a full-employment Britain; the refinancing of the then down-at-heel but precious NHS; the pension credit to ensure even the poorest pensioner has dignity and security in retirement; and radical changes that, in different but often complementary ways, Tony Blair and I pioneered to drive opportunity in education and make our public services personal services too.

I write frankly about the tragic conflict and the post-conflict tragedy in Iraq, and the long and endlessly frustrating intervention in Afghanistan. I write too of the challenges of writing off unpayable African debt, of creating a G20 group of world leaders to revive the world economy, and of striving to deliver the radical changes I saw – and still see – as fundamental to the global financial order.

Where in my life and our times I made a difference, and where I fell short, is for the reader to decide.

INTRODUCTION

You do not usually wake up to news of four deaths of people for whom you feel responsibility; or to a newspaper allegation that you are corrupt; or to a denunciation by a predecessor.

Friday 8 May 2009 might seem at first sight an unusual day. It was tragic. But such were the dramas and controversies in my three years as prime minister that it was not so out of the ordinary: it was just part of the messy, untidy tapestry that defines the work of modern government and, in the case of a country permanently at war from 2001 to 2014, inevitably heart-rending too.

As was normal, I got up at around 5 a.m. and, as I tried to do on as many weekdays as possible, I ran for half an hour on the treadmill I had installed in the Downing Street flat we occupied at No. 11.

Before 6 a.m. I was at my desk in the downstairs, open-plan office we had created in No. 12 Downing Street. The No. 10 clerks brought me breakfast from Downing Street's basement café. I found throughout my thirteen years as chancellor and prime minister that an early start was the best way to prepare for the long day ahead. I used the time before the staff arrived to organise my thoughts for speeches, articles and the succession of meetings that usually occupied every hour of the working day when I was in No. 10 and the Treasury. Or, if I was about to travel on a visit out into the country or overseas, I could use the time to leave instructions on what needed to be done.

While I used a small private office to entertain visitors, I preferred to work from a desk surrounded by the private secretaries and political advisers. And that morning I was typing out changes and corrections to two important speeches I would make the following Monday and Tuesday. A speech was, for me, usually the culmination of a hundred drafts constantly rewritten, updated and refined. On Monday,

I would speak in Harrogate to the Royal College of Nursing Congress – I would be the first prime minister to address that prestigious nursing conference – and on Tuesday I would speak on law and order, and launch the next wave of our partnerships between the police and the public aimed at cutting crime. No Labour prime minister could be silent for long on how we sought to improve on our party's greatest achievement – the NHS, the most-loved institution of our country. And no prime minister of any party could fail to reinforce the message on law and order that the first duty of government was the security of the people.

But nothing can ever prepare you for what I was about to be told.

To end the previous day reading a note that there had been yet another death in the eight-year-old war in Afghanistan was wrenching enough. But to start the next day being told we had lost three more men in two further attacks – miles apart from each other in Afghanistan's Helmand Province – was not only heartbreaking: it was so shocking that they needed a full inquiry and explanation.

Sergeant Sean Binnie, who had been shot early on the Thursday, was from the Black Watch, 3rd Battalion, the Royal Regiment of Scotland. He had attended school in my home town of Kirkcaldy. I had gone to bed thinking of his wife who had just received the news of her husband's death at 4.15 that afternoon, and of a Scottish family who had lost their son. He had died from an enemy gunshot wound in a firefight near Musa Qala, a Taliban stronghold that we were now trying to control.

As the hours passed, further notes were put before me – tragic news from the front that three more brave men had died. I was to be told later that two soldiers – Sergeant Ben Ross of the Royal Military Police and Corporal Kumar Pun from the Gurkhas – had been murdered by a suicide bomber the night before while on routine patrol miles away in Gereshk. And late that Thursday evening, in yet another part of the province of Helmand – just outside a key stronghold, Sangin, where we had been taking heavy losses – a fourth soldier, Rifleman Adrian Sheldon, was blown up by the most common weapon the Taliban were deploying to murderous effect: an improvised explosive device which had been planted on the road ahead of the Jackal vehicle he was driving.

I recalled what the then Defence Secretary had said three years before, when we first moved in to protect Helmand: that we might leave without ever a shot being fired. Sadly, the opposite had happened: Helmand had turned into a killing field. Less than a month later, on 6 June 2009, I had these sacrifices in mind when I spoke on Normandy beach, with presidents Barack Obama and Nicolas Sarkozy, in commemoration of the sixty-fifth anniversary of D-Day. I was addressing our Afghan and Iraq heroes as well as our Second World War ones when I said that 'the threads of your lives . . . are already woven into the fabric of the world'. The losses hurt even more because we had left Iraq permanently a week earlier and were hoping that, with the end of one war and the redirection of resources to Afghanistan, we would begin to see a reduction in fatalities. In fact, we were to lose 456 of our best soldiers in Afghanistan by October 2015.

War seemed always with us. Lady Eden said of the Suez conflict in 1956, when we were up against President Nasser's Egypt, that she sometimes felt as if the Suez Canal was flowing through the No. 10 drawing room. During the three years I was prime minister, Lashkar Gah, Musa Qala, Kandahar, Sangin, Marjah and Nad-e Ali were names I woke up to most mornings as news of casualties on the Afghan front flowed in. Almost every day in the three years from June 2007 was filled with reports of death or woundings, raids or bombings, ebbs and flows – but mainly the ebbs of a conflict that even the mightiest armies of the world could not bring to a successful conclusion.

That day, as I digested the latest news I felt nauseous: I thought of the families across Britain – mothers, fathers, wives, sons and daughters – who were about to receive a visit; of the moment when the doorbell rings and they already sense the terrible news they are about to be told. I thought of the sheer chaos of war – the mud, the scratched gravel paths, the exposed roads that I myself had travelled on during many visits to the quagmire Afghanistan had become. Going through my head were the images of those dedicated young men, getting up that day, with no sense of the fate that would befall them. And then you think of their colleagues, now grieving because they will never see their friends again, but who have to dust themselves down and continue to put their own lives at risk. War is always grim and never truly glorious. And it is impossible to separate two emotions: the pride you have in the service our forces have given to the nation, and the sense of obligation you feel to ensure that young lives have not been sacrificed in vain.

We were at a delicate point in the Afghan war. Having identified the critical border between Afghanistan and Pakistan as the 'epicentre of world terrorism', we were waiting on an American decision by President Obama on a new troop surge in that area. An email I was reading that morning from Tom Fletcher, my diligent and highly intelligent foreign affairs private secretary, set out how we would prepare the ground with Pakistan's new president, Asif Ali Zardari, Benazir Bhutto's widower.

But, just at this point, I was also having to rebut an allegation by the *Daily Telegraph*. The night before, I had been alerted to questions from the *Telegraph* about a new series they were doing on MP's expenses. Until I saw the first editions, with the front-page photos of my brother and me under the headline 'The Truth About the Cabinet's Expenses', I did not know the full gist of their allegations. It turned out to be a fabricated charge that I was claiming House of Commons expenses to pay cash to my brother under the guise of submitting bills for cleaning my flat. The *Telegraph* had not bothered to check the real facts in the claims forms given to them by their whistle-blower: that all the money had gone to the cleaner; that these were expenses solely for cleaning my flat; and that all my brother and I had done was join together to pay her one lump sum to make sure she had enough overall income – when our two payments were taken together – to qualify for National Insurance and a state pension. There was nothing untoward in what we had done and everything we did was to keep our cleaner within the law.

The expenses crisis had been a slow-burner. Its roots lay in the Freedom of Information Act 2000, and the requirement that came into force in 2005 on public authorities to divulge, if asked, where money had been spent. With its introduction came the inevitable request for dis-closure of MP's expenses claims – what was received to cover food, accommodation and travel when on official business away from home. There had been court actions and parliamentary debates, including an attempt I had made to impose tougher new rules which MPs foolishly voted down. However, just as the authorities were preparing to release more information in the summer of 2009, the *Telegraph* was offered a computer disc containing the full files, with further details, paying

£110,000 to a whistle-blower. There then followed an entirely justifiable outpouring of public anger about out-of-touch and, in some cases, corrupt MPs who had let the country down.

After more than a quarter of a century in Westminster politics that had seen everything from suicides to sex scandals and stories of money in brown paper envelopes being passed to MPs in exchange for asking parliamentary questions, it was hard to be surprised any more. Yet, as the scale of wrongdoing by MPs on their expenses claims dawned on me, I felt angry and ashamed.

That morning I had in my email inbox a note done at midnight after a phone around of members of the Cabinet. We had asked them to agree to publish their complete expenses claims immediately. Most were happy to, but because two or three objected it was impossible to go ahead.

Some say that as prime minister I should not have been so deeply involved in what was a matter for the whole Commons and not just the government. But I was stunned by some of the over-the-top claims MPs had made. This new scandal went to the heart of an already threadbare trust in politics.

The Telegraph's article about me, however false, was a distraction on a morning when my attention was on the fallen soldiers. You think that you can put the episode down to politics – a right-wing paper choosing to hit at you simply because you are a Labour prime minister – and indeed that morning, as I flicked through the pages of the Telegraph, I found an opinion column carrying a highly personal attack on me from John Major. But it all leaves a terrible taste. Suddenly you must be on guard. My wife Sarah had inadvertently submitted the same receipt twice – making a double claim on a quarterly electricity bill. The money had immediately been paid back but the story also threatened to be headline news. In the atmosphere that was about to pervade Westminster, a small oversight could be magnified into a major offence.

At my instruction, members of my team spent most of Friday retrieving obscure documents to prove we were telling the truth about expenses claims that had been submitted years before. We even had to contact the cleaner, who had long since left our employment, and check her contract and National Insurance registration. We had to show that, while originally from the Philippines, she was a British citizen paying tax and National Insurance. Yet, whatever steps you take to clear your name, the mud sticks and the damage is done.

Keen to see an immediate correction of the *Telegraph*'s story, I asked to speak to its editor, Will Lewis. By the time the call from him came through I was on a train headed for Bradford. I was standing in the cramped space between two carriages that were bouncing up and down as passengers squeezed by on their way to the buffet bar. It seemed absurd that I was having to clear my name on a mobile phone halfway up the line to Yorkshire. I asked why I was the person they were choosing to target when there was nothing untoward in what I had done. 'It's because you're prime minister,' he said. 'We had to start at the top.' 'Even if there's nothing wrong?' I replied. They had to back down. On Sunday, an editorial in the *Telegraph*'s sister paper carried the headline 'Gordon Brown: no suggestion of impropriety'. On Monday, they had to publish a grudging correction described as a 'clarification'.

I was travelling to Bradford to be present at the unveiling of a memorial in honour of Sharon Beshenivsky, a local police officer who had been fatally shot at the scene of an armed robbery in 2005, aged only thirty-eight. In front of a large crowd which had assembled in the open air, I paid tribute to her as 'a wonderful wife, a wonderful mother, a wonderful servant of the community, a courageous woman'. Events as poignant as this move you to tears – the sacrifice of heroes like Sharon and the pain and resilience of the family she had left behind who were now struggling to get by. It was one of the most emotional moments of my prime ministership. The crowd fell silent when Sharon's ten-year-old son was introduced by his father and said he knew his mother 'would be very proud'.

I recall many instances of pride and emotion during the years I was in government. Almost all of them involved people who would consider themselves ordinary members of the public who had done extraordinary things. Families of the war dead came to Downing Street and Sarah and I talked with them about their losses. One or two had set up charities in honour of their loved ones and we tried to support their efforts. I recall too meeting cancer patients with only weeks to live who had asked to see me because they were determined to press for improvements in the treatment of others and so give meaning to the last days of their lives.

Some time before, I had visited one of the oldest surviving First World War veterans on the day of his hundredth birthday. He had been in the trenches at the age of seventeen and gassed in 1917. He had outlived all his children. And I will never forget the look I saw on the faces of those who were given long-overdue veterans' medals for their service in the armed forces. In my time in office I presented hundreds of such medals and had written a book of essays, *Wartime Courage*, that celebrated heroism and raised money for veterans' charities. The Bevin Boys – young men conscripted to work in the coal mines after 1943 – were also recognised, the first official acknowledgement of what they had done for their country. Perhaps most moving of all was the joyous reaction of now elderly women, who in the Second World War had served in the Women's Land Army, coming to Downing Street to finally receive medals that honoured a unique but previously unheralded contribution during 'our finest hour'.

If my visit to Bradford had been to commemorate and honour the past, my next visit of the day to another Yorkshire city, Sheffield, was all about the future – performing the opening ceremonies for some of our newest educational investments: an academy school and a Sure Start children's centre. My good friend Ed Balls, our dynamic and reforming Children's Secretary, himself an MP for a Yorkshire constituency who had worked with me since my days as shadow chancellor, was present for both. Before formally opening the £27 million new academy in Sheffield, I walked in on a GCSE maths class – joking about the training I might have benefited from in their subject before being chancellor – and then chatted to pupils during their art lessons and watched budding musicians in the school's recording studio. After this, visiting the superbly equipped play facilities at the Aughton Early Years Centre, Ed and I marked the opening of what was now the 3,000th Sure Start children's centre under our government. I talked of the 'real and lasting impact they can have on families by providing them with services which can transform children's lives'.

On my way out of the city, I visited one of Sheffield's oldest businesses, Sheffield Forgemasters, whose steel-exporting business was threatened by the recession. The night before, Christina Scott, an incredibly diligent private secretary who went on to become governor of Anguilla, had sent me an email which summed up the state of the steel industry: 'Corus's Teesside plant is under threat from closure, with an announcement as early as tomorrow, with the potential loss of up to 3,000 jobs (and up to 8,000 in the supply chain).' Luckily, we managed to head off these redundancies but only until December that year. I was, however, able to offer Forgemasters an £80 million government loan, a lifeline later rescinded by the incoming coalition government.

As I travelled back from Sheffield, I read another email prepared that afternoon by Tom Fletcher about talks the next week involving all the Northern Irish parties, as well as the Taoiseach, Brian Cowen. The Good Friday Agreement was a historic achievement delivered, to his great and enduring credit, by Tony Blair. But in spite of the peace settlement – and perhaps also because of it – Northern Ireland was on the prime minister's desk every day, every week and every month, and even ten years on it was a never-ending negotiation.

Progress on the devolution of policing and justice – the final part of the Northern Ireland peace process – had stalled. While Westminster had legislated for the transfer of powers to a new justice ministry, the parties could not agree on who was to be the minister. The Democratic Unionist Party (DUP) had dug in and said they would never allow Sinn Féin to occupy the Justice Ministry. This blanket rejection put the whole agreement in jeopardy. After a period of successful cooperation between the First Minister Ian Paisley and Martin McGuinness, the Deputy First Minister, the new First Minister Peter Robinson and McGuinness rarely talked. Just a few weeks before, in March, at Massereene Barracks, two off-duty British soldiers had been shot dead and four people were seriously wounded. This tragic and depressing outbreak of violence reminded me once again of what Churchill had said nearly a century before: that God is always crying over Ireland. We knew that while officially the men of violence were reported to be in the low hundreds, the real figure was closer to 1,000. Shaun Woodward, our ever-vigilant and effective Northern Ireland Secretary, feared that, amid recriminations and bitterness at the top, Northern Ireland was descending yet again into ungovernability. In our view, the first step away from this was for the Alliance Party to take the Justice Ministry. My task was to lead all parties towards an agreement on this.

I knew the negotiating formula from my time as chancellor. As usual, if there was to be a deal, everything had to be agreed, or nothing was agreed. Matters already on the agenda included – from the DUP – a new Parades Commission, a gratuity for thousands of part-time Reserves in the Royal Ulster Constabulary, a Police Museum and a bailout of the crisis-hit Presbyterian Mutual building society. And – from Sinn Féin – there were demands for a new Bill of Rights, support for the Irish language and pardons for past offences.

The DUP negotiating tactic was one I was familiar with. When I met Peter Robinson, he would say, 'But have you talked to Nigel Dodds? He has some real worries.' And then when I met Nigel Dodds, the deputy leader, he would say, 'You have to talk to Jeffrey Donaldson,' now chief whip, who then referred me to Sammy Wilson, another senior DUP figure, who had been finance minister. And so it went on: never one negotiation but round after round of negotiations. No side felt the need to be pushed into a final decision on any one day; each calculated that they could gain more if they could hold out for many days. And yet almost as quickly as the two sides could walk out on each other, they could band together when it came to money. There was a famous story of the eighteenth chancellor visiting Ireland whose Treasury red box had blown open in a blast of wind, only to reveal he had nothing in it. No modern chancellor or prime minister could go to Belfast empty-handed and survive. As I joked with our team, referencing Tony Blair's famous remark before the Good Friday Agreement: 'I feel the hand of history on my shoulders, and the hand of Peter Robinson in my pocket.'

I was dealing with another issue that, through a catalogue of errors, had become an embarrassment – the failure to accord Gurkhas a right of residence in the UK. This had sparked a campaign led by the actress Joanna Lumley, whose father had served as a regular officer with the Gurkhas. It was not lost on me that yet another Gurkha, loyally serving our country, had just been killed in Afghanistan by a suicide bomber. The Gurkhas' campaign was the inevitable result of a misguided decision to restrict a right to residence only to those who had finished service after 1997. Consumed with the financial crisis, Iraq and Afghanistan, I had given the issue too little attention and the Home Office was worried about a surge in immigration if all the Gurkhas and their families could settle in Britain. I had not altered our position in time for a Commons vote, which we lost. But when I had met Joanna on the Wednesday of that week, I had resolved that a change of policy was right.

I was now looking at an email from Joanna saying, 'I wish we could have met sooner.' Sadly, her supportive public and friendly private statements – and my relief that we were finally close to a solution – were undermined overnight when, unknown to me, Home Office letters prepared days before rejecting appeals from Gurkhas to enter the country, had landed on their doorsteps. So, as I returned from Yorkshire, I was having to pick up the pieces after a wave of hostile coverage. I was at least philosophical enough to remark that the over-whelming level of public support for the Gurkhas showed it was possible to persuade millions of the positive benefits of immigration. Within two weeks our new policy was announced. The Home Office had estimated that applications from soldiers, wives and children could go as high as 100,000. In the event, only 8,000 applied.

By Friday evening I was back in Downing Street. Between making and taking phone calls from foreign leaders about the continuing fall-out from the financial crisis and reviewing what might be recom-mended by the new Calman Commission for extending the powers of the Scottish Parliament, I held a strategy session on our election plans for June. In normal times, 8 May would have been the day after the local counts, but polling had been postponed so that local elections would coincide with those for the European Parliament. The month's grace looked, on the face of it, like a small stroke of luck.

In April, we were caught up in a storm that led to the resignation of one of my political advisers, Damian McBride. He had been a car-eer civil servant in the Customs and Excise Department who had worked his way up on sheer ability to become a Downing Street media adviser. But on his own admission, in emails that he never expected to become public, he had smeared the Tory leadership with salacious personal attacks repeating gossip that had no basis in fact. After his resignation, he wrote a very honest and penitent book blaming only himself for what he called 'the power trip' he had been on; and to his credit he then spent two years working in his old secondary school and then another few years helping CAFOD, a world-renowned Catholic development charity.

The grace period of four weeks saw things go backwards rather than forwards. I had thought our handling of the financial crisis would help us. In April, just before the McBride email fiasco, we had overseen a successful G20 summit in London, where – with Barack Obama, Angela Merkel, the Chinese premier Wen Jiabao, the UN secretary general Ban Ki-moon and others present – leaders had agreed to a British-initiated plan to underpin the world economy with $1.1 trillion of financial support. Now, in a series of phone calls in advance of meetings we would have at July's G8 in Italy, I was trying to persuade leaders of the world's main economies that we needed a second-stage push on growth. With a boost from the London agreement, the global economy was finally starting to turn around. But by then the Conservative opposition, who had been silent on the economy during the G20, mounted an escalating set of attacks.

For them, the issue was no longer UK jobs and growth – growth, although returning, was still fragile – but the UK deficit. I was still worrying about the threat of unemployment, mortgage repossessions and bankruptcies, which had been graphically brought home to me on Friday by the threat of another steel-industry closure. Yet now I was being asked all the time not about jobs – the media had virtually lost interest in that – but about the deficit and debt. Try as I did, I could not persuade the public that running a deficit at this time was critical to – and indeed the precondition of – sustained growth and continuing recovery from the recession, and therefore entirely rational. Neither could I persuade the Americans to join in the more radical pro-growth initiatives I was lobbying for as the agenda for September's forthcoming Pittsburgh G20 summit. In April, coming out of the G20 London summit, we had thought we were winning the argument about how best to rescue our economy. By that Friday evening in May, I feared we were losing it.

At the end of the day, Kirsty McNeill, my ever-alert and insightful adviser and speechwriter, who was always up to date on the concerns of the day, sent me a poem by the English poet Wendy Cope, a widely tipped contender to become Poet Laureate. It is a morality tale based on a tribute to the American baseball star, Ted Williams, and includes the lines:

> Watch the ball and do your thing.
> This is the moment. Here's your chance.
> Don't let anyone mess with your swing.

Thinking ahead – perhaps to what I might say in my next speech – I replied: 'Brilliant poem. We need a British version of it. Perhaps the image is – Don't let anyone turn our strength into a weakness.'

As prime minister, Disraeli found time not just to read poetry but to write it. Gladstone disappeared for weeks to translate Homer. Even amidst the carnage of the First World War, Asquith played long after-dinner games of bridge, and spent hours of his day writing love letters to a young nurse, with whom he was infatuated and who, to his desolation, eventually married one of his Cabinet colleagues. Even amidst the fiercest of fighting in the Second World War, Churchill was famous for his morning drinks and afternoon naps. Such was the leisurely pace of government even in the early 1960s that Harold Macmillan had time to read the works of Austen, Trollope, Scott, Dickens and Thackeray.

As my diary of Friday 8 May reveals, none of that was now possible. What was new was the 24/7 news cycle; the speed at which, in this media-conscious age, decisions have to be made; the minute-to-minute focus on every aspect of a prime minister's life; and an expectation that, even if every problem does not land on their desk, it is they who must respond. To the outsider, what I describe will look like a work schedule not only packed to breaking point, but with a pace that seems breathless, a weight and breadth of issues that is difficult to comprehend, yet alone control, and a speed at which you have to work and make decisions that almost defies belief. And although every day was different, this was not an abnormal day. Simply to recount the events of that day may give the impression that, as prime minister, I was overwhelmed. This was not how I felt at all. I relished everything – the meetings, the speeches, the preparatory reading, the strategising – and I felt in command, with one exception: my public communication.

The world had changed dramatically since the time Winston Churchill spent twenty-one days away from London in the White House, or since the time embarrassing details of a presidential visit to the UK could go without comment – when, for example, John F. Kennedy arrived in London to visit Harold Macmillan and the prime minister was not waiting to greet him but in bed asleep. The president was parked in a waiting room and given a copy of *The Times* to read while he waited for Macmillan to dress. Today, if there was but a minute's blip in the scheduling of a presidential visit, TV reporters outside would be declaring a crisis and the prime minister would be ridiculed – in the case of a Macmillan-type incident, told he was too old and worn

out to retain office. But that day – and for years after – no one even
knew that the prime minister had slept in. How things had changed.
Each time I met President Obama, as I recount, every aspect of our
encounter – the number of minutes we spoke, the time given to the
press for questions, the length and warmth of the handshakes, even
the presents we exchanged – was the subject of extensive reporting.

Of equal significance is the speed at which decisions have to be
made and communicated. When in 1949 the Labour government made
its decision to devalue the pound, it set its announcement for three
months ahead, so that the chancellor, Sir Stafford Cripps – then hos-
pitalised in a Swiss sanatorium – could be informed in person. If a
Cabinet today delayed announcing such a sensitive decision for more
than a few hours, or even just a few minutes, markets would be in
turmoil. More likely someone would have tweeted the decision within
seconds of it being made.

In this media-drenched world of the twenty-first century, prime
ministers must be on guard all the time, ready to react and comment
on a multiplicity of daily events, ranging from the most important to
the most trivial. Unless you can offer a view on each and every issue
of the day, you are immediately accused of indecisiveness. Your views
are not just sought on political issues: you are pushed to venture
opinions on sport, films, theatre, pop groups and even the soap operas
that dominate evening TV. I was uniquely unqualified to comment
on all of these subjects – with the exception of football. Indeed, on
that Friday morning in May 2009, an article I had penned appeared
in the *Independent* on my joy at the successes of my family's two
favourite local football teams, Raith Rovers, whom I support, and
Cowdenbeath, my father's team.

But when I ill-advisedly ventured an opinion on any other aspect
of popular culture, it usually backfired. I learned this the hard way
when, just before I became prime minister, a casual question turned
into a PR disaster. At the end of an interview for *New Woman* magazine there was a round of quick-fire questions. One was: did I prefer
the Arctic Monkeys to James Blunt? Not knowing much about either,
I said I preferred Coldplay, but added: well, the Arctic Monkeys would
certainly wake you up in the morning. That throwaway remark led
to a political storm: 'Brown gets up to Arctic Monkeys' the papers
wrote, at which point all hell broke loose about me trying hard to

present myself as someone I was not. A myth was born and years later I would chuckle when invited to present a lifetime achievement award to the group.

The mystery of monarchy – and the success of what is called the dignified part of our constitution – is built on the Queen never venturing an opinion: indeed, the magic of monarchy is that no one really knows what the Queen thinks. But the modern prime minister has to have a view on everything and can never keep silent for long.

This book is not only about the cacophony of decisions, crises and everyday rhythms of politics that I am describing through the kaleidoscope of one day's events. It is about the great underlying questions that marked all my thirteen years in office. Across all the separate issues during my years in politics, I believe there is a common thread: a modern battle for Britain.

At first and in the main, the task has been to build a prosperous and fair country. The question we come back to all the time is: what kind of Britain do we want to create? But at both the outset and in the twilight of my time, the questioning has been of a more existential nature. When I was first politically active, the overriding issue was the decline of Britain. Now, fifty years on, the issue is the very survival of the United Kingdom. Then we were dealing with the fallout from the end of empire and how Britain could reposition itself. Today we are threatened with the unravelling of the Britain we know – literally whether we can survive as one country – which was an unthinkable prospect just a generation ago. For increasingly there was, and is, something else that has clouded our public life and had to be confronted: the long shadow cast by the rise of nationalism.

Every country depends for its sense of identity on a story about itself, a narrative that draws on history and reminds us of who we are and why we belong together. I have witnessed and indeed been part of many attempts to construct a post-imperial story, one that gives definition and purpose to a Britain rediscovering itself after two centuries of global hegemony.

It was once said that in the Britain of the 1950s we managed decline, in the 1960s we mismanaged decline, and in the 1970s we declined to manage. It was this narrative, and the recognition we needed to change, which set the context for our application to join the European Economic Community, the rise of Mrs Thatcher, the advent of New

Labour and the controversy over two political unions: Scotland's place in the United Kingdom, and Britain's place in the European Union. At different times, governments have tried to renew Britain by elevating the UK–US special relationship, asserting leadership in Europe, pioneering a monetarist revolution, and by creating a New Labour for a New Britain.

By far the largest of the European empires, the British Empire also defined Britain's identity and it follows that its end strained the bonds forged in the centuries-long historical experience that Scotland shared with England. As I can see from living in Fife, our sense of who we are is becoming more and more localised and inward-looking, even as our range of experience is becoming more and more global. The last thirty years have seen an explosion of interest in Scottish, as distinct from British, history. Scotland is in the process of rewriting its own story, and the same is true of England and Wales. In a world which is at the same time more globally connected and more locally focused, to be British seems to many less relevant.

Today's battle for Britain is not being fought out on the old terrain of empire, the Industrial Revolution, two world wars, or a country that once confidently felt it was sufficient unto itself. Instead Britain has been, and is being, reshaped by three great forces: wave after wave of globalisation; the neoliberalism with which our economy was managed, or more accurately mismanaged; and the struggle of progressive politics to offer an alternative. These forces drive and explain the day-to-day comings and goings. They conditioned the decisions we made in government – and they will impact the quality of life for generations to come.

This account of my time in public life tracks how we were influenced by, and how we sought to influence, globalisation; how we tried to swim against the neoliberal tide; how we developed and advanced a progressive view of Britain and sought to make the Labour Party a credible and radical instrument of change.

Time and again, in each generation, we see power accumulate, vested interests entrench and seize too much control – and the historic task of political leadership is to stand up and tackle selfish concentrations of power, whether business elites forming cartels or monopolies; pressure groups adopting restrictive practices; and – especially – in this age of mega-wealth, individuals who abuse their financial might to manipulate government to their own narrow advantage. The task of leadership is to discover where power lies, to ask how justified it is and, where it is unjustified, rein it in.

In our time, overhanging all else has been the most dramatic global economic transformation the world has ever seen – an economic revolution that has been 1,000 times faster and deeper than the Industrial Revolution. Globalisation triggered a decades-long transition to a predominantly knowledge and financial-services economy, in which the pace of change constantly accelerates. It is now well understood that globalisation – the opening up of global capital flows and the global sourcing of goods and services previously manufactured here – has created millions of winners who have better-paid jobs, higher standards of living and more material possessions than ever before. But it has also created millions of losers whose skills and wage expectations cannot compete with cheaper labour economies. We have seen occupations that employed millions – from secretaries, clerks and typists to miners, ironworkers and shipwrights – virtually disappear. Traditional jobs like boilermakers, draughtsmen and electricians – and some of the newest, such as radiologists, computer operators and financial analysts – are repeatedly being reconfigured by technology. Since the 1980s, this has destroyed one third of our manufacturing jobs, challenged us to adapt to modern technology, opened a wider gulf between rich and poor than society should tolerate, and sown seeds of insecurity even among professional workers in well-paid jobs.

It is hardly surprising that in the old industrial communities, people complain, indeed cry out, that the country is not what it was, that it no longer belongs to them, that it is no longer theirs. Understandably, they want someone, somehow to protect them from what they see as akin to a runaway train.

Taming globalisation – and redirecting it to meet the interests of working people – has been and is the defining political challenge of our era. But for progressives the task has been doubly difficult: year after year, we have had to confront what is best described as neoliberalism. Even now, many of the public have never heard of the term; but, starting out from attempts to control the money supply in the 1980s, versions of it gained credence when Keynesian economics and the corporatism it spawned appeared exhausted and unable to cope with inflation. When neoliberalism was dishonestly cast as analogous to prudent family budgeting, celebrated as an economic expression of what it is to be free and packaged in a public form as 'popular' share-owning capitalism, it had a more compelling appeal than it deserved – at least for a time. Over four decades, versions of it – from the failed monetarist experiment to austerity – were often dressed up in communitarian clothes, whether it be John Major's Citizen's Charter, David Cameron's Big Society or Theresa May's civic conservatism.

Throughout my years in Parliament, we were up against what it really meant – to liberalise, privatise, deregulate and tolerate high levels of unemployment as the price for keeping inflation down. Not only did privatisation replace nationalisation – as in telecommunications and railways – but the radius of market influence expanded into areas like education, healthcare and even defence, often sweeping all before it. In its unbridled form this state-shrinking, tax cutting, free-market fundamentalism meant, for many people, the pain of unemployment, poverty and being left behind.

Markets may be a good servant – but, in my view, they are not such a good master. They can and must be made accountable. The progressive measures Labour introduced – from our New Deal funded by a windfall tax on utilities to restoring recession-hit Britain by stemming business bankruptcies, mortgage repossessions and job losses – were our alternative to that neoliberal ideology and an attempt to make globalisation work in the interests of the British people. We were determined to show in practice that, in mastering the challenges and opportunities of an open global marketplace, we could deliver both a strong economy and a fair society; that prosperity and social justice were not at odds with each other but inextricably bound together. In these pages, I recount what we did, in good times and bad, to try and promote a high-employment economy and a more equal country. I also tell why, in a world where a country's freedom of manoeuvre is constrained by global trends, events and pressures – where, in effect, our independence is now limited by our interdependence – there is a ceiling to what can be achieved without cross-border cooperation and coordination.

This book is also a lesson in how the fortunes of a progressive party can rise and fall. All throughout my thirty-two years in Parliament, and in the years since, the question the Labour Party has had to answer has been: can it be trusted with the economy? During the post-war years, every economic expedient in sight was tried in turn – tariffs, wage controls, national plans and social contracts, as well as full-blooded monetarism – but none prevented us falling down the international league table as other countries moved up. Neoliberalism held sway for a time because it offered a simple framework within which to understand the bewildering changes summed up in the word 'globalisation'. I write here of how we set out new approaches and how they succeeded or failed.

And from the vantage point of the second half of the second decade of the twenty-first century, we see that Britain's fundamental challenges are closely linked: the struggle to manage globalisation in Britain's interests is also the struggle to define Britain and its place in the world – and, indeed, hold Britain together. Economic pressures wrought by globalisation not only make people worry about what they have, but also about who they are and what might become of them.

Certainly we celebrated and continue to celebrate great triumphs in our recent history: from Churchill's wartime indomitability and our gallant VC and GC heroes to all the great British post-war medical breakthroughs – from being the first country to produce a test-tube baby to transforming X-ray technology with magnetic resonance imaging. And no one growing up in my generation can forget that Britain gave the world the Beatles, the Rolling Stones, years of pop-music dominance and great British Oscar-winning films from *Chariots of Fire* to *The King's Speech*. We rightly boast of our leadership in art, classical music and literature. Britons have won ninety-five Nobel Prizes since 1945. So much of the new world we live in has been created by great Britons I have had the privilege to know such as Tim Berners-Lee, inventor of the World Wide Web, Jony Ive, designer of many iconic Apple products such as the iMac, iPod, iPhone and iPad, and the world-famous writer and philanthropist J. K. Rowling. We are equally right to have celebrated days of triumph from the Falklands conflict to the Queen's Jubilee and then London's Olympic Games. We can take pride in how empire became Commonwealth; how British ideals of tolerance, democracy and respect for human rights became a guiding light around the world; how Britain has led international development for the poorest countries; and how British institutions, like the BBC and its World Service, reach and are respected on every continent.

Our post-war history is adorned with glittering achievements, but throughout my life, I have been aware of a gnawing sense within our country that we have fallen from a great height. With typical hyperbole, Boris Johnson, Foreign Secretary at the time of writing, described the scale of our influence as a country in a way that foreshadows the extent of our decline: 'Of the 193 present members of the UN, we have conquered or at least invaded 90 per cent of them – 171,' he said. A country that oversaw an empire that held in its hand the destiny of one quarter of the human race now seems in retreat even from its nearest geographical neighbours in Europe.

During the first half of my life a whole industry developed around explaining and lamenting our perceived decline. 'Declinology' – the search for what and who was to blame – led us to focus, in a painfully self-conscious and often self-defeating way, on allegations of 'poor' productivity, 'amateurism' in management, 'rampant' trade union power, 'suffocating' corporatism, and 'restrictive' entanglements with Europe. An objective view would remind us that, as the rest of the world converged, a first mover – the Britain that had led the Industrial Revolution – was bound to see others catch up. As America is now finding, the hegemony of one state can be temporary and transient. David Frost, the late journalist and television host, once joked that the newspaper banner 'England collapses before lunch' was not just the familiar headline reporting another batting failure of the England cricket team, but a caption that would not have been out of place when the pound crashed, the stock market tumbled, or our 'stop-go'-prone economy succumbed again to recession.

We, in Labour, took a different view which did not dwell on the reality of relative decline but looked to building a New Britain fit for a new age. We would change Labour so that Labour could change Britain. Persuading the party to change was often a daunting and wearing task, but as an American writer put it, 'If you are not willing to spill blood between elections, you'll spill it on election day, and it'll be yours.'

We were not the first to talk of a New Britain and we will not be the last. It was a theme of turning-point elections in 1964, 1979 and then for us in 1997. The sense of decline was not our theme but it was the backdrop: we would not have needed a New Britain if the old Britain had not faltered. The modern politics of America is also replete with the word 'new' – from the 1930s 'New Deal' to John F. Kennedy's 'New Frontier' and Bill Clinton's 'New Covenant'. Obama was presented as new both in relation to the Republicans and his Democratic opponents. But the 'new' in America is quite different from the 'new' in Britain. 'New' for America means moving on from one successful but passing era to another. 'New' in Britain means breaking out from a troubled past.

The contrast between Britain and America is even more apposite when we consider not just the different implications of the word 'new' but what each country has understood by the word 'change'. Growing up, I like others witnessed the power of the idea of change with John F. Kennedy – 'the torch has passed to a new generation' – and, as an MP, with Bill Clinton's summons to 'make change our friend and not our enemy'. This is a time-honoured political appeal that Barack Obama took to a new height with 'change we can believe in'. In America, changing from the old to the new is about a self-confident nation leading the world in adapting to new times. But in Britain change was required not just because we, like America and every nation, needed to rise to meet the challenge of new realities. Our country needed to change not because we wanted to abandon tradition, but because we had to stop falling behind.

By 1997, Britain was tired of, and ready to move on from, the neoliberal experiment. In the 1970s and 80s, it was fashionable to talk of the evils of collectivism – to lament the ever-increasing power of the trade unions and the state – and to salt criticism with horror stories about red tape, bureaucracy, corporatism and the public sector crowding out the private sector. By the 1990s, Britain was suffering – according to any opinion poll – from an inflation-prone economy, a shrinking industrial base, run-down public services and an outdated twentieth-century infrastructure that left us ill-equipped for the twenty-first century.

If the Tory view had been that we had too much state and too little market, the Labour view was we had too little investment, too little fairness, too little social cohesion and too little community. But we were not posing the old collectivism against Tory individualism; we were calling for a new kind of common purpose. We felt we were in that part of the cycle described by the American historian Arthur

Schlesinger, when the pendulum swings towards progressive politics. And on the global stage, we countered the Conservatives' turn from Europe towards isolationism with a vision of international cooperation. This made sense of a post-Cold War world where Russia was throwing off Communism, a post-analogue world where the digital revolution was sweeping all before it, and a post-insular world where globalisation seemed to bring more opportunities than risks. Not surprisingly, Tony Blair's eloquent summons to 'a new dawn' captured people's imagination. At our best, we in Labour viewed ourselves as applying enduring ideals to a new world.

But Britain did not want change for its own sake or merely as a symbol: 'Cool Britannia', one of the slogans of the day, is now best remembered for a raucous party of celebrities at No. 10. And after £1 billion spent on the Millennium Dome to welcome in the year 2000, the night is best remembered not for some new affirmation of Britishness but for a queue of newspaper editors unable to get to their plastic chairs in time to hear the clock strike midnight.

Things like this stood in sharp contrast with the authenticity of Danny Boyle's opening ceremony for the 2012 Olympics. It was a shining display of a Britain that honoured liberty, fair play and social responsibility. While the Conservative culture minister – now the health minister – complained that there was 'too much NHS, too little armed forces', the tribute to nurses, doctors and a health service free to all captivated the world.

Britishness is not a simple idea because ours is a multinational state where four distinctive nations, with their own distinct cultures, have to find a way of living together. But it cannot be grounded just in institutions, no matter how ancient and prestigious. I used to recite a joke about our institutions when they were accused of underperforming: 'Don't worry, the first 500 years of any British institution's history are always the most difficult.' Even our pride in the longevity of our institutions is not enough to bind us closely together if the values that shape them are not widely shared.

For all the time I was in government, I was also acutely aware that we could not base our Britishness on ethnicity either: we are not only a multinational country, but a diverse one. Nor could we be a united country if some claimed to be more British than others or claimed that patriotism was their preserve and theirs alone. If we fell back on ethnicity as the foundation of national identity we would quickly be divided up into English, Scottish, Welsh and Northern Irish. So I tried to root our sense of Britishness in the values we – all four nations – shared in common. This I believed was the only way to win the battle for Britain against nationalist pressures that have risen not only in Scotland and Wales but, more recently, in England as well, where the 'take back control' movement was undoubtedly central to us leaving the European Union. In this book, I chart the battle for Britain – the out-come of which is still in doubt.

In writing, I am conscious that we approach history on three levels. The nineteenth-century historian Thomas Carlyle, who for a brief time taught in my old school, then Kirkcaldy Burgh School, saw history only as the story of the lives of great men – the ambitions, calculations and manoeuvres of those at centres of power. But I cast my net beyond the usual tales of who said what to whom and try to explain our driv-ing ideas and the deeper forces which shaped our actions in govern-ment. History – even a memoir – will be incomplete without an understanding that there are economic, social and cultural tides flowing across society which decision-makers have to take into account. Then there are competing ideas that sculpt the contours of our society which both open up and limit what leaders can do. Only then can we set out an account of what a political leader did and attempted to do. My hope is always to place the account of my experiences within this much broader context and so shed light not just on what happened dur-ing my time in politics, but also what happened during that time in our country and is still happening at this pivotal moment in our history.

In the years after 1997 the speed of change intensified with enor-mous, previously unheard-of, and once unimaginable social progress – the advance of women's equality, the enfranchisement of the young, the vindication of gay and lesbian rights and the reduction of sectarian divisions with a long-elusive peace in Northern Ireland – all within the context of a revolution in communication and social media which has changed the way we interact with each other. This has also been accompanied by the growth of protectionist appeals, anti-immigrant sentiment and identity politics, the weakening of the centre and the strengthening of the extremes. And all of this has happened on a canvas coloured by one phenomenon that historians, years from now, may view as perhaps the most important shift affecting our country – the decline of religion.

In our social-media age, judgements are instantaneous and often brutal – and then people quickly move on. It will take a generation before events and people are put into perspective. If journalists have given us the first draft of history, the most I can offer is a second draft. It is, however, a truism that all political careers ultimately end in failure. Harold Macmillan did not rebound from his failed efforts to take Britain into Europe. Having achieved what Macmillan could not, Edward Heath was humiliated when he called an election on 'Who governs Britain?' and the people responded, 'Not you.' Economic crises undid the premierships of Harold Wilson and Jim Callaghan. Margaret Thatcher was summarily rejected by her own party after a decade in power. Support for John Major collapsed when his party's reputation for economic competence evaporated over Britain's departure from the Exchange Rate Mechanism. Despite all his other considerable achievements, Tony Blair is remembered above all else for a war that few now think should have been fought. David Cameron will be remembered for Britain leaving Europe and may yet also be blamed for setting the stage for Scotland leaving Britain. Theresa May will go down in history for gambling on a snap but ill-thought-out general election and enfeebling herself and her party by losing a parliamentary majority in the process.

My own biggest regret was that in the greatest peacetime challenge – a catastrophic global recession that threatened to become a depression – I failed to persuade the British people that the progressive policies I pushed for, nationally and internationally, were the right and fairest way to respond.

We have now lived through seven years of austerity and face isolation from Europe, and historians will assess these years economically – both for Britain and Europe – as a lost decade. But perhaps the most important lesson I wish to share from my life and our times is that the story need not end this way. We are defined by our times but, at important moments, we can define them too. I write both of how we went about changing Britain and where we fell short. It is a story of victories, defeats and lessons learned. This is my account of that endeavour.

CHAPTER I

GROWING UP

I was born in 1951 in one era and came of age in 1967 in another. I entered a world with a very particular order – empire, industry and religion. It was a world of pride, confidence and unity. People could still be forgiven for believing that the British Empire was going to last forever. The country of the Industrial Revolution was in the throes of a manufacturing revival: an Indian summer for cities, such as Glasgow, where life began for me, and whose shipbuilding industry was dominant on the world stage. And we, the British, could still think of ourselves as a chosen people: a churchgoing nation with its own special brands of Anglicanism, Methodism, Presbyterianism and British Catholicism. In the early 1950s, Scotland – where my father was a church minister – was described as the most religious country in the world.

It was fitting that the Govan parish in Glasgow that my father ministered included one of the world's biggest shipyards, which every day saw an army of highly skilled craftsmen building vessels that were sold to every continent. It seemed a confirmation of the ties that bound industry, empire and religion. So too did my father's next church, in what became my home town of Kirkcaldy, Fife, a church that stands tall just two streets away from what was, as I grew up, one of the world's biggest linoleum factories. Between them lay the Adam Smith Halls, a tribute to Kirkcaldy's most famous citizen, the economist who in the 1770s had first sketched out how the new global marketplace would develop to the benefit of Britain. That I grew up in the shadow of this building – donated and officially opened by Fife's other renowned global citizen, Andrew Carnegie – made me and my school friends aware, even at a very young age, of a wider world of which Kirkcaldy was but a small part.

Fife was where my father's family had lived for three centuries, and the town of Kirkcaldy, to where my family moved in the spring of 1954, had such engrained religious traditions that I could step out my front door and, in a matter of minutes, walk past nine churches that were within only a few hundred yards of each other. They claimed most of the population as adherents. Kirkcaldy was not alone: family life for millions of Scots and English was built around not just churches but religiously inspired organisations – like the Boys' Brigade and the Life Boys – and the sports teams they spawned.

In 1951 we were just six years on from the second of two catastrophic world wars whose traumas, carnage and loss of life shaped a whole century. However, while mainland Europe had to be rebuilt again, virtually from scratch, and Britain suffered a long period of austerity, the pillars of our domestic order remained intact.

The 1945–51 Labour government, still in power when I was born, had momentous measures to its credit, creating a welfare state and a free National Health Service that was unique in the world, and nationalising coal, steel and the Bank of England. Simultaneously, the post-war period saw a restoration of traditional social values, so much so that when the new Queen was crowned in 1953, an event televised for the first time, the ceremony was a pageant of ancient regal and religious forms reflecting coronations centuries before. The empire still loomed large. We were post-war but not post-imperial. In retrospect, the 1950s seem like an old world waiting to be lost – one far away from where we are now.

America is enthralled with the idea that anyone can grow up to be president. Britain is different. As I grew up it never occurred to me that I could or would become prime minister. Some colleagues can point to diaries, letters or essays that reveal such an ambition or have school friends who would later testify that they had been in on the secret all along. Not even when I became a Member of Parliament in 1983 did I think I would ever live in Downing Street.

I had visited London only half a dozen times in the thirty-two years before I became an MP. In fact, before I went to university, I had been there only once. My father's cousin Jack and his wife Maureen invited my brother and me to spend Christmas in 1963 in London. They entertained us with visits to the theatre, football grounds and to the Tottenham Court Road, where I remember buying my first transistor radio by selling off my stamp collection to Stanley Gibbons, the famous philately dealer. We did not tour any of the centres of power. We went to the Tower of London but not to the Houses of Parliament. There is no photograph of me as a boy standing outside No. 10 – like the young Harold Wilson. Before I became an MP, I had never been near it.

My childhood was focused more on sport than on studies, with more leisure time spent outdoors than indoors, and for every half hour doing homework there was an hour kicking my football against the wall in our garden. My earliest memories, in fact, are all of one thing: running. Running to play football in the park that was within minutes of our home; running to play with friends on Kirkcaldy's many other green spaces, including the famous Volunteers' Green – named so in the nineteenth century when people were asked to volunteer to thwart a feared invasion by Napoleon III; running to the High Street, an area where we loved to play street football, though we were often chased away and on one occasion gently booked by the police; and, of course, running to and from school as we could do in those days unsupervised.

Normal and commonplace, but parts clearly were not so ordinary. I did not quite understand why but I was sent to primary school at four and secondary school at ten. I remember sitting my eleven-plus exam just after my tenth birthday. As a result, I did my O-Grade exams at fourteen, my Highers – the Scottish near-equivalent of A levels – at fifteen, and went to university at sixteen.

My great-grandfather on my father's side was a local councillor, and an uncle on my mother's side was the provost – the equivalent of an English mayor – of his home village. Other than that, no one in my family had ever been involved in politics. For a time, I dreamed not of politics but of professional football. When I found I had none of the skills to go that far, I had to think of something else. And so, brought up on the stories of Roy of the Rovers, the famous fictional football star who went on to become a manager, I dreamed a new dream of managing my local football team, Raith Rovers. Then, when that looked difficult, I moved on to aspiring to be a football-club owner – a dream that has now faded but does not die.

I think I was seven when I pressed my father to take me to the Raith Rovers New Year's derby match. I was so keen to support Raith Rovers that I could not understand why my father was applauding good play on both sides; I thought he should be as partisan as I was in supporting our local team. By the time I went to secondary school, I was earning pocket money by selling match-day programmes at Raith Rovers – one shilling and sixpence for every hundred sold, plus free admission to the match. It was my first introduction to economics.

Adam Smith was so attached to Kirkcaldy that he regularly came home to Fife from his European travels, from a stint at Oxford and from a professorship at Glasgow University. It was at his home, just yards from my father's church, where he wrote *The Wealth of Nations* and *The Theory of Moral Sentiments*. In them he explained how the new economy of the eighteenth century worked – trade as the engine of growth, a global division of labour and comparative advantage for countries that produced the goods the world wanted.

If Smith had grown up in a landlocked community, we might never have heard of him. But he was the son of a customs officer, and his mother's home overlooked a mile-long seafront with an expansive view of the North Sea. He saw ships coming in and out of the port of Kirkcaldy every week, bringing new goods to the town – both staples and luxuries – and then exporting locally manufactured products like nails, leather and tiles on to the Netherlands and the rest of the continent. What he observed in the port of Kirkcaldy was the basis of his argument that nations would prosper if merchants were allowed to sell freely, unburdened by government-imposed mercantilist restrictions. This was a radical not conservative view, one that called for an end to monopolies and protectionism.

Two hundred years on, the fate of the Kirkcaldy of my youth was still being determined by its economic position. The town was one of the very special close-knit industrial communities at the heart of our coal-mining industry. We literally walked on top of aeons of coal. Once there had been sixty-six pits in the county of Fife, employing nearly a quarter of all adult men, and as recently as the 1950s there were more than thirty pits. A super-mine was sunk not far from where we lived to exploit the vast reserves of coal lying underneath the sea. But then as cheaper energy sources were becoming increasingly available, Fife – and all of Britain – started to experience a catastrophic fall in mining employment. Hundreds of families were suddenly leaving Fife to find a new life in the diminishing number of minefields that were still thriving – in Yorkshire and the Midlands. Their migration foreshadowed the fight for jobs that would become the central

economic issue in the area for the next fifty years and for all the time
I was a Member of Parliament.

Not only was the mining industry in decline but so too was the town's
other mainstay, textiles. Built from the late nineteenth century around
linoleum, a Kirkcaldy invention that became a world-leading product,
the industry was about to give way to the products of a new age, like
fitted carpets. It was still too early for entrepreneurs and health experts
to appreciate the value of linoleum as an easily cleaned floor covering
which helped in the prevention of hospital infections like MRSA.

I remember to this day the announcement in 1963 – I was twelve
years old – of the closure of Barry, Ostlere and Shepherd, the nearby
linoleum factory where the use of linseed oil sent out an aroma that
permeated the town centre. That huge factory, just beside Kirkcaldy's
main rail station and another set of linoleum factories to the north
and east of the town, employed thousands whose jobs were about to
vanish. Some of the friends I made at school had to leave with their
families for England so their fathers could find new work.

Because of its exposure to the North Sea, Kirkcaldy was regularly
battered by storms and floods. In 1958, thirty-foot waves broke through
the sea walls and poured into houses which had to be evacuated. I
went with my father to see some of the families who had to be moved
out of their homes and watched him give each of them money to
help them through. For decades afterwards, despite large investment
in building stronger coastal defences, there were sandbags stored on
the esplanade as a precaution.

In my memory my father still towers before me like a mountain.
I am sure I always thought of him as far taller than the six feet he
was. I seldom saw him in anything other than a suit – a trait he clearly
passed on to me. His bespectacled face was normally smiling and
gentle, but he did not need to say anything when he disapproved of
my behaviour; his frown told me everything. Looking back, I marvel
at his sense of contentment with life. Coming from a modest
background – his father was a shepherd who had gone without full-
time work in the 1930s – he often said: 'Be grateful for what you have.'
And then he would add: 'It's remarkable what you can do without.'
My father was in constant motion, visiting parishioners at home,
ministering in hospital and organising local events, often well into the
evenings. Sunday especially was a time for work not rest. He was on

duty almost all the time. He taught me to treat everyone equally –
subservient to no one, and condescending to no one. Remarkably, he
went through his life without an enemy, something I cannot say of
myself or anyone in politics.

His ministry was woven into my life and the lives of my older
brother John and my younger brother Andrew. We often answered
the doorbell to find homeless beggars to whom he always gave
money – which is why they returned again and again. I sometimes
took his call for charity towards the poor too far. I remember being
at home on my own when a 'beggar' arrived. Not only did I offer
him a few coins, but I invited him in to help himself to the food in
our kitchen. When my parents returned, they found me entertaining
the town's best-known burglar.

Any photograph of my mother in her youth is still striking: she
was a very tall, black-haired and shy woman. She went grey in her
early forties in an era when it was thought self-indulgent to dye your
hair. As a young woman, she had been caught up in the war effort;
she would someday joke that she was the first in our family to work
in Whitehall. She described how, barely out of school, she helped in
a very small way with the codebreaking operation at the rank of sergeant and recalled being part of the enormous throng that gathered
outside Buckingham Palace when the war in Europe ended.

Her father had run a very successful family business and she was
one of three children who became directors, a position she held for
at least forty years. But she was self-deprecating and always regretted
to her life's end that because of the war she had not gone to university. Even when she was in her sixties we were discussing whether she
would do an Open University degree. It was the stereotype of the
time that my brothers and I always thought of her as there at home
and assumed she would be there whenever we needed her. I was fortunate to have had parents insistent on good behaviour, founded on
what I now consider the best of values, but who also saw the benefit
of letting their children find a path for themselves.

Mine was a middle-class upbringing in middle Scotland in the middle
of the century. Our family was never well off enough to afford luxuries,
but we never worried about being without anything we really needed.
I remember my disappointment when my father did not get me the
famous Subbuteo football game for Christmas. I remember, too, my

yearning to own my first pair of Adidas trainers, unfulfilled until I left
secondary school and earned my first week's pay in a summer job as
a labourer. Our summer holidays were with relatives in Scotland, not
visits to hotels or travels abroad. Our first car showed up in 1958 – a
gift to my father from my grandfather – and our first TV arrived in
1959 as a gift from our uncle. The TV was supposed to be there in
time for the *Sports Personality of the Year* programme in 1959 – but it
had been damaged in transit. We had anticipated the night for months.
Luckily, someone lent us a temporary replacement and we watched
the world motorcycling champion John Surtees claim the prize.

At the age of four, when I was enrolled at nursery school and then
at the West Primary School, I first met Murray Elder, a classmate who
was to become a friend for life. Lord Elder, as he now is, was himself
a central figure in Labour's period of success in Scotland from the
1970s to the early 2000s. Over the years he was to give me very good
advice and he has often reminded me of something I had forgotten:
that we were taught to write not with pencils and notebooks but on
slate with slate pens and given rags to wipe the slates clean. No matter how long you live you never forget the names of your first school-
teachers: Miss Mason, Miss Donaldson and Mrs Munro.

My brother John was almost two and a half years older than me
and much more dynamic and entrepreneurial than anyone I then knew.
He went to the front of any meeting while, shy and thought of as
shy, I always occupied the back row. But he brought me into his youthful charity work and media projects. In the spring of 1960, inspired
by one of my father's sermons, John set up a charity shop in the
family garage and soon started a newspaper. The first article, in the
unoriginally entitled *Local News*, covered the annual Ravenscraig Park
sports festival. I became the sports editor and, in an early edition, I
wrote about Scotland's 3–3 draw with Hungary. All the editions were
produced on a Gestetner machine, where we hand-turned the drum
to duplicate the stencils we pecked out on my father's typewriter. My
two-finger typing was as bad then as it is now – living proof, as I
would be told years later by a university lecturer, that typing could
be as illegible as handwriting. So my brother and I had to buy a lot
of correction fluid. I remember that the paper was sold for threepence
with all money not spent on correction fluid going in aid of the
Freedom from Hunger campaign.

Two years later, the *Daily Record* and *Scottish Daily Mail* featured a story about my brother's next venture, the *Gazette*. We sold 500 copies, and raised six pounds, three shillings and ninepence for African charities. Significantly, the first story in the *Gazette* was on threatened pit closures. A second edition carried a leader criticising the Tory Budget of the chancellor Selwyn Lloyd who had just introduced a tax on children's sweets. In April 1963, the fourth edition of the *Gazette* appeared under a new and bold strapline: 'Scotland's only newspaper in aid of the Freedom from Hunger campaign'. It was in this edition that a school friend Stephen Salmond and I wrote about the loss of those 1,500 linoleum jobs.

My brother was nothing if not bold: in July of that year, John secured an article by Harold Wilson, the new leader of the Labour Party, headlined 'The Battle Against Poverty'. We also wrote to John Glenn, the first American astronaut to orbit the earth, and persuaded him to write what we called an exclusive for us. Some of our mistakes were comical: 'UNEMPLOYMENT HOPES' was one of our less-considered headlines. There was also a story entitled 'WOMAN KILLED BY M. HENDERSON AND G. BROWN'. We thought we had learned how to write news, but our piece about the Eichmann trial in Jerusalem described the notorious Nazi overseer of the Holocaust as 'Adolf, 56'. But there were also moments I cherish. For the Christmas edition of another magazine my brother created, called *Zeal*, I contributed an article denouncing the persecution of the Jewish people. It is a concern to which I would often return.

In November 1963, as my family and I had a rare weekend hotel break at Crieff Hydro in Perthshire, I had my first taste of politics on the ground. I already knew where I stood. Never did my father try to push his views on us, but my brother remembers my father talking of the wave of optimism after Labour won in 1945, and a member of his congregation repeating a well-used phrase, 'we are all socialists now'. He also remembers my father's disappointment at the October 1959 election result, which they watched together on TV but which Labour lost. My older brother and I quickly became committed to the Labour cause. I wrote an obituary for my school magazine on the Labour leader, Hugh Gaitskell, who died prematurely, and another article praising another Brown, George Brown, who stood unsuccessfully to be his replacement. In debates and arguments at school, I became a firm supporter of Harold Wilson, who talked of the 'white heat of the scientific revolution' and promised to clear the 'dead wood out of the boardroom'.

And it is not difficult to see the appeal he had at that time. There was no better example of his theme that Britain was changing than the Beatles, who I and millions of other teenagers first followed from 1962 – young, unconventional, from the north, and awash with a new energy. I was to argue with my history lecturers that the 1964 and 1966 elections were won on a wave of enthusiasm for change and that no one illustrated this mood better than the Beatles. Without their fame Harold Wilson might have struggled to popularise his theme: creating a vibrant, dynamic Britain free from the stuffy establishment living in the past. The Beatles helped Labour win in 1964.

That was a few months off. When we arrived at Crieff Hydro, a critical by-election in the constituency of Kinross and West Perthshire was under way. The new prime minister, Sir Alec Douglas-Home, was standing for Parliament, because in his new role he had to move from the Lords to the Commons. At the local Labour offices, John and I offered our services to the campaign of a youthful candidate, Andrew Forrester. He was up against it in a crowded field. There was a strong Liberal candidate, while the Scottish poet Hugh MacDiarmid stood as a Communist, and the famous comedian Willie Rushton campaigned as an independent. Rushton – well known for his appearances with David Frost on the television satire *That Was the Week That Was*, a late-night programme my father actually allowed us to watch – addressed a meeting I attended and made fun of the now 'commoner' fourteenth Earl of Home. Asked whether he would be buying a home in the constituency, Douglas-Home replied: 'No, of course not. I have quite enough homes already.' I heard him speak in some of the villages. He delivered exactly the same speech wherever he went – something that shocked me then but which now I quite understand.

That month, Labour lost but a more bitter taste of politics was to come. I was sitting in the living room with my mother on a Friday night when regular TV programming was interrupted with a bulletin that President Kennedy had been shot, and soon the news came that he had died. What happened seemed like a blow against democracy itself. I was only twelve, but John F. Kennedy had captured my imagination and that of a generation. In the years to come, he and his brothers would have a profound influence on the way I saw and spoke about politics – and decades on, Ted Kennedy would become a good personal friend.

I was part of an experiment called the 'E stream' at Kirkcaldy High School. Concerned about the failure rate at Scottish universities and worried that Fife pupils were failing because they were not sufficiently prepared for university courses, our educational authority decided to give some pupils a seventh university-preparation year at secondary school. To make that happen, we were taken out of primary school a year early. The first 'E stream' class contained twenty-five girls and eleven boys; more girls had higher IQ scores.

I was merging with pupils two years older than myself and it was tough adjusting in my first year. I did not help myself by letting my team down when I dropped the baton in the annual school sports day relay race. But I did have one starring role that year which convinced me acting was not my forte. It was, I suspect, because I had the loudest voice that I was chosen to be the young footballer in a French-language play. I had a very small role bouncing my ball onto the stage to answer a query from grown-ups, cheekily telling them that I did not know the way to the station – 'La gare? Quelle gare? Je ne sais quoi' – because I always travelled by car – 'Je moi, je voyage en auto.' Unbeknownst to me, a few of my fellow actors, sixth-form pupils, were plotting a daring real-life drama. They were some of the brightest pupils in the school, but amazingly they had drawn up plans for two robberies – one of a shop and one of the local golf-course bar. It became a comedy of errors. They would have been successful if their getaway car had not broken down. Police traced the planning of the raids to maps left on tables in the local café frequented by teenagers. The sixth-form boys ended up in court, but in later life mostly became very successful in their careers. None of the dramas on the stage could compete with that drama off stage.

For many of the thirty-six secondary-school students channelled into it, the E-stream experiment turned out to be a painful failure. They were put under too much pressure. In the end, less than half of my classmates went straight from school to university. I felt strongly enough about what had happened to my friends to write what now seems an overly earnest article, complaining that 'I was a guinea pig, the victim of a totally ludicrous experiment in education . . . I watched as each year one or two of my friends would fall under the strain. I saw one girl who every now and then would disappear for a while with a nervous breakdown.' I wrote that 'the strain of work, the ignominy and rejection of failure could have been avoided'.

Kirkcaldy High School was one of the best in Scotland and I benefited from a dedicated headmaster, Robert Adam, and inspirational teachers whose names I still remember, like Sid Smith in English and Tom Dunn in history. We were encouraged to argue and to challenge one another as well as the teacher. In a school debate, I argued the case for the motion: 'That the Smith regime in Rhodesia should be crushed.' At fifteen, I secured the five A grades I needed in my Higher exams to be accepted for Edinburgh University. A year later, I came first in history in the university bursary competition, but had not been told before I entered that no money was available for my subject area. The following year, however, I was lucky to win a prize – £200, a stunning amount in the 1960s – in a nationwide competition run by the *Daily Express* for an essay describing 'our country' in the year 2000. It was one of the few good things the *Express* ever did for me. I foresaw that, 'By 2000, Scotland can, for the first time in history, have found her feet as a society which has bridged the gaps between rich and poor, young and old.'

It was also a difficult time. My mother was unwell; she had had a terrible year after suffering appendicitis and peritonitis. One evening, just before I sat my school exams, I visited her in Victoria Hospital in Kirkcaldy. My father thought he was taking us to see her for the last time and that she would not make it through that night. But she had an inner strength that defied the odds.

Months followed when she was either in hospital or recuperating. My father could cook only one thing, omelettes, another trait I inherited from him, and so we had a very limited diet. Most Sundays, a family who lived across the road invited us for Sunday lunch; the price was having to listen to their Tory denunciations about the 'evil' Labour prime minister, Harold Wilson. On returning home, I asked my father why he did not argue back, and he always replied: 'How can you do so when you are guests of people who are being so kind in making you lunch?'

At sixteen I moved from Kirkcaldy to Edinburgh. The two communities were just thirty miles apart, but the Firth of Forth which separated them was also a boundary between the old and the new. The Edinburgh of 1967 was about to cast off its Calvinist past and Edinburgh University would become one of the centres of radical student protest. It was the age of personal liberation. Edinburgh reminded me of what Mark Twain said of his youthful journey from his Presbyterian home to a frontier town in Nevada, from which he wrote that it was no place for a puritan and he did not long remain one.

The students were in a culture war with Edinburgh's austere city fathers. Within a few days of starting my studies, the campus news-paper, the *Student*, was castigated by university authorities for featuring a drawing of a nude woman that could be completed by filling in the dots on the page. At the same time, the students' union passed a motion demanding that the rector, Malcolm Muggeridge, advocate free supply of the contraceptive pill by the University Health Service. He refused. The rector was elected by the students and Muggeridge's radical past had ensured his elevation to the rectorship. But in January 1968, when he invited us all to a sermon in St Giles' Cathedral, he stood up and denounced the youthful generation that had elected him. He pronounced that the world was falling apart amid declining moral standards and ended his sermon by dramatically resigning. I was there that night to hear this fiery and dramatic jeremiad of my generation, and it was written up as if there had been nothing like it at St Giles' since the Protestant Reformation was sparked by a woman, Jenny Geddes, throwing a stool at the dean. Only long afterwards did I learn that in his youth – and even after – Muggeridge had enjoyed a notoriously active private life.

Within months, Edinburgh was engulfed in protests against the Vietnam War, against apartheid, and against overly rigid university rules that seemed to deprive students of the new freedoms they craved. The city was awash with its own student counterculture. One day in the local pub, frequented by workers as well as students, I listened to one of the Edinburgh University Labour Club leaders urging local workers to read and follow the Marxist philosopher Herbert Marcuse.

A sixteen-year-old at university could not fail to notice that alcohol was everywhere. I certainly did not, but drugs passed me by. Students whom I knew would later write the Edinburgh pub guide, noting that while the city had a hundred churches, it had 500 pubs.

My first days at university brought more drama than I expected.

I arrived on a Tuesday and occupied my hostel room in Lee House of Pollock Halls – room 114 if I remember correctly. I did the first two days of Freshers' Week – the usual round of talks, meetings and parties – on the Wednesday and Thursday. And then I went to see a consultant surgeon on the Friday for a prearranged appointment about a problem I had been having with my eye. It took the eye surgeon no more than a second to diagnose a retinal detachment.

Because of a misunderstanding, I left with the impression that I was about to lose my left eye – to have it removed altogether – and not just my sight. By Sunday, I found myself in a hospital bed next to elderly cataract patients, in what seemed one of the most ancient wards in Edinburgh's Royal Infirmary. I was ordered to lie flat for a few days before I was operated on. Both my eyes were bandaged shut for what seemed to a sixteen-year-old an eternity – actually around a week or ten days – during which I had to lie flat again – no pillows allowed – to give the retina a chance to set itself back in place. I would be out of action for the whole of my first university term.

How had it happened? In April, before leaving for Edinburgh, I had been kicked in my head during my last rugby match at school. I had been playing for the school's rugby team as a winger and then as a wing forward. Only fifteen when I had joined the first team, I had been knocked around for most of the season, though to my delight I scored the winning try in my debut match. My speed – I had run in the Scottish schoolboy championships – did not compensate for my lack of weight. Often, we played Edinburgh schools, where our opponents were sometimes eighteen years old. In the last match of the season, we were playing former pupils of our school – some of them friends of mine – who wanted to teach us a lesson or two by being overly physical during the opening minutes. I went down on the ball right at the start of play and then was surrounded and buried in a loose scrum. A boot landed on my head and I got up dazed, probably concussed. But, since it was the first few minutes of the match, I did not want to go off. Despite being more than a little hazy, I was so proud to be playing in this prestigious match that I just ploughed on.

Afterwards, I thought nothing of it. Only gradually, during that summer term of 1967, did I start to sense a problem. I felt as if I was always looking into the sun and the sun was reflecting on my eye. But if you have one good eye, you do not really notice how bad the

other one is. I went to see an optician, who could not find anything
wrong. Then I went to see a doctor – a family friend who was a kind
and generous man. He could not find anything wrong either; perhaps
that was not surprising because the batteries in his torch were dead.
He suggested I go to a consultant and agreed to fix up the appointment. Unfortunately, this was May, and the appointment was not until
October – five months away, during which time, as I later discovered,
my eye deteriorated beyond the point at which an operation was likely
to succeed.

Ironically, I could have gone right away to an eye consultant at my
local hospital; but not knowing my way around the NHS at the time,
I simply took the advice of the GP who directed me to his consultant
friend. It would be the last time I would ever go private. I spent what
would have been my first month at university a few hundred yards
away from it, lying flat and blinded in the hope that the retina, once
operated on, would stay flat. As I recuperated I joined fellow patients,
mainly there for cataract operations, and I remember how every night
at nine o'clock a trolley came around the ward, offering each patient –
thanks to a bequest to the ward – a choice of Guinness, beer or wine,
which was open even to a sixteen-year-old. I knew the NHS was free – but
I had not expected free beer.

I was told the retina had been reattached but there was no improvement in my sight. A few days after I returned to university – January,
to start the second term – I went back to the hospital for a routine
check-up and was told the retina was not in the right place. I had to
have another operation, but the prospect of it working was, I was
informed, remote. The surgeon agreed I could finish my third term,
then spend the summer holidays in hospital and recuperating.

I took his advice. But back again at the university in the autumn,
when I went for a precautionary check-up I arrived fearing the
worst. And I was right. I was suddenly back in hospital for a third
operation. The surgeon said he and his colleagues would try one last
time. Just before I went under a general anaesthetic he told me: 'Okay,
Gordon. We'll have a bash.' 1968 was one of the most tumultuous
years of the twentieth century, but I saw very little of it.

When the third operation did not work, I finally accepted I was
permanently blind in my left eye. At least my right eye was fine. Or
so I thought. I did not expect that two and a half years later, I would

find myself back in hospital, when that eye suffered its own retinal detachment.

In university but out of the classroom for much of my first two years, I had to renegotiate my course of study. I was advised to do an arts degree, the MA that I was awarded at nineteen, and then I prepared for an honours degree in social and economic history. I had some great tutors with whom I kept in contact after my studies, including Paul Addison, the prize-winning author of *The Road to 1945*, and the supervisor who eventually took me through my PhD, another John Brown, who sadly died a few years ago. I thought I had worked hard but my other activities led me to miss some lectures. When I was awarded my degree, the head of history wrote to me saying: 'Absurd and reprehensible an admission though it may be, I am not sure I know what you look like. So I very much look forward to meeting you.'

I also followed my brother John in another marginally more serious journalistic enterprise. John had worked at the university student newspaper and in the summer of 1969 I was elected editor. We concentrated on seasoning the usual campus gossip with investigative journalism which brought us the UK student 'Newspaper of the Year' award. We exposed the case of a professor who tried and failed to finagle his son a first-class honours degree. The professor was removed as head of his department but, rather than being sacked, benefited from an all-too-familiar university stitch-up. He was appointed to a personal chair in Romance linguistics.

Apartheid was now at the top of the agenda. Students, including some of my friends, had been arrested when protesting against the visit of the Springbok rugby team to play Scotland. Following a sit-in at the university careers office calling for the university to sell its shares in South African companies, we had also found papers showing that its director was a recruiting agent for MI6 – we kept it secret that one of the brothers of a school friend was exposed as a spy – and then in December I returned to guest-edit the *Student*. In a special edition that sparked national headlines, we exposed how the university had lied when it denied shareholdings in companies with interests in South Africa. Out of the blue, we had been handed a document which proved beyond doubt that the university held half a million pounds of investments in a range of corporations operating in South Africa, including De Beers and Anglo-American. Far from divesting, the university had been amassing a bigger portfolio. After our special edition, 'Sell the Shares' stickers and posters blanketed the university. A month later, the administration capitulated and sold the shares.

In 1971, as I prepared for my final year, my eye problems flared up again. In June, while playing tennis during a stay at a university study centre in the north of Scotland, I suddenly detected a blind spot – one part of the court where my right eye could not follow the ball. I finished the match, told no one that something was wrong and immediately went back to Edinburgh and the Royal Infirmary.

This time the surgeon – the same consultant who had done the other three operations – did not have to tell me what was wrong. I knew I had a retinal detachment in my good eye. Having seen three operations fail in my left eye, I feared for the first time that I would end up losing my sight altogether. An emergency operation was scheduled for the next day. To my surprise, Dr Jackson – highly esteemed in his own right – said that this time he was not the best person to do the operation; the best hope was his young protégé, Hector Chawla. But Dr Chawla was about to go on holiday. He delayed his departure and saved my eye. Had I waited even a day in rushing to the Royal Infirmary, he would have been gone and I doubt that I would have any sight today.

Hector had recently returned from a year in America and I was blessed to be the beneficiary of his newly acquired techniques. A lifelong friendship followed. Born in Scotland, the son of an Indian-Pakistani army doctor and a Scottish mother, Hector Chawla is a polymath, a writer of novels as well as the author of many books on the eye, and a world expert on the retina. Partly due to his breakthroughs, the success rate in reattaching retinas rose in forty years from 20 per cent to 90 per cent.

Since then, my good eye has had its bad days. Every now and then the same symptom I experienced on the tennis court recurs and forces me back to the surgeon for further checks. When I woke up in Downing Street one Monday in September 2009, I knew something was very wrong. My vision was foggy. That morning, I was to visit the City Academy in Hackney to speak about our education reform agenda. I kept the engagement, doing all I could to disguise the fact that I could see very little – discarding the prepared notes and speaking extemporaneously. Straight afterwards, I was driven to the consulting room of a prominent eye surgeon at the Moorfields Eye Hospital in London.

To my shock, in examining my right eye he discovered that the retina was torn in two places and said that an operation was urgently needed. He generously agreed to operate that Sunday. I asked him on the way out if my old friend, Hector Chawla – whom I had last seen briefly on the day he retired as a surgeon – could be invited to give his opinion too. I emailed Hector who was in France on holiday but he offered to come to the hospital that Sunday morning on his way back home.

I was already prepared for surgery when Hector examined me and said he was convinced that the tears had not happened in the last few days. They were not new but long-standing. His advice was blunt. There was no point in operating unless the sight deteriorated further. Laser surgery in my case was more of a risk than it was worth. If my sight worsened, doctors would have to operate within the eye as before – not with a laser. Both surgeons agreed that this was not the time to operate.

I am grateful that the retina has held to this day and I feel lucky beyond words. From that moment on a tennis court in 1971, when I thought it inevitable I would go blind, I have to date had forty six years of vision. I would never again have perfect sight, not even in one eye, but the sight I have has got me through.

Despite Jeremy Clarkson calling me a 'one-eyed Scottish idiot' (by no means the most offensive words uttered by the former *Top Gear* presenter), and Andrew Marr bizarrely suggesting in an interview in 2009 that my partial blindness would be a reason for standing down, I have always been open when asked about my eye injuries and never tried to hide them.

Nonetheless, it was after losing the sight in my left eye, and then some of the sight in my right one, that I started to think more about my future. There were certain things I couldn't or shouldn't do – playing the sports I loved, and driving a car, despite having a licence – but I was not going to be deterred. Even if I felt fate had dealt me a hand I would not have chosen, my time in and out of hospital – and the fight for my eyesight – gave me a perspective that I still feel helps me to be more understanding of difficulties facing others in a far worse position than me. I have nothing but admiration for those like my friend David Blunkett, who has overcome the challenges of blindness with such distinction.

For a while I thought my future lay in an academic life – lecturing and research. But I had come alive politically. Shocked by the levels of unemployment and deprivation in my home town and across the central belt of Scotland, I felt something had to be done to address these injustices. I dreamed there could be no greater privilege than representing my home area in the House of Commons.

CHAPTER 2

INTO PARLIAMENT

My first elected office would not be in Parliament. In 1972, having graduated for the second time, I secured a bursary for a three-year postgraduate course. My tutor Paul Addison encouraged me to apply to his former college, Nuffield in Oxford, but by then I had agreed to stand as the student candidate for the vacant rectorship of Edinburgh University. It was a post previously held by five prime ministers – Gladstone, Rosebery, Lloyd George, Churchill and Baldwin – and usually reserved for the great and the good in their later years. The rector chaired the University Court and I had urged my fellow students to take the unprecedented step, theoretically possible because of a loophole in the rules, of electing one of their own. We had done exactly that when I was an undergraduate by electing a friend of mine, Jonathan Wills, and when he and other friends pressed me to stand one year later – and I then found out the university had sought legal advice to try to delay the election – I felt obliged to agree my name should go forward. I was elected rector for three years in November 1972.

What I wrote of at the time as 'the return to the libraries' had begun. As a student of the 1960s, I and others had worried little about future careers: something that changed in the 1970s as growing economic pressures and the threat of graduate unemployment hit home. The political mood of students was best summed up as apathy punctuated by sit-ins. But even the protests were quite different from the heady days of the 1960s: less about the great issues of the day, such as apartheid, and more about mundane matters like student accommodation.

I had become rector on a platform that called for the university to extend student representation, to build closer links to the local community in the extramural courses it offered and the research it did, and to tap the widest pool of talent by recruiting more students from poorer backgrounds. This final theme – widening university intake – was one to which I would regularly return. We did secure stronger student representation on the Court – and my younger brother Andrew, who became president of the Students' Association, was one of the first to benefit. As an undergraduate I had successfully run a campaign to raise the wages of cleaners and catering staff, and I now called for non-academic staff to be represented on the university's governing body. We pressed for more community representation on the Court and I nominated the secretary of the local residents' society and chairman of the local trades council: they secured four and three votes respectively against nine each for the headmaster of a private school and a local businessman. Nevertheless, when I stood down from office in 1975, I was able to give an interview saying the Court was no longer 'a rubber-stamp body', and that while I kept 'getting knocked back' I was proud to be the only student chairman of a university governing body in the world.

The rector was able to appoint one additional member of the Court. But when in the spring of 1973, I appointed Allan Drummond, the outgoing president of the Students' Association – who had at one time organised a sit-in over student rents and the shortage of flats – the Court voted to debar him as unsuitable. And for good measure they also voted for a law change to prevent me being its chairman. Two High Court judges, both of whom sat on the Court, argued that it was within their rights to ban anyone they disliked. Indeed, when we took them to Scotland's supreme civil court, the Court of Session, it was almost impossible to find a lawyer among the Edinburgh legal establishment who would stand up to the judges by taking my case. This was the first time I saw the power of an establishment at work. When their case came to court they could cite only one precedent where a nominee had been refused membership of a public board because they were unsuitable: the Admiralty Board, which in the 1830s had barred a three-year-old. They were overruled by a fellow judge. And when university officials then tried to change the law to remove me as chair of the Court, they were overruled yet again, this time by the Privy Council. I'm told that Prince Philip, then chancellor of the university and formally consulted on their proposal, sided with me. We will never know why, but perhaps it was because he had been lobbied by a friend of mine and one of his royal cousins, Margareta, the crown princess of Romania, who studied alongside me at Edinburgh.

There were further disputes, most notably in 1973 over an Association of Commonwealth Universities conference in Edinburgh at which Rhodesia and South Africa were to be represented. I argued success-fully against their attending – and ironically debarred from the con-ference my father's closest school friend, Robert Craig, who was principal of the still multiracial University of Rhodesia.

While the title of rector is grand, the work is gritty. I spent many hours dealing with the minutiae of internal university matters. I found this particularly frustrating during the two general elections in 1974 – the first amidst the frenzy of a miners' strike and the three-day work week. At the time, I was also, at least in theory, working on my PhD, while being employed as a part-time tutor and lecturer.

My formal involvement in Labour Party politics had started when I joined the university Labour Club. It was a hive of activity. Through it, I met friends whom I still know today: Neil Davidson, now a mem-ber of the House of Lords; Ian Davidson, later a fellow MP; and George Foulkes, a popular and successful minister after 1997 in the Labour government. I canvassed for a twenty-four-year-old Robin Cook in the election he fought and lost in Edinburgh North in 1970. Then convener of the Edinburgh City Council Housing Committee, Robin was seen by me and many others as one of Labour's brightest and most promising politicians. Friends at the outset and friends at the end, our political relationship was to endure through testing times in between.

I became chairman of the Labour Club in 1971 and endeavoured to engineer a revival in its fortunes by separating us from the International Marxist Group and the Trotskyist factions. And then after I became rector I was, for a time, also a member of the Edinburgh Trades Council. I remember the very first time I was asked to stand as a Labour Party candidate. It was for a city council seat in the local elections in Edinburgh. The suggestion came from a trade union offi-cial. I was still a student and I replied honestly that I knew little about council funding and what were then rate-support grants. 'Look, pal,' he brusquely admonished me, 'if we're going to win the seat you wouldn't be the candidate.'

When the general election of February 1974 came along, I worked long hours to meet my rector's responsibilities while serving as a ward organiser for Robin, who won Edinburgh Central, albeit with a small majority of 961. Although Labour polled 220,000 fewer votes than the Conservatives, the party managed to form the government in Britain's first hung parliament since 1929.

During the next few months, as everyone prepared for a second election, my university friend Ian Levitt, later to become the best researcher of twentieth-century Scottish social history, asked me to stand as a Labour candidate at the nomination conference in Edinburgh North. I thought it worth a try, not least to show I was around and to let people know I was interested in more than student politics. At the selection meeting I gave a fairly decent speech delivered without notes, but this was never good enough to take votes from my friend Martin O'Neill. However, I did help Robin defend his slim majority in the election of October 1974, working to get the vote out in one central Edinburgh ward – Gorgie and Dalry. Robin increased his majority to nearly 4,000, bucking the trend in Scotland towards the nationalists, who surprisingly secured eleven out of seventy-one seats. Labour, with a majority of only three seats, formed a precarious government.

A further general election seemed likely, and the parties quickly got down to the business of putting in place parliamentary candidates. I was secretary of the Edinburgh South constituency when I was selected in April 1976. It was a close-run thing. I prevailed by just one vote over an opponent with more experience than me – and, for that, I was grateful to Nigel Griffiths, who eventually became the local MP. He had persuaded one of the few undecideds – and thus the single swing voter in the selection conference – by assuring him I would support a new sports centre for his ward inside the constituency. In the words of the former Massachusetts congressman and Speaker of the House Tip O'Neill, all politics is local.

My term as rector had come to an end the previous year, though I was still yet to complete my PhD, and I needed to get a job. I applied for three: Scottish research officer for the Labour Party, an organiser for the Workers' Educational Association, and a lecturer at Imperial College London. None of them panned out. And I had burned my bridges with Edinburgh University, not least because when a part-time tutor I joined the protests against the conditions under which we worked. At twenty-four, in a year when unemployment was rising, I was out of work. Fortunately, a few months later, in early 1976, I was appointed to a lectureship at Glasgow College of Technology, later to become Caledonian University. The head of department who appointed me, David Donald, and his wife Christine would become lifelong friends. When I spoke at his funeral, I reminded his family that he had championed me over a favoured internal candidate who would go on to be a distinguished professor of politics and the author of scholarly works that won wide acclaim.

As we digested the first onrush of the Scottish National Party and grappled with devolution, I edited *The Red Paper on Scotland*, persuading people as diverse in their political views as Robin, Jim Sillars, Vince Cable and Tom Nairn to contribute. At the Scottish Labour conference in 1976, held in Perth, I entered into perhaps the most divisive debate I had seen in Scotland – championing the case for devolution. A large number of Labour leaders whom I respected saw devolution as a diversion from the effort to secure a Labour government in the UK. In response, I argued that a commitment to devolution was rooted in Labour's ideals, going all the way back to 1888 when Keir Hardie first committed Labour to 'home rule all round'.

The resistance inside the party was fierce. Later that year, I heard Neil Kinnock tell the Labour Party conference in Blackpool that some are born devolutionists, some achieve devolution, and the rest of us – 85 per cent of the people of this country – would have devolution thrust upon us. He was having none of it.

Being a Labour candidate between 1976 and 1979 – out on the doorsteps every week – was, to put it mildly, hard going as the Labour government, engulfed by both inflation and recession, became increasingly unpopular and the SNP, the Conservatives and Liberals all rose in strength. In the May 1977 council elections, the SNP gained their first foothold in Labour's traditional working-class constituencies. Glasgow was widely regarded as a write-off for Labour. When Donald Dewar took the nationalists on in the famous Glasgow Garscadden by-election of April 1978, everyone thought he faced a steep uphill climb. I saw Glasgow Garscadden as pivotal. If we could show that the SNP were not the progressive force they claimed to be, we could re-establish Labour in industrial Scotland. I enlisted as a foot solider in the campaign and, after lecturing each day in Glasgow, I spent the evenings canvassing. Donald, with his masterful debating skills and indefatigable campaigning, won the unwinnable election and forced the SNP onto the back foot.

I might have joined Donald in Westminster earlier than I did. Another high-profile by-election loomed, in Hamilton, a constituency that ten years earlier had been carried by the SNP. The local Labour Party was anxious to avoid a repeat of that fiasco. The party concluded that they needed someone who was both young and had Lanarkshire connections. My father, who had moved from Kirkcaldy to minister in Hamilton eleven years before, was a popular figure. More because of him than me, I looked like a viable candidate. I had spent a lot of time in Hamilton and knew many people in the town. The local councillor, Alex Reid, asked to see me personally. To my surprise he not only offered me his support but named all of the delegates who would back me, virtually guaranteeing the nomination.

Events unfolded badly. My father was about to spend months laid up following a complicated gall bladder operation. He knew he was ill but didn't tell me when the two of us spoke before the selection. I asked for his counsel about my standing. He had always been supportive, but on this occasion advised me not to run. When he was rushed to hospital, I decided it was not right to impose what would be a highly public and fraught election contest on him and my mother. George Robertson, a very good Labour candidate with more experience than me, went on to win the by-election. Nineteen years to the month after his victory, George was to sit with me in Tony Blair's first Labour Cabinet and he would later serve as secretary general of NATO.

The argument over devolution continued throughout the late 1970s and showed just how difficult it was to hold the Labour Party together. I was determined to push the case for what was then called a Scottish Assembly. And when, in 1978, it was decided to hold a referendum on this, I was chosen to chair Scottish Labour's Devolution Committee.

Despite Labour divisions, I threw myself into this new role: in the last seven days of the campaign, I addressed thirty meetings. I had also prepared one pamphlet which set out the Labour case for the new body and a second focused on what the new body could do. I wanted us to run as positive a case as possible on the difference a Scottish Assembly could make to people's lives. I also chastised the Conservatives for turning their back on devolution, arguing that they were putting party politics before the constitutional future of the country and 'playing into the hands of the extremists and wreckers who want to break up Britain'.

The Labour leadership wanted to exploit what they saw as the personal popularity of the prime minister. It was even decided that our main poster of the campaign should be a picture of Jim Callaghan urging people to vote 'yes', a move that made Scottish devolution appear like a diktat from a prime minister based in London with a parliamentary seat in Cardiff. It might have worked in his adopted Wales but it could not work in Scotland – and it didn't. Voters' decisions in a referendum tend to deliver a verdict on the government of the day. With the Labour government more unpopular than at any time in its tenure, a Lib-Lab pact had done little to enhance the party's reputation.

During the passage of the Scotland Bill through Parliament, Labour had accepted an amendment that required the approval of 40 per cent of Scotland's electorate to pass the referendum, rather than a simple majority of votes cast. So, while the final result showed a narrow majority in favour – with 51.6 per cent supporting an Assembly, a majority of about 77,400 – only 32.9 per cent of the total electorate actually voted Yes. Afterwards, the SNP joined the Tories in a motion of 'no confidence' that brought down the Labour government.

Could events have worked out differently? Absolutely. Approached after the 1979 devolution debacle to co write a book – eventually entitled *The Politics of Nationalism and Devolution* – with my one-time politics lecturer Henry Drucker, we were in no doubt that, despite the recent defeat, devolution was ultimately inevitable. We argued that the Scotland Act had been deficient and in a section of the book written by Henry he proposed a more radical settlement: reducing the number of Scottish MPs, introducing proportional representation for a Scottish Assembly and devolving tax powers, all of which later came to pass.

A divided party entered a difficult election campaign in 1979. When the chancellor, Denis Healey, came to Scotland to meet the Scottish Labour Executive, he came under attack. I was one of the few to defend his economic record. And when in a later meeting Jim Callaghan was criticised by a prospective Labour candidate from an unwinnable seat, he told her to come back to challenge him when – and if – she was elected. 'Sunny Jim' was how he was portrayed, but in private meetings he could be tough and uncompromising – and unsmiling.

My Conservative opponent in Edinburgh South at the election was a young ex-MP and Tory aristocrat, the Earl of Ancram, who contrived a popular touch by always insisting: 'Call me Michael.' He was also known in local circles as 'Norman Crum' having been announced as such at one formal occasion by a deaf official who hadn't quite got 'Lord Ancram'. I tried to fight on local issues. But as is often the case in politics, there is one point in the campaign when you just know you have lost. For me, it was a Friday-night candidates' debate in a Morningside school. I had been speaking to small public meetings of fifty or so people, three times a night. On this occasion, when the earl, myself and the other candidates took questions and answers from a church-group forum in the most prosperous part of the constituency, an audience of several hundred turned up. After we drew lots, I stood up to deliver what was, on reflection, a fairly bog-standard speech – from the table behind which our chairs were placed. I sat down and Ancram was called. He walked beyond the table right to the front of the stage, clasped his hands and began by reciting the words Robert Kennedy had quoted from George Bernard Shaw, words I knew and suddenly wished I had used: 'Some see things as they are and ask why. I dream of things that never were, and ask why not?' The one word he never used was 'Conservative'.

With more students than ever living in the constituency, I had hoped we could win with the help of undergraduate voters. We did increase the Labour vote by 4,000, at a time when Labour support was falling nearly everywhere. I still lost by 2,460 votes. I had tried everything. Late into the night of election day, just before the polls closed, we had been rounding up those who had not yet voted. Alistair Moffat, a close friend who was director of the Edinburgh Festival Fringe, spent hours on the campaign trail with me alongside his wife Lindsay. After we knocked on the door of a very elderly constituent who needed persuading to come out to vote, Alistair said to her, in utter frustration, 'But this may be the last time you will ever vote . . .' She got her coat on and joined us. It was not enough. Edinburgh South had never been anything other than a Conservative seat for seventy years, and it would take until 1997 – and a brilliant campaign by Nigel Griffiths – for it to be won. Only in 2017, thanks to the hard work and popularity of his successor Ian Murray, has this once Tory seat become a safe Labour seat, the safest in Scotland.

For a while I took a new route. I was still a lecturer but did some television work to gain experience in an area I knew little about – broadcast media. Scottish Television, prompted by ever-generous friends Russell Galbraith, Bob Cuddihy and Ken Vass, offered me the chance to produce programmes. Although this was never a long-term prospect for me, I remain proud of some of the shows we did. We were the first to expose how little revenue was flowing from North Sea oil and how little tax had been paid on land deals around Glasgow. And we led the way in consumers' rights television producing a series, *What's Your Problem?*, which uncovered malpractice and championed viewers getting by on tight family budgets. I learned a lot about TV – but given my experiences later on, clearly not enough. I suspect my work at STV was more helpful to me than to them.

At that time, independent TV was pretty much a licence to print money, but even so, it would be fair to say that it was a licence to save as much money as they were printing. For instance, STV broadcast live golf, as you would in Scotland. But their version of live golf was not tournaments involving Sam Torrance, Tony Jacklin or Sandy Lyle. STV thought they could save money by broadcasting live amateur – seven-handicap – golf. This sounds fine in principle, but the problem was that the cameras had to follow people into fields, in and out of ponds, out of bounds into people's gardens and beyond. It was taken off air by popular demand.

I worked too on the Edinburgh Festival programmes, which again saved money by bringing in amateur acts. One night the programme ended not with the ordinary news headlines of the day but with a satirical alternative. When the news that was broadcast was 'The world will end in three minutes' and then 'The Queen's corgi has rabies', there was understandably a mountain of complaints. Elderly viewers were fainting in old people's homes. However, when we analysed the calls, the biggest concern seemed to have been for the Queen's corgis, not that the world was ending. By that time the channel had a technique for dealing with complaints. We asked viewers who phoned in for their details, starting with their television licence number. Many hung up.

In 1982, near the end of my time in television, I covered Scotland's World Cup journey to Spain under the great manager Jock Stein. I was present at the Estadio Benito Villamarin stadium in Seville when

Scotland faced off against Brazil. I was standing right behind the Brazilian goal when, after eighteen minutes, David Narey, who played for Dundee United and later joined my local team, Raith Rovers, put Scotland into the lead with his famous 'toe poke' from outside the penalty box. There was a moment of hope. Then, and to the ever-present drumbeat of Brazilian supporters, Brazil scored four goals, including a free kick from the majestic Zico. After Scotland's exit from the World Cup, I flew back with the dejected team on their plane. It was the only time I met Jock Stein – who led Celtic to their European Cup victory in 1967, making them the first British team to win the trophy. Even though he had a reputation for being dour, I found him affable and full of humour, despite his obvious disappointment.

Just before the World Cup, I had submitted the final work for my PhD and was awarded my doctorate while volunteering for an education project in Fife involving union members at Rosyth Dockyard, which employed 15,000. Our aim was to explore an alternative economic strategy to the Conservatives' monetarist economics. Our classes aroused the ire of Norman Tebbit and the Department of Employment. The department wondered why so many trade unionists had signed up to education classes and started to investigate the curriculum we were using. Fife was instantly considered to be the most dangerous place in Britain and Mr Tebbit's department monitored us all the time.

I was still, however, living in the Edinburgh student flat that I had occupied since 1976 – with all the untidiness associated with an undergraduate existence. After being away in London doing some PhD research at the London School of Economics, I arrived back at my flat to find the police looking round following a burglary. When they came to my study, they said to me: 'Totally ransacked, sir.' I had to tell them that the study had been undisturbed by any burglar; it was in exactly the same chaotic state it had been when I left for London.

I became vice chair of the Scottish Labour Party in 1982 and chair the following year. The Labour Party was sharply split between the Bennite left and the mainstream. Denis Healey had won an acrimonious contest for deputy leader in the autumn of 1981 by the narrowest of margins; the bitterness spilled over into Scotland. When Callaghan's successor as leader, Michael Foot, made a courtesy visit to the Scottish Labour Executive just two months later, the Bennites, led by the then chair George Galloway, castigated Foot for excluding Benn from the shadow Cabinet and assailed Healey for refusing to support the recently adopted party policy on unilateral nuclear disarmament. I disagreed with George and said that we needed to reach the middle ground to win the support of voters: 'Anything which prevents this is not only needless but harmful,' I said. I proposed that a draft manifesto be issued immediately and that we campaign on it in what would be an eighteen-month run-up to the general election. Years later, we would adopt a plan similar to this in advance of the 1997 general election with *Road to the Manifesto*, a document that was voted on by the party membership.

The Bennite group on the Scottish Executive persistently tried to thwart any initiatives I took. In 1982, matters had got so bad that they voted to prevent me, even though I was vice chairman of the party, from addressing the Scottish Labour conference. But they could not stop me from becoming chair in 1983 because I had the support of all the major unions in Scotland.

Friends in Fife were pushing for my selection as parliamentary candidate for the newly created constituency of Dunfermline East. Luck played its part. My selection as a candidate had nothing to do with me being a lecturer or working in television – it was about local connections, local people, local trade unions and local Labour Party supporters. I was friends with a great trade union official, Jim McIntyre, who understood the need for on-the-ground organisation and not only endorsed my candidacy but helped me greatly with wise advice.

Jim had surrounded himself with a group of young shop stewards from Rosyth Dockyard and the surrounding open-cast mines of Fife. They included Charlie Boyle, Helen Dowie, Jimmy Dyce, Charlie Logan, Margaret Logan, Bert Lumsden, George Manclark, Derek Stubbs, Peter Young and also Alex Falconer, who later moved from trade-union shop steward to the European Parliament. It was, however, Jim who had told them that, while in time they might find their own parliamentary candidate from the shop floor, at this point I was the person best suited to represent them at Westminster.

There were two remaining barriers. After a boundary review, the county of Fife, which previously had four constituencies, now had a fifth. The sitting MP, Dick Douglas, wanted the safer seat of Dunfermline East but his roots were in the other constituency of

Dunfermline West. He had underestimated resistance to the idea that he could simply move east. Such was the independence of the new Dunfermline East party that, at their very first meeting, they voted against his automatic endorsement and for a selection conference.

Second, although my family had been in the area for 300 years, some insisted that I was not the local candidate. One headline in a newspaper published a week before the selection conference read: 'Local Man Challenged by Brown.' The selection conference was chaired by David Stoddart, a retired miner. Of the fifty-two votes cast, I won thirty-four in the first round. With polling day only twenty-four days away, I needed an agent and I asked David. When he said he had not even voted for me, I replied that was an even better reason to pick him – if he was my agent, I told him, we could reunite the local party quickly. David was to be my agent over three general elections, and he became a close friend and invaluable adviser as we clocked up thousands of miles driving to and from the many towns and villages in the constituency.

Over the remaining three weeks of the 1983 campaign, I never stopped addressing public meetings, then still an important feature of election campaigns. Audiences ranged from a handful in sheltered accommodation to hundreds at the dockyard, where I was allowed to speak only in the presence of the rear admiral. It was faintly possible, I joked with my team, that he was a floating voter. Others came to canvass on my behalf, including the long-serving general secretary of the National Union of Mineworkers, Lawrence Daly, and Jimmy Reid, who led the internationally renowned Upper Clyde Shipbuilders' work-in. Only once did I venture outside my constituency. This was to claim at a Scottish Labour Party press conference that there was a secret National Coal Board plan to shed 10,000 Scottish mining jobs. Sadly that leak turned out to be right. In my first successful count as a candidate, I tallied 18,515 votes, an overall majority of 11,300. But I would be a member of an even smaller Labour Party in Parliament; around the country we had lost fifty-two seats.

I was known in Scotland, if only slightly. But outside of Scotland I was completely unknown. When I arrived in Westminster, my anonymity was rammed home to me when The Times wrote about new MPs. According to the article, I was born in 1926: it reported that I was fifty-six years old and described me as a veteran. It was bizarre;

while they had mistaken me for an elderly colleague also named Brown, the article was accompanied by a photo of me aged nineteen with my hair spilling over my shoulders. Showing the power not so much of the press as of the press cutting, another newspaper labelled me an old Labour stalwart. A few days later, a letter arrived from a private pension company, saying I had entered a new job late in life and should make provision for impending retirement. I was thirty-two.

CHAPTER 3

PERMANENT OPPOSITION?

Early on in our parliamentary careers, I told Tony Blair that, from my reading of history, no great friendship among the senior ranks of politicians had ever lasted. I said this not because I believed a break-up of our friendship was inevitable; on the contrary, I said it to convince him that, if we had the chance, we should do things differently from our predecessors. The wars between Harold Wilson and his deputy George Brown in the 1960s; the rivalries in the wake of Wilson's resignation between Roy Jenkins, Anthony Crosland and Denis Healey all vying to replace him, allowing Jim Callaghan to slip in as his successor; and the recent debacle in which Tony Benn had attempted a coup against Michael Foot's deputy, Denis Healey: these recurring internecine conflicts were counterproductive and damaging. I thought Labour could do better.

I now feel that Tony drew the opposite conclusion: that because past political friendships had not endured, no political friendship could ever endure; that friendships in politics, even if they start out real, become instrumental, a means to an end. I don't accept the stereotype that people at the top of politics fall into two types: those who use and those who are used. Nonetheless, while there is always talk of the team, the tendency to rivalry is often inevitable.

I had met Tony only once, before the 1983 election, when John Smith, then a member of the shadow Cabinet, introduced us in the bar of the House of Commons. We did not have a chance to talk. I was actually familiar with only a few MPs outside Scotland. I had, however, met Michael Foot, who at one stage considered asking me to work for him in the run-up to the 1983 election. I also knew Neil Kinnock, having met him on his regular visits to Scotland. That was about it.

I couldn't help but notice that the Parliamentary Labour Party was anything but young. Even among the new intake only a few of us – Tony, Nick Brown, Sean Hughes, Tony Lloyd, Clare Short, Jeremy Corbyn and Ron Davies (together with Harriet Harman, who had arrived in 1982) – were in our early thirties.

I also arrived to what was for many a familiar story in the life of a new MP: no office, no telephone and no facilities – just nothing. Within a few months I might be able to get a desk and then later share an office. For the moment, I would have to make do with the House of Commons Library or tables around the corridors near the Chamber where there were also some phones. That was one of the reasons why I did not deliver my maiden speech to the House until July, two months after the election.

I was very aware of Aneurin Bevan's view of the Houses of Parliament as set out in his book *In Place of Fear*. The building – erected before there was a right to vote in this country – had housed for most of its life either an unelected elite or one elected by the narrowest of constituencies. For that reason, I was never much attracted to the argument that Westminster as an ancient institution was entitled to resist change in the name of our great traditions and noble heritage.

Some of these traditions were ludicrous. It took me some time to adjust to naming my opponents and colleagues in the third person, or to speak from a standing position without a desk or rostrum on which to rest notes. It is said that when called to give his maiden speech, Dennis Canavan, a fellow Fifer who was a Scottish Labour MP for over twenty years, walked to the front of the House towards the Dispatch Box, thinking that was what everyone did. It is, of course, reserved only for frontbenchers. As Dennis walked towards it, the shadow Scottish Secretary Willie Ross waved him back to his seat. 'Not yet, son, not yet,' he said.

As Tony and I talked, we discovered we shared a fierce passion to see the party reform and recover. He had first been given an office with Dave Nellist, the Militant MP for Coventry South East, who was in effect running a separate party. Tony wanted out and I needed an office, having not yet been offered anything at all. So we linked up to get one – a room without windows, with erratic heat and air conditioning, hidden away off the first floor of the committee-room corridor. I was there more than Tony, who because of the rather spartan circumstances understandably preferred working from home in London.

My first few months in Parliament were a strange time: no fixed abode, often staying with friends, living out of a suitcase. Partly because of this, I came up with my own version of Tony's solution. I spent a lot of time in Scotland, coming to London on Monday or Tuesday, and then leaving on Thursday. This was a blessing in disguise. I got to know my constituency inside and out. I built up enduring friendships. And away from Westminster I learned more about what we needed to do as a party to win back the country's trust.

London was still an awayday for me. I cannot remember a full weekend between 1983 and 1997 that I spent in the capital. Even when my brother later joined me in London, almost all of my friendships were in Scotland. My early interventions at this time were often hit and miss. Perhaps one of my most embarrassing moments with the media came not long after becoming an MP. Gerald Kaufman was shadow Foreign Secretary and he was always getting requests for interviews from radio and TV around the world, but he liked going to the theatre in the evenings. I was just along the corridor from Gerald and one evening he asked me to stand in for him on an inter-view for a radio station 'down under'. They wanted to hear about the new Labour Party. I was told by Gerald to await a call, which duly came, and the technician patched me through to the programme. 'Do you not think you're making great changes to your Labour Party? When we're stuck here?' I said this was simply not true, as the Australian Labor Party was also making great reforms at the time. 'I've just met your prime minister Bob Hawke and we have talked about the reforms we have in common.' The interviewer responded: 'Mr Brown . . . this is Radio Auckland . . . Our prime minister is David Lange . . . and you're talking to the people of New Zealand.' I was not invited back.

The 1983 election had been a watershed for Labour. With the SDP–Liberal Alliance splitting the progressive vote, not only had the Conservatives increased their majority to 144 seats, despite a slight decrease in their popular share, but Labour had come within an inch of falling to third place in votes cast. Michael Foot's parliamentary party was down to 209, the lowest number of Labour MPs since 1935. The campaign, as I remarked at the time, had started badly – and then fallen away. The manifesto – a prolix 22,000-word document described by Gerald Kaufman as 'the longest suicide note in history' – was read only to seek out the nuggets of political disaster. The manifesto slogan 'Think Positively' elicited a negative response. The message was reminiscent of the Latin American finance minister who is said to have told his Cabinet that 'past policies have brought us to the edge of the abyss, and now it is time for a bold step forward'.

When I attended my first meeting of the defeated Parliamentary Labour Party, Michael Foot, who had announced he would be standing down, gave a speech that was magnanimous and witty. He summed up Labour's performance by quoting George Bernard Shaw's remark about the first night of a play he had written that had gone down badly: 'The show was excellent, but the audience was poor.' Some months before in Glasgow, I had heard him make a similar joke: 'In 1945, the good people of Plymouth Devonport elected me as their MP. In 1955, the bastards threw me out.' Finally, pointing out what had to be done under new leadership, Michael echoed the words of Bertolt Brecht: you could not re-elect the electorate; you had to live with their judgement.

The race for the new Labour leader was already on. The two main contenders were Neil Kinnock, representing the so-called 'soft left' of the party, and Roy Hattersley, a former member of Jim Callaghan's Cabinet, who was on the party's right. Some of my Scottish colleagues – John Smith, Donald Dewar and George Robertson – were supporting Roy. I was for Neil. While I liked and admired Roy, Neil was one of the few MPs I knew well before I arrived in Westminster and I felt he had the eloquence, charisma and pragmatism to inspire our recovery. Neil asked me to join his leadership campaign team. He had a wide range of supporters from Robin Cook, who ran the campaign, to the later UKIP MEP Robert Kilroy-Silk. I was the only new MP to be part of this team.

The contest was the first to be decided by an electoral college made up of MPs, constituency parties and trade unions – a scheme agreed at a special conference at Wembley in 1981 – rather than by MPs alone. But any candidate had to be an MP. The fact that Tony Benn, who had lost his seat at the election, was unable to stand was a boost to Kinnock. Neil steered a course between the old establishment and the hard left. It was an appealing strategy for a party yearning to be reborn and win again. With majority support among MPs, constituencies and the unions, he won an overwhelming 71 per cent of the vote. Roy became deputy leader. I joined the Tribune Group of MPs that supported Kinnock and progressive centre-left policies, and persuaded others – like Tony, who had also voted for Neil – to do so.

As I prepared for my maiden speech, Robin Cook, who had entered Parliament some ten years earlier, advised me that one speech a month was about right: to do many more would make you a Commons bore; to do any fewer would make you irrelevant. It was sage advice.

Maiden speeches are set-piece events. As such, they can be stressful. In his 1869 novel *Phineas Finn*, Anthony Trollope's eponymous hero worried so much about his maiden speech that, after overpreparing, he lost his nerve and did not deliver it. Finn's second attempt was equally unsuccessful. He delivered an off-the-cuff and incoherent speech to a stunned and rapidly emptying Chamber. Later in the nineteenth century, Benjamin Disraeli made a disastrous maiden speech in which he assailed the Irish leader, Daniel O'Connell, and sat down to hisses, boos and the drumming of feet.

I represented a constituency in which there were more people out of work than there were people employed in manufacturing industries. One in seven of my constituents were dependent on means-tested benefits. So I felt it imperative that I make my maiden speech in a debate on social security. I said I would raise in the House the full scale of unemployment every month that it remained as high as it was. Norman Tebbit had previously advised the unemployed to 'get on their bikes'. That day, the minister on duty was the ultra-right-wing former headmaster, Rhodes Boyson, who had infamously attempted to blame the poverty and unemployment of the poor on their laziness. He claimed there were plenty of jobs for them as window cleaners. I now realised, I said, what the Conservatives meant when they talked about ladders of opportunity. I finished my relatively short speech with a simple question: 'In 1948 . . . the welfare state was created to take the shame out of need. Is that principle to be overthrown by an ever-increasing set of government assaults on the poor that are devoid of all logic, bereft of all morality and vindictive even beyond monetarism?' As is usual practice in the House of Commons, the response was to praise the speech and fail to answer the question.

The Conservatives' rightward drift was to be a major theme of mine all throughout that parliament, and I started to write regular articles in national newspapers about jobs, social security and the NHS. In February 1984, I exposed a government plan to pilot a scheme in Cowdenbeath forcing eighteen- to twenty-five-year olds to accept any low-paid job on offer or lose their benefits. The following year, in July 1985, I highlighted so-called 'snooper squads' who were making early-morning calls to the homes of young single mothers to check for the 'presence of male items'. A friendly civil servant later passed on to me the details of the Tory government's 1985 welfare reforms. I used the computer printout to show that 7 million people would lose out. While we could not reverse the policy in the face of an overwhelming Conservative majority, we did manage to water it down.

I loved my constituency work – most of the time. In my last pre-election meeting in Cowdenbeath, I was asked by a voter to confirm I would live in the constituency when elected. I said I was planning to move home and open an office. On the first day after the election, I was phoned by a man who said he had to see me urgently but that I had to visit in person. I duly arrived at his home to discover he was the voter who had asked that question. I exchanged pleasantries, sat down and then he enquired: 'How do you like it?' 'What do you mean?' I asked. He answered: 'It's worth £55,000, but I'll give it to you for £50,000.' I made my excuses and left.

Later, after I moved into what is now my home in Fife – I have only lived in two Scottish houses over the last forty years – I was burgled, perhaps not surprisingly because the house was empty for days on end when I was away in Westminster. All electronic items of any value – TV, video and stereo – had been stolen. A few days later the burglar was arrested. When he came to court his father wrote me a letter apologising; if his son had only known it was the Labour MP's house, he wrote, he would never have broken into it.

While I mostly found my work on behalf of constituents both interesting and enjoyable, I did once come close to a major embarrassment when I took up the case of a widow in her mid-seventies who had gone for a private hip operation on the advice of her NHS surgeon. He then performed the operation at the nearest private hospital in Edinburgh. The woman showed me a stream of bills she had received doubling the original estimate for the hospital stay. I remember the items included several pounds each for an aspirin and a cup of tea. I took her case up with the BBC and ITV. I said the widow was a hard-up pensioner who had been conned into draining her life savings to pay for this operation. The cameras gathered at her home in a cul-de-sac in Crossgates, a village a few miles east of Dunfermline. Just before they started to film, I casually encountered the neighbour next door, who had come out to watch and suddenly asked: 'What's this about? Has she won the football pools again?' I played up her age and played down her wealth, and no one was any wiser. But more serious – and indeed in some cases tragic – issues took up more of my time, including securing justice for a constituent whose husband had been murdered in Spain as he tried to fend off thieves. I demanded the Spanish authorities prosecute the guilty assailants.

In October 1984, when Neil reshuffled his front bench, he invited me to join as Scottish spokesman under Donald Dewar. I was pleased to be asked but declined the offer. Still a new MP, I told Neil that for now I thought I could learn more – and make more of a difference – from the back benches. Neil replied that if he was in my position he would have done exactly the same.

There were local campaigns to be fought for those losing out from the second Conservative term. In addition to raising social security issues, I opposed the downgrading of Fife's regional development status and stood by mining families trying to survive the terrible deprivations of the year-long miners' strike.

During these difficult times, it is often said, the miners under Arthur Scargill were 'lions led by donkeys'. Indeed, Scargill turned the dispute into a political strike personalised around himself. I had spoken with him once or twice at meetings in Fife before the crisis. I noticed that when he was before an audience he talked only about himself. A settlement was possible in the summer of 1984. But because of Scargill, the strike dragged on for a further nine months through a bitter and cold winter.

The Conservative government were well prepared for this confrontation. In 1981, they had rejected the National Coal Board's recommendation to close uneconomic pits, while the Energy Secretary, Nigel Lawson, set in train a plan to build up coal stocks by converting power stations to oil. By refusing to ballot his members, Scargill made a fatal mistake. Deprived of legitimacy, the miners lost the battle for public opinion.

In my own constituency, we now had no pits, but a high number of people living there worked elsewhere in mines across the rest of Fife, Clackmannanshire and the Lothians. There were ten strike centres locally and most Fridays I visited them to give whatever financial help I could. There was grinding hardship such as I had never seen before. The Department for Social Security even slashed the only benefit payment for miners' children and their mothers by £15 a week.

Under Section 12 of the Social Work (Scotland) Act, a local authority could give loans to families facing destitution. This is exactly what Fife did. In retaliation, social security officials cut benefits even more for those receiving small loans from the council. Later the government surcharged Fife Council for daring to prop up mining families.

I spoke to the miners in Cowdenbeath in March 1985, on the day the strike ended, pledging that we would continue to fight in Parliament for justice. And the struggle was far from over. Within a few days, nearly 300 Scottish miners were dismissed by the Coal Board, many of them for being arrested picketing a company moving coal through my constituency during the strike.

I resolved to lead a campaign against this cruel ideology of kicking people when they were down. It gained the support not only of all the Scottish churches but also of police chiefs who had overseen the arrest of the miners in the first place. They understood the need for reconciliation more than the Coal Board did.

As a member of the Select Committee on Employment, I persuaded the chairman, Ron Leighton, to organise hearings into the dismissals. By the time the head of the Coal Board, Ian MacGregor, was called in, I had assembled all the evidence I needed. At the hearing, I asked him why he had not given the dismissed miners a right of appeal as was laid down in their terms of employment. MacGregor replied that the chaos and unusual circumstances of the strike prevented proper procedures being followed. I then asked how many miners had been dismissed during the strike and how many since the end of the strike; most had been fired afterwards. MacGregor then had to admit there was no reason why they could not have been allowed their right of appeal. The Coal Board was forced to back down. All of the miners, with the exception of one, got their jobs back. I tried hard to persuade the odd man out to accept the deal. But he had expected a big cash settlement for unfair dismissal and not even his union could convince him to return. Though I disagreed with Scargill, I stood with the miners. I am proud of their decision to make me an honorary member of the Scottish Mineworkers' Union. To this day, I proudly display in my home the plaques and lamps that were given to me after that harrowing time.

Mrs Thatcher offered up a gift by promising she would meet any MP who complained about redundancies in their constituency. I met her every six months over two or three years and every time I went in to see her she said: 'This is your meeting, Mr Brown, to talk about the concerns you have.' Yet within a few seconds of me starting to speak she would cut across my speech with a soliloquy citing her favourite theme of the moment. It was more difficult to accept when she tried to rename the towns in my constituency. 'You have come to see me about the problems of Rosyth and Cowdenbeath.' she said. 'Cowdenbeath,' I replied gently. She said, 'You call it Cowdenbeath. We have always referred to it as Cowdenbeath.'

The cold winter of 1984 was not just a catastrophe for the miners and their families, it was also a harsh season for millions of poorer pensioners. Money that should have been given to pensioners in 'exceptionally severe weather payments' was being denied because the government had arbitrarily changed the qualifying temperature for payments to just a few degrees above freezing. In place of a flawed formula, depriving old people of help, I proposed that low-income households be awarded an automatic payment to defray crippling fuel bills. Years later, I would be mindful of this when as chancellor I introduced the Winter Fuel Allowance and then as prime minister was able to triple cold-weather payments from £8.50 to £25 a week.

Around this time, I had been leaked an internal government document showing that the Defence Secretary, Michael Heseltine, was planning to close the Rosyth Naval Base and to privatise the dockyard that refitted many of Britain's submarines and warships. Now far from the brevity of my maiden speech, I set a record three-hour speech in the committee stage as we attempted to delay the bill from going back to the House of Commons for its third reading. During that mini-filibuster, I read out every statistic I could get hold of about ship-repair protocols around the world – even in landlocked states.

An ideological government – with a big Commons majority – ploughed ahead despite the fact there was some public support for the concerns about privatising key elements of our national defences and security. Having lost that battle, I had a modicum of success in pressing for financial incentives for companies replacing the lost Rosyth jobs and investing in a Fife that had persistently higher unemployment than the rest of the country.

By now, I had the good fortune that my younger brother was working with me in the Commons. Taking three years off from his work in television, Andrew was an invaluable adviser and we worked to expose the Conservatives' indifference to the fate of the industrial regions. We had discovered that, to secure regional funding from the European Community, the government had to submit honest accounts of the state of each area, and by publishing extracts from what were massive documents we demonstrated the need for more support for the depressed areas.

In November 1985 John Smith asked me to join his shadow trade and industry team. The new post demanded that I make regular trips to the north-east, north-west, the Midlands and Wales as we took our campaign – 'jobs and the economy first' – around the country. Breaking with the past, we reached beyond traditional Labour supporters and drew in members of the business community, and I was fortunate then and over the following years that my work had the support of the Labour Finance and Industry Group and, in particular, three industrialists – Simon Haskel, John Gregson and Swraj Paul – without whose backing for the group I could not have researched and published the reports I did. During that time I also began working with John Prescott – who proved to be the most energetic and consistent advocate of economic devolution – in making the case for Regional Development Agencies, which to his great credit he would later establish in government. The Confederation of British Industry was initially sceptical but our message on industrial policy increasingly gained traction.

Labour appeared to be making progress in 1985 and 1986, particularly after Neil launched his attack on the Trotskyist group Militant Tendency. As he delivered his famous speech denouncing Militant at the Labour conference in 1985, I watched Eric Heffer, the hard-left MP for Liverpool Walton, heighten the drama by storming off the stage. This played into Neil's hands. Not only did Heffer walk off the stage, he walked into political oblivion. I joined Neil's fight to expel Militant from the party.

The 1987 election campaign, run by Bryan Gould and Peter Mandelson, was the first in which I had any national role – small as it was. 'Labour won the campaign, but lost the election,' it was later said. In fact, the reality was somewhat different. If you do not get the policy fundamentals right, no amount of good political presentation – from red roses to new anthems – can make up the difference. If the 1983 manifesto had been too long, the 1987 manifesto was a mere seventeen pages, set in a large bold type. It did not do enough to answer the concerns voters had about Labour's position on defence, taxation and economic management.

It was this election that taught me and my colleagues that we still had a long way to go to establish our economic credibility as a party of government. I spent my days travelling round the regions. I did only one national press conference – with Gerald Kaufman and Tony Blair. It did not go well. All the coverage Labour might have received from my employment initiatives was swept away by a comment Tony made alleging that Mrs Thatcher's policies on private rented housing were the result of 'an unchecked and unbalanced mind'. Michael Brunson, ITN's savvy political editor, instantly asked if Tony was suggesting that the prime minister had psychiatric problems. I knew – everybody knew – that this was not what Tony meant, but the press reported his comment as a desperate gambit by an increasingly desperate party. Tony was despondent as he got pilloried; I told him these things happened and it would pass.

In Scotland, Labour gained an additional nine MPs and increased its share of the vote by over 7 per cent. The Conservatives lost half their seats and it was now clear that they were a waning force north of the border. My own majority in Dunfermline East doubled to nearly 20,000. But across the UK, Labour secured only an extra twenty MPs. The Conservatives still held a parliamentary majority in excess of a hundred.

The year before, I had published a biography of the Scottish socialist James Maxton, perhaps the most gifted orator of his day and, according to Churchill, the best parliamentarian of his time. In his review of the book, Michael Foot described Maxton's rhetorical skills: 'Until the deed was done no one could tell which instrument he would choose – laughter or tears. Like all the very greatest artists he was the master of both.' He had taken the slums into Parliament, was one of the first to call for a National Health Service and a welfare state, and was labelled by some as the 'Children's Champion'. But the real message of my book was that to hold to an ideological purity at the cost of political impotence served no one. Labour – now destined to be out of power for another ten years – had to change even more radically if we were to return to government.

First, I thought we had to widen Labour's appeal and make it a mass-membership party through the recruitment of many of the country's 5.5 million trade-union-levy payers – members of unions affiliated to Labour. For 'this army of supporters now waiting in the wings', I argued in an article, 'individual membership should be inexpensive to buy and attractive to hold'. I followed this with a more detailed pamphlet a few years later, *Making Mass Membership Work*, focusing on an active, directed recruitment strategy in local communities. I was clear about the party's uninviting culture: Labour needed to locate itself at the centre of community life. In my own constituency we had great success thanks to the work of my election agent, Alex Rowley, and a friend who died all too young, Helen Dowie. Having already doubled membership in the late 1980s, we set and met an ambitious goal of 1,500 members by 1993.

I thought I could play my part in shaping change and decided it was the right time to stand for the shadow Cabinet. In these elections, deals were often made across the party's regional factions that made no sense of the party's ideological divisions. Some who would always have got a place on merit, like Gerald Kaufman, moved to the very top of the ballot because he was a master of sophisticated manoeuvring. Gerald elevated his campaign to such an art form that he was able to tell you how many times he had talked to each MP; indeed, he allocated each of his colleagues a quota of time-limited conversations over the course of the year.

I had to broaden my support beyond an admittedly larger than usual Scottish constituency – now one-quarter of the Parliamentary Labour Party. I did so thanks to my friend Nick Brown, the Newcastle MP who was a genius in mastering the byzantine machinery and assembled a coalition that won me eighty-eight votes. I was elected joint eleventh on the ballot, a decent enough result for someone standing for the first time.

While the election for the shadow Cabinet was in the hands of the

Parliamentary Labour Party, the allocation of portfolios was in the hands of the leader. In the ensuing reshuffle, Neil appointed me shadow Chief Secretary to the Treasury, under John Smith, the new shadow chancellor. I spent the next year thinking through how to modernise Labour's approach in the area that had become our Achilles heel – taxing and spending. None doubted our willingness to spend money, but too many doubted our capacity to spend prudently.

I argued that we had to become wise spenders rather than big spenders. John Smith, also keen to transform Labour, developed a mantra of a Labour Party committed to economic stability. We were up against Nigel Lawson as chancellor and the now rising star John Major as Chief Secretary. A former whip, Major was also an expert in parliamentary tactics – and, although this is not how he is now best remembered, an adept Westminster operator. In the last stages of the Budget debate in the spring of 1988, for example, at a time when most MPs would normally be standing in the bars rather than sitting on the benches, he flooded the House of Commons with supporters to shout me down; they were louder than ever, having just come from the bars.

Neil Kinnock continued to spearhead the efforts to make Labour acceptable, with reworked policies and a measured statement of aims and values. He insisted that we had to become more disciplined and more professional. The question, as he put it at the 1987 party conference in Brighton, was 'whether this party wants to achieve victory or to settle for offering the British people nothing but sympathy'. We were moving ahead, when Tony Benn suddenly launched a challenge to Neil's leadership. Eligible because he had returned to the Commons, Tony cobbled together enough nominations to stand. It was a classic case of tilting at windmills. Neil won by a landslide of 89 per cent. But since we always seemed to be looking inwards, out in the country we were failing to win support. In November 1988, a little over a month after the leadership contest, Labour lost the Govan by-election to the SNP. A majority of 19,509 in one of Labour's safest Scottish seats gave way to an SNP majority of 3,554.

The Budget of 1988, when Nigel Lawson infamously reduced the top rate of income tax from 60p to 40p, marked something of a turning point. On the spot, I concluded that Lawson had handed us a weapon that could eventually help us get back into power. As I pointed out at

the time, 95 per cent of the British people would gain nothing; in one
swoop, he had given billions to the wealthiest people in the country.
As I said, 'No Budget this century has given so much to so few.'

Such a huge and offensive redistribution of wealth from poor to
rich had economic consequences too. These were compounded
when, the next day, Lawson did what he often did: reduced interest
rates and then claimed the economy could afford this because his
policies were working and inflation was under control. It was this kind
of cynical ploy – the chancellor pronouncing favourably on his own
economics and rewarding himself with an interest-rate cut – that was
discrediting the conduct of monetary policy. In my own mind, I started
to question Treasury control of interest rates and remarked to John
Smith that there could be a case for Bank of England independence.
But Lawson had made a grave error. His tax cuts, followed by his
interest-rate cuts, helped fuel an unsustainable housing boom which
was eventually to bring recession.

Everything was to change for me in October 1988. On the Saturday
after our party conference, suffering from a severe headache, John
Smith went to see his GP, who sent him straight to hospital. When a
cardiogram failed to identify any problems, John went back to his
Edinburgh home. The next day, while getting dressed, he suffered a
heart attack. When I had been with John at the conference, he clearly
was not 100 per cent well. Having been stricken, John was now
instructed to take time off, cut out alcohol and lose weight. He would
be off for months. Parliament was returning within a few days. Bryan
Gould, the trade and industry spokesman, was the next senior person
with an economics portfolio and the obvious stand in. But to my
surprise, Neil asked me to take over temporarily as shadow chancellor.
Throughout the next three months, I kept in close touch with John,
visiting him frequently, but trying not to overburden him and simply
getting on with the job in hand.

My new role came just as interest rates started to rise and economic
issues took centre stage. Within a few days of taking over, I had to
confront Nigel Lawson across the Dispatch Box for the first time.
Seven months ago, I said, he had proclaimed he was presiding over
an economic miracle. What miracle? These had been seven months
during which real interest rates and inflation had soared to among
the highest in Europe; and every major forecast and assessment that

the chancellor had given was proving to be wrong. He was wrong about inflation, wrong about interest rates, wrong about imports, wrong about savings, trade deficits and the money supply. And his response, I said, was to tell us that what we needed was self-discipline – not from him, of course, but from everyone else. I went straight for Mrs Thatcher: 'Historians will be interested to know what special powers the chancellor has over the prime minister that she should witness these appalling errors and then describe them as brilliant, wonderful and marvellous.'

The press coverage was positive. I was described as a new Labour star, and Conservative strategists were so annoyed that, on the day after my speech, a rising Tory MP, Tim Yeo, was instructed to introduce a Point of Order claiming that I had gone to *Hansard* and tried to doctor the transcript of my speech. I had done nothing of the kind.

The Opposition can stage a debate almost every week in the autumn and Neil continuously put me on the front line during November. I again did battle with Lawson during the Autumn Statement. I was fortunate to be facing him in 1988. By now, after five years as chancellor, he came across as overconfident, complacent and growing indolent – perhaps even stale. Up against him, any thirty-seven-year-old might look dynamic and fresh. My accidental promotion pushed me from eleventh place to top position in the next shadow Cabinet elections in November.

John Smith resumed his shadow chancellorship in February 1989. Back to my old post as shadow Chief Secretary, I thought I had the time to write a book about the right-wing drift of the Tories. The title was *Where There is Greed*. Looking back on this, I missed a chance: while it was important to reveal what was wrong with the Tories' policies, I should have done more to define New Labour, set out a detailed agenda for change and provide a stronger intellectual framework for the modernisation movement within the party. Old-style national corporatist strategies, such as nationalisation, exchange controls and capital controls could not now work in an increasingly globalised economy. We had to move on from them. Labour had to be the party of aspiration but, even after Neil's major reforms, it was still seen as a party that prevented people fulfilling their ambitions.

The 1989 conference was to mark the completion of the Kinnock policy review process. In advance, Neil published *Meet the Challenge,*

Make the Change, a comprehensive document of seven chapters covering every aspect of party policy. It is best known for the decision to keep Britain's nuclear deterrent. By 1989 we had abandoned the three most unpopular policies of our decade out of power – unilateral nuclear disarmament, old-style nationalisation and high taxation. Thanks to his leadership, Neil's new policies were approved with relatively little dissent and they would form the basis of the 1992 election manifesto.

In November 1989 Neil promoted me to the trade and industry brief. I wanted to make the case for a modern industrial strategy for Britain but first I had to deal with a thorny problem: our continuing commitment to renationalising telecommunications. It was not only unpopular; privatisation was all but irreversible because of the fast-changing nature of the industry and the fact that so many millions had already bought shares in the privatised companies. By now, I was thinking of an alternative policy which would secure benefits for the country through regulation without the expense of renationalisation. In due course this was to lead to my proposal for a windfall tax on the privatised utilities to fund a welfare-to-work agenda.

Being the trade spokesman offered huge openings in the House of Commons because of the mistakes of our Tory opponents which led to a high turnover of Trade and Industry Secretaries. The first I was up against, the anti-interventionist Nicholas Ridley – who was ultimately forced to resign after saying that giving up sovereignty to the European Union was as bad as giving it up to Adolf Hitler – was well known as a heavy smoker. To make the point that he regarded his departmental brief as that of abolishing his department, I told the House that his desk had no in tray, no out tray – only an ashtray.

The next two years saw some dramatic events on the floor of the Commons as Mrs Thatcher's leadership faltered and then ultimately imploded. She was already under pressure from Scotland because of the flat-rate poll tax which was leading to demonstrations and potentially riots. None of the parliamentary dramas we would see under our own government would ever match the no-holds-barred Tory civil war that brought the resignation of Nigel Lawson as chancellor and the denunciation of Mrs Thatcher by Geoffrey Howe in his resignation speech as deputy prime minister in November 1990. There followed quickly the rejection of the prime minister who had brought the Conservatives back to power. We were well positioned to run against her in 1992. John Major's sudden premiership – his shift to the centre and his rags-to-riches story – created a new set of challenges for which Labour was less prepared.

Tony and I made a long visit to Australia in 1991, not just because we wanted to see a Labour government in action – we toured eight cities and met the Australian prime minister and treasurer, Bob Hawke and Paul Keating, and other future leaders too – but because we were rethinking some of the basic assumptions which animated progressive moments. On the long plane journey out, Tony and I started with a blank sheet of paper and tried to set down from first principles what a modern social democracy would look like. The world was changing. Both Tony and I were in no doubt that we had to endorse markets, competition and the essential role of the private sector in achieving economic growth, and that we also had to change from a tax-and-spend party that appeared willing to borrow, no matter the circumstances. Neil Kinnock had fought a long battle against those who opposed nuclear weapons, council-house sales and public-private partnerships to rebuild our infrastructure, and had to convince doubters that it made no sense to renationalise British Telecom.

Tony and I recognised that there were also such things as market failures. Effective as markets are as mechanisms for creating material prosperity, they come up against limits. Markets could not on their own account address pollution or deliver public goods, and even if the market could achieve a much-vaunted equilibrium – balancing demand and supply – that did little to counter inequality. Markets did not have the inbuilt mechanisms – that only government can provide – to correct their tendency to self-destruct. Getting the balance right between the public and private sectors and, if possible, ending the self-defeating territorial stand-off between the two was the challenge. We had to recognise that while markets need rules to underpin them, the public sector can be paid for only by a productive market sector. In future, public spending had to be judged not by how much we spent, but by what it achieved. On all of this, Tony and I agreed and we were to follow through these ideas in party policy reforms a year or two later. Where we found it more difficult to agree was on what to do about poverty and inequality. Both of us favoured promoting opportunity and felt that equality of opportunity was a goal that no one was yet delivering. But on equality I think it is fair to say that I gave more emphasis to prosecuting a war on poverty and addressing inequalities of income and wealth.

More immediate issues had to be tackled on our return. I was sure we should fight the 1992 general election by focusing on the state of the economy. Unemployment was rising sharply, the recession hitting hard, and higher mortgages were driving people into negative equity. At last, I believed, we could successfully attack the Conservatives for their mismanagement of the economy and credibly position Labour as the party of economic competence. None of this, I am afraid, happened.

Only once have I made a private forecast about the outcome of a general election that was predicted to be close – the 1992 election, when I was unhappily convinced the Tories would win. I anticipated a Conservative majority of thirty. I was too pessimistic: in the end, Major had a majority of twenty-one. The expected Labour breakthrough never happened. Why? Because we failed to stress the one issue that mattered most to the country. In Britain, too, as with Bill Clinton's successful presidential campaign in 1992, it should have been a version of 'it's the economy, stupid' – as I argued, 'jobs and the economy first'.

I could understand the calculation that Neil's pollsters were making, even though I did not agree with it. Their view was that people would come to us if Labour looked fresh, modern and free of extremists. By announcing Neil's support for constitutional change and his open mind on proportional representation, it was felt that we could show Labour represented the future and the Tories were now the past.

Labour had worked hard since 1987 to counteract its image as a party of high tax-and-spend. As shadow Chief Secretary, I had set up a system to ensure all policy commitments were vetted to prove we could be trusted with the nation's finances. Margaret Beckett then took over the role, determined to prevent the Tories frightening voters with claims we would be profligate. Yet in the summer of 1991, Conservative Central Office launched their usual attack on Labour's spending plans, this time falsely costing our proposals at £35 billion. And when John Smith published *Made in Britain* – which proposed to abolish the upper limit on National Insurance contributions – the Tories unveiled their 'Tax Bombshell' poster, falsely charging that Labour's plans would mean tax rises of more than £1,000 for the average family.

Perhaps most damaging of all, a few days before the start of the campaign, the party was caught out by Norman Lamont's pre-election Budget. He dramatically introduced a new 20p tax rate which took 4 million lower-paid workers out of the 25p tax band. The ingenuity of the Lamont plan was that, in effect, Labour now favoured higher taxes on the low-paid than the Conservatives did: our plans cut far less ice than the Lamont proposal.

John believed we had to neutralise Tory attempts to magnify fears in voters' minds about hidden Labour tax rises. Just six days into the campaign, and with all the pomp of a Budget day, John delivered a 'shadow Budget', publishing a host of figures as if he were already chancellor. He assumed that if we were upfront about the gains from a Labour government – rising pensions, increased child benefit, more for the NHS – then the public would accept tax rises to pay for them. But any talk of fairness got lost in the instantaneous Tory bombardment alleging that his shadow Budget hit ordinary families.

Months before, I had argued to John and Neil, who was also worried about John's tax plans, that we should recognise that we were in a recession, talk about the issues we were studiously ignoring – jobs and the economy – and sideline all talk of tax rises. I wanted us to argue that the economic problems of the country were now so severe that they would be our first priority, and an anti-recession programme – scrapping all previous unfunded commitments and all tax increases – was by far the best way to deal with the downturn. The Conservatives, I said, were finally vulnerable on the economy.

The American consultant Bob Shrum, hidden away in a London hotel, shared my apprehension. Bob and his wife Marylouise were later to become close friends of our family. But at that time, I didn't even know he was there and he had contact only with Labour's pollster and strategy adviser Philip Gould and the team around him. Party officials were afraid that the presence of an American would provoke a media storm about a foreign takeover. It was absurd; in 1997, 2001 and beyond, Americans including Bob were sitting in the middle of our election war room. It simply wasn't an issue.

Bob's view, like mine, was that day after day we should be hammering on the Tories' economic record. All this time, I kept asking to do national events highlighting unemployment. To illustrate the parlous state of the economy, I devised a clock that showed we were losing a job every seven seconds. I did unveil the clock, but spent most of my time travelling the regions.

And as we focused on the constitution and our spending plans but not on the economy, the Tories went for the jugular on tax. They plastered the country with two posters – 'THE PRICE OF LABOUR: £1,250 A YEAR FOR EVERY FAMILY' and 'LABOUR'S DOUBLE WHAMMY: MORE TAXES, HIGHER PRICES'. The calculations were crude and simplistic, but they were effective. Despite all our work, Labour was less trusted on tax than a Conservative Party that had recently tried, and failed, to impose a poll tax and had already more than doubled VAT. I was frustrated: the Tories had made the shadow Budget and tax-and-spend the issue.

For me, two images stand out from the last few days of the campaign: on the one hand, John Major on a simple wooden soapbox making his final campaign speeches; on the other, Labour's big-budget, triumphalist Sheffield rally that resembled a US-style political convention. With 10,000 party members in attendance, Neil's human and emotional response to the adoring crowd – 'We're alright! We're alright! We're alright!' – came under fire from the right-wing press. And when Roy Hattersley exulted that the result was a forgone conclusion, the press had another field day. It was a classic political error: you can't tell the voters you have won; they have to tell you.

The polls continued to show a marginal Labour victory – or at worst a hung parliament. By chance, on election night, my older brother was producing the TV coverage from Scotland and had linked me into a three-way interview with Kenneth Clarke and the Liberal Democrat, Alan Beith. Just as we were about to go on air, the programme dramatically switched to the count at the marginal seat in Basildon, where Labour had achieved only a 1 per cent swing and the Conservatives had held on. It was a bellwether outcome. As the camera turned to me, I dutifully retreated to the standard holding line that it was 'still too early to say'. But my worst fears had been confirmed.

CHAPTER 4

THE ROAD TO GRANITA — AND
GOVERNMENT

John Smith was the obvious successor when, after the 1992 general election, Neil Kinnock decided to step down as Labour leader. He was also my close friend. I had worked side by side with him in his team for many years. And I admired his abilities.

For nearly a decade, with courage and unstinting determination, Neil had taken the party into the modern world. He had confronted Militant entryism, transformed our policies from defence to the economy, and given the party back a belief in itself. Both Tony Blair and I believed it was urgent for us to build on what Neil had achieved, to push ahead with Labour's reform process and to move without delay. Once it was clear that Neil would resign, I told John that I would support him. And when Neil phoned asking if I would consider Bryan Gould, I politely declined to do so.

Not only was John Smith head and shoulders above his colleagues, my personal friendship with him was long-standing. It did not occur to me that I would be anything other than loyal to him and I wanted to give him all the help I could. I had not agreed with him over the shadow Budget, and I would push him to move more quickly on Labour's modernisation, but he had immense credibility born out of a natural integrity and years of public service. I had no doubt that he had the strength, ability and desire to take on John Major and win the next election.

On the day after the election, I travelled to County Durham to meet Tony at the Blairs' home in Sedgefield. I'm not sure Tony was serious when he said to me in his living room that I should stand for leader — and I did not take it seriously. He and others would later suggest that by 'hesitating' at this moment, I missed my chance. In fact, it was a contest I never had any intention of being drawn into, would not have won, and could not have entered out of loyalty to John.

For his part, Tony told me he wanted to run for deputy leader. His argument for standing was not without merit. As deputy, Tony could act as a powerful advocate for reform. If he ran, I would – I immediately said – support him. But I had to tell him honestly that I did not think he had any chance of success against Margaret Beckett and John Prescott, and that he would be accused of jumping the gun. Nick Brown, who was a former union official with unsurpassed knowledge of the unions, as well as the parliamentary party, offered the same advice, telling Tony bluntly that he could not win the trade union vote, then a third of the electoral college. A Smith endorsement of his candidacy could have given Tony support among his parliamentary colleagues, and I agreed to check this out with a phone call to John. But when I put Tony's case to him, John was unequivocal in his response. He did not want him to stand and preferred Margaret.

It quickly became clear that John was the overwhelming choice for leader in the minds of most MPs, party members and trade unionists. Such was his status that, at first, many suspected there would not even be a leadership contest. In the event, John's challenger, Bryan Gould, won only 9 per cent of the vote. And in the deputy leadership contest, John's preferred candidate, Margaret Beckett, won an outright majority over John Prescott.

At the shadow Cabinet election afterwards, I finished in first place while Tony ended up second. New recruits to the shadow Cabinet, like David Blunkett, Harriet Harman, Tom Clarke and Mo Mowlam, signalled a sweeping changing of the guard. John Smith named me shadow chancellor. I had expected Tony to want the post of trade and industry spokesman but, to his credit, Tony saw the opportunity as shadow Home Secretary to present a modern view of Labour on law and order. I pushed John to give him this post.

We were still in the post-mortem phase after our election defeat. That July, I delivered the annual Tribune lecture setting out my own view on how Labour could reshape itself and win the next general election. I emphasised that we had yet to persuade potential supporters that Labour reflected their values in a way that was relevant to their everyday lives. I pointed out that Labour's constitution was written in 1918 in response to the very different challenges of that time.

The implication was that reform of the party's constitution, including its blanket commitment to public ownership in Clause IV, was an issue we had to take up. My point was that the party now had to break with a one-dimensional centralist view of state power. If there was a public interest at stake, it did not require public ownership and a public bureaucracy directly overseeing provision – governments could be sponsor, partner, catalyst and coordinator of services or industries: they did not always need to be owners.

Four months after becoming shadow chancellor, I was elected by the party membership to the National Executive Committee for the first time. This was a breakthrough – the places had been monopolised for years by Tony Benn, Dennis Skinner and others on the far left – and it provided me, and Tony too, with the platform we wanted to push for more and faster change. And when John took up the case, which Neil had first advocated, for 'one member, one vote' in the selection of parliamentary candidates – a long overdue reform – I backed him to the hilt.

John knew 'one member, one vote' was totemic as a demonstration that Labour was changing. But in private, as he told me, he wished it was something he did not have to deal with. It quickly became a test of his leadership. So adamantly against this reform was John Edmonds, the general secretary of John Smith's own union, that he announced he was not inviting him to address their 1993 conference. But over the summer months John manoeuvred with exquisite subtlety to persuade other unions, most of them previously hostile, to go along with him. At the TUC conference in September 1993, John did not promise to repeal all Conservative trade union legislation, but he won many unions over by offering them a new Charter of Rights on the first day of a Labour government, and implied – to my dismay – that he would be prepared to tax, spend and borrow more. Even then it was still touch and go as to whether, a few weeks later, John would have enough votes to push 'one member, one vote' through; but so committed to winning this test of leadership was he that, as he told me, he would call for a vote of confidence and if necessary resign if he lost.

His last move was a masterstroke – and I witnessed his manoeuvres at first hand. Even as lunchtime delegation meetings were being held at the Labour conference on the day of the vote, John and his chief of staff, Murray Elder, had figures showing they might lose. John and

Murray considered asking me to make the final appeal to wavering delegates but they were right to instead call on John's erstwhile rival, John Prescott, to sum up the debate. A trade union negotiator to his fingertips, John Prescott could assure them that Labour had no intention of breaking its links with the unions. And so it was that with great passion he convinced delegates that John had 'put his head on the block' and that the conference must trust him. Not all speeches matter. But this one did. While lunchtime meetings had delivered further union support and Murray now calculated we had won, not for the first time a Prescott speech gave delegates the confidence to be positive about change. John Smith carried the day by the thinnest of margins, a little over 3 per cent.

While John was reforming Labour's constitution, I was reforming our economic policies. First, I persuaded him we had to ditch his own shadow Budget. Having convinced him, I bluntly announced we had got it wrong. This had to be awkward for John, but he understood that the defining mistake of the last campaign was not the one on which to fight the next. When a Labour MP demanded to know why I had dropped our tax pledges so brutally, I replied simply: 'Because we did not win the election.'

The change was officially announced in a document entitled *Campaign for Recovery*, which, of course, had a double meaning: not just the recovery of the economy but the recovery of the party. In it, I didn't avoid the issue of tax. For once, I had been able to find a popular tax. I now set out a plan for a one-off levy on the excess profits of the privatised utilities. It was an initiative that, unlike some others, stood the test of time and was eventually enacted five years later as the windfall tax to finance the New Deal for unemployed workers. We were able to offer something more. I launched an attack which made headlines about what I called the 'undeserving rich' – the privatised-utility bosses, tax avoiders and 'something for nothing' executives, who paid themselves far too much at the expense of the public. But in the detail of my attack and my justification of the windfall tax, I was careful to distinguish between those who made money because of the monopoly that they enjoyed – who ought to pay more tax – and those who did well competing successfully in a harshly competitive marketplace.

My proposal had an added advantage that tax increases rarely do:

it was difficult for the Tories to successfully attack this policy. Not only were the profit levels and remuneration systems of the privatised utilities deeply unpopular – with many chief executives awarding themselves lavish salaries and share options – but the Conservatives had created a precedent by introducing a similar one-off tax on the banks in the early 1980s. While many of my shadow Cabinet colleagues were sceptical, John backed me and I stepped up the public pressure on the government.

I also took a tough line with colleagues announcing unfunded spending commitments. That was the only way to overcome the perception that Labour would be reckless with the public finances. It was a long, hard fight. In my early years as shadow chancellor, it seemed that every interview I did, from the usual politics programmes to Radio 4's *Today* and breakfast TV, focused on the allegation that taxes would inevitably go up under Labour, and for a simple reason: we planned to spend more, they claimed, on public services and almost everything else. Our plan was to avoid willy-nilly spending commitments, and to deter them the Treasury team set up a private contest among members of the shadow Cabinet: who could spend the most for the least publicity? Michael Meacher won hands down, when he called for billions of extra spending and secured only one column inch. The lesson was being learned – but I suspect because of my uncompromising stand on tax-and-spend, I never did as well again in shadow Cabinet elections as I had in 1992.

I was working hand in hand with Tony. We seemed to be of one mind and, at times, we could each anticipate what the other was thinking. It was almost as if we still shared the same office. In January 1993, Tony launched a new counteroffensive on crime using a phrase I had suggested: 'Tough on crime and tough on the causes of crime'. For the first time in years we had a position on law and order around which the whole party could unite, and this rewriting of Labour's approach, focusing both on the victims of crime and the causes of crime, rightly earned him great plaudits.

I think it is fair to say that I was the reformer who at that time felt the most heat from within the party. My hard-line stance on public expenditure provoked continuing divisions. For example, in March 1993 Peter Hain, later a good friend, published a demand from the Tribune Group, of which I was a member, for a £20 billion boost to public expenditure. That would have required a huge increase in income tax or a resort to old-style borrowing. I rejected the proposal unceremoniously, and in unvarnished terms I told party conferences that our New Jerusalem could not be built on a mountain of debt. Our approach was to be 'prudence for a purpose'.

An economic issue as important as tax, devaluation – one that had haunted Labour in the past – came to the fore early in my shadow chancellorship. This time it would haunt the Conservatives for years to come. My first two months as shadow chancellor coincided with the last two months of Britain's unhappy membership of the European Exchange Rate Mechanism.

The recession demanded interest rates be brought down which would have put downward pressure on the pound. But trapped within the ERM this was impossible: the whole point of the ERM was that you had to maintain the value of your currency relative to other members. The initial purpose of the ERM had been to create stability between European countries in order to pave the way for the eventual adoption of a common currency, but it had increasingly become a straitjacket stifling the British economy.

Labour had gone along with the principle of a managed currency within Europe. In October 1989, John Smith and I had visited European capitals and developed a fourfold strategy: entry to the ERM at an effective rate; adequate central-bank arrangements to ward off specu-lation; a pro-growth initiative; and increased support for regions left behind. It was part of our effort to reassure the country of Labour's economic competence.

By autumn 1992, however, all the logic pointed to the need for a devaluation of the pound within the ERM. It was now clear we had joined at too high a rate and our economy was being throttled by inter-est rates set to keep the exchange rate stable. While I made the predict-able calls for pan-European reflation and measures that would have eased the pressure on Britain, the truth was that we were in an impossible position. In any sensible world, we would have had only two choices: get our European partners to agree to a devaluation, or get out.

But Labour had an additional problem of its own: people thought we would always devalue the currency when the going got tough, as Labour governments had done in 1931, 1949 and 1967. Harold Wilson had famously been ridiculed after the 1967 devaluation for saying the 'pound in your pocket' was worth as much as it always had been. As shadow chancellor, I was determined that Labour should not to be seen as the party of devaluation and I stood out against this for longer than I should have. But my political logic was sound. If the Conservatives devalued they should get the blame for it – and not us. I faced criticism from some of my Labour colleagues but that is exactly what happened.

On Black Wednesday, 16 September 1992, the Conservatives abruptly took Britain out of the ERM. John Smith then made his first speech in the House of Commons as Labour leader in a special session. Despite his past support for membership of the mechanism, he brilliantly skewered Major as 'the devalued prime minister of a devalued government'. Major and his chancellor, Norman Lamont, suffered irreparable political damage from this fiasco; Conservative support plummeted in the national polls. It was a remarkable turnaround.

We now had a chance to build a new economic policy and I was building a team to deliver it. At the centre of my new operation was Sue Nye, who at a very young age had run the office of Jim Callaghan, and went on to do the same for Michael Foot and Neil Kinnock. Sue came to work with me after Neil stepped down as leader. Her loyalty was beyond any call of duty; and her knowledge of the Labour Party, broader and deeper than that of anyone I know, has subsequently been put to good use in the House of Lords. She was to be head of my political office until the day I left Downing Street in 2010.

With Geoff Mulgan leaving to form the new and highly successful think tank Demos in 1993, I had begun talking regularly to the brilliant economist Gavyn Davies, who happened to be Sue Nye's husband and was to later help with valuable advice during the Great Recession. In tandem, I also began drawing on the advice of Ed Balls, the very young leader-writer and columnist of the *Financial Times* and probably the most gifted economic thinker of his generation. Now a national celebrity in his own right, he is, in my view, a future prime minister. In 1994, Ed joined my Treasury team full-time. In the same year, I appointed a press secretary, Charlie Whelan, who was head of media for the Amalgamated Engineering Union and had helped ease the passage of 'one member, one vote'. Ironically, given the intense fights they would have later, he came at the recommendation of Peter Mandelson, who was now MP for Hartlepool. In the summer of 1994,

Ed Miliband – whose wide range of talents and leadership qualities I had spotted when he was working for Harriet Harman – signed on and focused on developing our anti-poverty policies. He was later joined by the very young but incredibly capable Spencer Livermore, who worked alongside another expert researcher, Nick Vaughan, for the Opposition front bench's rapid rebuttal unit. By then I was also drawing on the part-time help of Michael Wills, a highly successful TV producer who would later become MP for Swindon. At various times in these years I also had the help of Ed Richards, later the head of Ofcom, and Neal Lawson, who set up the think tank Compass.

Tony and I had an extraordinary close working relationship during this period. Together, we felt we had to pay attention to, and learn from, what was happening to social democratic parties around the world. In January 1993 we went to Washington DC, meeting key figures in President-elect Clinton's team, including Larry Summers, Robert Reich and Paul Begala. They explained how Clinton had gone about making the Democrats electable – the party's previous election victory had been Jimmy Carter's in 1976 – through putting the economy front and centre of the campaign, recognising they had to win over Middle America to their cause and emphasising responsibilities as well as rights. Clinton had focused on welfare reform, changed the perception that the Democrats were soft on crime, and overcame the narrative that his party was always in favour of taxation for taxation's sake.

I returned strengthened in my resolve to modernise our economic policy and to win the debate for change not just with the public but also within the Labour Party, publishing *How We Can Conquer Unemployment* in September 1993 – setting out the case for a New Deal to tackle youth and long-term unemployment – and *Fair is Efficient*, which argued that greater equality was the prerequisite for economic efficiency. I wrote of what I called the economic illusion that prosperity had to be bought at the cost of fairness.

Such was the conflict between the traditionalists and modernisers within Labour that Tony and I were barraged with criticism even for visiting Washington. Following on from our dialogue with the Democrats, when I proposed we adopt public-private partnerships to fund much-needed infrastructure, I similarly came under fire. The attacks only served to bring Tony and me closer together – just before events would begin to drive us apart.

On Wednesday 11 May 1994, I arrived back home late from a fund-raising dinner at the Park Lane Hotel. The event had been held to raise money for the upcoming European Parliament elections in which Labour was expected to do well. In keeping with the European focus, John Smith shared a platform with former French prime minister Michel Rocard. I sat at the front table directly across from John, who was on stage. He looked grey and exhausted. John had been travelling up and down from Scotland to sort out what was a parochial problem in his constituency that he should never have had to deal with: an inquiry into local government boundaries in which his council had asked him to act as their lawyer.

Later, I was one of those who frequently quoted the words he ended his speech with that night: 'The opportunity to serve our country – that is all we ask.' That eloquent finale will be long remembered, but I could see how tired he was. As I joined in the standing ovation – some of the business leaders present that night did not stand, something all of them must have regretted the next day – John and I caught each other's eye. He gave me a look that said, 'I got through it, and I did what I had to do.'

John then stayed up late to have a drink with Rocard. Early the next morning at his flat in the Barbican, as he prepared to leave for a campaign visit in what was now one of our target seats – Basildon in Essex – he collapsed from a heart attack. While being rushed to St Bartholomew's in an ambulance with his wife Elizabeth by his side, he suffered a second attack. The accident and emergency unit to which he was taken was one he had visited only a few weeks before to campaign against a threatened closure. That was where he was pronounced dead.

I was up early that morning to get ready for Treasury Questions against the chancellor, Ken Clarke. Around 9 a.m., I got a phone call from Murray Elder. Murray, who had had a difficult but successful heart transplant in 1988, was himself in hospital. He phoned me twice: first to tell me that John was very ill and had been rushed to hospital; then, a few minutes later, with the news that John had died. The medical staff had been unable to resuscitate him. The devastating news, Murray added, would not be announced formally for two hours while John's family – including his three daughters, Sarah, Jane and Catherine – were informed and given time to come together. The death was announced to a shocked public at a press conference in the hospital's Great Hall at 10.40 a.m.

Tony was on a trip to Aberdeen, campaigning for the European elections. After I hung up with Murray, I instantly phoned Tony and told him the news, and said that it would be announced to the public two hours later. Soon Tony was on his way back to London to confer with Alastair Campbell and others.

I tried to contact Elizabeth, started to pen an obituary and began preparing a statement I would make in the House of Commons, hoping the Speaker would give me permission to deliver it at the outset of Treasury Questions. Writing the tribute to John took longer than I thought, not least because I wanted to do his life and achievements justice. I struggled that morning with genuine grief; I had known John and his family for nearly two decades. The obituary later formed the start of a book that I edited with the journalist Jim Naughtie on John's life and work.

A shell-shocked party decided to postpone the choice of a new leader until after the European elections; Margaret Beckett became acting leader. In truth, though, the starting gun had already been fired. I believed that I was the best candidate to take over from John. As Murray Elder reminded me at the time, John had told him that he shared that view. And I assumed Tony would support me.

But events were to work out differently. In the days that followed John's death, my brother Andrew took time off from his TV work to help me and kept a full day-to-day record of what transpired and, in particular, of conversations he and I had with Tony.

When Tony and I spoke by phone on the evening of 12 May, he made it clear that he wanted to stand. I was surprised. He had always told me that he had never wanted the leadership: he would be happy to be chancellor and then take a top job at the European Commission. At one point he had even told me he might leave politics to work in television.

When we came to the Commons together, I had worked to broaden Tony's appeal within the Parliamentary Labour Party. I had helped write speeches for him and advised him on how to win over the trade unions and the Labour Party membership. More than once, he said I was the senior partner in our relationship.

But the campaign for Tony had already started the night of John's death. Alastair Campbell, then assistant editor (politics) of the mid-market tabloid *Today* and Tony's closest friend in the press, appeared on *Newsnight* to announce that Tony would be the next leader. In the *Evening Standard* on the afternoon of John's death, Sarah Baxter, another apparent Blair sympathiser, published an article entitled 'Why I say Tony Blair should be the next Labour leader'. The next days' newspapers were full of stories from writers like Trevor Kavanagh of the *Sun* favouring Tony.

The vacancy had come at a difficult time for me as I fought to make the party economically credible. I was not only in a bare-knuckle fight with John Edmonds, leader of the GMB union, who wanted Labour to commit to borrowing more to go for growth, but with members of the parliamentary party who favoured this approach to economic policy. Nonetheless, I believed that, in any choice between myself and Tony, I would have the support of the Labour grass roots and I knew that I could secure the majority of MPs.

But I made a fateful decision: that either Tony or I had to stand down. The Labour Party was still in a fragile relationship with the public. And the public, I thought, would never understand how two leading reformers could stand against each other with daggers drawn. With Margaret Beckett and John Prescott both likely to stand for leader and Robin Cook considering doing so, I took the view that, if Tony and I both ran, we would split the modernisation vote and neither of us would win. I knew that in any contest with Tony I would have to draw a dividing line, for example, by making a distinction between two forms of modernisation. I would argue that my policies were not only the best for winning an election but were the best reflection of our enduring values. I would have to argue that Tony could not pull this off and, perhaps more damaging to our future as a party, explain how his ideas of the future were not exactly the same as mine. I was not aware then of how important this distinction was to prove to be to the future of the Labour Party.

By Saturday, the Murdoch press were all backing Tony. The following day, they would publish a series of polls that reinforced this. I told Peter Mandelson in a call that most MPs and the unions would oppose Tony and I had the best chance of winning. Even so, I was worried: the media was writing Tony up as the only moderniser. It was wholly unfair but predictable. And if I forced Tony out of the contest, then the press would say that Labour had written off Middle England. According to Andrew's account of these days, I speculated that, if I became leader, we would have to signal radical change later that year including further party reforms and an end to Clause IV.

On Saturday, Margaret Beckett phoned with a plea she was making to each potential candidate to avoid discussing the leadership until after the European elections on 9 June. But no one, I'm afraid, paid attention. That day, I visited Elizabeth Smith at her Edinburgh home. She took some comfort from having been with John that fateful Thursday morning. I reminded her of John's achievements and of the respect in which he was held across the whole country. 'It's up to you now,' she said as I left.

The Sunday papers not only contained pro-Tony articles but also a story by Andy Grice of the *Sunday Times* which claimed that there was a 'secret pact' between Tony and me not to stand against each other. The article implied not only that I was involved in a backroom deal but also that I should be the one to stand down. My desire to avoid a split vote had been turned against me. I decided that I would fight on and make a leadership speech the next Sunday in Wales after John's funeral. John had been due to speak to the Welsh conference; I would take his place. And support for me was growing. Donald Dewar, John's best friend, had already offered me his support for the leadership. George Robertson, then shadow Scottish Secretary, also came to me to pledge support. He did so even though his political outlook had always been closer to Tony's than to mine. Indeed, half the shadow Cabinet told me they were with me. I was heartened that I was commanding a broad spectrum of support, left and right. I had no doubt I could and would win.

The *Sunday Times* piece, however, now set the context. On Monday, Peter faxed me a note about Tony's 'southern appeal'. At the time, when I and others read it, we thought that it was putting Tony's case. But it appeared to end with an offer: 'My fear is that drift is harming you . . . You have either to escalate rapidly (and to be effective I think I would need to become clearly partisan with the press in your favour) or you need to implement a strategy to exit with enhanced position, strength and respect. Will you let me know your wishes?' The irony about Peter is that, for all his gifts for seeing an opportunity and creating a positive story about New Labour, he was his own worst enemy: perhaps it was a personal modesty that meant the one person he could not brand successfully was himself. Often, I too misunderstood his motives.

That evening, Tony arrived in Edinburgh, ahead of visiting Elizabeth the next morning, and asked to see me. There was a touch of comedy about the meeting. I agreed to meet him at the home of one of his friends, Nick Ryden, a property developer, who lived in the well-to-do Edinburgh suburb of Merchiston. It was a rambling mansion that Nick was in the process of renovating. At the meeting, Tony introduced a new argument for his candidacy – that Robin Cook, Margaret Beckett and John Prescott would stand down in his favour and the election would be uncontested. It was wishful thinking. But he also wanted to assure me that, if I would stand aside, I would not only stay on as shadow chancellor but have complete autonomy over economic and social policy. This had some appeal, as I would have overall control, in a way I had not under John, of what I was to call the 'fairness agenda'.

At this point, I went to wash my hands before going on to another event. After eventually finding the bathroom amidst the building works, I shut the door and it locked behind me. The door had been replaced but there was no handle on the inside. I was locked in the house of Tony's close friend. For a few moments, I was literally out of the contest. Luckily, I had an early mobile phone – the size of a brick – and was eventually rescued from my imprisonment.

Tony asked to see me again the next morning after paying his respects to Elizabeth. My brother Andrew, who was now in Scotland with me, collected him from outside the Smith home and wrote up his impressions from the details of their conversation in his diary:

> It had been years since I had chatted to him for more than passing pleasantries. But immediately we talked at ease. With a pinch of salt, I hear his eulogy to GB. He's the 'greatest political mind the Labour Party has had', he says – and TB 'couldn't do it without GB'.

Yet Tony was determined, noted Andrew, that I should make a decision that day. And indeed when he arrived at my home in North Queensferry, his mood was close to desperation. He reiterated that he wanted me to stay on as shadow chancellor and would give me control over economic and social policy. This time, he added another promise – that if elected as prime minister, he would stand down in his second term. He said this was a family choice that he had already made. He wanted to be free from day-to-day politics to be with his children in their teens – the time of life when parents are most needed. It was a promise he repeated on several occasions. In between our talks, I went off to take a call and, as Andrew also recalls, Tony said to him that if he did not stand 'he would look like a monkey'.

When Andrew drove Tony back to the airport after our meeting, he wrote that Tony was 'much more tense than earlier'. He was talking to Andrew in the full knowledge that his offers which he had already made to me personally would be reinforced through repeating them to Andrew. The diary continued:

> He showed the desperation of his position when he reveals that GB could win if he stood. What he doubted was not that – but whether GB could win the general election. It's the trump card to play – especially against GB who believes above all else that, after four defeats, nothing should come in the way of Labour winning the election. TB also talks about how all of this has come 'too soon' for his young children. Only aged 10, 8 and 6 years old, he's worried about the prospect of media attention on them. Talks about how if he goes for the leadership now, he would want to spend time with them later before they're too old – perhaps in five years' time.

This accorded with what Tony was telling me directly: that he would stand down in his second term. But he now added two reasons why he, rather than me, should be leader at the next election. I was Scottish, he said, and I was unmarried. We could not, he said, have two leaders in a row from Scotland. I reminded him that he too was Scottish: born in Scotland of a father raised in Glasgow, and also educated at a school in Edinburgh. The only difference seemed to me that people knew I was Scottish and assumed he was not.

The 'being single' charge was more insidious. At least one or two of Tony's adherents went out of their way to imply to the press that they knew more about me than the public did. In conversations with colleagues, some MPs were persuaded to raise questions or cast aspersions about my private life. In the dark world of rumours and counter-rumours that swirl around Westminster, people believed what they wanted to believe and what suited their purposes. This was echoed in a low moment for the BBC two years later, when I was interviewed for *Desert Island Discs*, and the presenter Sue Lawley insinuated that being unmarried meant I was gay. I was not. But the insinuation was born of prejudice: that somehow there was something wrong with being gay. The allegations were as untrue as they were unworthy, but during these years damage was done.

On the Friday, I attended John Smith's funeral at Cluny Parish Church in Edinburgh. Donald Dewar, who had been closer to John than almost anyone outside his family, spoke movingly. He was emotional, but with a twinkle in his eye, talked of the John 'who could start a party in an empty room'. On that day, when the mourners assembled after the funeral, Tony was also seeking another meeting with me. But so immersed was I in talking to John's family and close friends that the meeting he wanted – which Sue Nye and Tony's assistant Anji Hunter were coordinating – had to be repeatedly postponed and rearranged. In the end, we met again at Nick Ryden's home, but the meeting was far shorter than Tony wanted.

Soon another story was planted, this time in the Scottish press, which attempted to take my strength and support in Scotland and turn it into a weakness. Scottish MP colleagues, the headline claimed, now wanted Blair and not me. In fact, when the *Scotsman* contacted forty-two out of forty-eight Scottish Labour MPs to ask their preference, twenty-one said they were already backing me and only six said they would vote for Tony. Simultaneously there was also a campaign to whip up anti-Scottish sentiment among English MPs, with a suggestion from some that it was time to ditch the 'Scottish mafia'.

Two days after John's funeral, I made my speech in honour of him at the Welsh Labour Party conference in Swansea in which I set out a vision of a party awash with ideas, vibrant with dynamism and purpose, that would reform the welfare state and appeal beyond our heartlands. It did not make the impact with the media that I had hoped for. I had an agreement with Tony that we would not attack each other's speeches, but a briefing went around that I had made my speech to appeal to what an unidentified briefer termed – without a hint of irony – 'forces of darkness' within the party. The phrase appeared prominently in the next day's *Times*. There was evidently a campaign under way to characterise me not just as unelectable but anti-reform too.

The briefing had its desired effect. In the days that followed, I attended a memorial service for John in his constituency and then criss-crossed the country – playing a full part in the European election campaign – from Morecambe to Aberdeen with a visit to Luton in between. On the way to Luton I had a further meeting with Tony. But my mind was already made up. I would accept his assurances. He would give me control of economic and social policy and would stand down during a second term. Unwilling to see the party divided in a way that would endanger the prospects for reform, in the days leading up to 30 May I informed those closest to me of my intention not to stand.

The rest was a formality. On 31 May, I sat down again with Tony near his home in London, at a restaurant called Granita. Ed Balls travelled with me to the restaurant and, after a few minutes, he left. I always smile when commentators write that we hammered out a deal in the restaurant. The Granita discussion merely confirmed what he had already offered and I had already agreed. The only new point was Tony's overture that he wanted to show that, unlike the Tories under Mrs Thatcher, Labour was not a one-person band but a partnership. As we walked out of the restaurant towards his home, he emphasised the word 'partnership' again and again, telling me it represented a new departure for British politics.

On Wednesday 1 June, I travelled to Nottingham with Ed Balls to honour a European campaign commitment. I penned a withdrawal statement that I sent in draft to Tony. At the same time, our usual 'lines to take' for any press enquiries were being hammered out – amended and re-amended in a process involving Tony, Sue Nye and Peter Mandelson, as well as me. They were there to reflect what we could explain publicly by way of background information when questions were asked by the press. This draft, leaked years later to the *Guardian*, contained Tony's guarantees about my control of economic and social policy. It was, of course, the part of the agreement we could allude to in public. The other part – that he would stand down in a second term – was an explicit, but private, understanding between ourselves and would, of course, not be referred to in public.

I made the formal announcement to the Press Association at 3.30 p.m. Originally, we planned to be photographed in public to affirm the strong partnership Tony had talked of. The plan was to walk between Westminster and Lambeth Bridge on the pathway overlooking the

Houses of Parliament. But immediately after I published my statement, Tony's team changed tack. Andrew's diary states:

> The whole episode was nearly a disaster. Tony had agreed to a photocall immediately after the statement was issued . . . But Tony's aides took cold feet. After GB had issued his press release withdrawing, TB threatened to break his agreement and not take part in a photocall. His advisers were suggesting that – even with no interviews by either TB or GB – he would be in danger of breaking shadow Cabinet rules on not making any pronouncements on the leadership question until after the European campaign. I suspected even worse than that. Without the photocall – particularly in TV terms – GB would have looked like a loser – and it would have been interpreted that way. After at least five phone calls between the two offices, Tony eventually succumbed to a photocall which took place much later than planned at about 1.15. The pictures themselves showed Tony looking very uncomfortable – and hardly acknowledging GB.

When I offered to chair Tony's leadership campaign, he demurred. And while I helped write his leadership speeches, I was frozen out of the campaign. Long into the future, the focus of the 1994 leadership race would wrongly remain on what was said at Granita. The restaurant did not survive; and ultimately neither did our agreement.

A week after his election as leader, Ed Balls and I visited Tony at his home in Islington. We were in for a shock. Sitting in the garden lapping up the sun on a very bright morning, we were both surprised when he announced that Labour must rule out forever any rise in the top rate of tax. I agreed that we should rule out a rise in the basic rate – indeed, we were considering a lower band, a 10p rate – but I said I didn't know how we could meet our promises unless we left open, for the time being at least, the possibility of a top-rate increase on very high incomes. I said we had to do in-depth work on the costing of our programmes – for example, the needs of the NHS – before we made such a unilateral move. He was adamant: no party he led would ever raise the top rate of tax. Of course, it made for good electioneering – the British version of 'read my lips: no new taxes' – but, as Edward Heath had pointed out years before, the better way of dealing with taxes was to say that we did not want to raise them but, if circumstances arose where it was necessary, we would take the action required. By putting a pledge never to raise the top rate at the centre of our modernisation, we did prove that we had changed, but it was not in the national interest to rule out the possibility of even a modest change in the top rate for the highest earners.

It was a fateful decision which meant we could do far less than I had hoped about the needs of our public services and the rising inequality in our country. In government, we would struggle to fund the NHS and education. We would need a great deal of lateral thinking: in addition to the windfall tax, we would raise National Insurance for high earners. It might have been better all round, however, if we had heeded Heath's advice. Levels of inequality were rising across the whole western world, not least in egalitarian Scandinavia. Our decision on tax meant that in the end we would be able only to stall rising inequality – not reverse it. As it has worked out, even the Tories now accept what Tony ruled out that day: a 45p rate at the very top.

For the next three years, I combined my duties as shadow chancellor with overall responsibility for election strategy, while day-to-day campaign planning was in the hands of Peter Mandelson and Philip Gould. Philip was more than a pollster: he was a strategist whom, before his tragic early death from cancer in 2011, I got to know well and came to admire greatly as a man of courage and humility. Every morning I presided over meetings to implement and finesse our message. Even so, I was not informed in advance of Tony's decision to announce the repeal of Clause IV of Labour's constitution, the iconic commitment to nationalisation of all industry. Others, like Jack Straw, had floated it in the past, but Tony masterfully delivered the change and positioned it as a hallmark symbol of the fresh approach of New Labour.

Our strategy group had a two-pronged approach: first to persuade the electorate that Labour had changed, with new policies to back that up; and second to expose the mistakes of the Tory government. To win an election we needed both approaches, the positive and the negative. Within weeks of Tony's election as leader, a plan I had been working on under John Smith came to fruition. It was to mark the most significant parliamentary defeat of the Conservatives since 1979.

Any rise in gas and electricity costs can have a dramatic impact on the personal finances of millions of families. So, when the Conservatives announced that they would impose an increase in VAT on fuel in two stages – 8 per cent in 1994 and 17.5 per cent in 1995 – I was determined to stop them in their tracks. The Conservatives successfully passed the first of their two VAT increases. Having done so, they assumed they would need no further parliamentary approval for the second rise. But our team, led skilfully by an ever-inventive Nick Brown, had devised an ingenious manoeuvre to force a vote by tabling a procedural motion. Our other weapon was the personal promises made by Conservative candidates in their constituency manifestos at the 1992 general election that they personally would never vote to raise VAT. With the help of a young researcher, Chris Leslie, who was later to become an MP and, for a time, shadow chancellor himself, we embarrassed the benches opposite by publishing the specific pledges each Conservative MP had made, constituency by constituency. Every time they stood up in the Commons to ask a question, we challenged them on their breach of faith with their constituents.

To head us off, Ken Clarke offered an extra £120 million to help the elderly. That was not enough. In a dramatic December vote, our amendment to stop the second VAT increase passed by 319 to 311. Just enough Tory members had defected. We could now argue that the only party which had delivered a major tax cut in the 1992–7 parliament was Labour.

We learned something from this episode. From then on, we relentlessly exposed the personal promises of Conservative MPs who had not only pledged never to raise VAT, but never to raise any other taxes, including National Insurance – which was exactly what they had just done. Clarke made matters worse when he said that no one should take seriously promises made in hustings 'on a wet Wednesday night in Dudley'. He was wrong: the public did.

Having put the Tories on the defensive, it was time to move on to the positive case for Labour on economic policy. But our attempt at a new economic policy had an inauspicious start. Ed Balls and I had organised an international conference on new economics with Larry Summers, Robert Reich and Richard Freeman of Harvard. Ed had prepared a paper setting out some of the new ideas in the economic literature and referred to 'neoclassical endogenous growth theory', by which he meant improving the supply side of the economy through R&D, training, the quality of investment and so on. Without properly thinking it through, I inserted the term in my speech. Although the media pointed the finger at Ed – and Michael Heseltine famously joked 'it wasn't Brown, it was Balls' – I was wholly to blame for the ridicule that ensued.

In the first half of 1995, Ed Balls, Ed Miliband and I hammered out a series of major speeches. Underlying them was a consistent theme: that a Labour government could deliver higher levels of growth and lower levels of unemployment. In a May Day lecture to Labour's Finance and Industry Group, I delivered the first speech, entitled 'The Dynamic Market Economy', setting out what I called my 'iron commitment' to macroeconomic stability and financial prudence. The second speech, two weeks later, was perhaps the most important I gave as shadow chancellor. Under the title 'Labour's Macroeconomic Stability', I set out the principles, based on a paper by Ed Balls, that would later underpin our decision to make the Bank of England independent. Side by side with a new monetary policy designed to maintain low unemployment and low inflation, I articulated the fundamentals of our fiscal policy on public spending and borrowing. The newspapers were to dub this 'Brown's Law'. Simply put, a future Labour government would borrow only to invest. In my third speech, at the end of May, I argued the case – controversial then in Labour circles – for using public-private partnerships to rebuild Britain's infrastructure, hospitals and schools.

In 1995, I also worked with Tony Wright on a book, *Values, Visions and Voices*, which aimed to make people even more proud of Labour. But therein lay an embarrassing story: we could not afford to pay fees to the publisher who had the copyright for Harold Wilson's speeches and writings, meaning we had none of his in the book. The day of publication in May coincided with Wilson's death. It made sense to retreat and cancel our press launch.

Even after setting out a new direction in economic policy – and our victory on VAT – we still had to offer repeated reassurances that showed we would be fiscally prudent. A few months later, I outlined the tax principles of a future Labour government – including a starting rate of income tax at 10p. Now I was being helped by Conservative mistakes: I could contrast their newly restated but costly ambitions to abolish capital gains tax and inheritance tax for the very wealthy with our measures to help low- and middle-income Britain. If the

Tories could spend money on helping high-income Britain, why could we not use the same money, I challenged them, to help low-income Britain?

Moreover, the outrageous behaviour in the boardrooms of the privatised utilities allowed us to put the windfall tax I had first proposed a few years earlier right at the centre of public debate. 'Fat cats' became a popular byword for such excesses, and I saw the errors of judgement of these privatised company boardrooms as both an outrage for the country and manna from heaven for Labour. For example, Cedric Brown, chief executive of British Gas, had awarded himself a 900 per cent pay increase during the ten years British Gas had been in private hands. Just as we were cranking up our campaign, he unwisely doubled his salary at the same time that he was cutting 25,000 jobs. I thought to myself that no announcement could be more persuasive than that. To be fair to him, there were many executives who had taken even bigger rises, but he had allowed himself to become the poster boy for their excesses. Millions who were paying high utility charges to British Gas could not fail to see the connection between his pay package and their monthly bills. I knew then that the tide that had turned away from the Tories over the exchange-rate fiasco was now turning even more sharply towards us on the economy.

Even more damaging for the government, several former Conservative Cabinet ministers had joined the boards of the very companies they had privatised. At the Labour conference, I only had to read out the names. Norman Tebbit, who privatised British Telecom as Trade and Industry Secretary, now sat on the board of British Telecom. Peter Walker, who oversaw the privatisation of British Gas when Energy Secretary, then went on the board of British Gas. David Young, who privatised Cable & Wireless as Trade and Industry Secretary, was now chairman of Cable & Wireless. Norman Fowler, who privatised National Freight as Transport Secretary, was on the board of National Freight. In total, there were sixteen Conservative ministers and MPs with well-paid directorships or consultancies linked to the utilities. It was clearly a milder form of what was going on in post-Soviet Russia.

What would a Labour government do with the proceeds of a windfall tax? We would meet the unmet needs of the unemployed by financing a New Deal that would offer qualifications and work. And the issue here wasn't just economic; it was also legal. The windfall tax would be liable to judicial challenge if it were justified simply on the grounds of corporate excess. I knew that we had to develop a watertight rationale: that the utilities had been underpriced when sold off; that regulation by the Tories had been too lax; and that the companies were now exploiting their quasi-monopoly power.

The work was led by Geoffrey Robinson, the MP for Coventry North, who would later be appointed Paymaster General in the Treasury. His help and advice was invaluable. Knowledgeable about industry from his time as chief executive of Jaguar Cars, and with contacts across business, Geoffrey was also willing to make bold and radical decisions. He never boasted of it but he put up £1 million of his own money to finance the research, the legal advice and the complex preparations needed for the parliamentary legislation. As it was market sensitive, the research was carried out in the strictest secrecy. The effort was given a code name, 'Project Autumn' – because we thought the Tories would call an election later in 1996 and we had to be ready to introduce the legislation as soon as we were in government.

Ed and Geoffrey assembled a small team of tax experts, including Chris Wales, who had vast experience in the private sector and an incisive and original mind that also helped devise the £6 billion a year reform of dividend tax credits we introduced in our first Budget. Chris had provided advice to John Smith and later joined me at the Treasury.

No papers about the windfall tax were ever circulated and meetings were held at Geoffrey's London flat rather than in the House of Commons or the Labour Party headquarters in Millbank. Any challenge under EU law, our advisers concluded, would fail and one of the reasons was that the revenues were being used to fund the New Deal and would thus be in the public interest. We now felt we had a watertight plan that could raise at least £5 billion.

Then, out of the blue, Tony told me that he wanted to exempt British Telecom from the windfall tax because of a separate arrangement he was negotiating with BT's chairman, Iain Vallance. The company would get a broadcasting licence if it provided free Internet links to schools, hospitals, libraries and other public buildings. I agreed that widening access to the Internet was an important advance, but I told him that if one company was arbitrarily exempted from the windfall tax, even for the best of reasons, our whole plan would be struck down and, without a consistent justification for our actions, we would be accused of discriminating against individual companies.

Tony was persistent: a few months before the election, in January 1997, he demanded BT's total exclusion from our Windfall Tax. I said that would mean the tax was not legally watertight. I said I would resign rather than abandon it. That March I was lobbied directly by Iain Vallance to drop the idea. I bluntly told him no. Iain was a decent man who would later become a Liberal Democrat peer, but his glib comment that the hardship of running BT justified his salary – being a junior doctor in the NHS might be more relaxing than his current position, he suggested – enhanced my confidence that this was a public debate we would win.

When the windfall tax was introduced after our electoral victory, BT threatened that they might take us to the European Court. In my desk in the Treasury, however, I had a note Iain had generously sent to me on the day I became chancellor that struck an altogether different tone: 'I write to offer my warmest congratulations on your confirmation as chancellor, and in what overwhelming circumstances. The tectonic plates have moved, in no small part due to your rigour on matters financial and economic. We are, of course very aware that Labour has a clear mandate for the windfall levy and I know from our conversation in March, that we fall within the scope of the tax.' It was clear to me that the BT PR team was bluffing.

All along, while formulating detailed plans on how to raise revenues, we also had to fend off pressure groups who wanted to spend them in many different ways. With an election obligatory by the summer of 1997, the 1996 Labour conference in Blackpool would be our last before polling day. The conference was designed to symbolise our unity, but a dispute about the level of pensions threatened to derail that and reveal glaring divisions.

Barbara Castle and Jack Jones, two of my best friends in the Labour movement, were leading a campaign to re-establish the across-the-board link between pensions and earnings that had been scrapped by the Thatcher government in 1980. By my team's calculations, re-establishing that link would now cost £5 billion and mean a substantial rise in tax. It was something that at this point we just could not afford.

Jack was no respecter of seniority. When he was shown around Windsor Castle on his appointment as a Companion of Honour during the 'Winter of Discontent' in 1978, he had observed that one of the paintings looked a bit amateurish. 'That's mine,' replied the Duke of Edinburgh. I spent the weekend before the conference thrashing out a compromise with Jack, who was one of the country's most successful negotiators. The breakthrough came in a late-night telephone call on the Saturday. I promised that the next Labour government would set up a commission to conduct a full review of pensions which would then report back to the government.

But while Jack offered me support, Barbara went ahead with her motion to conference and won the vote. Always principled and passionate, Barbara perhaps did more than anyone else to break the glass ceiling faced by women in British politics, and her loyalty to the Labour movement never faltered. I remember joking at the conference that she was both my 'mentor and tormentor'. She was a great politician right to the end. A few years later, Barbara kindly asked me to be present and speak at her eighty-fifth birthday party. She said that in return she would not speak about pensions at the next Labour conference. I attended the birthday party. She spoke about pensions at the conference.

In government, we created the pension credit which boosted the incomes of poor pensioners, and this was the biggest reason why pensioner poverty was halved between 1997 and 2010. We later established a Pension Commission, which recommended the restoration of the earnings link, financed by a rise in the age for receipt of the state pension for men and women from sixty-five to sixty-six by 2026, to sixty-seven by 2036 and to sixty-eight by 2046. The Pension Act 2007, which incorporated the main findings of the Pension Commission, was made law one month after I became prime minister. The reforms included the introduction of automatic enrolment, minimum employer contributions and new personal accounts for people saving in a workplace pension scheme, making it possible for every employee to have a work pension guaranteed for the first time.

Still, despite all our efforts, as 1997 began, the Conservatives, who had nothing else left, were accusing us of being a tax-and-spend party. Only Tony, Ed Balls and I were present at Tony's home on 5 January, the first Sunday of the year, when we discussed how to counter this. Tony was due to launch the party's New Year campaign at a Westminster press conference three days later. He wanted to say there would be no rises in personal tax rates, but accepted that, to keep room for manoeuvre, he would refuse to rule out an overall increase in the tax burden. In speeches and interviews, he had already been moving ahead with his pledge on the top rate, insisting that there was nothing in the party's programme that required or implied an increase in personal taxation, and the newspapers understood that as ruling out a new top rate.

I knew we were boxed in on what taxes we could raise but that meant we had also to be clear about what spending we could afford. This was the problem we now had to resolve – and quickly. If we merely promised to hold taxes down but still pledged more spending, the policy would be incoherent. This was the attack the Tories were preparing. I now had to make the announcements that locked in beyond any doubt our commitment to prudence.

The way to do so was to stick with current Tory public spending totals and to do so for at least two years. It was, of course, not an actual freeze, though it was often portrayed that way. It was an announcement that we would hold to the Conservatives' already published spending totals, an undertaking that we not only upheld but met with tougher discipline, as Ken Clarke has conceded, than the Tories themselves would have imposed. Indeed, Ken subsequently admitted that he would have relaxed the discipline if in power, whereas we tightened it.

By simultaneously ruling out an income-tax rise for the whole parliament and freezing spending for two years, I could dispose of the Tory tax-and-spend attack, at least for the coming election.

Once I had thrashed out the details of my speech I tried to contact Tony over the weekend to review it with him. He was not taking calls, something unusual for him. We then faxed the details to him at home. He did not pick them up. But we had already committed to the speech, and my most significant announcement of the campaign was now to be made without approval or even his prior knowledge.

The evening before, Charlie Whelan had already contacted Jim Naughtie, the BBC *Today* presenter, saying it would be worth his while to ask me about tax. The story we had given to the Monday papers was the freeze in overall public spending levels for the next two years; but Charlie then lined up all the main broadcasters to alert them to my *Today* interview.

My colleagues had to know where I was heading. During Sunday, I personally explained to each of them our tax-and-spending plans; those who wanted to see it were faxed the speech itself. But John Prescott was staying that night with the governor of Hong Kong and former chairman of the Conservative Party, Chris Patten, and we felt we could not fax him there. Senior union leaders, such as my friends John Monks, the TUC general secretary, and Rodney Bickerstaffe from UNISON, were also alerted.

It was not until the second half of the *Today* interview that Naughtie finally broached the tax question. He was startled when I responded: 'I will be making commitments for a parliament, and the basic rate and the top rate of tax will remain unchanged.' Naughtie's voice rose incredulously: 'For the lifetime of a parliament . . . that's a very important announcement.'

After that the election campaign went smoothly. And every day, after I sat down to chair the Strategy Group, we rolled out a series of attacks that put the Tories on the back foot – for example, on their plan for the abolition of capital gains tax (which would benefit the wealthy) and their last-minute change of policy on pension reform (which, we argued, had simply left people confused). But most of all our clarity on tax-and-spend made it easy to focus on their record and on the condition of Britain. It was like a political symphony, with an overall theme running through it but different sub-themes emerging each day.

In 1997, there was no TV debate between the prime minister and leader of the Opposition, but there was one between the chancellor and the shadow chancellor. Ken Clarke was the most formidable Tory debater of all. Fortunately, for me, he was off form on the night we went head to head, constantly on the defensive in the face of my references to the VAT shambles and my attacks that the Tories could not be trusted on tax. I fought him to what I considered a draw. Most commentators concluded I had won.

And I did not doubt that we would win on election day. Tony deserves great personal credit for the verve, eloquence and determination with which he fought the campaign from beginning to end. And for the first time in twenty years, we had not only put the Conservatives on the defensive on the economy but were confident in every answer we gave about our economic policy. We had largely put to rest doubts about our economic competence. We had utterly reversed the political equation of previous elections, taking step after step to position ourselves as the party of fiscal responsibility. Our standpoint on the economy was so strong and our victory was so decisive that I believe that we would have prevailed even if we had announced a top-rate tax on earnings above £150,000.

From 1994 to 2007 I worked for and with Tony in opposition and in government. There were fallouts and reunions, but our relationship was never again to be anything like the partnership we had built in the previous decade when together we were making the argument for change. After Labour won power, we still talked almost every day, sometimes four or five times. The meetings were not formal usually: we rarely talked to a written agenda. Most of our important discussions occurred with no one else present. Most of what was said between us is not recorded in minutes or documents. We didn't exchange letters or communicate by email. We talked on the phone or face-to-face.

The tensions between us reflected not only disagreements over substance but our very different styles too. Tony seldom told you exactly what he was thinking. On the other hand, I am probably too direct, usually blunt and sometimes uncompromising. While I said exactly what was on my mind, he was often reluctant to commit – and people could go away from his meetings with varying interpretations of what was agreed. There were to be fallouts over advisers, press briefings, leaks, personalities, appointments – for example, we were to row over my promotion of Douglas Alexander as the candidate for the Paisley South by-election and over some of my appointments to the Treasury in 1998 – but on the big issues, with few exceptions, we worked well together. The fact we worked side by side in opposition for fourteen years and in government for ten years – a remarkably long time given our histories with each other and the intense atmosphere at the top level of British politics – shows that the stories put around about an impossible relationship were vastly exaggerated.

A clear division of labour – I did the economy, tax and public spending – and my decision not to engage with him on every issue, especially foreign policy, made things more manageable. Tony deserves credit for great reforms our government brought in. His role in the Northern Ireland peace process, humanitarian intervention in Kosovo, many public sector reforms, the Human Rights Act and in introducing civil partnerships delivered lasting benefits. Still, I think he would agree that many of the changes we made – like funding for the NHS, tax credits to tackle child poverty, the push for increased overseas aid, and of course Bank of England independence and the eventual decision on the euro – were driven by the Treasury.

CHAPTER 5

TAKING POWER AND GIVING IT AWAY

While I had been a Member of Parliament since 1983, I had never once, in those fourteen years, crossed the road from the House of Commons into the Treasury. I had never been inside it or sat down with any of its senior officials. On the Friday afternoon, following the general election in 1997, I entered the Treasury building for the first time.

To my surprise I did so to a warm and enthusiastic welcome from civil servants lining the lobby, the stairways and landings above. TV cameras pictured me shaking hands with my new officials and acknowledging the cheers of a normally reserved group of economic experts. Within minutes of arriving at my new office, accompanied by Ed Balls, I met Terry Burns, the permanent secretary, and Nick Macpherson, now my principal private secretary and later to hold Terry's job. On my arrival, I handed Terry an important paper on the reforms we intended to implement.

My day had started late. It was not until early Friday afternoon that Tony had called me to confirm my appointment as Chancellor of the Exchequer. I had not seen him on election night. I had flown down on a chartered plane from Edinburgh to London after 3 a.m. with Robin Cook, who had also retained his seat, and we then dropped by the celebrations at the Royal Festival Hall at around 5 a.m. The atmosphere was unqualified exhilaration; not so long before, it had seemed Labour might never be back in power. But I did not stay long. I had to get some sleep so I could be ready for work later that day.

The Monday before the election, I had said to Ed Balls that if I became chancellor on Friday I wanted to go ahead immediately with Bank of England independence. Prior to that conversation, we had been working on the assumption that we would deliver independence sometime in a first term. I asked him to draw up a letter for the governor of the Bank of England which we would send to him in the event of winning. By the time we arrived at the Treasury, Ed had a draft setting out our new policy framework. This draft evolved into two letters over the next few days: one on monetary policy, one on financial stability.

On Saturday, we sat around an oval conference table in a gigantic oak-panelled meeting room unlike any I had ever been in. The table was so expansive that somebody speaking at normal volume at one end of it could not be heard by anybody sitting at the other end. This room, with its panoramic views of Whitehall, was also my new office. It certainly was a step up from the windowless cubicle I had shared with Tony in 1983. When we later renovated the building, I took the first opportunity to move to a more convenient office just down the corridor – which was actually one of the smallest in the Treasury.

The way the Treasury then worked was, in my view, unmanageable – gatherings of countless officials assembled around this massive oval table. It was also a waste of valuable time for senior officials, since only one or two of them were ever expected to speak. Almost immediately, I put decision-making on a more focused and professional basis – small meetings, with only relevant officials and advisers present – and I made a point of inviting the person doing the actual work on a project, rather than their superior two or three rungs up, who in the past would attend on grounds of seniority.

There were around twenty senior civil servants at that Saturday meeting: with Terry Burns and Nick Macpherson were the second permanent secretaries, Sir Nigel Wicks and Sir Alan Budd, alongside the department heads. Apologising for ruining their bank holiday weekend, I instructed them to prepare for a Tuesday announcement declaring Bank independence. I left them in no doubt that whatever hurdles we had to cross, we must do so to be ready for the day after bank holiday Monday. That weekend we went through a rolling series of meetings to prepare the ground on all aspects of the change.

For most people Bank independence came as a bolt from the blue. A week before the election, I had read with interest *The Economist*'s editorial 'Labour doesn't deserve it', in which the venerable magazine offered a lengthy explanation as to why it could not support Labour. Not that an explanation was necessary; they had invariably opposed us. But on this particular occasion the reason they urged a

Conservative vote was because, in their view, a Labour government would never make the Bank of England independent. They could not have been more wrong.

In 1995, I had undertaken a hard, detailed reading of everything I could get my hands on about independent central banks. But the argument that convinced me independence was essential was a basic one – that for too long in Britain, political expediency had dominated economic decision-making. Too often interest-rate decisions were made cynically for the here and now to deal with a political problem or in response to just one economic event. An operationally independent Bank would depoliticise the process. The long term would take precedence over the short term.

I agreed with the standard criticism of post-war British economic policy: that our economy was inflation-prone, slow-growing and weighed down by unnecessarily high levels of unemployment, under investment, poor infrastructure and, hence, low productivity. Whenever recession hit, it always seemed the case that Britain was 'first in and last out'. Inflation had averaged 12 per cent in the 1970s and 6 per cent in the 1980s. The overriding priority was to move Britain from its post-war stop-go economic volatility towards a new macroeconomic stability.

I do not blame any individuals – Labour or Conservative – for earlier failures to make the Bank independent. Their forbearance was inherent in our political process. In the 1980s, when Nigel Lawson challenged Margaret Thatcher to make the Bank independent, he found her 'wholly unreceptive'. 'So far as she was concerned,' Lawson thought, 'she really was going to go on and on and on . . . [and] while she was there, she was not going to give up the levers of power which the control of interest rates, as she saw it, represented.' When Norman Lamont twice tried to persuade John Major to establish an independent Bank – first when Britain was in the ERM, and then after Britain's humiliating exit – he was rebuffed. Later, Lamont created what seemed to me to be a cumbersome hybrid committee of chancellor and governor, who met every month to determine the level of interest rates. The informality of these meetings between Lamont's successor, Ken Clarke, and the governor, Eddie George, led some economic commentators to christen it the 'Ken and Eddie Show'. But an indication of how political the process remained was that, in the months before the 1997 election, the chancellor repeatedly rejected the Bank's advice that interest rates had to be raised. This was the kind of partisanship and short-termism from which I had already determined we would break free.

In the early 1990s I had talked to my friend, the economist Gavyn Davies, who made a compelling case for independence. But it was in 1995 that Ed Balls, who was also already committed to that view, came up with a detailed and sophisticated plan. Long before we came into government, his plan had been written, rewritten, reviewed, finessed, tested to destruction, completed and filed. So why did we not announce this bold new initiative before the election? It was for one simple reason: if we had done so, the Tories would have alleged that, under the new system, interest rates would immediately rise and homeowners would have to pay far more for their mortgages, and businesses more for borrowed capital. Our pre-election silence was caution for a purpose.

Ed Balls's plan was a decisive break with the past. By fettering our discretion and accepting operational independence for the Bank to decide interest rates, it would give both the public and the markets confidence that we had put in place a framework to ensure stability and keep inflation low.

In the blueprint for independence, we made a crucial decision: we had chosen not to go for what was called 'goal independence' – the right of the central bank to define price stability and set the inflation target – but 'operational independence'. This meant that, subject to parliamentary oversight, the chancellor would set the inflation target and the Bank of England would be charged with reaching it. And unlike the targets given to other central banks, the Bank of England's target would be 'symmetrical'. Instead of the original Lamont target of 1–4 per cent or the current Clarke target of 2.5 per cent or less, we set what we considered to be a target conducive to growth. Inflation 1 per cent below 2.5 per cent would be as unacceptable as inflation 1 per cent above it. Although I applaud the post-ERM changes introduced, to their credit, by Lamont and Clarke – inflation targeting, a joint Bank–Treasury committee to set interest rates and the use of outside advisers – and believe this represented substantial progress, Bank independence was not just 'putting the roof on the cathedral', as some have suggested, but a fundamental change.

On the morning of Saturday 3 May, I met Tony to talk about the timetable – I had told him on election day I was thinking of moving quickly – for proceeding with Bank of England independence. We did not meet in Downing Street. At this point, Tony was still working out of his London home and so, over cups of coffee and seated in comfortable chairs, we discussed the change. What would become known as 'sofa government' was quite literally starting in the informal atmosphere of his living room in Islington. With him was his new private secretary, Moira Wallace, a Treasury civil servant, who moved seamlessly from serving a Conservative government to working for a Labour one. Moira, who was as intelligent as she was forceful, had a very different view from mine – and I think Tony's – on how the issue should be handled. She advised us that we ought to wait until we had run the gamut of a whole series of formalities. To be fair, she had been advised by the Cabinet Secretary, Robin Butler, that this was proper procedure, and it was in normal circumstances.

But on that day it sounded more like a delaying tactic that would have undermined the fresh start I proposed. Believing Bank independence would forever lock in our commitment to low inflation, I was determined to move quickly. At our Saturday meeting, Tony concluded our discussion with one word: 'Fine.' We would meet again on the Sunday evening when I proposed that I would phone every Cabinet member on the Tuesday prior to our formal announcement of the decision. Because of the historic significance of our plans – which I thought would be headline news in almost every serious paper around the world – I assumed Tony might request that the decision be announced by him from Downing Street. But Tony, I think, recognised that this was my initiative and left it to me.

Later on Saturday, back at the Treasury, Terry Burns now repeated Moira's advice to Tony and urged a pause. When I reiterated my decision that we would act immediately, Terry retreated into a more modest request: a one-day delay so we could get what he called 'all our ducks in a row'. I replied that Tony and I had already agreed to hold to my timetable, and that prior to our announcement we would bring forward the usual monthly meeting of the Treasury and Bank on interest rates to 8 a.m. on Tuesday. At that meeting, I would propose an interest-rate rise which was clearly needed in the face of rising inflationary pressures. There was an important reason for this. Interest rates had to rise and, before handing responsibility for them to the

Bank, I wanted to send an unmistakable signal that Labour would never shirk a difficult economic decision.

I do accept that that weekend we broke with all the conventions – detailed Civil Service papers, long subcommittee meetings of officials then ministers, a Cabinet discussion and decision. While Robin Butler, Terry Burns and Moira Wallace were justified in their reservations, I was absolutely convinced that Britain needed this new start, and the best time to make it was at the very beginning of our first days in power. I was also learning about leadership. Without a clear vision and determination to see it through, you could easily be knocked off course.

As we worked through the weekend, we found that the Treasury also had a Bank of England proposal on the stocks. A year before, the Treasury Management Board had considered a paper on what would happen to the Bank of England if we joined monetary union, put together by one of the ablest civil servants of all, Jon Cunliffe, later deputy governor of the Bank of England. I subsequently learned that Terry had a sense the day before the election that this earlier work might be needed and brought it out of the filing cabinet. So, on the day after the election, Burns met with Cunliffe. The two decided that Tom Scholar, then a young official and later the Treasury's permanent secretary, should prepare a paper overnight. The Treasury proved, as it would in the future too, agile, fast-moving and on top of all the detail. There were some changes to Ed's original draft. For example, Ed and Sir Alan Budd, the Treasury's chief economic adviser, now agreed we should add what was to be called the 'open letter' system: the governor of the Bank would be required to write a public letter to the chancellor to explain why any deviation from the inflation target occurred and what policy actions were needed to rectify this. I later found out that officials in the Treasury anticipated receiving such a letter once every fifteen months or so: the first letter was not sent until ten years later. But to all intents and purposes, Ed's original letter – and plan – remained unchanged.

First thing on Tuesday morning, at what would be the last joint meeting of the Bank and Treasury to determine interest rates, we went through the motions, agreeing to a 0.25 per cent rise. We then called time on the last meeting of this hybrid group. The last episode of the 'Ken and Eddie Show' had aired a month before. There was

not to be a 'Gordon and Eddie Show'. Eddie and his staff then returned
to Threadneedle Street while I went back to my office to phone each
member of the Cabinet to inform them of our plans. With this done,
I went straight to the press briefing at 11 a.m. in the Treasury's Churchill
Room – the room from whose balcony he had greeted the cheering
crowds of well-wishers when peace was declared in 1945.

The press conference itself was something of a surreal experience
that at first confounded our expectations. I started by announcing the
interest-rate rise and then proceeded to announce that the Bank of
England, which the Labour government had nationalised in 1946,
would become 'operationally responsible' for interest-rate decisions.
Because I used the word 'responsible' and not 'independence', some
journalists thought the interest-rate change was the real story. It took
an hour before the media came to realise what a fundamental shift
the announcement represented: politicians would no longer make
interest-rate decisions in their partisan interest; an independent Bank
would make decisions in the national interest.

That morning I had phoned all Cabinet members that I could track
down and explained our decision to them one by one. I also called all
previous chancellors. Ken Clarke, by then a challenger for the Tory
leadership, politely told me he would publicly and strongly oppose
the move, and later the Conservative Party voted against it in
Parliament. In contrast, Nigel Lawson and Norman Lamont made it
clear to me that this was exactly in line with their own thinking and
they wished their party had done this when in office. I did not get
through to John Major, but I knew his views. Denis Healey was luke-
warm, while Jim Callaghan was – as always with me – very supportive.
Jim had given me his first-edition copy of John Maynard Keynes's *The
General Theory of Employment, Interest and Money*, originally a gift to
him from a previous Labour chancellor, Hugh Dalton, and it is a prized
possession, a symbol of the common ground between the Keynesian-
led rethinking of the 1930s and what we were now attempting.

Our success would depend on the effective operation of the newly
created Monetary Policy Committee (MPC), five of whose nine members would come from the Bank's staff: the governor, two deputy
governors, the executive director for financial markets and the chief
economist. The other four would be nominated by the Treasury. The
appointment of 'externals' was our plan – conceived in opposition – and

it was one we implemented boldly by choosing from the broadest possible group of members, including, to the dismay of many, two non-British citizens.

When I met Eddie George on 5 May, I was able to remove the main fears he had in his mind. He was wary that the MPC would be representative of various 'sectional interests' – code for representatives from industry and the unions who he thought, perhaps unfairly, had no experience of macroeconomics. But I was later to learn that Eddie was 'thrilled' about the symmetrical target as it demonstrated a commitment to both stability and growth. In fact, when he addressed the TUC in 1998 and explained this benefit to the economy, Eddie was applauded enthusiastically – a first for any Bank of England governor.

But it was not all smooth sailing. In our draft letter to the Bank, we said we would legislate to transfer the Bank's responsibility for financial supervision to a new statutory body and that consultation would now begin on that basis. Unfortunately, in his exchanges with Terry Burns, Eddie seemed to form the impression that the change would not happen quickly, or perhaps not at all. So, two weeks later, when I prepared to go to Parliament to announce the creation of the Financial Services Authority (FSA) as the new supervisor, I first learned about the scale of Eddie's concerns.

Prior to 1997 there were nine separate financial regulators. In my long years of opposition, I had seen how the Bank had run into problems – in 1991 over the collapse of BCCI, and in 1995 over Barings. These two embarrassing banking disasters had resulted, at least in part, from an inadequate regulatory system that was essentially an informal old boys' network dealing more in private assurances than professional monitoring. There was a strong case for locating the prudential supervision of all regulated firms in one place – the FSA, as the new single regulator – with the Bank of England, as the central bank, responsible for stability of the system as a whole.

Eddie was later reported as saying that on hearing of my plans he had thought of resigning. But there was no substance to this; he was undoubtedly angry, but I found Eddie more intent on using the initial misunderstanding to claw back some of the powers we were to give to the FSA. After a long summer – during which, to his great credit, a very patient Alistair Darling, the Chief Secretary to the Treasury, did most of the negotiations with an irate Eddie – a memorandum

Wearing my Kirkcaldy High School rugby shirt before the game where I got injured, resulting some time later in the loss of sight in my left eye.

Aged around four with my mother and big brother John.

My father holding the book of his sermons that my brothers John and Andrew and I had published for his 80th birthday.

As a young MP with my friend (and former boss) Labour leader
Neil Kinnock at a 1989 press conference.

With three great figures of Labour politics (left to right) Robin Cook, Donald Dewar and
John Smith in the 1992 general election campaign with Stirling candidate Catherine Phillips
This seat was won from the Tories in 1997 by Anne McGuire.

On Budget Day 1997 with the new Budget Box and the Rosyth apprentices who had made it for me.

At work on a budget speech in the Treasury with Beth Russell, Ed Balls and Ed Miliband and US political advisor and strategist Bob Shrum.

Filming the 2001 general election party political broadcast with Tony Blair.

My wedding to
Sarah at home in
North Queensferry
on 3 August 2000

Staff Christmas party in the
No. 11 flat sometime after
entering government

Back Row (left to right): Ian
Austin MP, Spencer Livermore
(now Lord Livermore), Sue Nye
(now Baroness Nye of Lambeth),
me, Carole Bird, Anita Ralli,
Rt Hon Ed Miliband MP,
Shriti Vadera (obscured),
Cathy Koester
Front Row: Jonathan
Ashworth MP, Ed Balls (in the
Santa suit), Nicola Murphy,
Damian McBride,
Matt Cavanagh

In the No. 10 flat
with Sue Nye,
the budget box
and my son John,
then two, in 2006

With football icon and lifelong Labour Party supporter Sir Alex Ferguson at a Co-op event.

With the 'real' Santa Claus, actor and director Richard Attenborough (Lord Attenborough) at a No. 11 children's charity Christmas party.

With Senator Ted Kennedy at the Kennedy compound on holiday in Hyannis Port, Cape Cod, in 2000.

With Afghanistan's President Karzai meeting British
and Afghan troops at Kandahar Airbase.

Enjoying the British wins at the 2008 Beijing Olympics with footballing legend Pelé.

Our official joint photograph taken by Tom Miller, who also took my picture that hangs on the No. 10 staircase today.

In the No. 10 Cabinet Room with John and Fraser in 2008.

The official Leaders photograph taken at the G20 London Summit for Stability, Growth and Jobs in 2009.

In South Africa with Nelson Mandela and Graça Machel.

of understanding was hammered out between the Treasury, the Bank of England and the FSA. But sadly, because it was a compromise, it was far less definitive on who did what than it should have been. It was an unhappy start for what proved to be a strained set of relationships. And while there was a marginal improvement with the appointment of the deputy governor of the Bank, Howard Davies, as head of the FSA, the tripartite system did not work in the way I had hoped. The irony was that little publicity was attached to another transfer of power from the Bank – its responsibility for managing and financing the national debt. This task, which the Bank had performed since its founding in 1694, was summarily passed to a new executive agency of the Treasury.

I was not entirely happy either; in my case, with the way the blueprint was translated into legislation. First, one other innovation I had hoped for was to rename the Bank of England as 'the Bank of England, Scotland, Wales and Northern Ireland'. This would honour its history – people would abbreviate the long name and still refer to the Bank of England – while leaving no doubt that it was there to represent the whole of the UK. However, I was told that this would have required a revision of thousands of statutes and regulations which referred to the Bank of England. Given the imperative of moving quickly, we did not have the time to do that. It is a reform that I still wish to see happen.

Second, I wanted the Bank to have a dual mandate to keep inflation low and employment high – one that was similar to that of the American Federal Reserve. But the lawyers advised that it was too difficult legally to have two primary objectives. We got around this as best we could. The legislation defined the Bank of England's objective as 'to maintain price stability and, subject to that objective, to support the government's economic policy, including its objectives for growth and employment'. Nevertheless, much of the heat was removed from this argument by the symmetrical inflation target, which promoted growth and thus employment.

The Bank performed well. Bank independence gave an immediate boost to the economy, as bond yields – and thus the price people had to pay for borrowing – fell by 0.5 per cent and the difference between UK and European rates narrowed to Britain's advantage. Our long-term interest rates would, for the first time in decades, come close to those of Germany. Eddie George proved to be a good choice as the first governor of the newly independent Bank. He not only held the confidence of the City of London but had a clear sense of the limits as well as the power of his new role. Sensitive to possible charges against the Bank of interfering across economic policy while being unelected, Eddie did not seek to interfere in any way with fiscal policy – privately or publicly. Over time, too, we also opened up the Bank's procedures to even more public scrutiny and gave the House of Commons a new role in scrutinising our appointments.

When it comes to big ideas in monetary policy, few are bigger than central-bank independence and, from the perspective of 2017, I am still convinced that it was, and is, the right policy. The timing was right – at the start of a new government – and the execution well prepared. We avoided endless press stories of a monthly tug-of-war over interest rates between a Labour chancellor and the City establishment. But the vision we had was about more than controlling inflation: it was about setting a stable long-term path for the economy that abandoned what I believed had been, despite all efforts to the contrary, fifty years of short-termism in economic management; and we ensured the choice on the euro was no longer between an unstable British monetary policy and a stable European regime but between two different regimes both offering stability. As a result of our decision, monetary policy decision-making now became more responsive to economic conditions and quicker and more flexible in reacting to problems. Interest rates were increased in 1997 to deal with inflationary pressures and lowered in late 1998 in response to recessionary fears and the near collapse of the massive and highly leveraged hedge fund LTCM at the time Russia devalued its currency. The Bank also acted expeditiously to prevent a British repeat of the American downturn after the tech-boom crisis in 2001–2 when interest rates came down fast.

British inflation was kept low after 1997, helped on by low world-wide inflation, not least because China and emerging nations were flooding western consumer markets with cheaper goods. From 1997 until 2003, inflation met its 2.5 per cent target, averaging 2.4 per cent, and in the next four years kept to the new 2 per cent inflation target, averaging 2.01 per cent. Inflation was so benign that, when he retired, Eddie George wrote me a letter explaining why he had not written an 'open letter'.

The years that followed were less smooth. UK inflation peaked at 5.2 per cent in September 2008 and troughed at 1.1 per cent in September 2009 before increasing to 3.7 per cent in April 2010. This volatility can be explained. It was in part due to the recession, in part a result of the violent rise and then fall in oil prices, and in part due to sterling's depreciation. The later rise reflected the return of VAT to 17.5 per cent in early 2010.

The 1997 settlement has proved durable and more successful than any other UK monetary policy regime in our post-war history. While some still favour complete independence, I believe that the Bank's greatest expertise lies not in setting goals but in putting them into practice. Our settlement struck the right balance between the use of experts and the need for public accountability. So I would still reject the idea that the Bank set their own target. But the singular focus on inflation   with one target and one weapon – was also a creature of a time when the economic priority was dealing with persistent bouts of high inflation.

In New Zealand and Australia – economies as open to external influences as ours – the exchange rate is taken into account in setting interest rates, whereas the system we designed was more suited to that of a less open economy like America – and we had renounced exchange-rate targeting when we left the ERM. For ten years the exchange rate was stable – but at a level 10 per cent higher than in the twelve years from 1984. In fact, the real effective rate, factoring in unit labour prices, was 27 per cent higher.

Should the Bank have taken into account not only the direct impact of our exchange rate on manufacturing but also asset prices, particularly when UK house-price inflation was high, in determining interest rates? Well-known economic thinkers Olivier Blanchard and Ken Rogoff believe that interest-rate decisions should reflect concerns about asset prices. However, while the Bank considered the issue of asset prices, they agreed with the more conventional view of the former chairman of the Federal Reserve, Ben Bernanke, that this should be taken into account only to the extent that it affected the inflation rate. These concerns – and the dangers flowing from a risk-laden financial sector – would become more pressing when the Bank and government failed to anticipate what became the worst global financial crisis in most of our lifetimes during 2008 and 2009. And as we approach the third decade of the twenty-first century, it is right to review our macroeconomic regime, as I propose later, and examine better fail-safe early warning systems to counter risk.

Nevertheless, Bank of England independence had a profound impact on how the Treasury operated: put simply, it allowed ministers and senior officials to focus on the long term. For years there had been televisions on in the corner of every Treasury office, as ministers and officials monitored the markets and their fluctuations because of the Treasury's role in setting interest rates. With Bank independence, we were freed to take a more strategic view – to ask how we might achieve our aim of full employment, higher living standards, better public services and higher productivity. It allowed us to target previously neglected areas like welfare-to-work, fiscal management, tax reform, modernisation of our public services, the reasons for slow growth and even Third World debt and international economic reform.

And from my first few months in the Treasury, when the Asian financial meltdown happened, there was no shortage of crises to address. On Christmas Eve 1997, as I prepared to take the chair of the finance ministers' and bank governors' G7 – the premier economic forum of the day – the Asian financial crisis hit us. Eddie George asked for an urgent meeting. As usual, he lit up his cigarette before he came to the point. His message was blunt: South Korea was bankrupt.

Britain was about to assume the presidency of the G7 group of nations. I was the newest finance minister, but as the chairman of the finance ministers' and bank governors' meetings, Britain would have to lead the response, and so I spent much of the next few months visiting Thailand, South Korea, Indonesia, Hong Kong and Japan. The roots of the 1997 crisis were not dissimilar to 2008: an unsustainable property boom, a rush for quick and easy yields, a wave of speculative foreign investment, and overleveraged financial institutions. One lesson I learned then was to act quickly and never allow an economy to sink so low that a recovery becomes more and more elusive.

Another was that the international economy was in urgent need of restructuring. Early on in my time as chancellor, one of our highly respected civil servants told me that the way of the world was that America did the big issues on the international stage and Britain the smaller ones. Another would joke that America led the thinking and we held the pen. I was not prepared to operate to that mindset. I saw that in Asia, but also in the West, the current systems of national regulation did not have the bandwidth to cope with the new complexities of international finance. In a series of speeches I was to give over the next few years, starting with Ottawa in September 1998 and at Harvard in December 1998, I was to challenge what was then called the Washington Consensus – a free-market approach that assumed that all we had to do was deregulate, liberalise, privatise and focus our attention on keeping inflation low.

Instead I proposed an interventionist approach – international supervision of the biggest financial institutions, a new set of global banking standards, the opening up of tax and regulatory havens to scrutiny, and a major reform of the International Monetary Fund (IMF) to make it more like an independent central bank – not so different from what Keynes had called for in 1944 – with a more explicit duty to monitor and advise on the condition of the global economy. To further these aims, in 1999 I became chairman of the IMF group of finance ministers that met twice a year, usually in Washington, to survey the world economy.

Travelling on Concorde with Ed Balls and my speechwriter Beth Russell to the IMF meetings in 2002, we heard the noise of an engine blowing out. Instantly the plane fell thousands of feet; passengers at the back of the plane started to scream. I now know you can tell when things are really serious: for minutes, there was no intercom announcement or explanation from the flight deck. Both Ed and I found out a lot about ourselves during these minutes, staying remarkably calm – 'Do you think there's any point in finishing the speech?' I remember asking – but we both felt our time was up. We talked about family and friends – until minutes later we were told Concorde had stabilised and would now fly at low speed to New York using its remaining engines.

On more than one occasion before I became prime minister I considered invitations to become the managing director of the IMF. But I would have had to give up my constituency and Parliament – something I was not willing to do – and, even then, I still believed Tony would keep to his promises.

But while we secured the creation in 1999, with German help, of the Financial Stability Forum to monitor global financial market trends and, with an American push, a G20 for finance ministers to take a strategic view of the global economy, we did not secure agreement on the reforms that would have prepared us for the problems we faced in 2008. The IMF did agree to submit to each of our twice-yearly meetings an analysis of the financial risks and uncertainties across the world. But the most important change I proposed – creating an early warning system for the world economy – did not win the support it required. An initiative by the IMF to deal with global economic imbalances also struggled to get off the ground. So, when the most severe global crisis since the 1930s hit, we had to make more progress in cooperation in a few weeks than we had made in the previous ten years.

CHAPTER 6

PRUDENCE FOR A PURPOSE

The Budget is one of the few parliamentary occasions when members of the public take any notice of Westminster. The minute the chancellor emerges from No. 11 Downing Street with the Budget box, people are on the lookout for – sometimes in fear of – the next tax rise, VAT increase or higher fuel, alcohol and cigarette duties.

At 3.30 p.m. on Wednesday 2 July 1997, when I was just about to stand up to deliver the first of my eleven Budgets, Conservative MPs interrupted with a complaint about Budget leaks. After the altercation had taken up more than a quarter of an hour, I remember turning to Tony, who was sat next to me on the front bench, and saying, 'We've waited eighteen years; I suppose we can wait the extra eighteen minutes.'

A Budget is usually a year in preparation. It is like painting the Forth Rail Bridge – as soon as one is delivered, work on the next begins. But I had less than two months to prepare for the Budget I delivered in 1997. In the past, chancellors had gone into Budgets after periods of 'purdah', when they had been silent for weeks and often months. In my first weeks in office, while our Treasury team of ministers and advisers were spending almost all waking hours planning, writing and preparing our Budget, I was very much in the public eye as we delivered the new settlement for the Bank of England and prepared the ground for the windfall tax to fund our employment programme for young people.

Bank of England independence had shown us to be fresh and full of new ideas. But it was not this that gave our team the most powerful sense of drive and purpose: it was the New Deal to boost employment. My first Budget itself was to be about more than the public finances: it was a Budget for Jobs. The New Deal would aim to help 400,000 young people with no jobs, nearly 100,000 of whom had been on the dole for longer than a year. Until we acted, many faced a life-time without work.

When in my first days as chancellor I visited a Job Centre with Andrew Smith, our minister for employment who would go on to manage the delivery of the New Deal with – like every other job he did in government – great distinction, we were left with a clear impression that we were not dealing with young people who were work-shy. They had just fallen through the net and were as keen to work as Andrew and I were. Our policy, I told them, was to match new rights to jobs with the responsibility to take up what was on offer. Even when we told them that the sanctions attached to the New Deal would be tough – that they could not just refuse to take a job – there was no resistance: they wanted jobs. Everywhere I went, I found a positive response to the New Deal.

In these first few weeks I also visited a children's hostel in Slough. This showed me another side of the jobs picture – the lengths to which we would have to go to help young people who had missed out on their schooling and whose problems were more than a dearth of skills. The young girl I met had nothing: in her small room, she had no radio, no CD player, only the clothes she was wearing. She had a violent father. She went back to him when she had no money. I have often asked myself what happened to that young girl caught in a cycle of despair with an abusive father, a stormy home life, temporary stays at hostels and nothing of substance to call her own. I left her what cash I had in my pocket but it was only £30. The New Deal had to offer her support, counselling and mentoring – tailored to her needs – but also the chance to earn enough to break free from a violent past.

In the 1980s and 90s, Britain had been blighted by a long period of mass unemployment. In two deep recessions unemployment exceeded 3 million. And when official unemployment figures which documented the number of registered benefit claimants came down, there remained 2.5 million people outside the workforce who were on Incapacity Benefit. Once those discouraged from registering for work were included, more than 5.5 million adults were workless.

Our detailed response was the brainchild of the Treasury team I had built up in opposition – in particular our policy advisers Ed Miliband and Spencer Livermore, who worked alongside Ed Balls.

The New Deal had first been announced in 1993, and was based on a careful and thorough analysis of international best practice of welfare-to-work policies. It incorporated lessons from the United States, and from successful labour-market policies in Europe, especially Scandinavia. Youth unemployment was such an emergency that we consciously borrowed the phrase 'New Deal' from Franklin D. Roosevelt's series of measures taken in America during the 1930s in response to the Great Depression. To get it up and running within a matter of months was an exercise of unprecedented scale and speed within the Treasury, only later surpassed by the work taken to deal with the global financial crisis in 2008 and 2009.

Creating the New Deal was one of the most challenging, satisfying and rewarding times of my political life. Securing full employment was a cause I believed in passionately from my own experience growing up in Fife. For most of the last century workers looked for stable jobs that would last a lifetime. A skill once learned would serve someone for fifty years until they retired. By 1997 the world of work had changed. Technological advance was already forcing a regular turnover of jobs and the restructuring of many occupations. Training could never again be confined to just one skill: it was now about building adaptable skill sets. And we were concerned about making work pay. It was not enough to create jobs for the unemployed if they just moved into poverty wages: with the minimum wage, we could start to make work pay, but if we were to cater for the full range of family needs even the minimum wage would need to be topped up. Ed Miliband and Spencer Livermore were, as a result, already discussing with highly motivated Treasury officials tax credits to complement the new minimum wage.

From May 1997, we met together almost every day to talk about how our plans could be implemented as quickly as possible. We worked to a tight and stretching timetable – legislation in July and the first entrants to the New Deal pilots in January 1998.

The New Deal for Young People was the starting point. Our plan was simple: to offer all eighteen- to twenty-four-year-olds who had been unemployed for six months or longer a range of options, all of which led to a qualification: a subsidised job with a private employer, full-time training or education, placement with a voluntary-sector provider, or work on a specially created programme to undertake environmental improvements. They could take up any of these offers, but could not choose to remain on benefits. With the New Deal, we were honouring one of our much talked about 'five pledges' in the manifesto – to get 250,000 under-twenty-five-year-olds off benefits and into work. I was to joke that the New Deal had been such a popular part of our election appeal that the first entrant to it had been one of our young researchers, the newly elected MP for Shipley, Chris Leslie, who was just twenty-four. And I was able to set out in my first Budget how the windfall tax on the privatised utilities would raise £5.2 billion to fund the New Deal.

The New Deal for Young People was rolled out nationwide in April 1998. A perverse rule that barred young people receiving benefits if they were studying for more than sixteen hours a week was relaxed. And young people who went into full-time education now received a discretionary grant to help with travel and other costs.

The next step was to extend the New Deal from young people to the country's long-term unemployed and then to lone parents, the partners of the jobless, and to the disabled. Here, too, there was a crisis. Four years after the recession, more than half a million adults had been on Jobseeker's Allowance for more than a year. When we came to office 2 million children were being brought up by 1 million single parents on benefits. Between 1979 and 1997 the number of people on Incapacity Benefit had trebled to 2.4 million. Emphasising capabilities rather than the incapacity of disabled men and women on benefits, we provided a 'pathway to work': offering not only training and a personal adviser but a return-to-work cash credit.

With the New Deal supporting an economy that grew strongly from 1997 to 2008, employment rose by 3 million, from 26.5 million to 29.6 million. We were praised by a normally critical IMF for our 'innovative efforts to use active labor market policies to help benefit recipients move into work'. According to the Institute of Fiscal Studies, the New Deal for Young People increased the probability of a young person finding a job by 20 per cent. There were also wider economic benefits: the National Institute of Economic and Social Research estimated that the New Deal benefited the economy by £500 million a year. The country's leading researcher on employment trends, Paul Gregg, who helped advise us, argued that it had 'a large and positive effect' on lone parents' employment rates, as well as their self-esteem.

In its first ten years, according to the National Audit Office, more than 1.8 million people were helped into a job through the New Deal.

The New Deal was, in truth, made possible by an emergency allocation of funds paid for by a one-off tax. The real story of our Labour government is of how we responded to other legitimate public demands for change but only after a period of restraint to ensure the country's financial position was secure. We imposed a rigid fiscal discipline in our first years precisely so that we could accumulate the financial strength to deal with the injustices that led people to vote Labour in the first place.

We knew the lessons of history. Previous Labour governments had spent more than they could afford in the first two years of their tenure to honour promises they had made in opposition, and were forced to retrench in their later period in office. We would not make the same mistake.

I was confident of being able to deliver a genuine improvement in public services, a reduction in unemployment and a stronger growth rate over the lifetime of the parliament. I knew this could be built only on a platform of sustainable levels of debt. But the state of the public finances, we discovered on entering the Treasury, was a further constraint. While the Conservatives had reduced the deficit from its earlier high, I found that they had underestimated by £20 billion how much the nation would borrow over the next three years. We found the public finances were indeed as bad as we had been saying they were.

In 1997, I announced two new rules on the public finances which went beyond the constantly changing fiscal promises that had characterised the Tory years: what I called the 'golden rule' on borrowing and the sustainable investment rule on debt. The 'golden rule' meant that, over the course of the economic cycle, government would borrow only to invest and not to fund current expenditure. The sustainable investment rule meant that national debt, in normal times, should never exceed 40 per cent of national income.

Behind the new rules and mechanisms put in place were common-sense truths that I hoped would shape public expectations: namely, that public consumption that brought benefits in the short-term should be paid for, but that borrowing was justified in normal times for investment that produced benefits in the long term – just like a family borrowing to purchase a home or a business to buy the seed-corn technology and equipment to become more productive. I felt strongly that previous governments, struggling to bring down public borrowing, had sacrificed the future needs of the country by cutting investment first and by most. I believed that a nation concerned about the future of the economy, public services and our national infrastructure could be persuaded to support investment for the future on this basis.

I was referred to as the 'Iron Chancellor', an epithet I welcomed as I was intent on overturning the past caricature of Labour as 'profligate'. But it was always important how we talked about prudence: not just for its own sake, but prudence for a purpose. This was the thinking that lay behind my first few Budgets. They were designed to prepare the ground for the long-term investments we planned to deliver further down the line. Critics argue that the prudence of 1997 and 1998 was very soon followed by excess and that this was merely a convenient device to obscure future spending. This is not true: the new investments in our social and economic fabric that followed would be paid for through growth and rises in taxation.

In my first two Budgets, we took money out of the economy, as we tightened fiscal policy and sent an unmistakable message that we would insist on 'iron discipline'. Total government spending, which stood at 35.8 per cent of national income before we took power, fell to 34.3 per cent two years later. Even then, we did not relax. We tightened further in 1999–2000 and brought the share of public spending to its lowest level – 34 per cent – since the late 1950s. By 1999, through holding firm against demands for additional spending, we had moved the deficit into surplus and debt was falling as a share of national income. In the next four years, we would be repaying debt. Indeed, such was our commitment to prudence that, when we invented a new form of auctioning for the next-generation mobile-phone licences in 2000 and secured a windfall of £22.5 billion, we used the proceeds to help pay down the national debt.

Even after we went into surplus, I made a presentation to the Cabinet about avoiding the mistakes of the past: of accelerating spending too fast and taking increasing economic strength for granted at a time when the UK still had a large productivity gap with its main competitors. Attempts to run the economy at too great a capacity, I warned, would stoke up an unsustainable consumer boom and force mortgage rates to rise. We needed a more staged approach: first, stability and prudence to keep interest rates low; second, tackling underinvestment, and then a focus on the nation's other priorities when they became affordable.

But there was one other change that we made early on. In 1997, average per capita income in the UK was among the lowest in the G7 group of advanced economies; and what income we had was far less equitably shared. The Wages Councils, which set minimum wages for agriculture, textiles and other low-paid occupations, were now ninety years old and had been reduced by the Tories to nothing more than shells. Their failure was the impetus behind the minimum wage, which was piloted through the Commons with speed by Ian McCartney and Margaret Beckett in the face of objections from a Conservative Party that seemed still stuck in the past. It was a landmark piece of legislation Labour had sought from the days of Keir Hardie more than a century before. But there were two outstanding issues we had to resolve. First, to ensure the minimum wage quickly gained acceptance, Tony and I agreed that we would start from a lower rate than we would have ideally wanted before raising it faster in successive years. Secondly, for fear of undermining the New Deal, we would only gradually bring young people within the scope of the minimum-wage laws.

We turned to wider economic policy matters and what we could do to enhance competitiveness, enterprise and investment. My analysis was clear: Britain had an inflation-prone, low-growth, low-productivity economy that was suffering from a chronic lack of investment.

Britain's poor productivity had been our Achilles heel: raising it and our levels of investment were at the forefront of our economic aims. In 1964, Harold Wilson and George Brown had created the Department of Economic Affairs to pursue the growth agenda; in contrast, we worked through the Treasury with a new Enterprise and Growth Unit overseen by Geoffrey Robinson. Our successes included the R&D tax credit which was taken up by 6,000 businesses, the ten-year science plan announced in 2004, enhanced collaboration between universities and business, and tax incentives to encourage investment in areas like information technology.

Having introduced an independent monetary policy, I pressed for an independent competition policy – arguing in the 1999 Budget that cartels and anti-competitive practices had to be broken if we were to expand opportunity for new competitors. And with the Treasury pushing a new Enterprise Act in 2002, we empowered two bodies independent of government – a beefed-up Office of Fair Trading and a Competition Commission – to clamp down on anti-competitive practices. We sought advice far and wide – not all of it was to prove useful. A 1998 review by the North American division of the management consultants McKinsey came out with one surprising conclusion. When they observed our well-known hotels were too old and used space inefficiently, we had to point out that ancient buildings and our heritage were among our most important tourist attractions.

In my first Budget, I reduced the rate of corporation tax from 33 per cent to 31 per cent and by 2007 had brought it down to 28 per cent. But I was attacked for simultaneously withdrawing the payable tax credit on dividends, and, while it was accepted that this removed what had been a disincentive to investment, I was to be accused for the next ten years of taxing pension funds and thus ruining final-salary pensions – an unfair allegation, as the evidence I brought before a rowdy debate in the House of Commons in 2007 proved. I wanted to do even more to help small businesses, reducing their tax rate to 20 per cent in 1998 and for some of the smaller start-ups to 10 per cent in 1999 – later lowering it to zero for some. In 1997 there were 3.7 million small businesses and 3.4 million self-employed. By 2010, the figures had risen by nearly 2 million in total – 4.8 million and 4 million respectively, despite a debilitating recession.

The annual cycle of economic decision-making now started with the Pre-Budget Report in November or December, months in advance of the Budget itself. Total public spending – previously decided year-to-year in constantly changing announcements – was now subject to a longer-term set of disciplines we had thought through in opposition: a system of public spending reviews which would plan and set limits three years in advance.

The theme of each review, starting with the Comprehensive Spending Review of 1997–8, was money only in return for reform. The Treasury may have lost one empire – the control of monetary policy – but it had assumed an even bigger task in long-term fiscal management and overseeing public sector reform. The success or failure of our delivery of public services was now measured not by the Treasury's traditional focus on inputs – what was spent – but on what really matters: outputs and outcomes. What counted now was not simply the level of spending but whether programmes achieved their stated purposes and what difference they had on people's lives. Each department would now have to sign a three-year contract with the Treasury, known as a Public Service Agreement, on delivery of specific and measurable targets. I chaired the relevant Cabinet committee to hold ministers to account. This was seen by many as a Treasury power grab. In reality, it was necessary to assess continually not just whether departments were coming within their budget limits but also whether they were delivering results.

By 1999, with debt falling and these new systems in place, we were now in a position to do much more to address the inequalities distorting Britain. The issue we would now tackle head-on went right to the heart of British society – tackling poverty, increasing investment in public services and narrowing the economic disparities between the north and south that were being highlighted by John Prescott. The prudence we had shown in our early years had been for an even bigger purpose. The outcome of our 2000 Spending Review – average real-terms growth in spending on public services of 5 per cent a year, compared to 0.7 per cent under the Tories – represented the biggest sustained increase in expenditure for thirty years. What's more, whereas in the period 1979–97 42 per cent of each pound of additional total public spending had been allocated to debt interest and social security expenditure, the figure was now only 17 per cent – leaving even more for health, education, transport and social policy.

There was one other set of initiatives vital for investment in our economy and public services – public-private partnerships or PPPs. For some, PPPs were simply a halfway house to privatisation. The public sector, they said, handed over control of projects to private contractors who, in return for paying upfront capital costs, charged exorbitant interest rates over the next thirty years. For me, PPPs looked different: they were a way of mobilising private funds for public purposes and offered a better route to building our infrastructure than the old ways of financing. After all, we had always hired private builders to construct our schools, hospitals, roads and public buildings. But we had enjoyed little control – leading to run-on costs, delays and often poor quality. With PPPs we were not only mobilising private sector skills for public purposes, ending the sterile and self-defeating battle for territory between public and private sectors, but building in tougher contractual requirements that secured far better value for money for the taxpayer. There were to be teething problems – some projects were poorly structured – and in an environment of low interest rates, legitimate issues about the rates of interest being charged. But, at their best, PPPs married the long-term thinking and ethos of the public sector with the managerial skills of the private; and, in truth, we could not have commissioned more than a hundred hospitals and built, rebuilt or refurbished 4,000 schools by 2010 if we had not.

Our spending reviews were not just about domestic services: they were designed to create the resources we needed for defence, security and international development. The first review of defence spending ended in what I was later to realise was the normal way of doing business – a threat to the existence of Rosyth Dockyard beside my constituency if the Ministry of Defence did not get the best deal. Nevertheless, we were able, in successive reviews, to finance both the strategic and day-to-day requirements of the Ministry of Defence.

The spending reviews also offered me a chance to begin the work I had set my heart on: increasing international development aid to the poorest countries. I had hoped to do something to make a difference on world poverty ever since I was a child contributing articles and raising money for the Freedom from Hunger campaign. But it was only when I started to make visits to Asia and Africa that I saw at first hand the scale of poverty and yet the enormous potential of these two great continents.

Like Tony, I wanted international development to have a far stronger profile. To this end, he had established the new Department for International Development under the dynamic leadership of Clare Short. It was not simply about projecting 'soft' power as was often the case in the past; it was about doing what we could to eradicate global poverty and improve development. Our approach stood in marked contrast to the Tories, who in the 1970s abolished Labour's Ministry of Overseas Aid and subsumed its responsibilities within the Foreign Office. It was Barbara Castle – Harold Wilson's first minister for overseas aid – who defined the role Clare now discharged as 'a guarantee that overseas aid was no longer to be regarded as a charitable donation from rich to poor but an essential element of world development'.

Clare and I worked well together. When we took over, overseas aid was only 0.26 per cent of UK national income, just a fraction of the 0.7 per cent target set by the United Nations. We were spending only one pound for every three needed to meet the target. To raise spending on international aid overnight to 0.7 per cent was an impossibility given the multibillion costs involved. But Clare and I devised a plan to raise spending gradually, first to 0.5 per cent, then 0.6 per cent and finally to 0.7 per cent; and, by reprogramming aid to focus on the needs of the most vulnerable and by untying it from defence and other contracts, we used it more effectively to reduce poverty. Our changes counteracted what was anyway a false claim that aid was taxing the poor in rich countries to hand over cash to the rich in poor countries.

Debt relief was a much more controversial issue. Thanks to the work of a very thorough and gifted researcher, Sandy Hunt, I had been able to argue from the early 1990s that interest now being paid on Africa's debt was syphoning off money that could be better used for education and health. Shriti Vadera, who would next help me plan for 100 per cent debt relief, was at once a master of the technical detail and awash with innovative ideas. In 1997, at the Commonwealth Finance Ministers' Conference in Mauritius, I made one of my first speeches as chancellor calling for widespread relief of debt. I argued that, under current plans, only one or two countries would ever secure the relief from unpayable debt that the international community had promised. I therefore proposed 90 per cent relief as a first step to eradication of all the debts of the poorest countries. At the conference, we also agreed to take on corruption in a far more sustained way. I had already acted in my first Budget to remove the tax reliefs that until 1997 had been available on bribes that companies paid to win foreign contracts. It was something of an irony that a few hours after my speech in Mauritius, when flying to Thailand via South Africa and refuelling in Madagascar, that the airport head demanded a bribe before allowing the plane to leave. The very civil servant who had helped write the speech demanding we outlaw all forms of bribery was preparing to pass his last dollars to the blackmailer when a Russian Aeroflot plane carrying hundreds of passengers – and thus more lucrative business for the airport head – arrived, and we were allowed to leave without charge.

When later that year the G7 finance ministers met, I once again tried to open the question of debt relief. I got nowhere – indeed, my fellow finance ministers said that the issue had been fully dealt with and initially even refused to countenance its inclusion on the agenda. Luckily, my international colleagues were coming and going at a rate of knots: I was the second-most senior of the whole G7 within eighteen months. So, step by step, we reopened each of the issues preventing full debt relief and won over France, Italy and Germany. Crucially, at a 1999 meeting of the World Bank, the Americans finally agreed to a 100 per cent cancellation. But then there was a change of US president, and we had to start again.

The battle over debt relief and the challenge of meeting our aid target galvanised my efforts to play a bigger role in international development from the Treasury. It brought a fresh purpose into our politics. I genuinely felt that the fiscal discipline we had shown in the first two years – and beyond – was for a worthwhile cause. Yes, we spent a long time telling people what we could not do, but I never gave up on the longer-term vision I had: supported by a new, tougher, fiscal framework, we could now sustain the increases in public spending, the improvements in public services that were desperately needed, and our plans for the reduction of poverty. A long and difficult battle lay ahead. But my mind was made up. The Treasury would next turn to addressing children's and pensioner poverty. I had in mind a bold endeavour to fight a war on poverty – to create a form of payment that would be neither a social security benefit nor a tax relief. First, though, we had to persuade the country that our tax system had to change.

CHAPTER 7

TAX AND THE BRITISH – AND THE BATTLE AGAINST POVERTY

Margaret Thatcher always saw them as symbols of the country she believed in. Try as they did, Nigel Lawson and Norman Lamont could not change them in the way they wanted. Tony Blair was reluctant to abolish them, though he recognised that they had no economic logic. Labour pollsters were aghast when we tried. But, in one fell swoop in the Budget of 1999, we swept aside two British institutions that symbolised a bygone age so we could use our nation's scarce resources for our priorities.

One was mortgage tax relief, the tax break given to homeowners by the state, and the other was married couple's allowance, the tax break that symbolised the importance our society attached to the institution of marriage. Attitudes to reform of both were indicative of something even more entrenched in society – the British people's suspicion of taxation. But our aim was not 'taxation for taxation's sake'. Spending, as we then did, £3.5 billion a year on these two tax reliefs deprived us of the resources we needed to meet a national emergency.

The changes we proposed on mortgage tax relief and married couple's allowance were the first skirmish in our longest battle, success in which had proved elusive for decades: to wage and win a war against poverty. First, we had to break the rise in child poverty – and then stage by stage eliminate it. At the turn of the century we would publish our timetable for the abolition of child poverty. By 2010 we would have binding legislation in place. The new law would require government to end child poverty by 2020.

And we would achieve our objectives in new ways. Working from ideas our team had formulated in opposition, we planned to introduce a wholly new line of support for millions of low- and middle-income families – tax credits. This new form of help was neither a social security benefit nor a tax cut. Why did we do this? The former – welfare payments – would not get to all of the low-paid households in poverty whom we wanted to reach. The latter – a tax cut or a rise in allowances – would be spread too thinly.

The same was true of the new benefit we introduced for the over-sixty-fives: pension credit for those below or just above the poverty line. A blanket rise in the old-age pension would give only a few pounds to 9 million elderly citizens, while a rise in supplementary benefits for the extremely poor would miss millions of pensioners at or just above the poverty line, many of whom had only small occupational pensions which deprived then of any means-tested supplement.

Year by year we would expand both tax credits and pension credit. By 2010, tax credits were worth £80 a week to the average family in receipt of them, and nearly 3 million pensioners would benefit from pension credit. It was as near to a revolution in our tax-and-benefit system as we have seen in Britain. Our reforms were for a purpose: to eradicate child and pensioner poverty in one generation.

But first we had to win the battle over tax – winning over a country that was naturally suspicious of any tax reform and which, in particular, attached importance to tax exemption for mortgages and marriage.

Mortgage tax relief commanded wide support because it was purported to signal our belief as a country in a property-owning democracy. It reflected the long-held belief that 'your home was your castle', that your property was an extension of yourself, its rising value the product of your own efforts and therefore not to be burdened by taxation.

Married couple's allowance had originally been offered in 1918 to married men as they returned home from the First World War. While their wives, most of whom were employed for the first time in war service, returned home to domestic chores and thus no longer in paid employment, it was seen as a form of compensation. The married couple's allowance would enshrine and financially underpin the idea of the traditional family – man at work, with wife and children at home. In the post-1918 period no more than 15 per cent of married women were in work. As recently as the 1950s, when I grew up, the figure was only 30 per cent. But by 1997, when we came to power, 60 per cent of married women were in employment. So, even when most married women were working, we continued to pay an allowance originally designed to compensate them for staying at home.

However, any hint of a proposed change to these taxes – other than downwards – led to letters of complaint to MPs and newspapers, a popular discontent which was reflected in opinion polls, conversations and even in the monologues of comedians. I had always remembered on my first visit to the USA in 1984 seeing the inscription on the front of the Inland Revenue Service building on Pennsylvania Avenue in Washington: 'Taxes are what we pay for a civilized society'. It was written generations ago. I could not imagine winning unanimous support today in any part of the West for inscribing such a pro-tax motto on any government building.

In the neoliberal lexicon, tax generally had come to be viewed less as the contribution we make towards funding a civilised society and more as an unfair restriction on a person's freedom to do what they wanted with their own money. I may have seen a justification for tax in righting wrongs: more people, though, seemed to see it as violating their rights.

It is part of our folklore that Britain's first poll tax in the 1380s and the second version in 1990 both sparked resistance and uprisings. Less well known is that the first income tax did too. An emergency levy introduced during the Napoleonic Wars in 1799, it was a graduated tax set from 1 per cent to 10 per cent. It was voted out in 1816 in a Commons backbench revolt against the chancellor of the day, even after he explained that the alternative would be harsher taxes on the poor. The House of Commons told him that either it would be removed or he would be.

Various other taxes – from the eighteenth-century window tax to VAT on gas and electricity bills – also proved unpopular. And, of course, the attempt to tax the colonies – a tax that famously included a levy on imported tea and the imposition of stamp duty – fundamentally changed the future of the British state. Colonists correctly claimed that the 1689 Bill of Rights had promised 'no taxation without representation', demanded seats in Parliament, and when this was refused protests, starting with the Boston Tea Party, led to the American Revolution and the creation of a United States of America – gone for good from the British Empire.

So no government can introduce even the smallest tax rise without weighing up the potential for a big backlash. Recent examples, none of them small, abound under the Conservatives – the proposed dementia tax by Theresa May which was dropped within three days; the planned tax on the self-employed by her chancellor, Philip Hammond, withdrawn within a week; and the cuts to tax credits intended by his predecessor, George Osborne, discarded within a month.

If anything symbolised the difficulties we had in balancing the need for revenue with the distaste for taxation it was high levels of fuel duty – the fuse that lit a set of protests which threatened to bring Britain to a halt. Even on occasions when the main culprit for the rise in petrol prices was the Organization of the Petroleum Exporting Countries – in my time in office the oil price varied from $10 per barrel to $147 – it was us, the government, that was always to blame. We had inherited a road fuel tax escalator – now raising petrol tax at 5 per cent more than inflation – to bring revenue into the Treasury and help balance the books. We risked alienating the public by raising fuel duty to 6 per cent above inflation, bringing an annual petrol tax rise close to 10 per cent a year. And while the oil price seems small in today's terms – it was rising from a low point of just over $10 to $30 – tax now accounted for about 85 per cent of the cost of petrol. So even when we abandoned the fuel escalator in 1999 – fuel taxes would now rise no faster than inflation – the oil price rise meant drivers in the UK were now paying over 80p a litre.

But the whole government was taken aback by the 'Boycott the Pumps' campaign, which kicked off on the first day of August 2000, after a Conservative-organised day of protest on 29 July. Threatening an autumn of unrest, British truck owners and farmers then adopted a traditional French way of protesting – the blockading of refineries and depots – in September. There followed an eight-day crisis when things got out of hand, with rationing and then panic buying of petrol; petrol stations closing; emergency services, including the NHS, running short and on red alert; and even the panic purchasing of food. Six of the UK's nine refineries and the main oil distribution depot were closed. I was adamant: Budgets not blockades made the decisions on taxation. At the risk of a backlash, I stood firm. Whatever we did had to be justifiable on wider policy grounds. When the public saw garages, shops and hospitals running out of supplies, support for the blockade, which in early September had reached nearly 80 per cent, fell to just above one-third.

With protests all over Europe, I went to a European finance ministers' meeting in Versailles. I refused to sign up to a communiqué that said Europe was united in refusing to cut petrol prices. My European colleagues thought it would strengthen their hand with domestic audiences if the EU ruled out a cut. I had the opposite problem: I said, if it was the EU telling us what to do, it would be a disaster for the Labour government in Britain. This would be seen as a European diktat coming from on high, carrying no weight with the British people.

Still, it was time for us to act. In my 2000 Pre-Budget Report, I spent £1 billion to cut duty on the more ecologically acceptable ultra-low sulphur petrol, froze fuel duties, radically reduced licence fees for smaller more environmentally efficient cars, cut vehicle excise duties and introduced a Brit Disc Tax for foreign lorries using British roads. The proportion of taxation in the cost of a litre of petrol subsequently fell from 85 per cent to 68 per cent. By 2010, it was down to nearer 60 per cent.

When in 2008 the oil price moved upwards towards $140 per barrel, and petrol prices went beyond £1 per litre, we might have expected a repeat of 2000. But the British people had looked over the precipice that year and no one wanted a repeat of halting fuel supplies to hospitals and emergency services.

We had raised fuel tax and paid a political price. Mortgage tax relief and married couple's allowance also seemed impossible to abolish without a political cost. So sacrosanct were these two taxes that even in the most difficult of times – in the 1960s, 70s, 80s and 90s – chancellors shied away from removing them. They had seemed simply untouchable. While Nigel Lawson had hoped to persuade Mrs Thatcher to cut mortgage tax relief during the 1980s, neither he nor his successors could overcome opposition to reforming it. By the time the Tories left office it was still worth up to 15 per cent relief on the first £30,000 of home loan mortgage costs. What made it even harder to tackle was that, unlike many tax reliefs or allowances, it was easy to claim: from April 1983, the homeowner got the benefit directly in their pay cheque. It was entirely unfair to poorer families who rented their homes, and added to inflation by contributing to higher house prices – which, in turn, led to higher mortgages, negating its benefits to homeowners.

The married couple's allowance had also been expanded – to accommodate rising divorce rates, increased rates of separation without divorce, and increasing numbers of single parents – meaning it was neither confined to those who were married nor even to couples. It was a tax credit paid at the same flat rate to married couples, single parents and unmarried parents who lived together. More perversely, far from recognising marriage, it was worth more in the year you separated or divorced because it was paid twice – at the full rate – to each partner in that year. Yet, wholly outdated as it now was, the relief was still held up as the affirmation of traditional family life that the tax system should support.

In 1997 resistance to change of these two taxes was shared by some of my colleagues. Tony was informed by Philip Gould that the abolition of mortgage tax relief was particularly unpopular with his focus groups.

I would have preferred all-party agreement to end these two tax anomalies. However, when we came to preparing our Budget of 1999, we found that, now in opposition, the Tories were even more dug in than they had been in government. In particular, married couple's allowance was championed by their new leader, William Hague, as proof of the Tory Party's commitment to the family. He made it a dividing line, trying to position the Tories as the party of the family, and Labour as the party of the permissive society. But Conservative opposition would not stop me.

In meeting after meeting, we tested our arguments and it was only after extensive preparations that I announced in my 1999 Budget that I would abolish the married couple's allowance from April 2000 and end mortgage tax relief. Even then I was cautious in the way I made the change: I did not interfere with the married couple's allowance paid to pensioners, which in the 2000 Budget I raised in line with inflation. But no new claims would be accepted for the next generation of pensioners. The Tories not only vigorously denounced our change, they also pledged to reinstate the allowance in their 2001 election manifesto. And in the run-up to the 2010 general election, George Osborne would promise to legislate a new version of the married couple's allowance – a costly, illogical and administratively difficult scheme that would be introduced in 2015.

Was it worth taking on the traditionalists? Did it merely remind people of the Old Labour that they associated with a ceaseless yearning for tax rises, or could we show people that our arguments were based not on old dogma but on new realities? Yes, I was anxious about how Labour would be seen; and I would probably not have taken the risk of triggering a political firestorm and losing support in Middle England if I had not had in mind the larger and more compelling objective that I have described. We had to take action on child and family poverty and I was determined to show the country that the money from these two outmoded tax breaks was needed to tackle poverty.

Child poverty had doubled under the Tory government. By 1997, one in three children were living in families whose incomes were less than 60 per cent of the national median, meaning they were officially in poverty and brought up in families unable to pay for even basic necessities. Child benefit had changed little for years and the system of supporting poorer families – family income supplement and its more recent replacement, family credit – was reaching fewer than a quarter of the 4 million children who should have been helped. By ending married couple's allowance and mortgage tax relief, we could release £3.5 billion per year to help tackle poverty.

I have always considered poverty an obscenity. I do not know why some images stay with you while others fade. While I recall details of meetings with some of the world's most prominent leaders, I remember to this day more clearly the faces of the most vulnerable people I have met. We had built New Labour on the idea that, to help those in poverty, we had to reach out to those on middle and higher incomes, showing our policies were in tune with their values, rather than at odds with them. Making ourselves electable was the only way we could get a chance to do that. But, once in office, our defining test was what difference we could make to the lives of the poor. When I veered from that, as I did by not thinking through all the ramifications of eliminating the 10p tax rate, I lived to regret it.

The poverty emergency was such that we needed to act as soon as we came to power. So, despite our commitment to freeze spending at previously planned levels for two years, I moved quickly to add £2.50 a week in child benefit for the first child, over and above the normal uprating. But child benefit, paid to every family and child, was not targeted on the poorest. While I believed there should be a universal benefit for children, I knew simply that raising child benefit would not do enough to help those most in need of help. A flat payment of what was then a little over £10 a week child benefit could not make the difference between being in or out of poverty. Even if child benefit was doubled to £20 a week – a rise that we would eventually deliver – it would still not be enough to make the difference for families in dire poverty.

That's why as soon as it was fiscally possible, in the autumn of 1999, I introduced the working families' tax credit, the first in a number of tax credits to help the poor, low-paid and vulnerable. The new children's tax credit followed in 2001, initially paid at up to £520 a year to 5 million families, offering three times as much support as the married couple's allowance had ever given them. In 2002, we added an extra £590 for the first year of a child's life. Then, in 2003, I replaced the children's tax credit with the child tax credit, which, along with child benefit, provided a single and seamless system of financial support for families with children, whether in or out of work, alongside the new working tax credit for those in low-paid work. Taken together, these two measures were to save 2 million children from poverty. But, of course, this was possible only because we were building upon the minimum wage: without it, tax credits would have ended up subsidising employers for paying poverty wages.

Our ambition to eliminate child poverty was our boldest objective and the most difficult to deliver. Why did we adopt tax credits as the way to tackle it? A team – with Dawn Primarolo working night and day as the minister in charge, and strengthened by the highly respected children's rights campaigner Maeve Sherlock and academic expert Paul Gregg – looked at all possible ways of making our society fairer for children, and we found that even if we doubled child benefit it would not be enough to make the inroads into the family poverty we sought to eliminate. To have raised it to £20 a week for every one of the country's 12 million children would have cost us £6 billion. The problem was we would spread resources so thinly that the poorest 4 million children would be only £10 a week better off – as, of course, would be their better-off counterparts. Targeting support through tax credits could give families with the poorest children up to £40 a week more; and, potentially, £80 more for two- or three-children families. These were the kind of sums needed to lift millions of children out of poverty.

Similar results came when we reviewed a measure said by its supporters to be the best way of tackling poverty – lifting the income-tax threshold. But while the same £6 billion would take several hundred thousand out of tax, no one would receive more than few extra pounds a week – hardly enough to take poor families to an even basic level of sufficiency. And, of course, people too poor to pay tax received no benefit at all. Raising tax thresholds would do very little to help Britain's poorest; indeed, much more of the benefit would flow to second-earners in the top half of the population.

We also studied the idea of a universal basic income, but found it was not only more expensive than tax credits, it was like another proposal, a negative income tax, not well targeted at tackling poverty. Again, for the same amount of money spent, poor people would receive far more from tax credits than if it were allocated to a universal basic income. While there will always be a debate between universal and selective benefits, there is no doubt about what achieves most for the poorest: a universal benefit with additional support for those who need it most.

Tax credits were designed not only to lift millions out of poverty: they could also help families just above the poverty line – families not too poor to receive social security benefits and not wealthy enough to feel secure. Stretched to the limit, they needed help too. Yet, here again, neither tax reliefs nor child benefit would have much impact. What's more, we recognised that many mothers had to give up work because they had no cover for the hours after school. For this reason, we introduced a special element within working tax credit to offset the costs of childcare. It was not to be seen as a handout; it was, rather, a genuine family income supplement to help with the costs of bringing up children. As I said at the time of its introduction, we worked on two principles: that parents or guardians had a responsibility for bringing up their children, but that, where it could, the government had a duty to help them in this difficult task.

Tax credits mattered because they unlocked the door to achieving our boldest poverty objectives. With the mortgage and married couple's tax reforms of 1999, we took the first steps to help Britain's lower- and middle-income families. We then pledged to cut child poverty by a quarter in 2005 – a target which we just missed – and then halve it by 2010. Our commitment was more ambitious than that of any other government of the day and inspired a later EU strategy for poverty reduction. After a series of increases in tax credits – including promised rises we did not withdraw during the global recession – we would, by 2010, be transferring £28 billion a year to low- and middle-income families.

Our approach on tax credits was underpinned by what I called 'progressive universalism': a floor of basic social rights for all, but with more support to those most in need. Our Child Trust Fund, a financial endowment payable to every child at birth, was also based on this principle. All children born from September 2002 received a lump sum of £250, and if from a low-income family, £500. The fund was 'topped up' by a further contribution from government when a child reached seven. Five years after its launch, the Child Trust Fund was showing real benefits: 4 million children had an open, active savings account giving them a financial springboard into adulthood, and 70 per cent of the government contribution was going to families on below-average incomes. This was social mobility in practice: we were reducing the over-concentration of wealth in our country. Until 1999, most low-income households were not saving anything at all, and the new individual savings accounts we introduced led 17 million people to buy in and would ultimately raise savings by £220 billion.

The pension credit was based on the same principle of progressive universalism as tax credits. An additional payment on top of the state pension, pension credit was designed to provide security in old age for the poor and nearly poor. It had a major impact in reducing poverty. Even after housing costs are taken into account, pensioner poverty fell from 29 per cent to 15 per cent between 1997 and 2010. By April 2010, all the single pensioners on the pension credit were above the poverty line.

We did not, however, always satisfy those concerned about pensioner incomes. I readily concede that when the inflation-linked rise to the state pension amounted to only 75p per week in 1999, it was a public relations disaster. By way of compensation, that Christmas we increased the new winter fuel allowance fivefold – eventually it would run to £200 a year for the under-eighties and £300 for the over-eighties. That may have made pensioners better off, but it did not end the accusation that we had shortchanged those on the basic pension, even after our introduction of free TV licences for the over-seventy-fives and free pensioner bus travel.

The most controversial source of revenue for any government is income tax. Our 1997 manifesto contained two main commitments on this: not to raise the basic and higher rates of income tax over the lifetime of the parliament; and a long-term objective for a new 10p starting rate. In January 1998, only months before my first March Budget, I was sent a memo from Tony's private office that contained an astonishing proposal: to abolish all income-tax reliefs and allowances, other than a small personal tax credit, and use the proceeds to reduce the basic rate of tax to 20p and the top rate to 35p. Many would lose out under his proposal. I still have the formal response of the Treasury, which showed that there would be 12.6 million losers and 700,000 low earners taken into tax. High earners would gain around £2,000 but more than 1.5 million pensioners would lose about £500 per year. The proposal went no further.

I had always considered tax credits the high-hanging fruit and the 10p rate the low-hanging fruit. The first was initially difficult to reach, almost an impossible dream until, at great difficulty, we created the billions in extra resources needed to make it an instrument for transforming the incomes of the poorest families. The second was easier to deliver but a necessary element of our anti-poverty strategy only, in my view, until we had introduced tax credits. Then it became optional but not essential: once tax credits boosted the income of families, particularly those with children, then the case for the 10p rate – which was spread thinly, benefiting every taxpayer, including the very rich and not just those on low incomes – became much weaker.

Not until the 1999 Budget was I able to announce the 10p rate would apply for the first £1,500 of each individual's taxable income. This was the lowest starting rate of tax for nearly forty years, and reduced the marginal rate of tax to 10p for 1.8 million people. But I also cut the basic rate from April 2000 as I abolished the 20p rate which Norman Lamont had introduced with such devastating political results before the 1992 election. Most of the gainers were on low incomes.

By 2006 tax credits were now making a significant impact on poverty and I saw a chance to both extend them further and simultaneously deal with another tax issue that bothered me. As long as the basic rate was 22p and not 20p, the tax issue remained a potent weapon in our opponents' hands. Indeed, I believed that sooner or later – probably sooner – the Conservatives would fight an election on cutting the basic rate to 20p. With inflation low, revenues high, the system of tax credits firmly established and the opportunity for reform now available, I believed it the right time to kill the income-tax issue for good.

In the 2007 Budget, when I cut the basic rate to 20p and extended tax credits for those on low incomes, I spent £1 billion raising tax allowances for those aged sixty-five and over, another £1 billion raising the child tax credit and an additional £1.3 billion bringing more people on modest incomes into tax credits. Taking the Budget package as a whole, the poorest third of the population emerged as the biggest winners, largely thanks to the increase in tax credits. As was now the norm, we tested our Budgets for fairness – how they shifted the distribution of incomes as a whole – and once again our Budget changes ensured that, while the highest 10 per cent saw their incomes reducing to pay for the reform, the lowest 10 per cent saw theirs increasing.

But I had made a mistake. Taxpayers on incomes between £5,435 and £19,355 lost more from the abolition of the starting rate than they gained from the cut in the basic rate. The loss from this one individual measure was greatest at £232 a year for someone earning £7,755, and though most of these taxpayers were receiving tax credits that wiped out any loss, they would see their income-tax bills rise. While we protected most poor pensioners and poor families with children, too little had been done for childless adults who did not qualify for a big enough tax credit and for earlier retirees who had lost their working tax credits when they left their jobs but were too young to benefit from the more generous tax allowances for the over sixty-fives.

Finding a solution was not easy. The 10p rate could not be restored because integral to its affordability was the cut of the basic rate to 20p. We found a way through only after examining every option available. In May 2008, Alistair Darling raised the basic personal allowance a further £600 and every basic-rate taxpayer gained an extra £120. By the time of the Pre-Budget Report in November, we were already in the throes of the downturn, so Alistair announced an additional increase in the personal allowance of £130 from April 2009. All but a few of the losers from the abolition of the 10p rate were now better off. A mistake had been made and rectified – but at a price. Abolition of the 10p rate was an error I made in a rush to boost tax credits and kill off the income tax 'issue' and I was wrong to assume that a rise in tax credits could compensate all of the losers.

Nevertheless, the tax credit revolution had changed Britain. People wanted both security – to know what their week-to-week income would be – and also flexibility, so that if circumstances changed – such as going on maternity leave, or losing income through the denial of expected overtime – tax credits could adjust for any loss of income. Without them and other measures, the Institute for Fiscal Studies estimates that child poverty would have gone as high as 31 per cent instead of falling to 18 per cent. Simulations suggest that had financial support merely risen in line with inflation from 1997 to 2010, child poverty would have increased to 4.3 million, instead of falling to 2.5 million children.

However, even when we were distributing nearly £30 billion a year in tax credits, I never succeeded in popularising them in the way I had hoped – despite many attempts to do so. Tax credits were, it was suggested, redistribution by stealth, but at no point did I have any desire to hide what we were doing. Indeed, when we launched tax credits we ran a massive advertising campaign to explain what they were and how they would help families.

The problem was that tax credits were difficult to explain. The general public understood cash benefits – money that came from government as a universal payment like child benefit, the state pension or as a means-tested giro cheque. They also understood taxes, perhaps all too well, as the money they paid to government. Tax credits were different: while this was money paid by the government directly, much of what came through was wiped out by the money going out in tax. And because tax credits were flexible – going up and down according to circumstances – there was never a flat payment easily identified like a lump-sum benefit. Our problem was not, in the end, a failure in policy. With tax credits, as on many other occasions, there was a failure in presentation. It was difficult to explain how we were helping millions, not because we did not try; it was because the new system would take years to be understood – and, on this, we were not helped by early administrative difficulties, which we eventually ironed out.

Perhaps we should have talked of our tax and pension credits in more populist terms – as a form of tax cut, or income tax in reverse, or as child benefit-plus or pension-plus. While cutting or raising tax thresholds does far less for reducing poverty than tax credits, it is more easily understood. It was only when the Conservatives tried to cut back on tax credits that a truly popular campaign emerged to defend them. Of course, some will always argue that all benefits should be universal; but I am in no doubt that the real challenge is to explain and popularise the more progressive policy of doing more to help those who need help most.

Like tax credits, environmental taxes were in their infancy between 1997 and 2010. We pioneered new environmental taxes – namely the climate change levy, a tax on the supply of energy to business – and increased the rates of air passenger duty and landfill tax. In opposition, I had promoted the concept of taxes on 'bads' and tax reliefs on 'goods' to deal with environmental pollution. Each reform was a battle in itself: hours spent persuading industry that all revenues from the climate change levy would flow back to environmentally efficient firms; time spent explaining how the landfill levy would work in practice; and dealing with pressure from interest groups everywhere – and giving into some, like remote islands which all wanted their own airport levies. And, of course, our policy on fuel taxation was heavily influenced by our desire to promote cleaner fuels and vehicles.

In Europe there is a new system of carbon trading through emission permits, and part of the challenge is getting the balance right between incentives – through the tax system and market mechanisms – and the imposition of standards through regulation. What is clear is that the fight for a more ecologically sound tax system is only in its infancy and future governments will have to do much more.

I also wanted to use the tax system to do more to encourage charitable giving. Accordingly, we introduced a new system of Gift Aid that gave charities and faith groups up to £30 extra for every £100 they raised. And while we had to root out abuses – commercial enterprises posing as charities – the change boosted charities' incomes substantially. The reform was welcomed by church groups, who sometimes came to me with requests. When Rowan Williams, the Archbishop of Canterbury, called me one day to an urgent meeting just before my Budget in 2003, I thought he was about to raise one of many ethical concerns then at the centre of our national debate. In fact, his concern was VAT. He wanted an exemption for church repairs – then impossible under European Union rules. I agreed to refund the VAT paid on church repairs.

There was another battle for fairness that had to be fought. In opposition, I had annoyed the tax avoidance industry by saying we would take it on, and in each Budget after 1997 I introduced measures to close the corporate loopholes that allowed smart accountants to reduce the tax bills of the wealthy and well connected. Our biggest confrontation was with UK-based multinationals who were exploiting the openness of the new global economy to escape corporation tax, in some cases paying nothing at all in the UK. Companies will always strive to minimise their tax bill. Governments, in turn, must show equal ingenuity and perseverance to keep pace. Economic activity should be taxed where it takes place. With an estimated $7 trillion held in tax havens, tackling tax avoidance – and its criminal cousin, evasion – is central to tackling inequality.

By the turn of the century more and more companies were channelling their profits through low-tax jurisdictions and wiping out their tax liabilities in countries like ours. The battle culminated in a head-on clash with the telecoms giant Vodafone, chaired by Christopher Gent, a well-known Tory. The issue came down to dealing with what we called a controlled foreign company, or CFC, that diverted taxable UK profits into low-tax territories.

We proposed to treat Vodafone's Luxembourg subsidiary merely as a holding company for much of the group's UK activities. After several tense meetings with Vodafone and other companies, some of which I chaired, we agreed that we would intervene only against artificial arrangements but refused to back down from the general principle that profits made in the UK had to be taxed in the UK. By the end of 2005 Vodafone's accumulated potential tax liabilities alone ran to £5 billion. Such was their scale that, when they finally disclosed what they might have to pay, there was a 10 per cent fall in the group's share price. The issue went back and forth in the courts, with the government winning in 2008 and being set back in 2009. In 2010, though, the new coalition government would make a deal to water down the rules – and then entered into private agreements with companies like Facebook and Apple. The battle to address the huge global tax avoidance industry was put on hold, at a cost to Britain of billions a year in lost revenues.

I was to find from the Panama Papers in 2016 just how widespread the scale of avoidance by both individuals and companies still is. The most notorious recent British example is Sir Philip Green, who reduced the UK tax liability of BHS by paying rent and interest to companies registered in Jersey and the British Virgin Islands and then transferring hundreds of millions of pounds of BHS profits tax-free to his wife, resident in Monaco.

In the wake of the financial crisis we did make some inroads on tax avoidance when we agreed a blacklist of tax havens that were not complying with international rules for the exchange of tax information, and proposed new global standards for automatic exchange of tax information, including greater transparency about who really owned companies and trusts. This advance was finally endorsed in 2013 at the G8 in Lough Erne, Northern Ireland. While most countries have complied and the UK will have country-by-country reporting by multinationals, America remains happy to demand tax information from other countries yet is immovable in its refusal to reciprocate. The state of Nevada, we discovered, was the eighth most mentioned tax haven in the Panama Papers.

Tax havens abound, and as Britain prepares to exit the EU some on the right have suggested the country should now become one. This would exacerbate tensions with our nearest neighbours, widen the gap between the top 1 per cent and the rest of Britain, and deprive us in future of the resources we undoubtedly need – and which we raised in government – for our public services, including the NHS.

And all too often, low-income Britain has been persuaded by those who have the most that the real problem is not those above them – even when they siphon off money needed for decent social services into tax havens – but immigrants and ethnic minorities. All too often, as I found, a tax rise for the wealthiest is rejected by millions unaffected by it because they are persuaded it is the thin end of the wedge of inevitable tax rises for all.

But we did have a vision of how a fairer tax system could underpin popular support for good public services. And we did make substantial inroads into the unfairness that disfigured the Britain we had inherited. Overall, as a result of Labour's tax and benefit changes, the average income of the poorest tenth of the population rose by 12 per cent, while that of the richest tenth fell by nearly 9 per cent to pay for the changes. This stood in marked contrast to the regressive policies that preceded and succeeded us.

Our top-rate tax rise came in April 2010 – just a month before we left power. It was accompanied by a 1 per cent increase in the employee, employer and self-employed rates of National Insurance. Even before these rises, our tax changes had brought a fairer distribution of income across the United Kingdom. We not only raised more money to pay for the NHS, education, defence and security, but through tax credits transferred substantial cash support from the top to struggling lower- and middle-income households. The higher-earning 20 per cent paid £48 billion in taxes on income in the last year of the previous Conservative government, and were paying twice as much, £95 billion, in the last year under Labour. As a result of these changes the top 20 per cent who were responsible for 54 per cent of all tax payments in 1997 were paying 63 per cent in 2010, and after the top-rate tax changes fully came through, 65 per cent. Once we include tax credits the share of tax paid by the top 10 per cent had risen from 34 per cent of all taxes in 1997 to 43 per cent in 2010. Britain was a fairer country. By 2010, the effective tax rate paid by the top 10 per cent was 24 per cent, higher than for four decades and higher than under the 1974–9 Labour government. Now the share has started to fall, making Britain more unequal again.

Even before our tax rises in 2010, Britain was one of the few countries to defy the neoliberal orthodoxy of the time. The tax system became fairer – not just between the top and the bottom, but all round. There was much still to do; but once tax credits were included, the top 40 per cent, who in 1997 accounted for 80 per cent of all taxes paid on income, were now contributing 90 per cent. But we could not reverse the rise in inequality because everywhere in the western world the pre-tax incomes of the top 1 per cent were rising so fast. However, if not reversed, the rise of inequality was stalled.

The charge of 'taxation for taxation's sake' is one that had to be constantly refuted. The lesson I have learned from my tax battles – from the windfall levy to tax credits – has convinced me that on every step of the road we have to persuade the taxpayer of the rightness of the cause, to hypothecate where possible the tax increase to the service being delivered, and to demonstrate, in detail, why the public provision that the tax rise covers is more efficient and fairer than any private alternative that forces people to provide for themselves.

At the turn of the century, with some of these lessons at the front of my mind, I approached the next challenge – finding a way to refinance our cash-starved National Health Service for the new century.

CHAPTER 8

RENEWING THE NHS

When, in summer 2001, Sarah announced she was pregnant and expecting our first child the next spring, we were overjoyed.

We had married in August 2000, when we had tried to avoid all publicity. This proved difficult. In Scotland, you have to publish your 'marriage banns', giving the names of the couple intending to marry, displaying them for fourteen days in a public place. Fortunately, a very helpful registrar of marriages, births and deaths in our local office in Inverkeithing positioned the banns in as inconspicuous a place as possible. So, for days, no one noticed. Our stay-low strategy worked, in fact, until the night before the wedding. Presumably news of the impending marriage made its way to more and more officials up the line, and from there, predictably, the story leaked to the *Daily Record*. As a result, just as we were holding a small dinner for family and friends in Edinburgh, I found myself dealing with what became a media frenzy. Friends I had not yet told about our marriage – and who we were planning to phone the next day – had to be informed that night and statements issued confirming the event. Eventually, I was able to tell everyone we would invite them to a party later in the year and none had been forgotten.

There followed a rush of TV crews to our local church. Fortunately, a helpful local policeman had placed traffic cones on the road outside the church reinforcing the impression that an event was about to take place. Few people realise that in Scotland, as long as your church minister agrees, it is possible to get married in a religious ceremony at home. I had the idea to do this when I saw a photograph of the wedding of my grandmother and grandfather almost a century before, which showed the ceremony taking place in one of their parents' home. Sarah and I planned to get married in the dining room of my home in North Queensferry, courtesy of our local minister, Sheila Munro.

We had another small diversion that would help keep publicity to a minimum: getting married on the eve of the Queen Mother's one hundredth birthday. We assumed the interest in us would quickly subside, overtaken by the more compelling and telegenic birthday celebration occurring in London. And we were right: we had about thirty-six hours of intense media interest after the leaked story, but once we had flown out of Edinburgh that evening we were able to enjoy our honeymoon in Cape Cod – with only a few snappers in attendance.

I was, however, taught one salutary lesson in my dealings with the press. Feeling sorry for the numerous cameramen and journalists camped for hours outside our home while we celebrated inside, I asked my older brother to pour them glasses of champagne. This backfired: one of the bottles was from Sainsbury's. So the event quickly became dubbed a wedding on the cheap with run-of-the-mill supermarket champagne.

Sarah's first pregnancy came almost a year later, and for the next few months we continued our lives as normal: spending weekdays in London and then flying up to Scotland for weekends in Fife. Suddenly, just after Christmas, when Sarah went to our local maternity hospital – Forth Park in Kirkcaldy – the routine twenty-six-week scan indicated a high heartbeat and low levels of amniotic fluid that could inhibit growth in the final seven weeks of pregnancy. That was the Thursday. On the Friday, Sarah and I drove back to the hospital, and after a thirty-minute Caesarean section, which seemed to go well, Jennifer was born at 12.16 p.m. on 28 December. Our consultant obstetrician, Dr Tahir Mahmood, who carried out the delivery, said the baby was 'crying healthily'.

Naturally there were some problems with a baby born seven weeks prematurely: Jennifer weighed only 2 lb 4 oz. The doctors told us she was doing well. Yes, she looked incredibly small and fragile in her incubator, but we were surrounded in the children's unit by other small babies in incubators. I assumed everything would work out fine, though I was concerned that Sarah herself was unwell. Outside Forth Park, the cameras had gathered and I gave an interview saying just how happy I was. Politics, I said, suddenly seemed less important, and, not normally prone to such statements, I declared Jennifer 'the most beautiful baby in the world'. Congratulations, toys and clothes were all arriving. It is difficult to describe the joy that comes from seeing your first child, even in fraught circumstances.

It took some days before I realised that there was something wrong. First, we were told that Jennifer would be treated with phototherapy lamps for jaundice, which is common in premature babies, and fed through an intravenous drip. Nevertheless, we still believed that, though very tiny, she would grow – and grow up. Sarah was producing milk for her. Even when we were told that Jennifer would need to stay in the incubator unit for six weeks until mid-February, and even though six days later Sarah came home without our baby, we still did not fear the worst.

Then doctors and nurses told us that she was not responding properly, and that she had to be moved from the hospital in Kirkcaldy to the Royal Infirmary in Edinburgh to be treated by specialists. She still seemed able to respond when we held her and talked to her.

But by the Friday night, exactly a week after her birth, I started to draw my own conclusion that there was little hope – and not because of anything anyone said. I just began to realise she was not responding to treatment. Finding yourself looking at your beautiful baby, who looks untouched by illness but with whom something is so fundamentally wrong that nothing can be done, is almost impossible to bear. That was the most terrible, terrible moment.

I called my friend Dr Colin Currie and asked for his advice. His medical expertise was a great source of wisdom, while his writing skills proved invaluable when I arrived in No. 10 and he took time off from his important medical research to work with me. He said I would have to talk to the consultant the next day, but warned me that I might have to face up to the worst. So, that Saturday we had a private meeting with Dr Ian Laing, who had come in specially to see us. An ultrasound scan, he explained, had shown that our beautiful daughter had suffered a cerebral haemorrhage. He told us gently that there was absolutely no hope whatsoever; all we could do was sit with her – which we did for twenty-four hours a day, sleeping at the hospital – as gradually the life support she had was withdrawn. Even then we did not realise how short the time we would have with her was. Although we knew that she would not live, we hoped that maybe she had more days.

She was baptised on the Sunday at her cot in the Royal Infirmary ward. Sheila Munro came in to perform the baptism and I held Jennifer in my arms – her beautiful face still unaffected, untouched by the scale of the tragedy that had befallen her. Sarah and I took our vows as parents to do everything to bring her up 'in the nurture and admonition of the Lord'. The baptism was not for us just a comfort or a ritual: it was a recognition that every single life, even the shortest one, had a purpose and every person is irreplaceable. The Saturday, Sunday and Monday were essentially a vigil. We spent Jennifer's last nights taking it in turns to be at her bedside and sleeping next door in a room set aside for the parents of critically ill children. There was nursing help to ensure Jennifer had no pain or suffering. We were with her all Monday afternoon as her life ebbed away. We held her in our arms as she died at 5 p.m.

It was unspeakable to come home without her. We actually did not want to leave the hospital. We could not bear to be away from her. But we had to leave. Some photographers snapped a photograph of us right after we got in the car.

I had to call my mother – she never saw our baby alive – who was now frail. My older brother John and his wife Angela had visited regularly. But my younger brother Andrew, who had come to visit, sadly arrived just too late. Sarah's parents, Pauline and Patrick, were – as they always have been – towers of strength and support, both then and in the months and years to come.

There was, perhaps understandably, huge press interest. We were personally grateful to Paul Dacre, the editor of the *Daily Mail*, and his wife Kathy, and Piers Morgan, then editor of the *Mirror*, who came to the aid of Sarah and me in the days when Jennifer was critically ill and dying. Following some intrusive and unfair reporting of her condition, they helped secure a period of restraint when it came to reporting on her death. For that we remain grateful to this day.

In the past when a baby died at ten days old, there was usually no funeral, but we thought it right to have one. And I wanted something to be said about her life. My brother John agreed to speak, but I spent hours writing the notes for his remarks: that was one way I grieved. John spoke about the ten days we had with Jennifer and how they had changed our lives – that 'never to see our baby grow up, take her first steps, talk her first words, have her first day at school, carve out her first friendships, was almost too much to bear . . . Jennifer brought great joy: joy so deep, a love so immediate and intense, that the anxiety, the loss that followed, are almost unbearable. So for Sarah and Gordon, their lives were transformed twice over: first as they wept tears of happiness and then of sorrow.' To this day, I draw strength as well as solace from rereading these words spoken in the Kirkcaldy church where my father was the minister.

Jennifer had died on 7 January and her funeral took place on 11 January. After this, I could not think of returning to London. Sarah was not well and I wanted to be with her. Life seemed empty. Westminster was the last place I wanted to be.

Sarah and I resolved that we had to do something that gave meaning to our loss. In Jennifer's memory, we would create a charity to find treatments that would prevent what we had suffered. The Jennifer Brown Research Laboratory at Edinburgh University has in its first fifteen years facilitated breakthroughs in a number of areas, such as the level of oxygen that is needed in an incubator if a premature baby is to survive and flourish. At the time of writing it is conducting a major new longitudinal study that will track some of the most serious problems that arise in pregnancy, including brain damage.

To raise money for the charity, I spent some of the next year writing a book of essays, entitled *Courage*. It featured the lives of men and women who had the courage of their convictions and also the willpower to stand up for them whatever the odds. I was grateful to a long-time family friend of ours, Lord Swarj Paul, who, in memory of his own daughter who had also died too young, distributed copies to every school in the country.

But just as Jennifer's birth and my becoming a father gave a sense of completeness to my life, so the sense of emptiness that came with her loss would not leave me. I was brought up to keep private emotions to myself – that was called for at all times. Never talk about your sorrows, I was taught, nor your innermost feelings. But even at the time, I noticed how it changed me. The day-to-day things that occupy so much of our lives seemed trivial and irrelevant. I had been accused of hardly ever smiling anyway, but I doubt if I smiled even once for months after Jennifer's death. I could not listen to music for more than a year.

Having returned to work in February, with great reluctance I had to travel to Canada for a G20 finance ministers' meeting. Despite the comradeship of fellow finance ministers who were so kind to me, I was reluctant to throw myself into the debates. In the weeks that followed, however, I found there was one task that I could wholeheartedly embrace. It comforted me to think that I could help all those who would need the NHS as much as Sarah and I had.

And so I immersed myself in writing the Budget of 2002, which was delayed by a month because of the death of our daughter. Its purpose would be to increase funding for the NHS. My personal commitment to the NHS, deepened by what happened to Jennifer, was long-standing. After all, I owed my eyesight to it, and as a son, I was grateful for the care it provided for my elderly parents. But Sarah and I were not alone. Millions of British citizens owe their lives, their health and, in Aneurin Bevan's phrase, their serenity to the existence of the NHS. It is our best-loved national institution. Any government which neglects or ignores it pays a heavy price. But while the performance of the NHS is a make-or-break issue for every government, the expectations faced by Labour governments are always especially high. This is not just because Labour created the NHS in 1948. It is because throughout the last seventy years we have always claimed that it is safer in our hands. When we fought the last day of the 1997 general election on the slogan '24 hours to save the NHS', we knew we were raising expectations even higher and I was determined to meet them.

The year of our election, 1997, had not been a good one to be sick and dependent on the NHS. The Major government's modest increase in spending was never going to be enough to prevent a winter crisis in the health service or satisfy heightened expectations. And because we had pledged not to exceed already announced expenditure targets, we had to be content initially with the most modest of promises: that we would reduce the numbers on waiting lists by 100,000. But after we came into power, I decided to announce an extra £1 billion for the NHS in my first Budget and then later that autumn I announced an additional £250 million to relieve winter pressures.

It is to the great credit of our first Health Secretary, Frank Dobson, that he not only accepted the economic logic of sorting out the public finances first but also persuaded nurses, doctors and patients that we had to do so. Frank was one of the best leaders of the NHS because nobody doubted his commitment to a free universal health service and to meeting the needs of the poor. His diplomatic and leadership skills, which should have won him the election for mayor of London, were critical in holding the government together in our first years. It was thanks to his patience that while the government started with a narrow aim – to avoid a winter crisis – we were later able to deliver the best-financed health service in our nation's history.

The historic significance of what we legislated in 2002 lay in the fact that the NHS had been recurrently underfunded and would finally be given the resources it actually needed. It would at last be able to prove that it was not a relic of the 1940s, 'created by fools to be run by saints', but was able to satisfy twenty-first-century demands for individualised treatment and higher standards of personal care. NHS spending rose from £60 billion in 2001–2 to £102 billion in 2007–8 and £118 billion in 2010 when we left office. To achieve this, we would have to take on those who wanted to privatise the NHS or introduce a system of charges and fees, and we would have to win public support for the biggest single tax rise for the NHS in its history: a National Insurance increase of 1 per cent in both employer and employee contributions, and an additional 1 per cent paid by top earners.

We had actually been working on these plans for some time – since the winter of 1999, in fact. In a series of discussions with Ed Balls, Ed Miliband, Spencer Livermore and Bob Shrum in Washington, we had agreed on a basic strategy. We would have to convince people anew of the uniqueness and value of the NHS as a free service – and also make a further argument about the risks families would face under a system of private insurance, which could not guarantee them access to the wide array of advances being made in medical technology and treatments. To do this, we would publish the costs of heart transplants, statins and cancer care in a way that allowed people to understand that the NHS was not there merely for minor ailments but as the best insurance policy in the world against catastrophe.

Persuading the public to let us raise taxes would be an uphill struggle, and we were all too aware of our manifesto promises that ruled out increases in the basic rate and top rates of income tax. So, over the next two and a half years, a group of officials and advisers within the Treasury worked on an intricate plan to refinance the NHS. First, I planned to announce in the 2000 Budget a five-year plan for the NHS with an unprecedented 7 per cent annual increase in spending. This, we said, we were doing in preference to the tax cuts the Tories were now proposing.

Our programme of research and public education was set back only once, when Tony – who knew our thinking and was keen to signal a fresh start in 2000 – announced in his New Year interview with David Frost that he planned to raise NHS spending to the average European level of 8.5 per cent of GDP. I knew immediately the problem we now had: as with John Smith's shadow Budget, the focus would be on the resultant tax rise, before we had had a chance to explain the logic of a National Insurance increase as 'something for something'. Tony had announced the gain – the spending increase – without explaining the pain – the tax rise, despite my insistence that the two had to be announced together. For the next few weeks the focus on tax and spending threw the very carefully organised sequencing of our campaign into disarray.

The public rollout of the strategy we had devised in Washington stepped up in the March 2001 Budget, delivered three months before the general election of that year. It was a sensitive juncture, with the Tories looking to pin us to the wall on tax rises. In the Budget, I announced the next stage of our strategy by inviting Derek Wanless, the former head of NatWest Bank, to prepare a report on future funding of the NHS. I found him to be a great colleague. I also discovered we had had similar experiences growing up. I told Derek that my father had told me story after story of the panic of families in the 1930s as they faced up to the crippling costs of treatment for loved ones. I shared with Derek my father's view that the NHS was a 'deliverance from evil'. Derek responded that he could remember his own parents telling him similar stories about the days before the NHS in the north-east of England.

Because of the foot-and-mouth outbreak, the general election of 2001 was moved from May to June. We fought it on the final line of my Budget speech from that spring: 'Schools and hospitals first.' Tony had started the year with a modest claim: 'A lot done and a lot still to do.' Some of my colleagues wanted to move on from that to a broader 'One Nation' appeal to Conservative voters, but we found this had no traction when we tested it. As chairman of the Election Strategy Group, I made our focus schools and hospitals. When, in the last days of the election, Tony and I campaigned from a battlebus festooned with the banner 'SCHOOLS AND HOSPITALS FIRST', we were working from a script that had been years in the making.

Given our plans for the NHS, Labour's 2001 manifesto had to be very carefully sculpted. It repeated the pledge of 1997 that we would not raise the basic or top rates of income tax in the next parliament, but I refused to rule out increases in National Insurance and other taxes, despite pleas from some in our election team to make life easier by doing so. This led to some difficult and tense moments. Whenever I was asked the obvious question – whether I would rule out a rise in National Insurance – I could only repeat that we had already ruled out changes in income-tax rates. When Patricia Hewitt, who was then a junior minister in the Department for Trade and Industry, announced that we would not raise National Insurance at all, I had to issue a statement denying this. We were now facing a major front-page story the next day and an embarrassing week of tax questions clearly lay ahead, when suddenly John Prescott threw a punch at a man who pelted him with eggs during a visit to Rhyl in Wales. This turned out to be a blessing in disguise as it became the front-page story for days. Some advisers panicked about the punch and thought John would have to resign, but the focus groups we held all cheered him on: it was about time someone stood up to hooliganism. Without knowing it, he had also struck a blow for us on tax.

In the event, middle-class voters turned to us to an even greater degree than they had in 1997. But, of course, elections are won not as a reward for what you did in the past but on how voters see their prospects in the future. And I am not alone in the view that while voters were not unhappy with the achievements of the first four years of Labour government, it was our pledge to improve public services, especially health and education, that did most to cement our vote.

As we moved towards the 2002 Budget, I decided that to win the argument for a tax rise, we had to prosecute our NHS case from first principles.

Our planning for this campaign was detailed, forensic and – for a few months – all-consuming. First, we would explain what was wrong, then we would look at every alternative model for rectifying the problems, and finally we would show the virtues of a publicly funded expansion as the best way forward.

Over the course of the next nine months, I went around the country arguing that there was no better way to finance healthcare than through the tax system. American and continental models for funding health would not work in Britain and I made the principled argument for the British model of pooling and sharing risks and resources to pay for healthcare.

Few people were in any doubt that the NHS we had inherited in 1997 was not fit for purpose. The UK had the fewest number of doctors for every 1,000 people in the population of all developed nations. The NHS budget we inherited amounted to only £975 per person a year – that is £19 a week to cover the full range of hospital and GP services – which was hardly enough to pay the costs of a single week in hospital or a standard operation. True, total health spending had risen in real terms over the past fifty or so years, but this increase was slight compared to the much greater advances in life expectancy, public expectations of what healthcare could offer and medical technology, all of which had major funding implications. Operations like heart and lung transplants under a privatised system could only be afforded by the wealthy. Only by sharing the costs through insurance, I argued, could we now pay for such advanced care.

Derek Wanless's assessment of funding needs had also to take into account that at least one-third of the hospital and community health services buildings needed to be rebuilt or renovated, as well as patients' demands for single rooms – or, at the least, small wards – in place of the long line of beds in old, oversize wards. As Wanless was to remind us: 'The NHS has not replaced and refurbished its assets at an appropriate rate.'

I also made an argument that no one could have imagined when Aneurin Bevan created the NHS: as genetics enabled us to identify in advance those most likely to require expensive life-saving treatments, a private insurance model was far more likely to punish those whose needs were greatest. Only the more inclusive and comprehensive model of public insurance that pooled and shared all risks was a patient's best guarantee for receiving the best care.

Popularising the idea of National Insurance for a new century was at the heart of our strategy. Originally, National Insurance had been set up in 1911 by Lloyd George, who had been inspired by seeing the German welfare system at work. The principle of National Insurance was a simple one: you paid in when able and received help when you needed it. Under this arrangement, a person paid National Insurance not into a general amorphous pool which might go towards paying off the debts of the past, but into secure tangible future benefits for their family in the event of unemployment and sickness.

However, National Insurance, as originally envisaged, was by now a fiction: it was guaranteed by the Treasury, and, to all extents and purposes, contributions went straight into the general coffers. There was now only a theoretical link between health funding, most of which came out of general taxes, and the National Insurance fund. But weak as the connection was, the little that remained of it was still important in people's understanding of the link between payments and benefits. And it was central to our argument on the NHS: a tax rise would not be used to pay off past mistakes or be lost down a general hole in the Treasury; it would be explicitly earmarked for funding a person and their family's healthcare.

We sought therefore to establish a direct connection between the taxation an individual paid through National Insurance contributions and the visits they and members of their family made to a GP or hospital. We presented it as a 'something for something' payment.

We had, of course, learned from the detailed preparations done when we abolished the married couple's allowance and mortgage tax relief – two sacred cows of the *Daily Mail* and Murdoch newspapers. Again, we sensed that the biggest resistance would come from the Murdoch press, so we made a special effort to meet their editors, correspondents and even their readers to explain what we were setting out to do. If taxes were raised it was important that people understood there was a purpose to it. We had had years of explaining 'prudence for a purpose', now we had to explain 'taxation for a purpose'. At the same time, we worked hard to secure the backing of the most popular public servants – nurses, midwives and doctors. I believe we will look far and wide to find a government that was better prepared for a Budget than ours was in 2002.

At the last minute, Tony attempted to force a change which would have ruined our Budget's carefully calculated arithmetic. This was not unusual. On the night before our Budget of 1998, for example, he had asked that we announce the abolition of inheritance tax, thinking we could do it at no sizeable cost. I had to tell him that loss of revenue would have been £2 billion. In the spring of 2002, at the final moment, Tony said he wanted a watering down of the National Insurance rate increase. He wanted us to announce that the rise would be followed by a tax cut. Frustratingly, I had to remind him that he was the person who had announced our commitment to matching average EU health spending in the first place – and this, as I pointed out, was a cost that had to be funded.

He came up with a proposal for a sliding scale for National Insurance, which meant that our 1 per cent rise would be followed by a 0.1 per cent fall every year thereafter until, eventually, the rise would be wiped out. Had we been budgeting for something with major start-up costs that would then fall over the years, this would have made sense. But the NHS was in the opposite position: it needed an ever-rising share of national income year after year to meet rapidly growing demographic pressures – people living longer yet needing a higher standard of end-of-life care – and the escalating costs of technological advances.

On Budget day, we published the final Wanless report, which recommended our eventual proposal: a cumulative increase of £40 billion in funding for the NHS, representing an average real-term growth of 7.3 per cent annually for five years until 2007.

The next day, Tony announced major reforms of the NHS that I had not been informed about – most of which I welcomed, but some of which led us into huge difficulties. One reform was to offer doctors a new contract. I had no doubt of the need for better remuneration, but I had wanted the pay rises to be conditional on reform, and I had not wanted to see so much of the new NHS budget consumed by pay. The eventual bill for the new doctors' contract came to £7.7 billion a year, and the cumulative overspend on this alone in the first three years was £1.76 billion.

At the same time, Alan Milburn, the Health Secretary, put forward proposals to establish new foundation hospitals. Under this model, managers of the best-performing hospitals and primary care trusts would no longer be subject to financial and managerial control from government and could set their own pay rates. In the original proposals, they would also be able to establish joint venture companies with private providers, perform private work and be subject to far less monitoring and inspection.

Of course, I worried that if we went too far in treating private patients and creating a pricing mechanism for services we would open up a two-tier health service, where there would be a premium service for the wealthy and a basic one for the rest, with private sector capacity replacing NHS capacity. More broadly, as I would later argue in a speech to the Social Market Foundation in January 2003, there were fundamental limits to the ability of markets to provide a public service such as healthcare: because nobody can be sure if or when they will need medical treatment or of what sort, the consumer is simply unable – as in a conventional market – to seek out the best product at the lowest price. The results of a market failure for the patient could be long-term, catastrophic and irreversible.

My main and specific concern, however, was that while the new hospitals would be permitted to borrow money against their assets, the government would remain ultimately liable for their deficits and debts. Alan thought he could reclassify the borrowing of foundation hospitals as belonging to the private sector and thus outside the government's balance sheet. But there was no doubt that if a hospital went bankrupt, it would fall on the Treasury to bail it out. In other words, the foundation hospital scheme meant government accepting all the liability while ceding almost all control. I made it clear to him that foundation hospitals would not be allowed to borrow 'off-budget' and that any debt incurred would have to come out of the health budget.

Whatever the validity of my reasoning, I was criticised simply for being an anti-moderniser, opposed to greater flexibility, freedom and choice. That August, Alan argued in *The Times* that 'the battle in the party is now between consolidators and transformers'. The implicit depiction of Tony and himself as 'transformers' and of me and supporters of my position as 'consolidators' was both disingenuous and vacuous. To make my concerns known to colleagues, the Treasury circulated a fifty-page document setting out the case against allowing foundation hospitals to run up debts. Tony was furious. He phoned me in Washington, where I was for an IMF–World Bank meeting. It was as if I had issued a declaration of war: No. 10 claimed that the Treasury paper 'had not been received', and ministers' private offices were phoned to be told that they were to say they had not received my document. It was to be treated as a non-paper. In his conference speech a month later, Tony made a defence of foundation hospitals, and the issue ran on until October, when I met with him, Alan and John Prescott at No. 10: it was agreed that the Treasury had to have control over how much foundation hospitals could borrow and that their debt would appear on the public sector balance sheet, as I had insisted, with a consequent reduction in the overall health budget on whatever they borrowed.

This debate about the role of the private sector in health raged over the next few years and often divided the party. Ministers argued about what percentage of operations and procedures the NHS should contract out to private providers. At one point in 2006, Patricia Hewitt, then the Health Secretary, sparked even more profound controversy when, in launching her latest reform plan, she said there would be no limit to the role the private sector played in the provision of services to patients. Her intervention raised fundamental questions about what New Labour stood for and what modernisation meant. I was not against the use of the private sector when it was in the interests of patients to secure services. I also believed it was impossible to achieve some of our objectives without mobilising private investment – specifically, to meet our demanding target of building a hundred new hospitals by 2010. While controversial, private finance initiatives allowed us to have the largest hospital-building programme the country has ever seen, and this could never have been achieved using only public funds then available. But I was against a definition of modernisation that implied the private sector was somehow better than the public sector and that the way forward for the NHS lay in deregulation and privatisation. There were, and are, real limits to the capacity of markets to deliver public services like healthcare, and limits to the desirability of them doing so. The test had always to be the public interest.

By 2010 the NHS had £118 billion to cover its costs, compared to £57.3 billion spending in real terms in 1997. Between 1997 and 2010, year-on-year growth in NHS expenditure meant that the percentage of national income going to health rose from 5.3 per cent to 8.4 per cent. It meant we were now spending on average just under £2,000 a year for every person purely on their healthcare. In 1997, we spent among the lowest share of national income on health of any European country, with the gap in spending much higher between the UK and our two major competitors, France and Germany. Raising overall health spending over the period of the Labour government by 5.8 per cent a year meant we outpaced France and Germany, whose health spending grew half as fast. And this happened because we presided over the biggest single rise in health spending in the history of the NHS.

CHAPTER 9

IN OR OUT? THE EURO AND AFTER

'Consider your position!' – the last words from Tony as I wheeled and walked out of No. 10 towards the sanctuary of No. 11, where the chancellor has both a flat and, conveniently, a second office just up the road from the Treasury. I didn't know how much longer I would be there, but I was not prepared to give way on a decision that could inflict damage on the British economy. In my view, you are in office to do a job, not to hold on to a job. The row with Tony that day had been brewing for months. It was 2 April 2003. At the time, joining the euro was portrayed in black-and-white terms: between a No. 10 over-eager to join, and a Treasury desperate to halt their ambitions. The reality was, as so often, rather more complex.

Of course, 2003 will be remembered in history more for the out-break of the Iraq War than any other single event. It was also a year when our health-service reforms were moving ahead with speed, and divisions over tuition fees were moving to centre stage. At a personal level, I will remember it best as the year when, after the loss of our daughter Jennifer and a later miscarriage, Sarah gave birth to our first son, John. His arrival in October was such a joyous event and his presence with us so precious that for months afterwards we could not bear to let him out of our sight.

There are some political events – like arguments over which tax to raise or what spending to approve – that are controversial but come and go because, for all the 'sound and fury' at the time, in the end they signify little difference except at the margins. But there are some choices which are so momentous that they are transformative. They can include decisions not to act as well as to act. So it was when Britain finally rejected a long-standing option to abandon the pound in favour of the common European currency – a decision that I knew was fraught with difficulty and in the end would damage, almost irreparably, my relationship with Tony.

Between 2001 and 2003, Ed Balls and Dave Ramsden – later the Treasury's chief economic adviser and now a deputy governor of the Bank of England – led a two-year Treasury assessment of the five tests we had developed to judge whether we could join the euro. The 2,000 pages of analysis, set out in eighteen separate studies and amounting to more than 1.5 million words – the most extensive review of its kind ever conducted, and certainly the only such one carried out by any country contemplating the euro – had just landed on Tony's desk ruling out membership. It was in the tense exchange immediately afterwards when Tony said that, if I would not agree to join, I would have to consider my position. 'I'll do just that,' I replied. Straight after I retreated to No. 11, Ed Balls asked if I was still chancellor. 'I don't know,' was all I could honestly say. 'In or out' did not just mean whether Britain would join the euro but whether I was in the government.

How had we reached this point? How did we overcome the deeply felt divisions on Britain's potential membership of the euro to reach the right decision for the British economy?

At no time has the idea of 'Little Britain' held any attraction for me. Born in 1951, I grew up in the shadow of the war and a Europe seized of the need for peace and preventing any return to conflict. My father was a committed European from the 1930s onwards. Like him, I believed that Europe should reach out as widely as possible.

I knew that to win support for the European Union, however, we needed to show the benefits to Britain. I felt I had a patriotic pro-British argument that could persuade people to be more enthusiastic about European engagement. The real challenge was to balance the national autonomy countries like ours thought right with the international cooperation we needed. On that basis, I argued for greater economic and security cooperation and favoured the immediate adoption in 1997 of the European Social Chapter that guaranteed workers' rights. But for the same reason I resisted European Union interference in our domestic tax affairs when they tried to block our cut in VAT. In our first month in government, I had waved aside European objections and reduced VAT on fuel to 5 per cent. Then in 2000 I had countered plans for a harmonised pan-European savings tax that every EU citizen might pay. Even when in a minority of one, I stood firm at countless European finance ministers' meetings when under pressure to accept a compromise; I insisted that a one-size-fits-all savings tax would merely shift savings out of Europe to Switzerland, Liechtenstein and even Hong Kong. The best way forward was to drop the uniform European tax and agree that each country had autonomy in its tax decisions as long as it exchanged information with tax centres across the world. This was the essence of the balanced approach to Europe that I championed in other areas too – in preference to a blanket imposition of uniform standards and laws, I wanted, wherever possible, the mutual recognition of national practices.

I did not object in principle to a single currency. It could cut costs for businesses and consumers, not least by reducing the high costs of currency conversion. It could deepen commercial links and, by getting interest rates and inflation down, ensure greater stability. When, in October 1997, I first set out the Labour government's position on the euro, I also said that, if we joined the single currency, Britain's trade could, under the right circumstances, increase substantially – perhaps by 50 per cent over thirty years. Overall, inside the euro, UK national income could rise over that time by between 5 and 9 per cent.

But without measures to mitigate the inflexibility of locking our exchange rates forever, the euro could not work for contemporary Britain – its housing market, its small-business sector and public finances. I was also mindful of how deeply the European project had divided Britain over time – both the country and parties. In the early 1960s, I had read the words of the Labour leader Hugh Gaitskell, who famously rejected Europe in favour of the Commonwealth, warning about 'the end of a thousand years of history'. At that time, it was the left who opposed joining the European project because they considered it too neoliberal. In the late 1980s, however, the president of the European Commission, Jacques Delors, with whom I spoke regularly, convinced the Labour Party of his vision of a social Europe with guaranteed workers' rights – a vision I already believed in. Anti-Europeanism then became a cause of the right wing who took up the argument that increasing integration meant the end of Britain as we knew it.

As we prepared for government – and dealing with the creation of a European single currency – I was fully aware that we would have to negotiate a difficult path. In February 1997, I invited the BBC's John

Sergeant to join Geoffrey Robinson, Ed Balls and myself to cover a speech I was giving in New York. In a pre-speech interview, I told him that we saw benefits in principle of joining the euro while also high-lighting issues of concern. Expecting me to say there were 'formidable obstacles' – as Tony and I had agreed – and frustrated by my unwill-ingness to say so, Sergeant exploded: 'That's it. I've had enough. I can't take this any more.'

In one sense, Sergeant was right: we had to be more precise about the conditions we would attach if Britain was to enter the euro. This would be the main subject of my speech the next day to the American European Community Association which we simultaneously issued in Britain. It was in this speech that I first set out the five tests that would determine whether joining the euro was in our best interests or not. These were to do with whether members would have the economic flexibility to deal with shocks, the potential for convergence between the UK and European economies, and the likely impact on financial services, investment and jobs. It has been reported that Ed and I scrawled these five tests on the back of an envelope while on a taxi journey across Manhattan. In fact, the five tests had been decided in advance of our visit to America. What did happen was that, while in New York, Ed briefed the story to the UK press from the back of a taxi.

But when it came to the general election in 1997, Tony felt it neces-sary to show the Murdoch press that he was sceptical about euro entry. He responded to entreaties from Rupert Murdoch and told the *Sun* that he 'loved' the pound. Against my advice at the time not to tie our hands, he promised that if we ever considered joining, there would have to be a referendum first.

Once in government a decision had to be made. There was only a brief honeymoon period on all issues European. Soon questions about the euro came thick and fast. With the mainland European states planning to join together in the single currency as early as 1999, the question was: what would we do in the new parliament? A further layer of complication was our upcoming presidency of the European Union in 1998, when all the main decisions would be finalised.

And yet big questions about the euro remained unaddressed. How would Britain converge with the different economies of continental Europe? On the way to membership of the euro, would we have to return to John Major's failed experiment of managing the exchange rate? How would our unique housing market respond if interest rates were cut? Even if we did satisfy ourselves on the merits of joining the euro, our opponents would inevitably recast our decision to make the Bank of England independent as a Trojan Horse for surrendering interest-rate decisions to the planned European Central Bank.

In July 1997, Tony was persuaded by Philip Gould that he should break with tradition and campaign as prime minister in a by-election in Uxbridge. In the event, the Conservatives not only held the seat but secured a swing of 5 per cent from Labour to their candidate. It was only a few weeks since the general election but it was already clear that if we opted to join the first wave of the euro, we could not assume a clear run in any referendum.

While people feared we would make a wholly political decision, I insisted, as I had done since well before the election, that whatever we ultimately proposed, a persuasive economic case was essential. The British people needed to know we had thoroughly tested the euro's viability for Britain before deciding.

For all my predecessor Ken Clarke's enthusiasm for membership of the euro, we discovered that few preparations for it had been made inside the Treasury, so we instructed officials to flesh out the detail of the five tests. I was taken aback when Treasury staff told me that, in their view, there were not really five tests at all but four, and that the fifth – would the euro promote higher growth and a lasting increase in jobs? – was an amalgam of the fourth and fifth and should be dropped. I told them no, and less than five months later they produced a forty-page assessment that provided the basis for the huge door-stopper document that was finally published in 2003.

Given the media's interest in all things European, murmurings quickly started about where we were headed. Our Foreign Secretary, Robin Cook, was pro-euro, as was Lord Simon – formerly head of BP – who joined the government as Minister for Trade and Competitiveness in Europe. Peter Mandelson, ensconced in the Cabinet Office and with Tony's ear, was also pushing its case. Even so, in his first months as prime minister Tony oscillated from unalloyed enthusiasm to musing that the euro was a dead duck. At one point, in a somewhat unlikely proposition, Tony said he would ring Chancellor Helmut Kohl of Germany to persuade him to postpone the whole project until Britain was ready to join.

At this stage, though, we were engaged in private discussions: there was no plan for us to make any definitive public statement. But soon we would have to do so; if we did not, as was becoming increasingly clear, the rumour machine would spin out of control.

The first signs that it was doing so came with a *Financial Times* article in late September reporting that the Labour government was moving closer to joining the single currency. Some days later there was a story on the front page of the *Independent* claiming that a war had broken out between Tony and myself over the euro. Their story – that I was trying to bounce Tony into what was portrayed as the early death of sterling – came out of thin air and the suggestion there were divisions started to threaten the credibility of the government.

I recalled how the Conservatives' handling of the same issue, saying they would join 'when the time is right', had split them asunder as they fell victim to press questions every day, every week, every month about whether the 'time was right'. I decided this new round of speculation now needed a definitive rebuttal. So, when we had our usual weekly strategy meeting on the afternoon of Thursday 16 October in Downing Street – attended by Robin Cook, Peter Mandelson and Jonathan Powell, the No. 10 chief of staff, as well as Tony and myself – we discussed how to handle the issue of UK participation in the euro.

It was accepted that we would have to make an announcement that Britain would not be joining in the first wave in 1999, and would have to do so by the end of the year – the last possible date we could apply for membership. Given these realities, I felt there was nothing to be gained in delaying the announcement and losing credibility as we let speculation mount and moved closer to the deadline. As a result, when Tony and I spoke on the phone just after the meeting, I offered to do a newspaper interview. This would end the speculation, clear the air and rebut the allegation that there was a split between the Treasury and Downing Street. Tony asked me to talk to Alastair Campbell, now his director of communications, who also supported dealing with the issue.

That Friday, Ed Balls called Philip Webster, the Westminster political editor of *The Times*, and it was agreed to give him an exclusive interview on the euro. At the time, Philip was out playing golf with his opposite number from the *Sun*, Trevor Kavanagh. Given where he was – on the links with the arch anti-European Kavanagh – there could be no interview over the phone. Instead we faxed him a statement which we had shared and agreed with Alastair. In the fax, I restated our five economic tests for euro membership, including the need for the British economic cycle to be in line with that of Europe. We also reminded Philip that in our manifesto we had said there were 'formidable obstacles' to Britain joining in the first wave in 1999. That remained our position. I was determined that we would not fall into the trap that the Conservatives fell into over the Exchange Rate Mechanism. We would not resort to the discredited Tory proposition of joining when the 'time is right' – implying we could join the next week or the next month, allowing that possibility to dominate every hour and day, and then eventually being forced to make a decision for short-term political reasons. We would, I said, join when we were sure the five British tests were met – our policy was 'prepare and decide'.

I had concluded, as I informed Webster, we would not join in the first wave of countries and that it was 'highly unlikely' we would join in the lifetime of the parliament. He interpreted this as ruling it out for the whole parliament. It is true that I believed that, if we did not take part in the first wave in 1999, we would not be in any position to join before 2001. Imagine having a referendum on the euro in either of the two most likely pre-election years, 1999 or 2000? It was inconceivable that we would have put the return of a Labour government at risk by calling a referendum so close to polling day in 2001. But I was also clear in my statement that we did not completely rule out the possibility of joining before 2001. However, *The Times* reported: 'BROWN RULES OUT SINGLE CURRENCY FOR LIFETIME OF THE PARLIAMENT'.

On the Friday evening, operating from his mobile phone on the pavement outside the Red Lion pub in Westminster, Charlie Whelan, and then Alastair Campbell, who was working from home, confirmed to the BBC and ITN that, while not closing down all our options, I was effectively ruling out British membership for the Parliament. According to one account, Charlie suggested to the *Sun*'s editor, Stuart Higgins, that the headline in his next day's edition should be 'BROWN SAVES POUND'. At any rate, Charlie's more general remarks outside the pub were overheard by two Liberal Democrat press officers who notified the Press Association. We were now rapidly losing control of the story.

That night, Charlie took a call on his mobile from a very senior – and very angry – member of the government trying to discover what was happening: the prime minister. Stuck at Chequers, Tony was desperate to discover what was being briefed to the newspapers. Unable to get hold of me – I was at constituency surgeries – or Alastair Campbell, Tony was only able to track down Charlie. The conversation, as Alastair records in his diary, went as follows: 'TB asked if we had ruled out EMU [Economic and Monetary Union] this parliament. Yes, said Charlie. "Is that not what you want?" No, it is not, said TB. "Oh," said Charlie.'

In a hastily arranged Saturday conference call between Tony and myself, involving Alastair, Ed Balls, Peter Mandelson and Charlie, we tried to deal with what was now a crisis of our own making. But we knew the cement was already set: we could not row back. Alastair later wrote that both he and Charlie believed that they were doing the right thing. Some of Tony's staff have written that 'the intention had been to rule out entry to EMU only for 1998 and 1999 and not beyond'. But Alastair, who was aware of the *Times* headline, had believed it right to rule it out for the parliament. Indeed he wrote later that while the Treasury drafted the words, he made changes to tone down its pro-Europeanism. There was not a conflict, in truth, between the Treasury and No. 10: it was between those who accepted the hard realities and those who wished they were different. It was obvious that if we did not join the first wave of the euro in 1999 we would not be in a position to join in the run-up to the 2001 election.

Following a fractious weekend dealing with the fallout from the *Times* story, I then had to face my own Black Monday – or 'Brown Monday', as it was dubbed. On 20 October, I was presiding over the opening of the London Stock Exchange's new computerised trading system but because of the turmoil over the euro I found that just as I did so the electronic screen turned bright red behind me – giving the press an ideal photo op suggesting that shares were in freefall.

When it came to the Commons statement on 27 October, Tony wanted to pull rank and deliver it himself. I replied that the issue was a Treasury matter. In any event, Tony was at the Commonwealth Prime Ministers' Conference in Edinburgh, making it impossible for him to do the necessary preparations for such a major statement. That did not stop his private secretaries drafting a very glib statement which I found unacceptable. I used my own words, emphasising our support for the principle of joining and stating our policy was 'prepare and decide', a position Tony agreed with. I announced a National Changeover Plan and the establishment of a Standing Committee on Euro Preparations, and made clear we could only join if the currency was successful and the economic case was clear and unambiguous. I said again that this was unlikely to happen before the end of the parliament and – adding some words that Tony wanted and I was happy to agree to – 'barring some fundamental or unforeseen change in economic circumstances'.

We went ahead to consult on and publish the National Changeover Plan in February 1999. In October, I was present with Tony, the Liberal Democrat leader Charles Kennedy, Ken Clarke and Michael Heseltine for the launch of 'Britain in Europe', which was aimed at countering the Conservatives' 'Save the Pound' campaign. I used my annual Mansion House speech in June 2000 to affirm that, while we found the mechanics difficult, we were still in favour of joining the euro in principle. At the same time, I said that the Treasury was the 'guardian of the policy' and thus the tests. I reminded people we had a triple lock: the British opt-out on the euro, the vote that had to happen in Parliament if we wanted to go ahead, and the referendum.

Tony returned to the issue of euro membership in the months leading up to the 2001 general election as he planned his second term. He was thinking about a possible referendum on the euro in autumn 2002 or summer 2003. While he didn't think we could do it with Britain's high exchange rate of 2.80 DM to the pound, he suggested we redefine the issue from 'whether' Britain should join to 'when'. Even if we did so, Tony and I agreed that the economic logic would have to dictate the timing as well as the argument for a 'yes' vote. There is absolutely no truth in any claim that I used the euro as a 'political lever' and told Tony that I would only consent to entry if he later stood down. The opposite was, in fact, to prove to be the case.

There was one hiccup. In February 2001, Tony said at Prime Minister's Questions that he intended to make the case for joining the euro 'early in the next parliament'. William Hague, the Conservative leader, asked him: 'Does early mean the first two years of the parliament?' To which Tony replied: 'Early in the next parliament means exactly what it says . . . within the first two years.' I don't think Tony was bouncing the Treasury or me into action we opposed, but it did mean that we would have to do an assessment, publish it and put it to the House of Commons by mid-2003.

Tony's language on euro membership became a lot more bullish after the 2001 election. In a speech he had prepared to give to the TUC but was cancelled because of 9/11 – the contents of which he delivered at the Labour conference later that year – his tone was decidedly more positive. He called on us to 'have the courage of our argument' on the euro and cemented the idea in people's minds that we had a timetable. We agreed that there would now be a 'full assessment' by 5 June 2003, though he still accepted my caveat, that the results of the tests had to be 'clear and unambiguous'.

Now well into the euro assessment, I kept asking myself: what do we do if I say 'no' and Tony demands a 'yes'? How could our partnership survive? Although Tony's preoccupation with the Iraq War overshadowed almost everything else, events made him more enthusiastic about joining the euro. He felt that after falling out with Germany and France on Iraq, he could rebuild alliances over the euro, and, of course, he also saw it as part of his legacy. He sent me messages – directly through John Prescott and Clare Short and indirectly through Sue Nye – that if he got his way on the euro he would be ready to leave and pass me the leadership. But I was adamant: I would not put what I considered to be the national economic interest second to my own political interest.

I had wanted to issue our euro assessment on the day of the 2003 Budget – scheduled for 9 April – but a disagreement between Tony and me on what tests had been met delayed the timetable. It was probably just as well: I was giving my Budget speech as Baghdad fell and Saddam Hussein's statue was symbolically hauled to the ground.

Our plan changed to publication in June. On 2 April, we sent the full results of the Treasury's assessment of the five tests to Tony along with the conclusion that I had already conveyed to him in our conversations – four of the five tests were not met. The document and its appendices were so heavy that they had to be walked over to No. 10 by Treasury messengers. That itself became a source of tension. Tony's staff felt that I should have handed all the papers over to him in person.

And so began a furious shouting match between Tony and me. We argued when our advisers were in the room, then cleared it and tried but failed to sort out our differences. In truth, the disagreement was not so much about the assessment itself as what conclusions we drew from it and how we should present these to the public.

Tony was of the view that I was sabotaging his efforts to get us into the euro. I was saying to him that, try as we might, we could not make the economic case. By the time I left the meeting we were still in limbo.

The stand-off was only broken a couple of hours later when Tony asked his principal private secretary, Jeremy Heywood, and Ed Balls to thrash out a new text of the document with language that was more to his liking, but which did not change the central recommendations. All that was now left to decide was whether we would keep the door open for a revised decision further down the line; and, if so, when that might be.

In mid-May 2003, Tony and I talked to Cabinet ministers one by one. Each was given the eighteen studies on 17 May to inform discussions, with a promise of a final decision by the Cabinet on 5 June. Then on 9 June, I would set out the government's position to the House of Commons. At the start, most of the Cabinet had been for entering the euro. I explained to each Cabinet member that, while I too was strongly pro-European, the evidence we had assembled showed that the economics of the single currency currently did not work for Britain.

On 22 May, I gave a detailed presentation on euro membership to the Cabinet. I said that it was clear that membership of the Eurozone would involve lower transaction costs worth 0.1–0.2 per cent of GDP, with the gains greatest for small companies. There were also real gains to be made from diminished exchange-rate volatility, with benefits for large and small enterprises, especially the latter. Intra-Eurozone trade had increased strongly as a result of EMU, perhaps by as much as 20 per cent. As a result of membership, the UK could enjoy a significant increase in trade with the Eurozone, boosting output by up to a quarter percentage point a year. The case in principle for joining, I said, was made very strongly by these examples. But we could not reap these benefits without sustained convergence. There had been convergence between the UK and the euro area since 1997, but sustained convergence had to be structural and long-term, not just cyclical and temporary. If we were to enter, we would have to do more to protect our housing market, secure price and wage flexibility so that we could withstand any shock, and in the absence of an ability to set interest rates we would have to use fiscal measures, like varying our taxes, to moderate the economic cycle.

On 5 June, the entire Cabinet agreed that membership of the euro was not right for Britain at this time. When it came down to what my Commons statement would say, Tony and I agreed to continue our 'prepare and decide' approach; we would publish a draft referendum bill in the autumn, and then a new Changeover Plan and possibly a paving bill to make it easier to join the euro if we chose to do so. We also agreed that in each annual Budget we would report on whether progress was sufficient to justify a further Treasury assessment of the five tests.

The conclusions that the Treasury reached have stood the test of time. Our economy was out of sync with the rest of Europe and was likely to remain so for some time. Our housing market – already overpriced – would overheat if interest rates fell further and might lead Britain into recession. So the decision on the euro, I believe, was right. The single currency could not have worked for us; increasingly it was not working for the rest of Europe. Ultimately, I came to the view that the euro, as planned, could not avoid regular crises and under its guidelines Europe would be pushed towards becoming a low-growth, high-unemployment economy.

Looking back on it now the euro decision was not just an economic but also a political turning point. My relationship with Tony never quite recovered. And all the time the government was bogged down by Iraq – the abuses and torture at Abu Ghraib prison, the Hutton Inquiry into the death of the weapons expert Dr David Kelly, and controversy over troops and equipment.

I had already sensed a change in No. 10 from the time Tony secured re-election in 2001. The arguments I recount in other chapters – over the NHS and tuition fees – now reflected a different interpretation of what modernisation meant. In the autumn of 2002, I had been accused of being a 'consolidator', not a 'moderniser', when the battle between ministers was, at least in the media, at its height. The truth is I was always up for modernisation. However, I was never up for a narrow interpretation of it that made the test of being a moderniser how much privatisation and liberalisation I bought into and whether I was now agnostic on inequality. The Treasury was, anyway, moving ahead with controversial public-private partnerships; sales, from the Royal Mint and Ordnance Survey to the nuclear company Urenco and Air Traffic Control; and with sweeping reforms to raise productivity and cutting capital gains tax to encourage entrepreneurship. Moreover, during 2003, we had commissioned a report by Sir Peter Gershon on efficiency in the public sector, whose recommendations – £20 billion of savings by 2007–8, including back-office efficiencies that would be used to improve front-line services – became the centrepiece of the Budget in 2004. They were highly controversial, involving the loss or relocation of 100,000 public sector jobs. We could not, I felt, have been accused of slowing down on reform. What's more, in 2004, we had appointed Sir Philip Hampton, later to become chairman of Royal Bank of Scotland after it became 81 per cent state-owned, to undertake a major review to reduce red tape and regulatory burdens on business. His final report was to become a central theme in the pre-election Budget of 2005. Once again, I felt, the Treasury was taking the lead with a common-sense approach to modernisation.

For more than six months from the end of 2003, Tony talked to me about leaving during 2004. Whether he intended to and simply changed his mind, I will never know. We actually discussed whether he would preannounce his intention in spring or wait for autumn; even though it was not to my personal advantage, I thought the latter the better option for the stability of the party and government.

But out of the blue in mid-July 2004, the *Sun* headlined a scoop that Tony would serve another five years. Of course, every story that does not contain direct quotations is deniable and Tony immediately assured me that this one was wrong and he would have it corrected. However, while it later emerged that he had spoken with the *Sun* editor Rebekah Wade only four days before the story appeared, no one could be sure what was going on.

Not for the first time, John Prescott tried valiantly to be an honest broker, but at a dinner he arranged the following Sunday, Tony now equivocated. He said that he had indeed changed his mind about resigning and would need the summer to decide how to proceed. His reasoning was that he did not want to look as if he was leaving because of problems over Iraq. By the time he returned from his summer holiday, he had clearly determined to do things differently – and to do something else as well. He announced that Alan Milburn would replace me as head of the 2005 election campaign. Although I was both sad and angry to be frozen out of election planning for the first time since the mid-1990s, I kept my counsel.

At the Labour conference in September, there was a light-hearted and seemingly unifying moment when Bono praised Tony and me as the 'John Lennon and Paul McCartney' of the global development stage. But after I addressed the conference and then, as usual, flew across the Atlantic for the annual round of IMF and World Bank autumn meetings, I arrived in Washington to find that during my flight Tony had given another interview, revealing that he was about to undergo a minor heart operation and that he had now decided to serve a full third term. This led to a sensational and what now seems comical headline in the *Guardian*, quoting one of my staff as saying: 'It's like an African coup. They waited until he was out of the country.'

Cabinet members had been informed of his change of mind by phone an hour before the news was broadcast – of course I had not. Tony's later interviews were to be covertly but transparently hostile to the idea of my succeeding him – 'There are a lot of people who want to do the job,' he now stressed – and it was clear his plan to serve a full term meant staying until 2010 or 2011. From being about to leave he was now intent, it seemed, on staying another seven years in No. 10.

I also did not know that around this time Tony had commissioned his strategy adviser, John Birt, to devise a plan to split the Treasury in two – with transfer of its public spending function to a new 'Office of Management and Budget' in the Cabinet Office and thus effectively across to him. This highly secret plan, which was developed over the winter and spring into a 200-page document, would, of course, inevitably be a prelude to my removal from the Treasury. Even if Tony had not sacked me, I would have resigned if he had attempted to impose such a change. His plan was in breach of the promises he had made to me as long ago as 1994 about my role as chancellor. The plan was such a closely held secret that only a few of his friends at the time knew of what he was planning.

For those autumn, winter and early spring months I was out in the cold. But in March 2005, as the fallout from Iraq rumbled on and criticism of a presidential style of leadership grew, Tony read opinion polls that suggested our majority was at risk. In particular a targeted poll of the marginals showed we were falling behind badly in seats we had to win.

Before that, on the assumption that our support was solid, Tony had planned to finish his 2005 general election campaign with a series of seaside visits with his family. Our strategy had to be revised and, on his pollster's advice, Tony changed tack. He now asked me to return to the work I had done for years on strategy and join him on Labour's battlebus in barnstorming the marginals together. At one stop, in a much-viewed television moment, he approached an ice-cream van and ordered two cones. One of the vendors asked who the other cone was for. He replied, 'Gordon,' before somewhat awkwardly passing the ice cream to me. I brought the economy back centre stage in the election campaign and held a series of joint events where ministers exposed in meticulous detail how the Conservatives' tax-and-spending plans did not add up. At one of the later press conferences I had to step in to defend Tony from heated interrogations about Iraq.

I think that our campaigning made a difference. At one point Tory posters had been put up across the country, saying: 'Vote Blair, Get Brown'. However, they quickly came down, presumably because the Tory focus groups showed they had no resonance. And our shift from some complacent final days of campaigning to a concerted push in the marginals may have averted an even less happy result than the one we achieved. In the end, there was a swing of 5.5 per cent against us, resulting in a Labour loss of forty-eight seats. While we had won a third term, we did so with the lowest popular vote of any majority government in British history. The Liberal Democrats took 22 per cent of the vote and, with sixty-two seats secured, their best performance for eighty years – and, as it was to transpire, a better performance under Charles Kennedy than they would enjoy in 2010 with Nick Clegg.

On the day after the election Tony delayed his Cabinet appointments for some hours. He had to consider – as he did – whether to bring out of cold storage his scheme to split the Treasury in two. When we finally met he had not given up on his plan: he offered me Foreign Secretary which I politely refused. I told him that I had no desire to leave the Treasury. He agreed – but with evident reluctance – and while I was reappointed chancellor, I wanted to convince myself there was a reconciliation: in practice, it was more like a truce. I am told that it was not until a meeting at Chequers in the winter of 2005 that the idea of dismembering the Treasury was finally killed off. The focus groups suggested the public did not like a divided leadership. All that came out of Lord Birt's review was the renaming of the Department of Trade and Industry as the Department for Productivity, Energy and Industry, but that plan also went wrong. Within days of taking office, it was revoked by the new minister, Alan Johnson, when we realised that the initials could be pronounced 'DIPPY'.

The Sword of Damocles thus hung over the Treasury for months. While we had fought the last stages of the election together, Tony seemed determined to strike out on economic policy on his own. But there was, I thought, scope for collaboration. The Treasury and No. 10 had worked together on the Hampton Review into red tape and regulation. This formed the basis of our agenda for our upcoming presidency of the European Union in 2005. Fed into it also was the ongoing work of the task force focused on the needs of small businesses led by David Arculus.

I was fascinated by, and determined to, push through a streamlining and improvement of our regulatory system. Our plan was founded on a new evidence-based approach to measuring and assessing levels of risk. The theme was regulation only when necessary and, where possible, the elimination of unnecessary red tape. What was called the Better Regulation Initiative was directed, in part, at what we saw as the blanket uniformity demanded by an increasingly bureaucratic European Union; and there was common ground between Tony and me in simplifying British regulatory systems and challenging our European partners to support a wider agenda for change.

But only a few days after the election, again out of the blue, Tony redefined the whole basis of our approach. In a speech, clearly long in its preparation and planning, he called for massive deregulation and a bonfire of controls. He appeared to be defending a financial sector 'free-for-all' and denounced the City's regulatory body, the Financial Services Authority, for being 'hugely inhibiting of efficient businesses'. He accused pension protection plans of 'inflating dramatically the cost of selling pensions'. All this brought a fierce response from the head of the FSA, Callum McCarthy, who in a letter to Tony and myself bemoaned the remarks as damaging to our influence and abilities to support the principles of better regulation. Little did Tony know that his remarks would be used by unscrupulous dealers trying to fend off the proper monitoring of their dubious transactions in the shadow banking system. His timing, only two years away from the biggest meltdown in modern financial history, was unfortunate to say the least. Tony's speech was billed as an attack on the 'compensation culture' forced on the City. It could be seen in retrospect as a defence of the City's 'non-cooperation culture' when it came to proper supervision.

What followed was an unhappy few weeks, with one part of the government wanting a better way of regulating, the other to get rid of regulating. This laid bare a larger difference in perspectives. Tony's speech was briefed by supporters as his bid 'to mark his third term with a wave of deregulation'. Instead I favoured basing regulatory requirements – not just in finance but health and safety, consumer protection and the environment – on a proper measurement of risk. That, in my view, was the modern approach: only the regulation needed. But for all the caveats he introduced into his arguments, Tony's speech exposed modernisation to the critique that it and an ideology of deregulation went hand in hand. The cement was being set. The question in No. 10 was no longer 'Are you for modernisation?'; it was 'Are you for my modernisation?'

By 2005 I was about to enter the stormiest period of any political relationship that I have had. It was not with Tony or with any Conservative, Liberal Democrat or SNP adversary, but with a few British newspapers. The hostility of some of the Murdoch press was, initially, an unwelcome distraction; then, as it intensified, it became a sad fact to be reckoned with; when in full flow, it was nothing less than a direct attempt to distort and suborn the policy of the government. While I never expected an easy run from the press, I could not have anticipated how much the *Sun* would effectively become the leader of the Opposition.

It was a force that had been long in the making. In 2000, one Murdoch paper, the *Sunday Times*, had run a lengthy campaign to suggest I was corrupt. On at least six occasions they broke the law by impersonating me in phone calls with my building society to gain access to my finances. They then employed someone who was to become a well-known criminal to deceive his way into obtaining information from my solicitors. And then their reporters reverse-engineered my phone, allowing them to trace my movements. The story they subsequently ran – that I had bought my London flat under-the-counter and at a knockdown price from the estate of the deceased and disgraced Robert Maxwell – was completely untrue. It would be a decade later, in 2011, that their then editor finally admitted to the Leveson Inquiry into the behaviour of the press following the phone-hacking scandal that they had used untoward methods. At no time, however, did they backtrack on their false claim that the flat had not been advertised on the open market, despite the fact that it had been advertised in the property columns of their own newspaper.

I understand the power and importance of investigative journalism. But the law-breaking of the *Sunday Times* was just the start of a sequence of unwarranted intrusions into my private life over the next few years. My tax returns were stolen. My medical records were hacked into by an NHS employee. A police officer was bribed by a private investigator to enter the UK's National Police Computer to check on me. I do not know to this day who was behind all this but well before phone-hacking the long descent of the media into malpractice and law-breaking was under way.

The *Sun*'s activities at this time were increasingly and overtly political as well. I could live with them taking sides against me as they invariably did, but after 2007 their editor Rebekah Wade (who took the surname Brooks after her 2009 marriage) began running campaigns – first on Europe, then on crime and then, as I describe later, on Afghanistan – directed against me in personal and often inaccurate terms. On one occasion, she put in a text to Sarah what she had been saying directly to me: that I had to sack one of our ministers, Tom Watson, immediately. Tom was not someone to take this lying down; it was the prelude to his leading role in the exposure in 2010 of media wrongdoing, especially by News International, in the phone-hacking scandal.

But that lay in the future. The *Sun* notwithstanding, there was in the summer of 2005 good reason for Tony and me to come back together in pursuit of a bigger cause that excited and challenged both of us. We worked closely together in June and early July that year as we persuaded the G8 countries to back our Commission for Africa and the doubling of aid to the continent.

In the run-up to the Gleneagles G8 meeting, I had risked a breach with President George W. Bush by pushing hard for an early decision on our ambitious programme to write off what was then a figure of $55 billion of unpayable debt – it was to rise closer to $100 billion by 2017 – owed by the world's thirty-eight poorest countries. It was a cause I had championed across two decades. To stress the urgency of acting, I asked to meet with the US Secretary of State, Condoleezza Rice, though she clearly felt I was putting unfair pressure on America. In the event, John Snow, the American Treasury Secretary, did not turn up for the all-important finance ministers' decision-making meeting in London, sending a deputy who said he had no powers to agree anything. The German and Japanese representatives, equally opposed to our bold plan to write off debt, threatened to walk out. But after days of telephone diplomacy, we secured a deal that included using IMF reserves to fund 100 per cent debt relief where it was most needed.

And while the Gleneagles conference was overshadowed by the 7/7 terrorist tragedy in London, we did create the momentum that spurred African economic development. In the next few months, I focused on our plans to raise £5 billion for the immunisation of 500 million children, and highlighted the neglected area of global education. I persuaded Nelson Mandela and his wife, the inspirational children's rights campaigner Graça Machel, to launch Britain's plan to get millions of children in Africa and Asia out of child labour. I visited them at their home in Mozambique, and with the Mandelas present at the announcement we promised the UK would spend $15 billion over ten years to ensure that 4 million children currently denied education would go to school. The visit brought some much-needed light relief: at the outset of his own speech, Mandela announced he was coming out of retirement in aid of this noble global cause and at the end of it he reannounced his retirement.

The next few months were consumed by our response to the tragic deaths of 7 July and our new measures to deal with the terrorist threat; and, as we worked though this agenda, my relations with Tony improved. Thankfully, he had made a complete recovery from his heart operation and the only noticeable sign of any difference in his health was that he now regularly came to No. 11 to ask for a cup of coffee – something that had been banned from No. 10. And so, we talked more. Nevertheless, in spite of Tony's energetic push for a new deregulatory direction in public sector reform, the two years that followed were more about him cementing his legacy and dealing with the fallout from Iraq. I still wanted a consensual transition; so when, without my knowledge, a group of ministers resigned from their posts because of their impatience to see a change, I helped put the rebellion down.

My preference had always been a Labour leadership election in 2004 or 2005 and a handover before what would have been a general election in 2005 or 2006. I was not expecting a coronation: I was happy to fight it out with any candidate when the time came. By 2004 Tony had already been Labour leader for ten years and prime minister for seven. He could, with my support, have stretched it to eight and a half by going to the second half of 2005 with an election in 2006. That would have been a longer period in office than any US president and he would have honoured his promise to me to stand down in a second term.

What's more, I felt I was running out of time. I wanted office not for the title but for the power to move forward progressive goals for the country. But I was very much aware that the public get fed up with politicians who have been in the public eye – and direct line of fire – for too long. 'I've already had seven years. Once you've had seven years, the public start getting sick of you,' I recall saying to friends in 2004. 'You've got seven years, but after that, you're on the down slope. I've tried not to be too exposed, but it's still seven years. Every year that goes by, the public are going to say: "Not that guy Brown, we're tired of him – give us someone new."' I had given my all to win in 2005 but I thought it should have been the last general election I fought.

I had also built a team for a handover in 2004 or 2005 – men and women experienced enough for government at the highest level, yet young enough to spend some time in No. 10 before planning glittering parliamentary or other careers in their own right. But they would not hang around forever. By the time I arrived at No. 10 in June 2007, I had lost a few of them and some would immediately become Cabinet ministers with their own portfolios. If we had changed over in 2004 or 2005, Afghanistan, as I will show, would almost certainly have worked out differently; so too perhaps the next stage of our relationship with Iraq. Some of the mistakes I made, like abolishing the 10p tax rate in my last Budget of 2007, would not have happened. And I had decided and told Sarah that if I became prime minister in 2005, and then fought and won an election, I would pass over to someone new by 2010. I knew the shelf life of leaders would be much shorter in the future than they had been in the past.

But that was not to be and I was realistic about what lay ahead. In 2007, I could still try to persuade the electorate that I was fresh and awash with ideas, but much of the political capital I had was expended in the difficult last weeks of the 2005 campaign. Roy Jenkins, who knew a lot from more than fifty years of Labour handovers, said that the worst time to become prime minister was in what he called the 'fag end' of a period in government. It is the moment when the decisions of the years before are coming back to haunt you and people simply crave change. This would turn out to be even truer than I ever wanted to believe at the time.

CHAPTER 10

FIRST DAYS IN NO. 10

As I was driven at speed out of the Buckingham Palace courtyard at 2.45 p.m. on 27 June 2007, I thought less about the fact I had just become prime minister than of the speech I was about to deliver on the steps of Downing Street. The day had started early with one final meeting with Tony Blair to discuss the handover. While generous with his time and advice, he was understandably focused on preparing for his final Prime Minister's Questions at midday. I then returned to the Treasury, making my way through hordes of assembled journalists and television cameras. There I had breakfast and turned to some final unfinished Treasury work before making my way to the Chamber. I sat next to Tony during Questions and, in a break with convention, he was given a standing ovation by all sides of the House at its end. It was there that I said goodbye to him as prime minister and he set out for Buckingham Place.

Back at the Treasury, I took a quick lunch in the staff canteen. And in my last act as chancellor, I signed the official papers that enabled Tony to step down as an MP. Under a procedure dating from the seventeenth century, MPs are not allowed to resign but must seek permission from the chancellor to be appointed to the temporary post of Steward and Bailiff of the Chiltern Hundreds, which is an 'office of profit under the Crown' and thus disqualifies them from sitting in Parliament. With this complete, I thanked the officials and staff I had worked with as chancellor over the last ten years. By then Sarah had joined me and we departed to applause from a large crowd of civil servants on all four landings of the Treasury building.

My path to No. 10, as I have described, had been anything other than smooth, but a few days earlier, on the Sunday, I had been elected unanimously as Labour Party leader at a special conference in

Manchester. I had long championed women's equality and I was pleased that we had a woman deputy leader in Harriet Harman. Harriet was a popular choice, narrowly beating off a strong challenge from a very able and likeable opponent in Alan Johnson.

I had never thought I would ascend to the leadership uncontested; and for many of the previous ten years never believed I would be there at all. No post-war leader had ever won without a contest. When Tony told me in 1994 he thought he could win the leadership without a contest, I had not believed him. Of course, I had been challenged – by John McDonnell, later the shadow chancellor – but he could not secure the necessary nominations. At the conference, I set out my agenda: widening opportunity in education, employment, enterprise and making our public services – the NHS, schools, policing – personal services too. As we left Manchester, with two hungry young children in the back of the car, we celebrated with takeaway chicken nuggets and chips from a motorway café.

Before becoming prime minister, I had read Churchill's account of the day he entered No. 10 in 1940. 'I felt that all my past life had been but a preparation for this hour,' he said with gravitas, before adding with a solemnity matched only by a sense of destiny: 'As I went to bed about 3 a.m., I was conscious of a profound sense of relief. At last I had the authority to give directions over the whole scene.' I had also read the historian A. J. P. Taylor's famous account of Lloyd George taking over from Asquith in 1916: 'He seized power,' Taylor wrote, quoting Churchill, 'perhaps the power was his to take.'

Others had been less sure than Churchill or Lloyd George about becoming prime minister. 'I think it a damned bore,' Lord Melbourne said upon being informed that he had been called to the Palace in 1834. He was, he told his secretary, 'in many minds what to do'. Others approached the position with foreboding: Harold Macmillan, when he took over from Anthony Eden after Suez, warned the Queen that he could not guarantee the new government would last six weeks – something she reminded him of six years later when he resigned. For a few, becoming prime minister failed to live up to their high expectations. Lord Rosebery, who had the unenviable task of replacing Gladstone as prime minister, remarked that there were 'two supreme pleasures in life. One is ideal, the other is real. The ideal is when a man receives the Seals of Office from his sovereign. The real is when he hands them back.' He later wrote that the greatest thing that ever happened to him was his horse winning the Derby. For my part, I was keen to get started in what I believe is the most important job in the country.

I knew too of Clement Attlee's matter-of-fact account that going to Buckingham Palace – arriving to meet the king in the little Hillman car, which his wife Violet had driven as he toured the country during the 1945 general election campaign – was not dissimilar to going to a business meeting at someone else's office. The encounter between Attlee and the king, both shy men, was perfunctory because neither knew what to say to the other. Apparently, the silence was only broken by Attlee observing, 'I won the election . . .' and the king replying, 'I know, I heard it on the six o'clock news.'

Contrary to myth, the Queen and her prime minister do not 'kiss hands': they shake hands. In a departure from past tradition, Sarah joined us at the end of my audience with her. The Queen and I had a congenial and businesslike conversation about the work that lay ahead, and I warned her that we were appointing quite a few new and young Cabinet members whom she would have to swear into her Privy Council during the next few days, this being the usual require-ment for sitting in the Cabinet.

However busy they may be, those who are sworn into the Privy Council must first attend its offices for a rehearsal, where they are taught how to kneel on a stool, how to raise the right hand with the Bible in it and take their oath, how to proceed forward three steps to kneel on another stool before the Queen, and then how to perform the difficult task of walking backwards without falling over either of the stools. Richard Crossman, who served as Lord President of the Council under Harold Wilson, wrote of the ceremony: 'I don't sup-pose anything more dull, pretentious, or plain silly has ever been invented.'

There had been nothing dull about the Saturday evening in May 1997 when I had visited Buckingham Palace with my new Cabinet colleagues, who were being sworn into the Privy Council, and I received the seals of office as chancellor. I remember well how my colleague and friend, Nick Brown, our new chief whip, was preparing to kneel on the first stool to take his oath when the Queen interrupted, saying: 'Not yet.' There followed what seemed an eternity. Was she, as Nick thought, about to refuse him membership? To his relief, the Queen explained that he had to wait until one of his colleagues had finished being sworn in.

Having arrived at the Palace in one car, the chancellor's Vauxhall, Sarah and I left in another, the prime minister's Jaguar, to give my speech on the steps of No. 10. I was determined to give my remarks without notes or a lectern. I wanted to speak directly to the British people. But with helicopters above, waiting press and TV cameras, and an expected posse of anti-Iraq War demonstrators only yards away outside the gates at the end of the street, we had anticipated that it would not be easy to be heard. So, somewhat farcically, I had rehearsed my speech in a Treasury anteroom while Damian McBride, my press officer, and Sue Nye hurled abuse in my direction, trying to distract me and shout me down.

In preparing my speech, I had the benefit of advice from Lucy Parker, a gifted author and highly successful social entrepreneur, who was to join us in No. 10 and lead our efforts to build bridges with business, as I tried to get the balance right between communicating my appreciation of the privilege that had been bestowed and my commitment to the work ahead. I ended my short remarks by reminding people of my school's Latin motto, *Usque conabor*, which I translated as 'I will try my utmost'. That, I said, was my pledge to the whole country. (The next day the newspapers were full of commentary about the relevance of school mottos. I was happy to have inspired such a debate.)

I then entered No. 10 for the first time as prime minister, to applause from civil servants who had lined up along the entrance hall to greet me. Less than an hour earlier, the same No. 10 staff had said goodbye to Tony, Cherie and their children after ten years of working together. I thought it must be a difficult day for them, as the departure of one prime minister whom they know well, and the arrival of a new one whom they have to get to know, happens so quickly. I walked to the end of the line shaking hands all round and found, to my surprise, my two young sons waiting for me. To our great joy Fraser had been born only eleven months before; John would be four in October. That moment they fell into my arms is one I will never forget.

A few minutes later, I was down to work. I began by announcing a set of changes that I was determined would send out a clear message as to what kind of prime minister I would be. I would immediately rescind the ten-year-old Order in Council that had given Tony's political advisers, Alastair Campbell and Jonathan Powell, the power to give civil servants instructions, restoring the constitutional practice that only elected ministers were entitled to do so. I also made a point of appointing a civil servant, Tom Scholar, as both my chief of staff and principal private secretary, ending the division of the two roles between a political appointee and an official. I was sending a clear signal that 'sofa government' was over and that a more formal process of decision-making was now in place, that while political appointees had their place, the Civil Service line of command would be restored.

Next came phone calls to world leaders. My first call was to US President George W. Bush, whom I spoke to for ten minutes, mainly about Iraq and Afghanistan. I then talked to the French president, Nicolas Sarkozy, whom I had known well since the time we were finance ministers together. We joked how few finance ministers had ever made it to the top spot. I phoned Angela Merkel, the German chancellor, to confirm arrangements already made to meet in Berlin on my first overseas visit as prime minister. During these latter two calls, I was sensitive to the fact that I had to get the right balance in our relationships with Germany and France – both were equally important to our European policy. I called the Taoiseach, Bertie Ahern, and we discussed the moves we would have to make within days to advance the next stage of Northern Irish devolution. Then I spoke to Romano Prodi, former president of the European Commission and now Italian prime minister. I also made courtesy calls to David Cameron and the Liberal Democrat leader, Menzies Campbell. Over the next few hours and days, I would have a succession of conversations with Commonwealth leaders – Thabo Mbeki of South Africa, Stephen Harper of Canada, John Howard of Australia, Helen Clark of New Zealand and Manmohan Singh of India – as well as with the Chinese leader, Wen Jiabao, and the heads of international organisations including president of the European Commission José Manuel Barroso, secretary general of the UN Ban Ki-moon, and director general of the World Trade Organization, Pascal Lamy.

In the early evening, before travelling to the House of Commons to appoint my first Cabinet, I brought together, at Sue Nye's suggestion, the Downing Street staff – ranging from the No. 10 secretarial staff, still referred to by some in antiquated terms as the 'Garden

Room Girls', up to the most senior officials – in the Pillared Room. I was now meeting the staff who would work hours far beyond the call of duty and with a strong sense of public service, all representing the best of what I had come to admire in the British home and diplomatic services. I told them that it had been an emotional day and they had said goodbye to a great leader and great family. I thanked them for the welcome they had given me and my family, and ended by saying: 'It's not every day you meet the Queen at 1.30 p.m., become the prime minister at 2.45 p.m., speak to the president of the United States at 4 p.m., and get told by Sarah to put the kids to bed at 7 p.m.'

When an administration changes hands in the United States, up to 5,000 staff come and go; in the United Kingdom, new appointees – political advisers as well as ministers – number at most around 200. In fact, as I moved in and Tony moved out, only forty or so new people would come into No. 10 – a team of the best policy researchers and advisers I could ever hope to work with and whom I mention by name in the Acknowledgements of this book. They were supported by our head of communications, first Mike Ellam and then Simon Lewis, both of whose sage media advice and unflappability I relied on, and by a Labour Party team expertly led by Fiona Gordon and later Joe Irvin and Jonathan Ashworth. But continuity in staffing was also the name of the game, and I asked some of Tony's younger advisers to stay on. Kate Gross – a wonderful civil servant, equally at home advising on UK social policy and international development, and who was to die all too young at thirty-six in 2014 – generously remained in her post to help me through the transition.

In addition to Tom Scholar, my new principal private secretary and later head of the Treasury, I was joined by a highly effective and popular economist, James Bowler, my principal private secretary as chancellor, and by Beth Russell, who was named speechwriter, but whose considerable talents, which extended far beyond speech-making, were of great value.

Simon McDonald, who was my foreign policy adviser, was on his way to becoming permanent undersecretary at the Foreign Office. He was joined by the brightest young diplomat of the day, Tom Fletcher. Tom became a highly effective ambassador to Lebanon at a critical time in the Syrian civil war and coordinated the education of more than 200,000 Syrian refugees in Lebanon. In his book *The Naked*

Diplomat, he showed how technology can transform old 'behind closed doors' diplomacy into a modern two-way communication with ordinary members of the public. Tom was later joined by another excellent foreign policy adviser, Nick Catsaras.

In January 2008, Jeremy Heywood – who in 2012 became Cabinet Secretary, and in 2014 head of the Civil Service – returned to lead on policy as principal private secretary and later took up a new position as permanent secretary to No. 10. Like Tony before me and two prime ministers since, I was able to draw on the support of Sue Gray, a senior official in the Cabinet Office, who was always there with wise advice when – as all too regularly happened – mini-crises and crises befell.

The Cabinet had to be announced within twenty-four hours; and, as far as possible, I was determined to avoid the increasingly common practice of issuing the names of appointees one by one just to feed the news cycle. Unbeknown to the media, I had decided to do my Cabinet-making in the Commons, rather than Downing Street. I did not want ministers who were resigning or being sacked to endure the glare of cameras as they walked along the street to and from No. 10. In my Commons office, I sat down in turn with Charlie Falconer, Patricia Hewitt and Margaret Beckett who would be leaving the Cabinet. I held meetings in the House of Commons until nearly midnight and in between made further courtesy calls to other Opposition party leaders – Alex Salmond, Ian Paisley and Martin McGuinness.

The next morning, 28 June, I made my way back to the Commons for further discussions – again, away from the cameras that were still outside No. 10, lying in wait for prospective ministers – and only then, once the Cabinet had been finalised, did I invite the new members to come to Downing Street to be appointed formally.

I replaced almost half of the Cabinet, with ten members departing. The average age had dropped to below fifty. Though none were as young as Harold Wilson, who joined Attlee's Cabinet at the age of thirty-one, the Cabinet as a whole was the youngest of the post-war period.

James Purnell and Ed Miliband, our new Secretary of State for Culture, Media and Sport and minister for the Cabinet Office respectively, were both thirty-seven; Douglas Alexander and Ed Balls, International Development Secretary and Secretary of State for

Children, Schools and Families respectively, were forty; and David Miliband, at forty-one, became the youngest Foreign Secretary since David Owen in 1977, while Jacqui Smith was one of the youngest MPs – and first woman – to become Home Secretary. Yet all these younger appointees had been at the centre of government, whether in No. 10, the Treasury or Cabinet Office, often since 1997. David and Ed Miliband became the first brothers to sit in Cabinet together since Austen and Neville Chamberlain nearly eighty years before.

I chose a young Cabinet that I hoped would mature and grow over the next three years. In it, I believed, was sitting one of the men or women who would be my successor. In that sense, the Cabinet was what my friend the author Doris Kearns Goodwin – sometimes called America's historian-in-chief – termed 'a team of rivals'. But not, at least for most of my time, did I see them as rivals to me. They were already competing with each other in a race for the succession; and, to be frank, they were sometimes distracted because of this.

Only Jack Straw, our Lord Chancellor, was over sixty. He would work with a new constitution minister, Michael Wills, who had been unfairly overlooked in the past and now brought fresh ideas to the debate about Britishness and our constitutional future. Harriet Harman was not only deputy leader of the party but became chair of the party, Leader of the House of Commons and minister for women and equality, in which post she was to pioneer the most ambitious equalities legislation in the world.

The full Cabinet was announced at lunchtime. At 2 p.m. we started what was to be a three-hour meeting. I glanced at Alistair Darling and said: 'It's very odd sitting across from the chancellor. I'm no longer the one who has to say "no".' This was to be the last Cabinet meeting on a Thursday: I moved our meetings to Tuesday because I wanted the Cabinet to prepare for the week ahead, not just review the week that had gone by.

Picking a Cabinet is even more complicated than it might seem. You have to focus on the jobs in hand, choosing the best person to deal with, say, education or health, and you also have to be aware of the overall balance – of ages, backgrounds, personalities and factions within the party – that needs to be struck. And, of course, there are the inexorable pressures of ambition: in the UK, unlike in America, if you are not a member of the government, you can hardly ever shape a piece of legislation, and so for most MPs the test of success is not achievement as a backbencher but whether they make it into the ministerial ranks.

I wanted a strong Cabinet, and I was happy to be surrounded by members who would challenge me with their own ideas. I recalled the words of Lord Curzon claiming that Lloyd George treated him as if he were a 'valet'. Instead, I admired Abraham Lincoln for his team of rivals. I would have wanted Robin Cook back in Cabinet and indeed had talked to him about a possible return to office before his untimely death in 2005. I considered bringing back David Blunkett, Charles Clarke and Alan Milburn too, but I saw no great desire on their part to come in.

To match Cabinet's youth with experience, I also brought talented men and women from outside politics into government. This had been tried in the past, with mixed success. On the one hand, there was Lord Chalfont, a lieutenant colonel who had fought in Malaya in the 1950s and later became a defence correspondent, who was not a notable success as minister for disarmament; C. P. Snow, the celebrated writer, lasted only two years as minister of technology; and Frank Cousins, who had been general secretary of Britain's biggest union, left within months. On the other hand, David Sainsbury was one of many successes under Tony and showed what could be done. He was a spectacularly effective minister for science – his work promoting innovation, science and technology deserves a book in itself.

I thought we could make outside appointments work by casting them in a new way. I singled out Ara Darzi, a brilliant surgeon whose work in reorganising the London hospital system was widely acknow-ledged to be path-breaking, as the man to speed reform of the NHS and complement the Health Secretary Alan Johnson's political acumen. Within a year, Ara was to complete a thorough review of staff prac-tices and patient experiences, recommending important reforms that have lasted to this day.

I also asked Mark Malloch Brown, former head of the United Nations Development Programme, to join David Miliband at the Foreign Office. Though their relationship did not get off to the best start – Mark gave an interview saying he would be 'the wise eminence behind the young Foreign Secretary' – the government, and David, greatly benefited from his exceptional knowledge of Africa and the developing world. The former head of the CBI, Digby Jones, with whom I had worked closely during my years at the Treasury, and Paul Drayson, a successful businessman in his own right, joined John Hutton and Pat McFadden at the new Department for Business, Enterprise and Regulatory Reform. Because Digby had made the transition from boardroom to the halls of a Labour government he was soon nick-named Comrade Digby. Sir Alan West, the recently retired First Sea Lord, came in as minister of security, working with Jacqui Smith. He gave invaluable service by helping to produce Britain's first ever National Security Strategy and Cyber Security Strategy. However, it did not help that he was wrongly accused in the newspapers of having an affair with one of the female members of Abba. I also considered Paddy Ashdown. Would he be willing to serve as Secretary of State for Northern Ireland – a job that I felt he could do on a non-partisan basis? Nothing came of it. But Alan Sugar, whom I appointed as Enterprise Czar in 2009 – and who became Lord Sugar – did brilliant and inspirational work encouraging young people to enter business.

In one further innovation, I appointed new regional ministers to act as champions within Whitehall and Westminster for each region of England. I wanted English regions to go some way towards match-ing the power that the Scottish, Welsh and Northern Ireland Secretaries and the devolved institutions enjoyed. We appointed high-calibre ministers – like Nick Brown in the north-east – who worked with regional development agencies and local authorities to strengthen the profile of – and resources available to – their areas. I saw this reform as the first step towards the much more extensive devolution of power within England that was my ultimate goal.

For the same reason, the Cabinet began a regular cycle of meeting outside London in the regions. I felt that we had to answer the charge from the rest of the country that no one in London listened. Prior to my becoming prime minister, only two Cabinet meetings in history had been held outside the capital. Lloyd George, who would not leave his holiday in Wester Ross, had summoned his ministers to Inverness Town House in September 1921 after Ireland renounced the British monarchy, and Harold Wilson held a full Cabinet meeting about his prices and incomes policy in the banqueting room of the Grand Hotel during the 1966 Labour Party conference in Brighton. In total, I would chair nine Cabinet meetings outside of London from Exeter in the south-west to Glasgow in Scotland.

On the morning of Friday 29 June, we had scheduled a Cabinet session to discuss our constitutional reforms, which were to be announced on the following Monday. These had been thought through largely by Michael Wills, who combined an understanding of what it was to be British with a strong sense of what a modern constitution should look like. He was to be the architect of the main reforms and many initiatives, like a new British Bill of Rights and citizens' juries, that were killed stone dead after we left power.

However, on that day, an unexploded bomb, packed with petrol, nails and gas cylinders, was discovered in an abandoned car at 2 a.m. in the West End. I was woken up at 4 a.m. and informed. The picture was unclear: we had yet to detain anyone and did not know whether there were other bombs in the area. I asked Jacqui Smith to make the initial public statement, and just after 10.30 a.m. I convened a meeting of the government's crisis response committee, COBRA – named after Cabinet Office Briefing Room A, in which its sessions are held.

After the meeting, we briefed the full Cabinet, and Jacqui again went on TV to warn of a 'serious and sustained threat', urging the public to 'remain vigilant'. While I went ahead with the appointments and meetings of the day, including my planned visit to a London school, we had another COBRA meeting later that afternoon, following confirmation that Park Lane had been closed off as police investigated a second suspect car. After the COBRA meeting, at 8 p.m., I spoke to the cameras from just outside the Cabinet Room, praising the fortitude and resilience of the British people. Later on Friday evening, police confirmed that a second car containing bomb material had been found.

A further COBRA meeting was held at midday on Saturday. Then, at around 3 p.m., a third incident – later confirmed as a terror attack – was reported from Glasgow. Two men crashed a burning Jeep into the entrance hallway of Glasgow airport. It was the first time Scotland had suffered a terrorist incident since the Lockerbie bombing of 1988. We invited Alex Salmond, the Scottish First Minister, to join the subsequent COBRA meeting on a video link but his initial statement was downright unhelpful – he wanted us to know that no Scot was involved in any terrorist act. Although no lives had been lost, we immediately moved Britain to the highest state of security alert, 'critical', meaning a terrorist attack was expected 'imminently'. It took four days until we were able to reduce the threat level back to 'severe', meaning an attack is 'likely'.

These were fearful but proud days for Britain, once again showing resilience in the face of a terrorist attack. One side effect of the attack was that it disrupted our careful planning for a series of ambitious announcements to herald the start of a new government. We had a raft of changes in train on the constitution, the NHS, student finance, drugs, welfare and gambling. Each of these announcements was designed to send a message about a new agenda in tune with the needs and aspirations of the people. Understandably that message was muted in the aftermath of the terrorist incidents when the focus became how we were responding to them.

In the days leading up to the summer break, I was intent on reinforcing the new government's commitment to the young. I had always opposed tuition fees but at this point we did not have sufficient resources to uproot and replace them with a graduate tax; which, even if it had been instituted in 2004, would still not have been yielding revenues by this time. Instead, we raised grant levels for poorer students. This was to be followed a few months later with an even more radical set of proposals to raise the minimum education leaving age to eighteen and bring into force the key findings of the Leitch Review, which recommended that training or education should be compulsory for all teenagers. Our aim was to ensure that the overwhelming majority of young people would have basic numeracy and literacy skills.

Another key signal I wanted to send in my first days as prime minister was about our democracy – and restoring trust in it, not least because it had been eroded over Iraq. I wanted our democracy strengthened by an extensive devolution of power from the executive to Parliament and the people. We announced that we would not invoke the ancient and outdated Royal Prerogative, relying instead on Parliament to declare on matters of war and peace. We simultaneously initiated a national debate on the case for a full British Bill of Rights and opened up public appointments and major policy decisions to greater scrutiny by the House of Commons. This included hearings on appointments to the Bank of England, hitherto the chancellor's prerogative, and greater parliamentary oversight of the intelligence services. The prime minister would also no longer play any role in selecting the Archbishop of Canterbury or other senior ecclesiastics. We would, too, relinquish our residual role in the appointment of judges who would henceforth be selected entirely by a non-partisan committee of experts. The rules governing the Civil Service were no longer to be set at the discretion of ministers but legislated by MPs. The executive would also give up its authority to grant pardons. We created citizens' juries to provide feedback on public policy, and new rights for people to scrutinise and improve the delivery of local services and vote on spending decisions in areas like neighbourhood and youth budgets. I had always thought we could extend the principle that underlay the jury system – that a group of ordinary citizens could be entrusted to make decisions – on aspects of policy wider than the criminal law. 'Power to the people' was the theme.

But there was a limit to that power. We were to later ban super-alcoholic drinks and toughen the classification of so-called recreational drugs that could harm mental health. Indeed, this measure is more remembered for the press's ensuing scurry to find out which ministers had smoked cannabis in their student days. Eventually nearly half the Cabinet admitted to it – not a great start to try to reduce its use; I never asked them whether they inhaled or not. Meanwhile, James Purnell, our Culture Secretary, announced that 1,000 online gambling sites based overseas would be banned from advertising in the UK. At Prime Minister's Questions, I told the House we would not go ahead with the proposed super-casino in Manchester. Perhaps my instincts were those of a son of the manse.

For over 150 years, what was called the annual Gracious Address, delivered in the Lords by the monarch, had been drafted inside government in private, far from the public eye, and then sent on to the Palace to be delivered unchanged. But in a statement to the House in July, I proposed to open up the government's legislative programme to nationwide consultation in advance of the Queen's Speech.

In total, I announced twenty-three bills and draft bills. One of the most consequential was the first ever Climate Change Bill which put Britain ahead of every other country in the world in enforcing tough anti-pollution standards. Our Counter-Terrorism Bill, meanwhile, proposed to give the government the power to impose travel bans on convicted terrorists and allow for post-charge questioning of terrorism suspects. At this point, suspects could be detained for only twenty-eight days. Tony had proposed a limit of ninety days, but I thought Parliament could be persuaded to accept a maximum of forty-two days in cases where there were genuine reasons to believe the detainee might be a terrorist. This incurred the wrath of civil-liberties groups and ultimately the Tories, Liberal Democrats and dissident Labour members blocked the bill. Our fallback was that in the event of another serious terrorist incident we would reintroduce the legislation.

As the summer holidays approached, I called the Cabinet together for a strategy session. I had often ruminated, even sometimes lectured, on the theme of Cabinet government. When I was a student at Edinburgh my professor, John Mackintosh, whom I had known well when he served as a Scottish MP, had argued in his lectures that real power in British government lay with the prime minister, not the Cabinet. This represented a major departure from the Victorian ideal, which held that the prime minister was simply *primus inter pares* – first amongst equals. While some had described the position in grander terms – Viscount Harcourt, the chancellor under Gladstone, described the prime minister as *luna inter stellas minores*, 'a moon amongst lesser stars' – most concurred with the assessment of the Liberal statesman John Morley, that the prime minister was no more than 'the keystone of the Cabinet arch'.

This was not how it looked by the middle of the twentieth century. In his foreword to the new 1963 edition of Walter Bagehot's *The English Constitution*, Richard Crossman famously argued that 'the post-war epoch has seen the final transformation of Cabinet government into prime-ministerial government'. Not long afterwards, George Brown resigned as Foreign Secretary claiming that Harold Wilson was 'introducing a "presidential" system' that was 'wholly alien to the British constitutional system'. Even without the authority that comes to the president of the United States from direct election by the people, Mackintosh pointed out the prime minister's powers in areas like appointments elevated him above his colleagues. But later the Scottish MP Tam Dalyell was considered to have gone too far when he compared No. 10 under Tony to the court of Louis XIV.

Having been in government for ten years, I wanted to avoid accusations of running a 'cabal' or the kind of 'court government' which people alleged had replaced Cabinet government. As I knew well, senior ministers could, and did, exercise a high degree of autonomy. But I wanted to empower them with more authority and establish a more collegial approach. I had empowered Jacqui Smith to lead our response to the terrorist incidents. Similarly, when I met George Bush, I was to surprise the Americans by taking our Foreign Secretary, David Miliband, with me. I did not want the focus for all major announcements to be on the prime minister: I wanted individual Cabinet ministers to play a far bigger role. I wanted the Cabinet itself to be more than a rubber stamp; more than just the sounding board it had often seemed – I wanted to see a rejuvenation of a more collective form of decision-making.

All in all, I felt confident in the abilities of those around me and ambitious for what we could achieve together. Even though the months ahead would turn out to be more challenging than any of us could have anticipated, I told Sarah during a few days back home in Scotland over the summer that I loved the job.

CHAPTER II

THE BEST-LAID PLANS. . .

Most of us in politics assume that the higher we rise, the more likely it is that we can acquire the power that enables us to deliver what we went into politics to achieve. This is true only up to a point. At the level of highest office, the array of unanticipated factors that can constrain your ability to exercise power dramatically increases. Even having the responsibility for a large department – with the Treasury as a good example – cannot fully prepare you for all the complex challenges ahead. For some leaders that may not be a problem – particularly if their main concern is to dominate the news cycle, for it is often those with the best-laid plans who are most at the mercy of events. As the previous chapters relate, I had a clear sense of what I wanted to deliver as prime minister, and this meant I had to fight even harder not to be thrown off course when the unexpected occurred. A leader's time in office should never be defined by such things, and although in some instances you can shape events to your designs, in others they shape you. If my first few days in No. 10 were dominated by security concerns, in the weeks and months that followed we were hit by one domestic crisis after another.

In July, Britain suffered some of the worst floods for years, with Hull and Gloucestershire particularly badly hit; in August, an outbreak of foot and mouth in Surrey; in September, we saw the collapse of Northern Rock and an outbreak of bluetongue disease in sheep and cattle; and in November the extent of avian flu became apparent, eventually leading to a mass cull. My hope that we might be able to shift attention from security to our agenda for reform would not be fulfilled as Harold Macmillan's famous comment – 'events, dear boy, events' – often sprang to mind over these months and beyond. Although there was welcome praise for our competence in handling the various crises, all talk of a new start would vanish from popular discourse by the time we entered the autumn. But even before all this, there were other pressing concerns to be dealt with.

Northern Ireland seemed to be in permanent crisis. There was a danger that, if we could not get all parties to agree a timetable for a second round of devolution, the Northern Ireland Assembly would collapse. At Stormont on 16 July, with the First and Deputy First Ministers, along with Bertie Ahern, I announced what I had spent months preparing at the Treasury – a new financial package worth £50 billion over ten years. The idea was to link the financial priorities of the competing parties to progress on issues like the transfer of responsibility for policing to Belfast. But, even with this on offer, it would take months of late-night meetings in Downing Street, discussions at Stormont and visits to Dublin to get the job done.

Russia was a rising international concern. After the meetings at Stormont I flew from Belfast to Berlin to confer with Chancellor Merkel who shared my worries about Vladimir Putin's increasingly assertive behaviour. We were in dispute with him over the murder of the Russian former KGB officer Alexander Litvinenko in London in November 2006, and I told her of our belief that the orders for the assassination had come from the top. The Director of Public Prosecutions, Sir Ken Macdonald, had already asked for the arrest of the main suspect, Andrei Lugovoi, who fled London for Moscow. When the Russian Prosecutor General ruled out extraditing Lugovoi, we responded by expelling four Russian diplomats on the very day I met Merkel. The next day's newspapers headlined a new Cold War.

There was approval, even on the right, for taking a firm line with Russia in what was seen as the first foreign policy test of my time in office, but Putin remained a constant source of provocation. I had met him twice when I was chancellor. On the second occasion, he spoke at a lunch of G8 finance ministers in the Kremlin. He threatened that if the West would not deal with Russia on his terms, he would no longer sell oil and gas to Europe and redirect exports to the East. When I looked into Putin's eyes, I did not see a good man; but I could understand his appeal to Russians who wanted to cast off what they saw as years of humiliation following the Cold War. He was prepared to go to any lengths to destroy any opposition – as we were soon to learn. Only months after the Litvinenko assassination, a second Kremlin plot seemed to be hatching – to murder yet another Russian citizen on British soil. Relations between Putin and me never recovered.

At this stage, Putin was prime minister while waiting to seize another term as president, so all my formal relationships went through his Potemkin president, Dmitry Medvedev. At his first meeting of the G8, Medvedev agreed to an initiative on Zimbabwe – only to find himself overruled the next morning by a Putin diktat. Later that year, when George Bush was leaving office, the wives of the G8 leaders toasted his wife Laura. In a further round of toasts, Medvedev's wife raised her glass in a toast not to her husband but to Putin: 'Once a president, always a president,' she said. The only other direct encounter I had with Putin was a frosty exchange at the joint NATO–Russia Summit in 2008. We merely shook hands and moved on.

When Parliament went into recess in July 2007, I headed to America for my first meetings as prime minister with President Bush. My destination was not the White House, as I would have preferred, but the presidential country retreat Camp David. George Bush told me he preferred an air of informality. But I wanted the public to see us working through detailed policy issues like Iraq, rather than appearing as though we were just exchanging pleasantries. The president was anxious to press me to keep British troops in Iraq. This evolved over our private dinner into a friendly but pointed exchange about numbers and timing.

Beyond Iraq there was another issue I had to raise – and I did so the next morning. Two of our ministers, Douglas Alexander and Mark Malloch Brown, had been widely reported as implying that the special relationship between Britain and the USA now mattered less than it once had. Douglas had given a speech in Washington emphasising the need for 'new alliances, based on common values', which was widely interpreted by journalists as a coded criticism of Bush's policies. A few days later, Malloch Brown said the UK and US were 'not joined at the hip' on foreign policy. I reassured Bush, satisfying him of Britain's commitment to our alliance, a point I reinforced in a session with the US Secretary of State, Condoleezza Rice, and David Miliband, who I had invited to attend the visit.

That morning the president drove me on a golf cart to our open-air press conference. Among the press corps was Nick Robinson, the political editor of the BBC. Six months earlier, Bush and Robinson had had a fiery exchange when Robinson asked him if he was in denial about Iraq. As our uneventful press conference ended, Bush asked Robinson: 'You still hanging around?' Referring to the fact that it was a hot and sunny day, Bush then suggested to him, 'Next time you should cover your bald head.' As Bush walked away, Robinson replied, 'I didn't know you cared,' to which Bush retorted, 'I don't.' This was yet another example of the storyteller becoming the story.

I was then helicoptered to Andrews Air Force Base and driven to Capitol Hill. Conscious that an American election was looming, I was anxious to cement our links not just with the Republicans but also the Democrats. Indeed, later that day in New York, I met with Bill Clinton. But I wanted my first few weeks in No. 10 to signal something more: so, my American visit ended with a speech at the United Nations. I promised to step up our aid efforts with the poorest countries, though my more urgent call was for joint action to end the conflict in Darfur and civil war in Sudan. I was sending a message to the Bush administration which, given all its troubles over Iraq, was reluctant to act: I saw the genocide in Darfur, like that in Rwanda, as a stain on the conscience of the world. I wish I could have done more.

Arriving back from my US trip, I had a private event in my diary: I took my young son John to the Hayward Gallery to see an Antony Gormley exhibition, the centrepiece of which was his room-sized installation *Blind Light*, a luminous glass box filled with mist. John was enchanted: even more than I did, he seemed to grasp what the shifting shapes and sizes conveyed. The apparent chaos reminded me of the Labour Party of old.

That same day, I welcomed to Downing Street the hero of the Glasgow terrorist attack, John Smeaton, a baggage handler who had helped police tackle the terrorist suspects, and after a planning session for my upcoming speeches to the TUC and Labour conferences in September, Sarah, the two boys and I left for a holiday. It would not go according to plan.

I had made a promise to stay in the UK in an effort to promote British tourism. Indeed, we would not travel abroad for any of our holidays when I was prime minister, deciding instead to vacation in England, Wales, Scotland and Northern Ireland. That first year our summer break was to be in the West Country near Sarah's parents, Pauline and Patrick. I arrived at their home around half past two in the afternoon, having stopped off en route to visit the Weymouth Sailing Academy that was to be a venue for the Olympic Games. But just four hours after arriving, I was told a phone call had come in from Bruce Mann, Director of the Civil Contingencies Secretariat, who reported an outbreak of foot-and-mouth disease in Surrey. Within a few minutes, I was talking to Hilary Benn, our Secretary of State for the Environment, and Debby Reynolds, the Chief Veterinary Officer. Damian McBride, who was with me as the duty press officer, had to brief newspapers and TV that we were doing everything in our power to identify the source of the outbreak and contain its spread.

The 2001 outbreak was still fresh in my mind; I recalled how slow the government's response had seemed and how much it had come under fire. This time we had to be proactive and swift to avert panic. I did not know the science of foot and mouth, although in the next few weeks I would be immersed in the details of the disease and its transmission. What I did know was that my holiday was ending before it had barely begun.

The next morning I left early for London, spending the car journey further reviewing the reports on the last outbreak, and thinking about how many animals we might have to slaughter, what would have to be done on footpaths and bridle paths, the impacts for horse racing, farm exports and tourism, and the potential return of exclusion and buffer zones.

When I arrived at No. 10, I chaired an emergency meeting of COBRA. By midday, I was doing a round of media interviews pledging that we would get to the bottom of the problem. On the phone, I updated the Opposition parties and devolved administrations. I had a further COBRA meeting at 5 p.m. and then discussions with officials and experts. Hilary was a tower of strength, particularly in reaching out to the farming community. A Surrey laboratory was quickly identified as the likely source of the outbreak. I found it strange that some in the press were blaming me for deserting my wife and children, leaving them with their buckets and spades on the beach. In any event, Sarah and I had decided to move our holiday from the south-west to Chequers, allowing me to stay with them over the break but travel each day into London as need be.

The next few days followed the pattern of the first: early morning updates to be read during the hour-long trip into London, then COBRA meetings and sessions with experts, followed by interviews with journalists and reports to the British people. While we might have expected all-party support for our swift action, bipartisanship went only so far: I briefed David Cameron, who went on TV to attack me, misusing the information I had passed to him in confidence.

By mid-August, with the epidemic being brought under control, I travelled to Scotland for a few days' actual break, visiting Alistair and Maggie Darling at their home in Edinburgh, as well as meeting up with J. K. Rowling, her husband Neil and their family. Sarah and I had known Jo and Neil for years, even before she had become the global icon she now is. I got to know her well after we both spoke at the National Council for Single Parents in 2000, and Neil had known my father years before that. In Scotland, I also found ninety minutes to watch a winning Raith Rovers team score three goals against Berwick Rangers, and after the match I made a presentation to the players, before we took John and Fraser to the local Chinese restaurant in Kirkcaldy.

In fact, I went to one more football match shortly afterwards – but this one was official business. Back in London, I took Angela Merkel to the opening of the new Wembley Stadium to watch Germany vs England. As part of her visit, we agreed a joint initiative to strengthen the financing of global health, a cause she was deeply committed to. But she may remember the visit more for the game, which Germany won 2–1.

There were two more ceremonial occasions before the end of the summer. The first, at the end of August, was the unveiling of a statue of Nelson Mandela in Parliament Square, with Mandela himself in attendance. Talking to vast crowds and with his wife Graça Machel at his side, Mandela said with great poignancy: 'Though this statue is of one man, it should in actual fact symbolise all of those who have resisted oppression, especially in my country.' As I later told the House of Commons, Mandela had visited London a few years before his arrest and imprisonment in June 1964. Touring Parliament Square, standing in front of the familiar statues of Gladstone and Disraeli, Peel and Palmerston, Lincoln and Smuts, he had turned to his friend Oliver Tambo and asked if someone who was black would ever be represented there. So, it was a very special honour for me to speak at that ceremony and say, 'Here Nelson Mandela now stands, forever, his hands outstretched, his finger pointing, as he did his whole life, upwards towards the heights . . . this statue is a beacon of hope. It sends around the world the most powerful of messages: that no injustice can last for ever, that suffering in the cause of freedom will never be in vain.'

Soon after there was a more traditional event: a visit to the Queen's Scottish holiday home, Balmoral, where you had to hope your children would behave. This was the annual visit of the prime minister and his family – arriving on Saturday afternoon and leaving on Sunday after lunch. The practice of prime ministers visiting Balmoral dates back to Queen Victoria. Not all of them have enjoyed the privilege. Disraeli complained that 'carrying on the government of the country six hundred miles from the metropolis doubles the labour', while Lord Salisbury referred to Balmoral Castle as 'Siberia'. In modern times, Harold Macmillan was as unsure as I was about whether the weekend should be treated as a social occasion, with discussion of business off limits, or as an extended version of the weekly audiences at Buckingham Palace. His successor, Alec Douglas-Home, was surprised to be woken by the Queen's official bagpiper early in the morning. It is said that Margaret Thatcher initially regarded trips to Balmoral as akin to 'purgatory'. In contrast, Harold Wilson enjoyed the informality of helping the monarch with the washing-up. Mrs Thatcher was so shocked that the Queen 'did the dishes' that she is said to have sent her a pair of rubber gloves as a present for Christmas.

The Queen was, of course, a gracious hostess. I was told that she personally checks her guests' rooms and selects books likely to be of interest to the prime minister and his wife, which are taken from the library and left by the bedside. Once we arrived, we travelled to Birkhall, the Prince of Wales's private residence in Scotland, for afternoon tea with Prince Charles. By 6 p.m., I was sitting down with the Queen to bring her up to date on events, in advance of the barbecue she had kindly organised for us. On the Sunday morning we joined the royal family for the service at Crathie Kirk, during which four-year-old John and two-year-old Fraser made a lot of noise, and after a lunch we introduced them to the Queen. She was surrounded by her corgis and the boys were delighted and shocked in equal measure when she told one of her dogs to 'shut up'.

It was time to return to London – and the various challenges that the autumn had in store for us.

I had decided that we would start the season with a major appeal for a 'new politics'. I saw this as essential if we were to tackle successfully the big challenges that we faced as a country: security, global competition, climate change, rising aspirations. I began the appeal with an interview in the *Daily Telegraph*, an attempt to reach beyond Labour's traditional base. Over the summer I had also talked at length to the Liberal Democrat leader, Menzies Campbell, inviting him to join us in a political arrangement that would see through the next stage of reform. My point to him was that the divisions between Labour and the Liberal Democrats over Iraq would soon be behind us – I told him we were about to leave.

My subsequent speech at the National Council for Voluntary Organisations called for a politics that drew on the widest range of talents and expertise, not the narrow circles of party or power. This was, I said, the politics of mainstream Britain and it was here that a new progressive consensus could be built. The day after my speech I showed up at a citizens' jury event at Bristol Brunel Academy, and at the press conference afterwards reaffirmed that Labour had to reach out to those who might not be thought of as our traditional supporters.

To his credit, Ming was enthusiastic about working together. The problem, I found, was the Liberal Democrats were a very individualistic and splintered group. Ming and I found plenty of common ground with each other but the two parties could not forge an alliance for common action. As a result, politics would continue to be dominated by the usual Tory–Labour fist fight.

Terrorism, floods, foot and mouth, and, as I recall in Chapter 15, the run on Northern Rock: the crises kept coming. And I was told in mid-September – just after I'd chaired a COBRA meeting on foot and mouth and before I left for the Labour Party conference – that we now had an outbreak of bluetongue, a viral disease spread by midges that had affected sheep and cows in Suffolk. New to the UK, it had been killing livestock across Europe where infected animals had been destroyed. I feared at that stage we were set for another controversial cull. However, following a conference call with Hilary Benn and the Chief Vet, it was confirmed that because the disease was not passed animal to animal, the mass slaughter was not needed.

Immersed in the business of governing, I had never wanted an early general election. So, prior to September, I had given no thought at all to calling an early election despite the gains we were seeing in the polls, and the apparently desperate state of the Conservative Party searching for direction under David Cameron. In early August as I left for holiday, Spencer Livermore, who oversaw strategy, had left a private note on my desk urging me to consider an early election, but I had put it aside and did not read it until September, by which time others would also be pressing me to take this path. Of course, I would have preferred my own mandate, but even as party conference season approached I had not looked at any internal polling figures, nor discussed the prospect of an election with any of my Cabinet colleagues. When we met as a political Cabinet at Chequers before the summer the issue had not even been raised.

After all the intensity of August, though, and with so many crises to deal with, I made an important error. As the party conference season got under way, I wrongly drew the conclusion that no damage would be caused by not explicitly ruling out an election, and I mistakenly allowed the speculation to mount. I was handed some polling but because I was not planning an election did not bother to study it in any detail. Things soon got out of hand: my mistake allowed MPs, delegates and, of course, ministers to begin to talk up the idea, and soon it was the talk of the conference. In a Sunday morning preconference interview with Andrew Marr, I ducked his insistent questioning by saying that whenever the time came for a decision the issues would be clear. And then, in an unguarded moment during a Q&A on the Labour conference floor, the journalist Mariella Frostrup asked: 'So when will the general election be, then?' I replied: 'Charming as you are, Mariella, the first person I would have to talk to is the Queen.' This offhand remark seemed to strengthen an already gathering wave of media speculation.

This conference, my first as leader, saw us announce major new policies: a more personalised health service, a reformed exam system in schools, and new employment opportunities for the disabled. After starting my speech with a tribute to the British people for the way they came through the crises we faced in the summer, I ventured into the personal by turning to what lay behind my commitment to public service. I would never forget, I told the audience, my father's words: 'we must be givers as well as getters'. 'Put something back,' he had said, 'and by doing so make a difference . . . this is my moral compass.' The phrase 'moral compass' led to a stand-up row with *The Times* who suggested I had stolen it from the American senator John Kerry, who had used it in his presidential campaign three years earlier. The link, they claimed, came via my friend Bob Shrum, who had assisted with the speech and worked as Kerry's campaign strategist. In truth, it was a phrase I had used repeatedly when talking about my father; indeed, when he died in 1998, I had invoked it in writing his eulogy. The article attacking me had been written by a well-known Conservative who also assailed my use of the words 'I will never you let down' – a sufficiently commonplace phrase that Donald Trump would later use it in his inauguration speech and no one alleged plagiarism. I was angry, as I told the editor of *The Times*, that his paper had chosen to make unfounded claims without first checking with me. But I spent far more time on what now seems a trivial issue than I should. A few days earlier *The Times*'s stablemate the *Sun* had launched a campaign against us demanding that we hold a referendum on the draft EU Treaty. These were the first two indications that even in areas where our approach would be the same as Tony Blair's, the Murdoch press would be my adversary whereas they had long been his friend.

I returned to No. 10 confident that the party was in good shape. We could afford just one billboard campaign at the time, but its slogan 'Not Flash, Just Gordon' seemed to have some resonance. Nevertheless, I was still not focused on the prospect of an election. As prime minister, though, you have got both power and responsibility. Your power is that you alone make a decision about matters like elections. The responsibility is to listen to advice.

On Sunday 30 September, Sarah and I had lunch at Chequers with the former chairman of the US Federal Reserve Alan Greenspan and his wife, the NBC correspondent Andrea Mitchell, and with Bob Shrum and his wife Marylouise. After lunch, I had a meeting with my key advisers – Ed Balls, Ed Miliband, Damian McBride, Spencer Livermore, Ian Austin, Gavin Kelly, Sue Nye, Douglas Alexander and Bob. This was the first time we had come together as a group to seriously examine the possibility of an early election. And for most of them it was the first time they had visited Chequers.

When we sat down, my question was: why not run the full term? This was my preference: with a guarantee of three years in power, there was no point in risking our already secure majority. Ed Balls said he would be the devil's advocate and set out the arguments against a snap poll – most, at this stage, were in favour. The American pollster Stan Greenberg, who had worked on Labour campaigns since 1997, had given us a poll that looked good but no one yet had the results of a poll that he was now undertaking that concentrated on marginal seats.

As we were meeting, the Conservatives were already briefing a pre-election, or perhaps an anti-election, ploy – one that would subsequently be dropped when they were in government – which was the abolition of inheritance tax for all but millionaires. Reforms in inheritance tax were certainly possible. We had contemplated reforming it the year before, but the Conservatives' proposal would give away £1 billion to the top 1.5 per cent in the country. We were too slow off the mark in deflecting what was an opportunistic move and the announcement gave the Conservatives a polling boost.

I had other things on my mind. The summer's foot-and-mouth outbreak had delayed my long-planned first visit as prime minister to Iraq. When I chose one of the few days available to me before Parliament resumed to make the trip, my decision was labelled a 'stunt' because it would coincide with the Tory conference. Even John Major was trotted out to complain about the 'cynical timing'. I was due to make my first statement as prime minister on the situation in Iraq the following Monday in Parliament. It would have been very strange if I had given such an important statement without having visited the country in person as prime minister.

In the event, on 1 October, I flew overnight to Kuwait, arriving at 6 a.m. and I was in Baghdad by 9.30 a.m. In rapid succession, I conferred with leaders of the different and divided factions; met with US General David Petraeus and Ambassador Ryan Crocker, who reported on the results of the surge around Baghdad; flew to meet our troops in Basra, where I went around shaking hands individually, and then, after an operational update from Brigade Operations Staff, I addressed them as a group. In interviews, I said that I expected 1,000 of our troops to be home by Christmas. By the evening I was on the way home, arriving back at Heathrow just after midnight.

On my return, I continued business as usual – visiting the Institute of Biochemical Engineering at Imperial College London, in advance of our launch of the Sainsbury Review of Science and the announcement of our intention to invest £1 billion over the next three years to boost business innovation and technology; holding meetings on the Pre-Budget Report at which we decided to proceed with the sensible reform of inheritance tax that we had postponed the year before; opening a new cardiac centre at a Basildon hospital ahead of the Darzi Review on the NHS; agreeing with the London mayor, Ken Livingstone, that the Crossrail project connecting London from east to west would now have the funding to go ahead. But all of this was portrayed as Labour gearing up for an election.

I cannot write about the events of 5 and 6 October 2007 without regret. Knowing that a Conservative election campaign would return to some of the anti-immigration themes of 2005, I spent the early morning of 5 October making notes for a speech on immigration, a speech that would recognise the issue as important, yet not brush it under the carpet as Labour had been accused of doing in the past.

However, within a few hours any idea of an early election was finally over. At 8.30 a.m., I convened a meeting in Downing Street. All my closest advisers were present, except Ed Balls, who was away in Yorkshire. Douglas Alexander, who from an early age had master-fully coordinated election campaigns in Scotland and the UK, had discovered that the party did not have the resources that were needed for an election. I now found, to my dismay, that I had inherited a party organisation where the parlous state of our finances put us one step away from insolvency: Labour owed £30 million in bank loans, overdrafts and in repayable loans given to us for the 2005 election by a small number of donors – and many were now pressing their con-tractual rights to be repaid. I had recruited Nigel Doughty, the highly successful head of Doughty Hanson & Co. who had doggedly stood by Labour through thick and thin, and my friend of many years, John Mendelsohn – now Lord Mendelsohn – to devise a strategy to stave off insolvency. A year later, J. K. Rowling and her husband Neil came to Labour's aid with a generous £1 million donation. But the rescuing of a near-bankrupt party was in its early stages. There was no chance that we could match previous election spending or even afford the advertising and staffing we would require. The final bill for the 2005 general election campaign had been £16 million: we had a third of that available in 2007.

I was also given the latest polling figures – which showed we were close or even behind in key marginal seats currently held by Labour in the south-east. This, the most comprehensive polling we had done, suggested we would win the election but only with a slender majority. 'Does anyone have anything else they want to say?' I asked near the end of the discussion. No one spoke, though Bob Shrum – who had changed his mind on the desirability of an election – said: 'Well, if the worst comes to the worst and you only have three years, there's a lot you can do. John Kennedy only had three years.' I then confirmed in telephone calls to each member of the Cabinet that there would be no election.

That day, I had agreed to entertain neighbouring residents at Chequers in the evening and allow local members of the community to visit for the first time. It was Sarah's idea: we were staying, at least for some days of the year, in what was, in effect, public property and it was right that the neighbours should have a chance to see it. I gave them a guided tour. They were keen to look at some of the historical artefacts, including those in its famous 'long room', which contains Oliver Cromwell's death mask and a journal kept by Lord Nelson. The next day, Saturday 6 October, I travelled back to Downing Street to plan how we would tell the country of the decision.

What followed was nothing short of a political catastrophe. Every Sunday paper was poised to cover our firing the starting gun of an election, so standing it down was going to come as a complete surprise. Conscious of this, I arranged for an interview with Andrew Marr at 4.30 p.m. on Saturday. We also needed to brief the political editors to enable them to hold their pages. This plan quickly fell apart amidst a leak. By the time Marr arrived for his interview, a vast media scrum was crowded outside Downing Street. The result was that we annoyed the entire media by giving an exclusive interview to the BBC while at the same time being unable to convey our message – a difficult one to deliver in any event – as the Tories would now be able to appear on television to blast me even before the interview was broadcast.

To Marr, and at the subsequent press conference, I said that there was too much work to be done to divert our attention to an early election. That had been my view all along. My instinct was always to get on with the job. But I went too far when, in the face of hostile questioning, I refused to concede that I had seen the public polling that lay behind the final decision. That was a mistake and much of the criticism was valid: I had mishandled decisions about an election that I had never wanted to hold in the first place. Harold Wilson said 'a week was a long time in politics'. I had gone from near-hero to near-zero in a day. Though I read the scorching criticism in the papers, I didn't have a lot of time for turning over the past.

I found that once things begin to go wrong, any mishap is blown out of all proportion and then a succession of mini-crises follows. Among them in the next three months were the loss of two computer discs containing personal details of 25 million individuals and 7 million families receiving child benefit; my late attendance at the signing of the Lisbon Treaty because of my appearance before the House of Commons Liaison Committee; the resignation of a very good Labour Party general secretary, Peter Watt, as a result of a party donor illegally contributing under a false name; and embarrassing Home Office leaks to the Conservatives about illegal immigrants – which allowed the Conservative leader to score points at Prime Minister's Questions using information he had but I did not. On top of all that there was a series of crises abroad, not just in Iraq and Afghanistan but inside the Commonwealth – with the expulsion of Pakistan before our November conference in Uganda, then the assassination of Benazir Bhutto, and at the turn of the year murderous violence in Kenya because of their disputed presidential election – in each of which Britain was called in to mediate.

I had tried to signal – and deliver – a fresh start, while realising how difficult that would be after ten years of the same party in government. I wanted to build a new coalition for change with a new focus on public service. I had widened our circle of advisers, bringing in former Tories Johan Eliasch and Quentin Davies as well as the Liberal Democrat MP Matthew Taylor. The idea of ministers who were part of a 'government of all the talents', or GOATS, was much talked (and joked) about. To that end, Mervyn Davies, the head of the bank Standard Chartered, was an invaluable addition as trade minister, and the well-respected financer Paul Myners came on board to strengthen the Treasury. But there were obstacles that stood between me and the new kind of politics I had in mind that I could not remove, and my outreach to the wider public never really got off the ground. Old and intractable issues such as Iraq and Afghanistan obscured the new. The array of mini- and full-blown crises that dominated the first few months cast a long shadow. It was these, rather than the initiatives which we had carefully planned, that would be remembered.

And in all candour, my attempts to move on from 'sofa' government perhaps inevitably fell short. As I explained in the previous chapter, I encouraged ministers to take full charge; wanted them, not the prime minister, to make major announcements; tried to promote less well-known ministers to the wider world as important decision-makers in their own right; and, to signal this, started my term with full strategy sessions designed to empower the Cabinet as a whole. At the same time, I had tried to revert to a more traditional No. 10 in which ministers alone made the formal decisions, and I held to a rule that all policy announcements were to be made by ministers to the House of Commons. But public expectations of the prime minister were different from what they had been even a decade or two earlier, and those expectations proved impossible to shift. When governmental responses were demanded to terrorism, floods, foot and mouth, avian flu or Northern Rock, it was the prime minister, not the responsible minister, who was the media's main port of call. In just about every area of central government, in fact, the media's questions landed on the doorstep of No. 10, no matter what the issue and which department was formally responsible.

So, when I now look back at the decisions we made in these first few months and how we made them, and compare this with the decision-making process of my predecessors and successors, I can see how and why the role of prime minister has kept expanding and that of the Cabinet has diminished.

Advancing his thesis of prime-ministerial government in his book *The British Cabinet*, John Mackintosh made the point that the prime minister's powers of patronage – his right to select ministers, advisers and officials – made his appointees far more dependent on him than ever he was on them. But Mackintosh was writing in the 1960s. Since then, the transformation of the media and public perceptions has magnified the role and personality of the prime minister as the public face of the government. This is even more true (as we shall see at the end of the next chapter) when it comes to foreign affairs where, in a departure from past practice, prime ministers are now in regular contact with their counterparts around the world.

Unlike the American president, Britain's prime minister is not directly elected and is certainly not the head of state. Nonetheless, the prime minister is now defined by their relationship with the public via the media rather than with Cabinet. Every day, twice a day, my spokesperson met the press and had to be ready not only to respond to every passing issue of the moment but also to convey my personal view of it. I had considered ways round this, such as the idea of sharing the role of spokesperson among a group of ministers on rotation and having them make their press briefings to camera rather than in a closed room full of journalists. Certainly it would have been considered a dereliction of duty on the part of the prime minister if at any point their spokesperson was unavailable to speak and answer questions for the government. A restoration of what we traditionally thought of as Cabinet government was simply not possible when the engrained expectation was for the prime minister's office to answer instantaneously the media's questions on any remotely important government action.

Our politics needs collective decision-making and, as I have suggested, no leader can succeed without an expert and committed team working alongside them. But no Cabinet – not even one sitting in permanent session – could keep up with the demands for such instant responses. Instead, the process of government came to rely even more on a close-knit team at the centre. Even if Cabinet was supposed to be the sole inner circle of decision-makers, there came to be another inner circle. Our critics referred to them as 'courtiers', a 'cabal', a 'clique', but someone had to deal with the stream of issues that constantly arrived on the prime minister's desk every day. Formally these advisers – who were, in the main, young, up-and-coming and very bright experts in their own right – may have had no power to make decisions but in practice they became among Britain's most important decision-makers. Indeed, much of what the Cabinet now does according to textbook constitutional theory is, in practice, done by these advisers acting as a kind of unelected Cabinet.

It was not, I found, a good system for governing, nor is it one that will endure without mounting criticism. The problem lies in the lack of accountability. Tony's solution was to use so-called Orders in Council to formally empower his top two advisers, but while this legitimised their decision-making power it did not make them any more accountable. We can, and perhaps should, devise rules that hold all those who take decisions to account. In my three years in No. 10 I tried, with varying degrees of success, to ensure greater ministerial control over the decision-making process. In May 2007, and later again in November, I asked Ed Balls to be minister in charge of No. 10 and the Cabinet Office, but understandably he preferred to be a departmental minister in his own right and I felt it wrong to deny him that chance. He was probably right to refuse: whoever I brought into that job would, I knew, be constantly accused of being an unelected second prime minister. But without more ministerial oversight than a prime minister or a junior minister or two can provide, government *with* advisers can all too easily become government *by* advisers, and even government *for* advisers. As the complexity and scale of government grows ever greater, the legitimate demands for accountability mean we will have to find new ways – a reorganisation of No. 10, reform of the Cabinet Office, a better system for appointing ministers and stronger parliamentary scrutiny – both to manage this century's new inner circle of decision-makers and to hold it to account.

CHAPTER 12

2008: REFORM BEFORE THE STORM

2008 was to bring the global financial storm, but in advance I had marked it out as the year of reform. I chose New Year's Day to make my first visit of 2008 – to Wexham Hospital in Slough – where I announced we would celebrate the sixtieth anniversary of the NHS by rebuilding it for the next sixty years. The NHS, I said, was not just a public service but a personal service. It was, and would remain, universal, but it could not be one-size-fits-all. Patients should be able to choose not only their doctor: they should have in their own hands a far wider range of choices about how, where and when they were treated. Health was on the agenda again. Then, unexpectedly on 2 January, a fire broke out at the Royal Marsden Hospital in London, a leading cancer treatment centre, destroying half of the roof. The next day, I spent time with patients who had been evacuated to nearby Royal Brompton Hospital and met fire officers at Chelsea Fire Station.

The following week, in a speech at the Florence Nightingale School of Nursing at King's College London, I set out what I saw as a consistent theme for the year: we could not rest on the advances made since 1997 but needed to drive a new agenda of personalisation in the delivery of public services. If the challenge since 1997 had been increasing capacity, the challenge now was improving quality. Instead of what were all too often run-of-the-mill public services – what some called 'bog standard' – impersonally delivered, I wanted all public services – the NHS, schooling, policing, welfare and housing – tailored to individual need, quick to respond, more professional in delivery, with, at all times, the focus on the requirements of those we served.

The priority of personalisation – as opposed to privatisation – was bound to be less exciting for the media, but I felt sure that public servants, most of whom were motivated to join up because they wanted to make a difference, would respond to this new agenda. It was radical because we were challenging the view that you had to go private if you wanted personal attention focused on your particular needs, with hands-on service tailored to your own individualised requirements.

In education, in particular, I was trying to find a way to ensure that the 93 per cent of children who were in state schools could enjoy the same educational advantages as the 7 per cent whose parents paid for schooling in the independent sector; and to do so without necessitating a huge increase in public spending. Our reforms to schools would include more emphasis on tutoring, mentoring and personalised learning. In housing, we would widen the range of individual choices available for buying, like shared equity mortgages, and offer new opportunities for those renting. In welfare – especially for the disabled – the emphasis would now be on the capabilities of the individual and the potential of each claimant. In policing, the general public, including victims of crime, would have more say in how policing and justice were carried out.

The agenda came alive in what we planned for health. In my January speech, I said the NHS had to be equipped to meet the higher individual expectations of the patient. With patients living longer, end-of-life care in need of expansion and higher expectations all round on the quality of care provided, we had to show how we could combine health and social care in a way that offered a service best suited to patients' needs – whether it be home help once a week or twenty-four hours a day bedside care in a hospital. By giving greater attention to an individual's diet, nutrition, exercise and habits like smoking and drinking, we could do more to prevent people from getting sick, rather than just treating them when they fell ill. And what seemed medical miracles accessible to only a few today should become medically routine and available to all who needed them tomorrow. Cutting-edge technologies, techniques from genetics to stem-cell therapy and life-saving drugs to prevent, alleviate or cure conditions like Alzheimer's – which no one but the very wealthy could afford – reinforced the case for the insurance-based, tax-funded service we had.

Alan Johnson and his deputy Ara Darzi proved effective partners in delivering health reform. My personal relationship with Ara got off to an unexpected start just before I became prime minister. One of his friends was my parliamentary private secretary, Ann Keen, a former nurse who as nursing minister chaired an excellent review of the profession. She told him of a cyst I had complained about on my back. Because I did not want questions to be asked about my health in the months leading up to entering No. 10, I wanted his confidential advice on what needed to be done. If the cyst was cancerous, I would of course have had to deal with it in a way that would become public. In any event, Ara agreed to operate. He came to my Downing Street flat one evening with his scalpels, needles and other surgical equipment, and for some reason the metal detector did not pick them up. I lay on the dining table and he gave me a local anaesthetic and removed the cyst. Ara soon reported back that the cyst, fortunately, was as benign as the metal detector.

Ara led the national review to plan the course of the NHS over the next decade. On his advice, GP practices and local health centres moved centre stage in the reformed NHS by expanding their range of health checks and screenings, ranging from blood tests to electrocardiography and ultrasound. 15 million people with a long-term condition, from asthma to diabetes, would have a personal care plan tailored to their needs and circumstances. Freely flowing information about results and league tables comparing performance would in future tell patients how hospitals, departments and doctors were performing and allow them to choose between them. The income of hospitals and GPs would in future depend on how much they improved their patients' health.

The focus on outcomes rather than inputs was the right test. By 2010 Labour policy had helped the NHS achieve a 22 per cent fall in cancer deaths, a 52 per cent reduction in fatalities from circulatory diseases among men under seventy-five, the lowest infant mortality rate ever, and all our waiting-time targets – no more than four hours for treatment at A&E, forty-eight hours to see a GP, sixty-two days before cancer treatment and eighteen weeks prior to hospital operations – were being met. The NHS was never going to be perfect – as graphically illustrated by the failure of effective regulation and supervision at Mid-Staffordshire Foundation Trust – but it now stood in marked contrast to the dilapidated Victorian hospitals, demoralised staff and chronic underfunding we had inherited.

I was committed to do far more on public health, especially in narrowing the gap between rich and poor, and in November 2008 we asked Sir Michael Marmot, a leading expert in public health at University College London, to review inequalities in health with a view to introducing a new Equality Act. Earlier equalities legislation had created positive duties on public authorities to give due regard to promoting equality by sex, race and disability. The new Equality Act, passed just before the 2010 general election, put increased emphasis on rooting out deeper social and economic inequalities. It was pioneered by Harriet Harman, who had, more than anyone, put gender equality on the map. But still a manual worker in a city like Glasgow had a life expectancy of ten years less than a professional counterpart in Surrey or Sussex. Infant mortality was twice as high in poorer income groups. This arithmetic of deprivation in the Britain of the twenty-first century was a disgrace – and, if I had stayed in power, closing this unacceptable gap would have been one of my priorities.

After he took over as Health Secretary in 2009, Andy Burnham and I discussed how we could take the next bold step in health modernisation: integrating health and social care. Colin Currie, who had joined as an adviser on health in No. 10, proved to me that the only way forward was to bring the two services together and expand their range. In 2010, we stood on an election manifesto that guaranteed to elderly citizens – no matter the state of their finances – a minimum level of care available to all. This, we knew, would not be easy or cost-free. But neither had been our transformation of the NHS after 2002. While we expected people to continue to pay for accommodation costs in residential care if able to do so, Labour's plan was a universal deferred-payment system. No one would have had to sell their home during their lifetime to pay for residential care.

The NHS should have been an important reason for voting Labour in 2010. But many had forgotten the pre-1997 NHS and did not fear a return to those dark days. While in the run-up to the 2010 election the Conservatives proclaimed they accepted our health settlement, the NHS is at the time of writing two-thirds of the way through the most austere decade in its history. Whereas health spending grew by an annual average in real terms of 4.5 per cent in the three years that I was in No. 10, average annual growth this decade has been only 1 per cent; and, with many health trusts in deficit, 4 million on waiting lists, targets on waiting times and A&E treatment missed, a £10 billion maintenance backlog, social care in crisis and staff morale lower than ever, many NHS services are close to breaking point. The issue today is not just how we improve performance through reform: it is how much we are prepared to pay for a good NHS. In future we will need to spend far more than we do currently – and we now need a similar kind of refinancing to the 1 per cent rise in employees' and employers' National Insurance of 2002. Once again, we have to explain what any new funding is for, why other ways of funding do not work and what it can achieve for British families.

The NHS has been a cause throughout my life and time in government. So, when Sarah encouraged me to join an online campaign when it was under attack, this time from opponents of Obamacare in America, I sent my first ever tweet to say what I had learned from my own life and believed heart and soul: 'The NHS makes the difference between pain and comfort, despair and hope, life and death. Thanks for always being there.'

Reform was even more central to our agenda on education. I wanted to prove that state schools could be as good, pioneering and geared to personalised learning as independent schools, giving each pupil as much individual attention as parents bought when they took their children into the private sector. Opportunity for all also meant supporting every part of a young life – from nursery and playgroups upwards right across to child health, youth crime and poverty prevention. Before I became prime minister, Ed Balls and I had thought through an innovation that would break down what we saw as self-defeating divisions between schools and other children's services. This led to our creation of the Department for Children, Schools and Families, which Ed led with enthusiasm and distinction. The aim was, as Ed said, to remove every barrier that prevented a child making the most of their abilities.

I was in no doubt that we could not create a modern egalitarian Britain without investing in the potential of every child. But if education is a moral imperative, it is also an economic necessity: we had to draw on the widest pool of talent.

In the past, countries in possession of raw materials enjoyed competitive advantage. Now what mattered most were skills, ideas, innovation and creativity. The old argument was that room at the top was limited so there was no point in educating everyone as far as their talents would take them: the economy didn't require it. This was encapsulated by Kingsley Amis's condescending notion that 'more means worse'. I believed Britain had been held back by this prejudiced way of thinking, whose arguments had since been decisively defeated by a fast-changing, knowledge-based global economy in which people continuously had to be trained and retrained. The rallying call for a successful modern economy could not be 'no room at the top'; it had to be 'no room at the bottom'.

Under Ed's predecesssors as Education Secretary – David Blunkett, Estelle Morris, Charles Clarke, Ruth Kelly and Alan Johnson – we had moved Britain from an education system which was below average to one that was above average, but as prime minister I wanted us to do much more. Our ambition, I believed, had to be nothing less than coming top of the global education league. While we had made major structural changes (academies being the most controversial) accompanied by huge new investments, our priority – indeed our stated mission – was always raising standards for all. That meant we could no longer accept any child nor any school falling behind. We had to aim high but also eliminate failure, thus Ed's controversial declaration that each failing school had no more than five years to prove themselves or be taken over.

As with the NHS and children's services, all of this required a more personalised kind of support. As I told the Labour conference in 2007, 'learning personal to each pupil – education available to all' was our mantra, 'not one size fits all, but responding to individual needs'. Our reforms included individual tutoring, customised teaching, personalised learning plans and where we could afford it one-to-one lessons for children falling behind.

At one of our events to make 'every child a reader', I read to a six-year-old at a school in Tower Hamlets who had been unable to make any progress until he had been given a personal tutor. He told me he wanted to be the best reader in Britain – reminding me that if we can capture the imagination of a child, anything is possible. These reforms went hand in hand with the early opening of 400 academies and more encouragement for universities to open them in deprived areas; the extension of Teach First, an American-born scheme that brought the best graduates into teaching within the inner cities; and the expansion of both the numbers and quality of teachers. By 2010, there were 50,000 more teachers than in 1997, now backed up by

190,000 support staff. Over 150 new schools were built with many more planned. Even after taking inflation into account we had nearly doubled total spending on education from just over £50 billion when we came into office to just under £90 billion when we left. In addition, as well as providing free nursery education for three- and four-year-olds we delivered by 2010 an amazingly successful innovation: Sure Start centres in every community – 3,500 in all – that combined health and educational services for the very young (all like the one I visited in May 2009, mentioned in the Introduction).

Having seen so many of my own school friends leave education for good at sixteen, despite having the ability to stay on, I had pushed for Education Maintenance Allowances – weekly cash allowances worth up to £30 that helped young people from low-income families stay on in school or college. This was something I had long thought important. As a young MP, I had run a 'Back to School' campaign with the Scottish *Daily Record* to encourage children to stay on in education. At one point, I had even considered removing child benefit from the parents of over-sixteens to pay grants directly to teenagers who stayed on at school. I won out against early opposition both from the Treasury and the Department for Education against the provision of maintenance allowances, and, by 2010, about 650,000 young people – a third of sixteen- to eighteen-year-olds in England – received these enabling them to stay on in education. It angers me to this day that in 2010 the incoming coalition government abandoned this help. In a decade when young people need skills and qualifications more than ever, too many British young people leave education forever at sixteen.

Of course, one of the best ways of continuing in education is through apprenticeships, and I tried to reinforce my support for them when, on the day of my first Budget in 1997, I refused to use Gladstone's famous red box and instead my photo call outside No. 11 revealed a new Budget box made by apprentices from the Rosyth Dockyard in my constituency. For some reason, the Treasury returned it to me after I left government and this treasured possession was, for a while, on public display – alongside the tie and suit I wore delivering one of my Budgets – in the National Museum of Scotland in Edinburgh.

In 2002, every sixteen- and seventeen-year-old with five GCSEs was granted the right to a Modern Apprenticeship. With the Apprenticeships, Skills, Children and Learning Act in 2009, we created an automatic legal right to not just qualified sixteen- and seventeen-year-olds but eighteen-year-olds too. By 2010, there were four times as many apprentices as in 1997. Side by side with this, 'Train to Gain' – financial support for in-work training – became a flagship initiative to upgrade workplace skills.

But there was one area where the Labour government got it spectacularly wrong and where I lost out when advocating a different course: the financing of higher education. On our desks when we came to power were the recommendations of the Dearing Committee to introduce tuition fees. In 1998, we accepted a watered-down version of this – £1,000 a year upfront fees for higher-income students, with tuition still free for 40 per cent. This did not satisfy the leading universities, who argued that their fee income was insufficient. I agreed that universities had to be properly funded, as we encouraged more young people to enter, and did not doubt that graduates should share in meeting the cost of tuition with parents and government. But at the same time, I was worried about who might be financially hurt or discouraged from university. As early as June 2000, I commissioned a Treasury paper which showed how a loan system to pay for tuition costs was the wrong answer. The Department for Education's proposal – and Tony's – was a version of the Australian system: variable fees capped at £3,000 per year.

This led to a battle royale inside government. At the Treasury, we had been investigating an alternative to tuition fees in the form of a graduate tax. Our analysis concluded that, with middle-class university entry almost at saturation point, our target of 50 per cent participating in higher education could only be met if we widened participation to those from less well-off backgrounds, who were traditionally under-represented. The advantage of a graduate tax – unlike the system of fees then in place – was that it would make university study genuinely free to students at the point of delivery: meaning students from poorer families, who were much more likely to be 'loan-averse', would be faced with incurring a future tax liability rather than having to take out a loan. The main drawback would be the extra cash cost in the short term – but this was something I would have been prepared to fund.

In the thirteen years after 1997, university admissions grew from less than 40 per cent to 46 per cent. This happened because of higher school attainment at secondary school, the removal of the cap on student numbers, and the increased routes to higher degrees, especially from further-education colleges, which now represent 10 per cent of all graduates. But while we increased participation from low-income groups, the relative chances of low- and high-income students getting to university barely changed, particularly at the most prestigious universities where entry rates for disadvantaged students changed little. My frustration with our lack of progress in widening access led to one notable incident.

Back in 2000, when we celebrated the thirtieth anniversary of the Equal Pay Act, which had been introduced by Barbara Castle, at a TUC reception in her honour, I raised the case that had already been publicised in the newspapers of Laura Spence, a young northern student who had been rejected by Oxford on the basis of examiners' notes which assessed her as not suitable for the university. I said her exclusion was a scandal and called on Oxbridge to reform its entry procedures. The minute I sided with Laura, the *Daily Mail*, the *Telegraph* and *The Times* – all of which had previously been sympathetic to her – reversed their positions. I was accused of dumbing down, of abandoning the objective of excellence, of denigrating the good intentions of our ancient universities. Faced with the hostility of Oxbridge and having little support from my colleagues, I fought the issue to a draw. Laura went to Harvard and I focused on widening university admissions, monitored by a new Office for Fair Access to ensure universities set out clear plans for recruiting students from under-represented or disadvantaged backgrounds. Spend on improving access for working-class students doubled from under £400 million to nearly £800 million, not least through the 'Aim Higher' programme – again, sadly, scrapped by the coalition government – which supported university outreach through mentoring schemes, masterclasses and summer schools.

The final decision on tuition fees was made at a meeting of the Domestic Affairs Cabinet Committee, chaired by John Prescott, in January 2003. During the committee's deliberations, Charles Clarke, the Education Secretary, conceded that his proposals for the introduction of fees were regressive. I said that my preferred option was to develop what I called 'a pooled, progressive tax', tapered according to the income of the graduate, so that over a time-limited repayment period, a higher-earning graduate would pay more than the lower-earning graduate who, for example, might have chosen to teach or work for a charity. The variable, deferred tuition fees advocated by the Department of Education would be unfair, I argued, especially for those taking career breaks to look after a child yet who would still have to pay back the full amount.

Friends of mine were prepared to vote tuition fees down because of the unfairness. In particular, Nick Brown, who had never voted against the government in his political life, warned me and others of the electoral consequences; and there can be little doubt that much of the youth vote moved towards the Liberal Democrats in 2005 because of the decision we made. In the Commons vote at the end of January 2004, the government won on tuition fees by only five votes – 316 votes to 311. In total, seventy-one Labour MPs voted against and nineteen abstained.

Despite my own doubts – and, more importantly, his – Nick and several of his colleagues who were opposed to the plans voted with the government out of loyalty. To help explain this decision to their constituents, I told them of a concession that had been won: maintenance grants to cover accommodation and food, which had been wrongly abolished in 1998, would be reinstated for low-income students, who would also receive some help with their fees.

When I became prime minister, I hoped to move the country from tuition fees to a graduate tax but the initial costs of such a move was prohibitive. Even if it were affordable, I also knew merely moving to a system of free tuition was not enough. We had seen that even without tuition fees in Scotland – it was a Labour administration that first rejected them – maintenance grants were being cut, hurting poorer students. The fee cancellation was being funded by reducing grants and dramatically cutting college places. In the absence of a better grant system to pay for books, accommodation and living expenses, free tuition had, in fact, become a benefit to students from higher-income backgrounds.

But there were changes we could make that would transform a loan into something closer to a graduate tax – and that is what we did. The key was to convert what was seen as a debt to be repaid in full to a graduate contribution more firmly based on the ability of the graduate to pay. If you started to pay back only on a fair share of your earnings, and thus after you were really able to do so, with repayments not charged at high rates of interest, then to all intents and purposes you now had a graduate tax – and, of course, it was collected like a tax linked to earnings, not by a collector running down your debt. Even so, we could only move in stages to a system where payments were no longer based on final debt but on actual earnings.

We announced graduates would be entitled to earn more before they started to pay anything and could have a longer period in which to pay. But because we had not yet moved to a full-blooded graduate tax, we hesitated to call it a 'graduate contribution'. We also took measures to ameliorate students' worries about what they had to pay in total: they would pay at fair rates of interest. And because we were worried that poorer students did not have enough money for their immediate expenses we increased the value of maintenance grants for poorer students.

The tuition-fee review Peter Mandelson had ordered from Lord Browne, the former chief executive of BP – which proposed raising the tuition fee ceiling from £3,000 to £9,000 – would have landed on my desk if we had been returned in 2010. It would have made the case for a graduate tax more pressing than ever, and so, at a later date, would proposals to raise the interest rate – to as high as 6.1 per cent in 2017 – at which students paid back their loans. For students starting in 2017 average debt on graduation will be just over £50,000. This is more than double the average debt students would have faced had the system remained unchanged after 2011. What's more, the starting point of repayment was meant to rise with average earnings after 2015. Yet by initially freezing it until 2021 at £21,000 and now at £25,000 for post-2012 students, and by retaining tuition fees at £9,250 until only 2019, the Conservatives have moved us further away from a graduate contribution towards a more rigid debt repayment system. Under the terms of the student-loan book sale, first-time graduates may now also find their loans reported on credit files – in breach of another promise. In time, we will come to the conclusion that what you pay should not be the so-called 'debt' you owe – 77 per cent won't clear their debt and interest charges within thirty years – but the percentage of your earnings that you can afford: in other words, a graduate tax in which the government shares the cost of higher education equitably with the graduate.

Before I became prime minister, my main role in decisions on law and order and policing was simply setting and settling the funding totals for police, prisons and the courts. But I felt that the public deserved a more personalised form of service delivery here too. As a result, I introduced our 'policing pledge', guaranteeing quick police response times, a more sympathetic approach to victims, and better neighbourhood policing. Under Jacqui Smith and then Alan Johnson in the Home Office – and Jack Straw at Justice – we worked to ensure local communities could do more to set their own local priorities: where to position police on the beat, CCTV, the lighting of streets, and how offenders discharged their community payback. We were innovative in other ways too: with the help of Britain's leading social entrepreneur Sir Ronald Cohen, we agreed to pilot what were called social impact bonds that paid charities by results – in this case a highly impressive success rate in rehabilitating young offenders in Peterborough.

Under the 1997–2010 Labour administration, crime fell by 40 per cent, with 7 million fewer crimes committed every year. Ours was the first government since records began under which crime went down and not up, a tribute not only to the professionalism of all our public servants but the 33,000 extra police – 17,000 more police officers and 16,000 new Police Community Support Officers – backed up by 26,000 extra prison places. Of course, problems remained – illegal immigration was one – but with police numbers rising and prison places expanding, why were we on the back foot on law and order? There were many reasons why we lost the battle – for example, one complaint from a victim of crime can send a more powerful message than any good set of statistics about cuts in crime – but a perhaps more important reason was that our record was easily traduced because of the damage done by a series of leaks over an eighteen-month period, emanating from the private office of the Home Secretary to the then Tory immigration spokesman and now First Secretary of State in Theresa May's government, Damian Green.

For what seemed to be the promise of a job with the Conservative Party, a young civil servant who had previously run as a Tory council candidate in his home town of Sunderland was handing Green highly sensitive Home Office documents, including detailed confidential figures and private advice to Jacqui (advice that I had never seen) – powerful ammunition to use at Prime Minister's Questions if it fell into the hands of the leader of the Opposition.

I could never understand why David Cameron appeared to have

information I did not even know existed. But from my very early Prime Minister's Questions, he regularly seemed to make use of this stolen information. The embarrassing Home Office memos, some of which went direct to the press, included internal data on illegal immigrants, stop-and-search, security breaches, operational codes for the police, forecasts of rising crime, even a list of Labour MPs rebelling over terrorist laws. It was no comfort that after the police traced them to Green and the civil servant, they botched their response, with the House of Commons' serjeant-at-arms sanctioning a police raid on Green's office without a warrant. What should have been a simple matter of dealing with a politically motivated leaker turned into a *cause célèbre* about the freedom of Parliament and the press. A problem others had created for us escalated into a public relations nightmare for the government.

But more important and wider lessons were being learned: it takes both reform and resources to assure high-quality public services. Reform without investment is a cynical slogan. Investment without reform will yield too little. 2008 proved we needed both.

In foreign affairs too, there was a period of calm before the financial storm. In the early months of 2008, before the crisis hit hardest, I was able to focus on international issues beyond Iraq and Afghanistan (which I discuss in the next chapters), undertake long-planned foreign visits and do something to restore Britain's international standing after the setbacks over Iraq.

There was a time when diplomacy amounted to the Foreign Secretary sending off telegrams and ambassadors on the ground doing the talking. The management of foreign affairs has been revolutionised since then. Now prime ministers regularly meet their counterparts at annual gatherings – the United Nations annual General Assembly, the G8, the NATO Council and European summits – and on any day you can talk by phone or video. It is yet another instance in which the direct involvement of the prime minister has so markedly expanded. Communications between governments that once took months, were highly impersonal and conducted in the main below the level of national leaders, now rely on constant personal contact at the top. This means that for a prime minister today, foreign affairs involve not only the calculation of national interests and ideas but the cultivation of a wide range of different individual relationships.

With the Asian economy on its way to becoming bigger than that of America or the West, I started 2008 with visits first to Delhi to persuade Prime Minister Manmohan Singh of the value of a world trade agreement, and then to Beijing to cement the strategic economic partnership with China that I had been building while chancellor. As always I stressed our human-rights concerns. For the first time Premier Wen held an open town-hall meeting where he and I answered questions from local citizens. Our talks ranged freely from the debt he owed to the Scottish moral philosophers David Hume and Adam Smith, to his prediction that the Internet would bring democracy to China. I asked him for China's support for the release from house arrest of the Burmese leader whose freedom I had long supported, Aung San Suu Kyi. Strengthening the relationship with China was even more imperative than I realised at the time. When the financial crisis struck with full force and Britain was to lead in forging an international response, securing Chinese engagement was essential.

Keen as well to strengthen our ties with our European partners after disagreement over Iraq, I conferred in Berlin with Chancellor Merkel and was in regular touch with Nicolas Sarkozy in Paris before his state visit to Britain at the end of March. Sarkozy and I formed a strong working relationship. Around this time he informed me privately of his upcoming marriage to Carla Bruni. Again, these European partners, as well as Prime Minister Zapatero of Spain and the Portuguese president of the European Commission José Manuel Barroso, were to become major allies alongside Prime Minister Kevin Rudd of Australia in fighting the global economic recession.

I flew to Italy to see Prime Minister Silvio Berlusconi who was at the time beset by court cases threatening his survival in office. I knew he would present me with a box of Italian-made ties, as he always did. My staff asked what he would welcome in return. 'A friendly judge,' I joked. But the meeting had a serious purpose. He was preparing to chair the G8 in 2009. It was important that I recruit the Italians to the idea of greater global economic cooperation. This would later prove essential: had the advanced economies clung to the G8 as the premier forum of economic cooperation, it would have been impossible to create the larger G20 without which we could never have halted worldwide economic depression.

Our Italian journey had another important but far less political purpose: to meet the Pope. I knew, of course, that Pope Benedict was theologically conservative, but Sarah and I warmed to him as a person. We found we shared a passion for bringing education to the world's poor. In private he had an ease of manner at odds with his rather austere public image and he struck up an instant rapport with John and Fraser. Both had baulked at wearing suits, shirts and ties for the occasion; John eventually struck a compromise, wearing a tie on top of his favourite T-shirt.

Like prime ministers before me I was drawn to the Middle East, asking myself what contribution Britain, historically so engaged in the region, could make to the peace process. In July I became the first British prime minister to address the Israeli Knesset; I spoke to mark the sixtieth anniversary of the founding of the state of Israel. My father had visited Israel twice a year for decades. In my schooldays, he had shown me slides of people and places in Israel on an old film projector that kept breaking down. Now I was lighting a flame at the Yad Vashem memorial to the Holocaust in memory of the victims – I would also later visit Auschwitz to pay my respects – and was addressing Israel's leaders. The widely respected historian Martin Gilbert and his wife Esther joined Sarah and me on the visit. Martin generously helped with my speech. I urged all parties in the Israeli Parliament to support a permanent peace with the Palestinians. The phrase 'Next year in Jerusalem', used every year at the Passover commemoration of the Jews' wandering in the desert, should not just mean 'home at last', I said, but 'free from war at last'. Swords should be turned into ploughshares in such a way that there was never a need for swords again.

This was one of a series of meetings that I held in the region to help promote the peace process – with the leaders of Saudi Arabia, the UAE, Qatar, Oman and, of course, the Palestinians. King Abdullah of Saudi Arabia had made a state visit to Britain in October 2007. Then and later, often through his ambassador in Washington, I acted as a go-between for him with the Israeli prime minister Ehud Olmert, a friend of mine who was determined to find an ever-elusive settlement. In fact, the outlines of a settlement – a viable Palestine and a stable Israel with shared occupancy of Jerusalem – were already there on the table. The issue was how we could get agreement. At this point Tony Blair was travelling back and forth from London as Middle

East envoy and America continued to take the lead in negotiations. Nicolas Sarkozy, however, favoured a European initiative. I felt that to deliver a two-state solution we also needed a twenty-one-state solution – all the Arab countries agreeing a settlement with Israel – to which the king of Saudi Arabia was the key.

As had become the norm, any progress was swiftly followed by setbacks. Hopes rose in January 2009 after the latest ceasefire between Israel and Hamas, when I was part of a delegation that included other European heads of government that visited Egypt to pledge funds for the reconstruction of Gaza and the West Bank. That same day we all flew to Jerusalem to dine with Israel's major party leaders. But in the end there proved to be no way forward. Despite or perhaps because of his bold plans for peace, Olmert was besieged by accusations of corruption. King Abdullah, meanwhile, was ageing and in poor health.

At that Jerusalem dinner, Benjamin Netanyahu, then leader of Israel's opposition and soon to be prime minister, made clear that his overriding objective was not a two-state solution but preventing a nuclear Iran. Netanyahu was an old friend and colleague – we had been finance ministers together. I knew he was influenced by his father's long-expressed doubts about Iran's trustworthiness. His views were not to change. Israel was and is utterly committed to a Middle East with no nuclear states except their own. With British support, the Israelis had secretly and unceremoniously bombed Syria's nuclear facility in the autumn of 2007. Later, Netanyahu would bitterly oppose the international nuclear deal agreed with Iran in 2015 for not being tough enough. By 2009, with Netanyahu newly empowered as prime minister and holding quite different priorities from Olmert's, a two-state solution was off the table. Sadly, at the time of writing it still is.

In 2008 I was also able to push forward our agenda for international development. Douglas Alexander, our minister for international development, had worked with me since the 1980s. He had been passionate about eliminating global poverty since his schooldays and was one of a line of very successful development ministers, following Clare Short, Valerie Amos and Hilary Benn. I was fortunate now to be able draw on his very considerable skills and judgement in this and in many other areas. In November 2007, Jens Stoltenberg, the Norwegian prime minister, had visited No. 10 to launch the Global Health Partnership, a concerted attempt to fund a worldwide effort against preventable and curable diseases. In September 2008 at a special United Nations global education event, I launched Education for All, our initiative to get every child in the world to school by 2015. By now I was working closely with the champions of global education, Nelson Mandela's wife Graça Machel (one of my mentors), John Sexton the visionary president of New York University who was now creating the first Global Network University, President Kikwete of Tanzania whose pioneering initiative Big Results Now would become a model for all Africa, and Jim Wolfensohn, the former president of the World Bank whose commitment to a world free of poverty had transformed that institution. Education supported by aid was, I said, the best route out of poverty for millions.

In August 2008 I visited China a second time for the last days of the Beijing Olympics. It was in part a family trip. John and Fraser came with us, but with so many official meetings to attend we were fortunate to have with us taking charge of the children Melanie Derby, who for ten years, in and out of Downing Street, in London and in Scotland, was the best carer, comforter and friend. Our family and hers became and remain very close. I knew this would prove a more difficult trip diplomatically as the Chinese had publicly objected to my decision to meet the Dalai Lama that April, the outcome of which had been my agreement that Britain would change its position from favouring Tibetan independence to supporting 'autonomy within China' – ironically, the Dalai Lama's own policy. Even though the Chinese leadership rejected this as well, they recognised that we had gone some way to narrow our differences.

Although we had come to Beijing for the closing ceremony of the Olympics we were there in time to cheer on Tim Brabants as he took kayaking gold, sit behind Pelé at the football final and visit the British team in the Olympic Village. I would also greet the victorious medal winners off their plane when they landed back at Heathrow. As we watched the track and field competition, one moment brought back a painful memory: we sighed when our men's 4 x 100 m relay team dropped the baton – just as I had on my first sports day at secondary school. But another handover went more smoothly: when Boris Johnson and I spoke to cheering crowds at the British compound as Beijing passed the Olympic baton to London.

It is said that in their first term prime ministers typically focus on domestic issues and only in their second do they shift their attention to foreign affairs. Leaving aside each of these overseas endeavours, I did not have that luxury, for overshadowing every one of them were the most pressing foreign policy issues of all: Iraq and Afghanistan. For four years before I entered No. 10, and for the first time in decades, Britain had been fighting two major wars, both of which were going badly.

CHAPTER 13

IRAQ: HOW WE WERE ALL MISLED

For those of us who are of a certain age, there are memories we share, some that will never die. They become indelible threads, tragic and triumphant, in the time-bound fabric of our lives. And for more than half a century, they have come to us almost instantaneously on television.

On 11 September 2001, I happened to be sitting with Sue Nye and Ed Balls watching TV in the small temporary office in the Treasury that I had while the building was being renovated. We were waiting for the coverage of Tony Blair's speech on Europe to the Trades Union Congress in Brighton when the programme was suddenly interrupted with the first horrifying images of an attack on the Twin Towers in New York. A little under twenty minutes later, a second plane crashed into the World Trade Center. We then heard news of a plane flying into the Pentagon, followed by one crashing into a field in Pennsylvania that was probably on its way to the Capitol or White House. In a little over an hour and a half after the first plane struck, both of the Twin Towers lay in ruin and thousands had died unspeakable deaths, including sixty-seven British citizens.

There are moments in history that once lived through can never be forgotten. On that November day in 1963 I remember being in Kirkcaldy when I first heard of John F. Kennedy's assassination. I vividly remember too the real anxiety across the world at the time of the Cuban missile crisis the year before. And, nearly thirty years later, there were the unforgettable scenes from Germany when the Berlin Wall – seemingly such a permanent scar across the heart of Europe – came crashing down. That moment in 1989; the execution of Nicolae Ceauşescu on Christmas Day the same year; Yeltsin standing astride a Russian tank in defiance of an attempted coup in 1991: these events and their accompanying images marked a geopolitical shift that transformed the balance of power not just in Europe but across the entire world, a process that is still under way. And most recently, and sad to say, I will never forget waking up in the early hours of 24 June 2016 to hear David Dimbleby's confirmation that the British people had voted to reverse our decision of forty years before and leave the European Union. The finality of his words will stay with me always.

So it was on 11 September 2001. I cried at the carnage that had been inflicted on our closest ally, America, a place I often visited on official business and on holiday. I worried about friends and colleagues in New York – indeed, there were a number of Treasury officials there on that day. Fortunately they soon phoned to say they were safe. We then had to consider the possibility that what had happened was a prelude to further attacks in Europe – perhaps London. The whole of Whitehall went into lockdown. I received a series of security briefings, and across government, far into the night, we reviewed what measures to take if a terrorist assault were to hit the UK.

I sensed that once more we were at a historic turning point, and remember saying to Sue and Ed that everything would now change. While economics had dominated the previous decade, security and foreign policy, I predicted, would be front and centre in the coming one. And so it turned out, as 9/11 was followed by 7/7 and further terrorist atrocities in the UK in the ensuing years.

We knew within hours that the terrorists were working out of Afghanistan, that their funding came from Saudi Arabia and that the epicentre of their activities was the border with Pakistan. Almost immediately, George Bush invoked Article 5 of the NATO Charter which states that an attack on one member is an attack on all, and assembled a coalition to invade Afghanistan that eventually included fifty-one countries. The first combat operations of Operation Enduring Freedom began less than a month later on 7 October 2001. In Britain support for the United States was instinctive – which Tony encapsulated eloquently when he said we stood 'shoulder to shoulder' with America. But this instinct would be severely tested in the maelstrom that followed.

The connection between 9/11 and the military invasion of Afghanistan was completely clear, but later, when I first heard that war in Iraq was being planned, I asked 'Why Iraq?' Fifteen years on, the decision to go to war there remains the most controversial foreign-policy decision of our generation.

There was nothing new about UK military intervention overseas. Britain had sent troops to the Korean War in the 1950s, and had briefly waged war to reclaim the Suez Canal later that decade, fought in Malaysia during the 1960s, re-established control over the Falklands in the 1980s, and acted as part of an international coalition to halt Saddam Hussein's invasion of Kuwait in the 1990s. More recently, we had deployed UK forces to stop ethnic cleansing by Serb militias in Kosovo in 1998, participated in the Desert Fox operation in Iraq during the same year, and intervened in Sierra Leone in 2000. But Iraq in 2003 was different: unlike these other interventions, we participated in a full-scale occupation of another sovereign state for the first time since the Second World War. While Britain had stayed out of Vietnam in the 1960s – Harold Wilson having rebuffed Lyndon Johnson's request for a token presence ('a few Scottish bagpipers', as the president put it) – we would become not only America's fellow combatants in Iraq, with the second-largest contingent in the coalition force, but their biggest cheerleader too.

I know there are times when conflict cannot be avoided. While war is evil, war is sometimes the lesser evil. Force can be justified on humanitarian grounds, as was the case in the Balkans in the late 1990s or – as should have been the case – in Rwanda earlier that decade. But we should never wage war unless the cause is just. War must always be the last resort, proportionate, solely for the purpose intended, and likely to do more good than harm. Or, as I said to the Chilcot Inquiry into our involvement in the Iraq War, you cannot fight a just war unless you have grounds to believe you can create a just peace.

When I consider the rush to war in March 2003 – especially in light of what we now know about the absence of weapons of mass destruction – I ask myself over and over whether I could have made more of a difference before that fateful decision was taken. Strange as it may seem, chancellors have seldom been at the centre of decision-making in matters of war and peace. Indeed, in 1915, the then chancellor Lloyd George had to become minister of munitions in order to play a central role in Britain's effort in the First World War. The chancellor has not been a member of most War Cabinets: there was, for example, no Treasury representative in Churchill's War Cabinet or Thatcher's during the Falklands conflict. My official role leading up to the conflict was to find the funds for it.

At the time, therefore, I had as much and as little access to security and intelligence information as most other Cabinet ministers. For that reason, when I went before Chilcot in 2010, I defended our decision to go to war. I explained that Iraq had systematically defied the resolutions unanimously passed by the United Nations. That was and remains true. However, in retrospect, having reviewed all the information now available – not just that revealed by the Hutton, Butler and Chilcot inquiries but in America too – I feel I now understand how we were all misled on the existence of WMDs.

In 2002 and 2003 I was on the road to a head-on collision with Tony over three matters: the euro, the NHS and tuition fees. All coincided with our decision to go into Iraq. Embroiled in these battles, I was, rightly or wrongly, anxious to avoid a fourth area of dispute, particularly one that was not my departmental responsibility but the province of Tony, the Foreign Office under Jack Straw, and the Ministry of Defence under Geoff Hoon. Most of all, there was nothing at the outset that caused me to doubt the threat Iraq posed to regional stability and global order.

Nevertheless, I did make a number of requests for information. At my insistence, I was shown more of the up-to-date British intelligence which seemed to prove that Iraq had WMDs. Indeed, I had a number of private conversations with Sir Richard Dearlove, the head of MI6. His officials reported chapter and verse the evidence against Saddam and impressed upon me that it was well founded. I was told that they knew where the weapons were housed; I remember thinking at the time that it was almost as if they could give me the street name and number where they were located. I also knew that two of my Cabinet colleagues, Robin Cook and Clare Short, had doubts. But in the build-up to war neither approached me with any contrary information. In retrospect, I regret that I did not press as hard as I should have. By not questioning the evidence with sufficient rigour, I let myself and many others down, especially the families of the soldiers who would be lost in the conflict.

The major formal government meetings in the lead-up to our war with Iraq revolved around an inner circle of officials from No. 10, the Foreign Office and the Ministry of Defence. In March 2003, I was invited into what was, in hindsight, a rushed and last-minute discussion on post-war reconstruction. The Treasury then worked with the US to devise a new currency for Iraq using the Bank of England's contractors to print the notes. Beyond questions of financing, the Treasury had little involvement.

I did not know until after I left office of the Blair–Bush telephone call in December 2001 in which Tony appeared to agree in principle to support the American-led intervention in Iraq. When in early 2002 I heard through the Whitehall grapevine about the secret 'Iraq: Options Paper' by the Defence and Overseas Secretariat discussing various strategies for 'regime change', I asked to see it. But the version I eventually received turned out to be different from the original document. I admired Robin Cook for raising tough questions at a Cabinet discussion on 7 March but the evidence I was being given appeared to be accurate – that Iraq did possess WMDs.

Between April and July important steps to war were taken – decisions that I did not learn of until much later: at Tony's meeting with George Bush at his Crawford ranch in Texas on 5–6 April (at which Tony did not commit Britain to war with Iraq, but discussed with the president the first quarter of 2003 as a possible timeframe for action against Saddam Hussein); at the pre-Crawford discussion at Chequers on 2 April (in which there was a discussion among Tony's closest advisers of whether WMD or regime change should be given as the justification if the UK went to war); with Tony's July letter to the president stating 'I will be with you, whatever'; and with the No. 10 meeting around the Defence and Overseas Secretariat paper of 21 July, 'Iraq: conditions for military action'.

That paper stated that when 'the prime minister discussed Iraq with President Bush in Crawford in April he said that the UK would support military action to bring about regime change, provided that certain conditions were met'; these conditions were that efforts were first made to try to eliminate Iraq's WMDs through UN weapons inspectors, that the Israel–Palestine crisis was quiescent, that there was a workable coalition and efforts undertaken to 'shape' public opinion. When the paper was discussed in No. 10 two days later, on 23 July, Tony said: 'If the political context were right, people would support regime change.' 'We should work on the assumption that the UK would take part in any military action,' the minutes said, with the caveat that 'we needed a fuller picture of US planning before we could take any firm decisions'. In retrospect, I should have barged my way into these discussions.

On the international front, progress was seemingly being made: in early August, Iraq's foreign minister invited the UN secretary general, Kofi Annan, to send the international weapons inspector, Hans Blix, to Baghdad. I and many others thought, wrongly as it turned out, that tensions were now easing. It was the calm that preceded the storm. When Tony came back from a summer holiday during which he read up papers on Iraqi weapons, he was convinced that we were at a disadvantage because the press were assuming war was inevitable and yet the public had been given no real reason why. Having sent George Bush a memo in July about the need to shift public opinion, he now spoke to him at the end of August and they met early in September. At a press conference in Sedgefield, just before his meeting with Bush, Tony was more explicit about the threat Iraq faced and promised a dossier. This would show, he said, that without any question Saddam was still trying to develop a chemical, biological and, potentially, nuclear capability.

Geoff Hoon simultaneously sought approval from me for six separate 'urgent operational requirements' – new equipment now needed as an emergency. In the first days of September I was sufficiently worried to ask for evidence of the claims Tony had made about Iraq's weapons of mass destruction. I was sent what I now know to be the same evidence Tony had been given over the summer. The first was the 500-page paper 'Proliferation Study of Iraq', providing an in-depth examination of each of Iraq's programmes to develop weapons, and what was called an 'aide-memoire on Weapons of Mass Destruction and Proliferation' addressing several countries of concern including Iraq.

In the first document there were claims that Iraq had 'begun development' of ballistic missiles with a range of more than 1,000 km, was 'continuing to carry out research into nuclear weapons development', and 'could begin the production of mustard gas on a significant scale at any time and the nerve agents sarin and VX within weeks'. According to the study, Iraq's chemical and biological weapons (CBW) production capability had 'been dispersed to survive a military attack and UN inspections'. The second report said the regime had 'the necessary command and control structure necessary to deliver CBW weapons' and that Iraq was on 'a worldwide drive to acquire production-level quantities of materials for making solid rocket motors and a continued emphasis on guidance and control technology'.

The facts I was being given were unequivocal – Saddam had a capability to produce chemical and biological weapons and was trying to acquire nuclear weapons. Just before Parliament was recalled and the dossier published I agreed to Geoff Hoon's equipment requests, setting an initial overall ceiling of £150 million. I felt the answer was to be safe now rather than sorry afterwards. Jack Straw was at this time indicating that a genuine offer from Iraq to comply with UN resolutions would reduce the arguments for military action. I dictated an official note saying that it was right to prepare for all eventualities.

But in these months before the war, I had no idea that key decision-makers in America were already aware that the evidence on the existence of WMDs was weak, even negligible. We now know from classified American documents, which became public in 2011, that in the first days of September 2002 a report prepared by the US Joint Chief of Staff's director for intelligence landed on the desk of the US Defense Secretary, Donald Rumsfeld. 'Please take a look at this material as to what we don't know about WMD,' Rumsfeld then wrote to Air Force General Richard Myers. 'It is big,' he added. So it was.

Commissioned by Rumsfeld to identify gaps in the US intelligence picture, it is now clear how forcibly this report challenged the official view: 'We've struggled to estimate the unknowns . . . We range from 0% to about 75% knowledge on various aspects of their [Iraq's WMD] program,' the report stated. It conceded that US knowledge of the Iraqi nuclear weapons programme was based largely – perhaps 90 per cent of it – on analysis of imprecise intelligence. These assessments, the report said, relied 'heavily on analytic assumptions and judgment rather than hard evidence. The evidentiary base is particularly sparse for Iraqi nuclear programs.' The Americans thought Saddam possessed a viable weapon design, though this was qualified with the statement: 'We do not know the status of enrichment capabilities . . . We do not know with confidence the location of any nuclear-weapon-related facilities.' The same lack of intelligence was true of biological weapons – 'We cannot confirm the identity of any Iraqi facilities that produce, test, fill, or store biological weapons' – and chemical weapons: 'The specific agent and facility knowledge is 60–70 per cent incomplete . . . We do not know if all the processes required to produce a weapon are in place.' The Iraqis, it was reported, 'lack the precursors for sustained nerve-agent production', confirming that US intelligence could not identify any Iraqi sites producing the final chemical agent. And as for missiles and the Iraqis' ability to target countries like the UK with them, which was to be the subject of dramatic claims only a few weeks later, Rumsfeld was informed: 'We doubt all processes are in place to produce longer-range missiles.'

While the British paper I had been given suggested a capability if not a production programme, this highly confidential US evidence was a refutation not only of the claim that Iraq was producing WMDs but also of their current capability to do so. It is astonishing that none of us in the British government ever saw this American report.

As we were later to discover, the intelligence had not established beyond doubt either that Saddam Hussein had continued to produce chemical and biological weapons or that efforts to develop nuclear weapons continued. Christopher Meyer, the UK ambassador to Washington at the time, who had meetings with US officials on 12 September, said that 'US interlocutors all pointed more generally to the need not to get trapped into juridical standards of proof. The bulk of the case should rest on history and commonsense argument, rather than specific new intelligence. When it came to Saddam's WMD, absence of evidence was not the same as evidence of absence. We should not be afraid to argue that, just as in 1991, Iraq's programmes were probably much further advanced than we knew.'

Some in the US had evidence which doubted even Iraq's capabilities. In public, the administration said something different. In October 2002, one month after the report to Rumsfeld, President Bush went on record for the first time with the assertion that Iraq 'possesses and produces chemical and biological weapons' and was 'seeking nuclear weapons'. Instead of investigating further the evidence held by the Joint Chiefs, the American administration produced a ninety-two-page National Intelligence Estimate, which made no mention of any counter-evidence and instead focused on what it called 'Key Judgements'. The key judgements were that Iraq had continued its WMD programmes in defiance of UN resolutions and restrictions, had chemical and biological weapons as well as missiles with ranges in excess of UN restrictions, and that, if left unchecked, it probably would have a nuclear weapon within the next ten years.

Papers subsequently declassified during the Chilcot Inquiry show that the Ministry of Defence presented Tony with a UK military-options paper on 15 October 2002, stating that an urgent decision had to be taken: 'We need to decide this week . . . US military planning for an operation in Iraq is gathering pace,' it said. Three basic packages were outlined, with the third – the so-called 'northern' option – being the most ambitious. If this option was followed, Britain would deploy more than 300 tanks and armoured vehicles and a total of 28,000 troops, which would enter Iraq from Turkey. It would be 'a major element of the northern line of attack which the US now judge as essential', officials reported. Two weeks later, a memo was sent setting out Tony's support for this option, with him stipulating that the US should be informed of this for planning purposes.

But still evidence of Iraq's possession of WMDs remained thin. The UK Joint Intelligence Committee had compiled one report on the threat from Iraq in May 2001 which was inconclusive. They had undertaken another review in March 2002, ahead of Tony's trip to Crawford, which assessed that Iraq had some stocks of chemical weapons. But neither of the reports contained details on locations or quantities. 'Actually, our knowledge of Iraq was very, very superficial,' a senior SIS officer later said. 'We were small animals in a dark wood with the wind getting up and changing direction the whole time. These were very, very difficult days.'

The data and intelligence which formed the basis of the September dossier, 'Iraq's Weapons of Mass Destruction: The Assessment of the British Government', were reviewed at the Joint Intelligence Committee during September 2002.

While the US report that was not circulated outside the Pentagon concluded 'we cannot confirm the identity of any Iraqi facilities that produce, test, fill, or store biological weapons' and that 'we do not know with confidence the location of any nuclear-weapon-related facilities', the British dossier said that 'Iraq continued to produce chemical and biological agents' and that Saddam 'continues in his efforts to develop nuclear weapons'. We had moved from the UK papers in the summer which warned of Iraq's capability to produce weapons, to claims around the autumn dossier that there were major weapons programmes under way.

How did this happen? After all, members and advisers to the British intelligence community had their own doubts and caveats. Of course there were mistakes, like the claim Iraq had sought uranium from Africa. But during September the intelligence communities believed they had found new evidence, including from an Iraqi defector code-named 'Curveball', who told the Americans of his certain knowledge of mobile biological weapons production facilities.

In Tony's foreword to the September dossier, in the executive summary and in the full document, the assertion was made that Iraqi military planning allowed for some WMD to be ready within forty-five minutes of an order to use them. This led to a sensational headline in the next day's *Sun*: 'BRITS 45 MINS FROM DOOM'. It might have been even more sensational. The JIC assessment from which the forty-five-minute claim was drawn suggested that CBW munitions could be ready for firing within twenty to forty-five minutes.

I have tried to recapture in my mind the atmosphere that prevailed at the time. There was a profound contrast between the view of the Americans that war was all but inevitable, and the view taken by some of us in the Cabinet that war could be avoided through negotiation. November 2002 seemed to hold the prospect of a peaceful solution when the Security Council unanimously adopted UN Resolution 1441, and although this stated that Saddam would face 'serious consequences' if he did not comply with weapons inspectors, France in particular made clear its view that Resolution 1441 did not give the US and UK an automatic right to attack Iraq. One week later, while denying that it had any banned weapons programmes, Iraq accepted the UN resolution unconditionally. The inspectors returned to Iraq later that month.

In early December, I agreed to a second tranche of £150 million for further urgent operational requirements, and then later in the month a further £500 million. Early in January 2003, Geoff Hoon announced his intention to call up 1,500 reservists, a figure that rose to 5,000 by the end of the month. That same month it was decided that if war came, the British invasion would launch not as originally planned from the north via Turkey but from the south via Kuwait. This change followed the decision of the Turkish Parliament to vote against allowing a land assault from Turkey.

But, just at this moment, Iraq agreed to the UN's demand for aerial surveillance, and the work of Hans Blix seemed to be yielding answers.

On 14 February, Blix told the UN Security Council that his team had not found any WMDs. This was followed by a statement by Dr ElBaradei that the International Atomic Energy Authority had found no evidence of ongoing and prohibited nuclear or nuclear-related activities in Iraq. A chance seemed to be there for avoiding war; and when, on 7 March, Blix delivered a new report to the UN Security Council saying Baghdad had made progress on disarmament, that seemed more likely. Further time was needed, Blix argued. 'Disarmament, and at any rate verification, cannot be instant,' he said. 'It will not take years, nor weeks, but months.' Our response was that Saddam could have ten days: after Blix's presentation, the US, Britain and Spain presented a draft resolution giving Saddam an ultimatum to disarm by 17 March or face the possibility of war. France, leading opposition to any war, said it could not accept the ultimatum.

But the march to war was now under way. I was receiving and approving an increasing stream of spending requests from the Ministry of Defence. I told a ministerial meeting on 6 March that the estimates for the humanitarian aid alone could be as high as £4 billion. The next day, unbeknown to me at the time, the Attorney General provided lengthy, detailed and unequivocal advice on the legality of the proposed invasion. Until this point, the British position had been that a second UN resolution affirming that Iraq was in breach of the previous resolution, 1441, was desirable if war was to be prosecuted. Indeed, when Tony met President Bush on 31 January at the White House he pressed him for support for a second resolution. Now, in Lord Goldsmith's assessment, British participation in the American-led invasion of Iraq could be declared illegal without a second UN resolution. This advice, not publicly known at the time, was only revealed in 2005. Goldsmith warned Tony: 'I remain of the opinion that the safest legal course would be to secure the adoption of a further resolution to authorise the use of force . . . We would need to be able to demonstrate hard evidence of [Iraqi] non-compliance and non-cooperation.' It was not until 17 March, at a meeting of the Cabinet, that I and others saw for the first time what was – although we did not know it – revised advice from Goldsmith stating that war would be legal without a second resolution.

The weekend of 15–16 March was tumultuous. At Tony's specific request, I went on David Frost's Sunday TV programme to urge the

French to support joint action. At this time, Chile and other Latin American countries proposed a new UN resolution that would have accorded Saddam Hussein a last chance to disarm. However, Britain argued that the French would never support intervention under any circumstances, and so the resolution was pointless, leading the Chileans to withdraw it. The No. 10 strategy was to focus on blaming France – that we should never have our decisions on national security dictated by them.

In his evidence to the Chilcot Inquiry, Hans Blix said that by this stage, with almost 250,000 coalition forces on the border of Iraq, the momentum for war 'was almost unstoppable'. He said, with some justification, that the UK 'remained a prisoner on that train'. It was around this time that the American evangelist Jim Wallis asked me to meet with him and a group of Christians opposed to the war. He had a middle way between war and doing nothing – a plan to indict Saddam Hussein that was later developed into a six-point plan for ousting him without violence. But as I told him, I could not see how this eleventh-hour proposition could be implemented in practice.

We have known since 2006 of a memo unearthed by Phillipe Sands, a QC and professor of international law at University College London, that in the weeks leading up to the war the US spent some time trying to make the case for action more acceptable to the public. A five-page memo, written some two months before the war by David Manning (Tony's chief foreign policy adviser and head of the Defence and Overseas Secretariat), reveals an American plan to 'to fly U2 reconnaissance aircraft painted in UN colours over Iraq with fighter cover', in the hope of provoking Iraqi forces into opening fire and thereby putting them in breach of the UN Resolution. According to Manning, the Americans still hoped that an Iraqi defector might be 'brought out' to talk about WMDs, or that someone might assassinate Saddam Hussein. Most of all, the memo confirmed the inevitability of conflict: 'our diplomatic strategy had to be arranged around the military planning', Manning said.

On 17 March, in a speech from the Oval Office, Bush told Saddam Hussein that he and his sons must leave Iraq within forty-eight hours. Their refusal to do so would result in military conflict, commencing at a time of America's choosing. The formal decision by the UK to invade Iraq if Saddam failed to obey the US ultimatum was taken by the Cabinet at 4 p.m. on the same day. Later that evening, Robin Cook resigned from government and delivered a powerful speech in the Commons against the war. The next day, Tuesday 18 March, saw the parliamentary debate and the biggest revolt that the Labour government was ever to face: 121 Labour MPs voted against the war, with even more – 198 in total – supporting an amendment arguing that the case for war had not yet been made. However, with Conservative support, the final tally supporting action was 412 for and 149 against. As I cast my vote, I was confident that the information we had been given about Sadaam's weapons was accurate. However, the more I learned about the suspect intelligence over the next few years, the more I started to feel that decisions were made on the basis of inadequate information and questionable assumptions.

The Iraq War began almost immediately afterwards, on 20 March, with a bombing campaign that was targeted at Saddam himself. The initial victory was so swift that on 1 May President Bush stood in front of a banner on an aircraft carrier that read 'Mission Accomplished'. But as we were now to discover, the main US initiatives – de-Ba'athification (i.e. removing members of Saddam's Ba'ath Party cohorts from positions of power) and disbanding the Iraqi army – would leave a power vacuum, administrative chaos, a vast number of armed ex-soldiers and a rapid descent into anarchy and sectarian strife. We failed to persuade the US of the advantages of a UN-led administration and then set a less ambitious goal of persuading them to accept UN authorisation of a coalition-led interim administration. The UK and the US, in effect, became joint-occupying powers.

In the years ahead, Iraq would be a cauldron of recurring turmoil. The country was governed officially by the Coalition Provisional Authority, which answered to the US Department of Defense. But while we were fully implicated in the Authority's decisions, I found, at least from my vantage point at the Treasury, that we singularly failed to have a decisive effect on its policies. If reconstruction was going to work in Basra and the south – the area we now had responsibility for – Britain, I felt, had to devise its own measures to secure a fragile peace and advance economic development. There now followed six years in which I and ministerial colleagues regularly visited Basra. There was a hope within the Treasury that the broken economy could be turned around. However, while we did everything we could – bringing in some very powerful business advisers, creating public works and jobs, supporting the rebuilding of the port and spending millions – we could never do enough. We were unable to bring the kind of improvement in living standards that would give the local population a big enough stake in their prosperity to stand up to the insurgents and resist a return to violence. There was, in addition, an ever-increasing danger of being viewed not as liberator but as foreign oppressor. As early as 2005, some of our officials, military officers and ministers were already worrying that we were heading towards 'strategic failure'. By that they meant a number of possibilities: a widespread sectarian conflict or civil war in Iraq; a victory for terrorist groups; or a failure to achieve a stable and secure environment in Basra.

When I became prime minister, I was of the view that we should end our four-year military presence in Iraq. Privately, I thought we should do so as soon as possible and set myself the task of leaving by the end of 2008. In my Camp David meeting with George Bush in July 2007 he pressed me to stay longer and raise troop levels. I told him I was not willing to see an endless British occupation, and I was clear that while we would not leave until security was improved, our deployments would have to be made in the British interest. Our plan was to scale down and withdraw. In the end, we left only sixteen weeks later than planned – on 30 April 2009.

In fact, for some time in Basra, we had started to do things differently from the Americans. Nevertheless, I would not explicitly position our departure as a break with the US and refused to convey the impression that we were distancing ourselves from America even at a time when the Iraq intervention was becoming more and more unpopular. There was never, I told my colleagues, going to be any public or private self-satisfaction in our leaving Iraq. At this time I made another decision: not to use our future departure from Iraq as an occasion to draw a contrast with Tony or score points against him either. Amidst all the second-hand accounts of the Labour years, what people sometimes forget is that during all my time in government, whether as chancellor or prime minister, I never engaged in public criticism of Tony. Inevitably there were heated words exchanged between us privately – and, in this respect, I hated what were too many off-the-record briefings to the press about these disagreements from each of our overly loyal teams – but neither Tony nor I ever publicly disparaged the other in government.

A Cabinet committee document presented to me in July 2007 observed: 'On paper, Iraq has the machinery of government in place, and security forces over 350,000 strong (Police 160,000, Army 157,000).' But, it added ominously, 'behind these outward signs of progress lie deep-seated problems'. The constituent parts of the Iraqi government were not yet working together and they were paying mere lip service to the need for reconciliation between them. 40 per cent of the Iraqi police service was thought to owe loyalty to militias, while other security bodies had become personal militias for ministers or provincial governors. Any gains, I was told, may prove unsustainable. The paper asked: 'Do we assess that we have reached the stage where the benefits of retaining security responsibility are outweighed by the downsides? Is there any prospect that by holding on, we can hope either to effect further positive change, or to provide the time needed by the Iraqis to meet the challenges themselves?'

In early 2007, President Bush had announced a major surge under the commander of the multinational force in Iraq, General David Petraeus, putting 20,000 new troops into the country with a mission to recapture lost territory and calm the insurgency. As I entered No. 10, our own mini-surge in Basra – an extra 360 troops deployed in what was called Operation Sinbad – merely confirmed the difficulty of our 'hold and build' strategy. My view at this time was that our best and only hope was to dedicate our efforts to preparing Iraq's provinces for the restoration of Iraqi control.

By mid-2007 we were up against sophisticated explosives made in Iran and finding it difficult to govern in Basra as the prime minister of Iraq, Nouri al-Maliki, started to press for our departure. Al-Maliki, meanwhile, was not in a strong enough position to lead without relying on the support of a variety of dubious groups, one of them being the Jaish Al Mahdi (JAM) militia, who operated in Basra. So, without my knowing it, security there had become dependent on a shady alliance, which involved the JAM terrorist leader, then in prison, negotiating early release for his members in return for delivering a more peaceful Basra. It took me months to get to the bottom of what was happening. This confirmed in my mind the view – shared by the new Chief of the Defence Staff, Sir Jock Stirrup, whose colleagues were divided two to one in favour of leaving – that the 'law of diminishing returns' was firmly in play and that there was an increasing risk that UK forces would become part of the problem, rather than the solution.

'Iraqification', an ugly term, best explained our objective: while the US led their surge, we planned to transfer control back to the Iraqis, province by province. We were already transitioning from 'tactical overwatch' to 'operational overwatch'. We would then transition to 'strategic overwatch' and then get out. We wanted to be seen by the Iraqis as supporting local forces exercising local control. But it was also true that we were increasingly worried by the rate at which military personnel were dying in battle or returning home injured. After the invasion in 2003 when we had lost fifty-three soldiers, deaths had fallen the following year to twenty-two, but in 2005 they had risen to twenty-three, in 2006 to twenty-nine, and we were to lose forty-seven in 2007. General Petraeus thought our position should be 'in together, out together', but I told him that autumn that the British task would be limited to creating enough stability to allow us to depart, and no more.

While the UK and US shared this same overall objective, we sometimes differed on the best means of achieving it. In essence, we tended to favour a more rapid transition to Iraqi control than the US did, not least as a means of forcing the Iraqis to step up to the plate. We agreed with the US that progress on political reconciliation was key to sustaining security gains and building long-term stability, but the US, under pressure to produce tangible results for Congress, were inclined to put greater emphasis than we were on the rapid passing of Iraqi legislation. By contrast, we wanted to avoid an unhelpful short-term focus on superficial benchmarks at the expense of more substantive and sustainable progress, such as reaching genuine consensus on the critical issues and building the political will necessary to ensure that any agreements that were eventually formalised would actually be implemented.

In line with this we were stronger advocates for holding early provincial elections: while not without risks, we believed elections were key to reconciliation between ethnic factions and maintaining political momentum across the country. They would help correct under-representation in many areas and provide a way into the political process – and away from violence – for those previously outside it.

The US, on the other hand, were nervous about holding provincial elections too soon, arguing that they could be destabilising.

I had told Parliament in July 2007 that UK troop numbers were already down from the initial 44,000 to 5,500. In Basra, our aim was to withdraw in phases, until we had a residual role in which we would only intervene in an emergency from an airbase outside the city. The Bush administration was worried about this, believing that if we moved forward with the plan too quickly they would be embarrassed during congressional questions on the surge in the autumn. Nonetheless, we evacuated Basra Palace – the base from which we commanded the whole province – in September 2007, handing responsibility to the Iraqis in December.

Despite disagreement with the Americans, Des Browne, our Defence Secretary, and I agreed that the time between leaving the palace and transferring power to local control should be as short as possible. And by the summer of 2007 – albeit for different reasons, not least his closeness to the Iranians – al-Maliki was adamant that he did not want or require UK military support in Basra for much longer. The Cabinet had already decided in principle on our departure, and the decision on timing was taken in consultation with the military on the ground.

On 2 October, I made my first visit as prime minister to Iraq, where I announced that UK troops in Basra were to be cut by 1,000 by the end of the year. After that, some 4,000 UK troops would remain, at the Basra airport base. A week later, on 8 October, I was able to announce that British troop numbers would be reduced to 2,500 the following spring. What was not announced was my hope that Britain would leave completely by the end of 2008.

Our plans were undermined by increased sectarian violence in Basra during March 2008. Al-Maliki decided on 23 March to launch independent military action, going into Basra with 15,000 troops. The operation – 'Charge of the Knights' – was aimed at driving the JAM and other Shia militia out of Basra. It was successful. Some saw al-Maliki's surprise attack on the militias in Basra during March as a blow to the British. However, it was exactly what was needed – an Iraqi-led government, and a Shia-led one at that, ready to take on the Shia terrorists in their midst.

While we paused our reduction of troops during these attacks, the security position in Basra was to improve significantly over the next few months. What's more, the Basra Development Commission, an independent body charged with promoting investment and economic development in the region, produced an economic plan in the autumn and local government elections would be held by the end of the year. I also expected the airport to be ready for handover to civilian control by the end of the year.

On 22 July 2008, I announced that I expected a 'fundamental change of mission' for British forces in Iraq early in 2009. Although the 4,100 UK troops would stay in Iraq for the next few months, their focus would be on providing Iraq's 14 Division with training, which was to be completed by the end of the year. Additional training, including in support of specialist functions and headquarters, would be required in early 2009. We would also have to seek a new agreement with the Iraqi government, requiring significant negotiation, so that our armed forces had a legal basis for operations after December.

This negotiation with the Iraqis was a long and drawn-out affair. However, before Christmas, we had an agreement. I travelled to Baghdad to meet Prime Minister al-Maliki, and we agreed that UK forces had completed their tasks and would leave the country by the first half of 2009.

We were right to move towards a limited form of overwatch and leave altogether when we did. Every time I visited Basra, I stood silently in front of the commemorative wall that had been built at the airport for those British soldiers who had lost their lives. I was deeply aware of their sacrifice.

We finally concluded combat operations in April, but as we wound them down the Conservatives, the media and some of my colleagues pressed for a full Falklands-style investigation. At some personal political cost, I proposed that an inquiry focus on lessons learned and not on apportioning culpability. I suggested that, like the Falklands Inquiry, the proceedings should be held in private. To many this seemed like an attempt at a whitewash or even a cover-up. This was a mistake on my part. To find a way forward, I encouraged Sir John Chilcot, whom we had chosen as the chair, to talk to all the political parties and relevant House of Commons committees to gather a consensus. While a Conservative attempt to make witnesses swear under oath was defeated, we agreed that the inquiry could range as wide as it wanted, criticise anyone it chose and ask witnesses to formally agree to stand by what they said in evidence.

In setting the course he did on Iraq, I believe that Tony had been intent on preserving the special relationship with America. In doing so, he hoped he would be able to advance the Middle East peace process.

At the beginning of this chapter I set out some of the conditions that have been debated throughout history under which war can be justified. With the passage of time, the evidence now accumulated allows us to assess whether reasonable thresholds were passed or short-circuited, and what lessons we can learn about how such grave decisions should be made in future.

I am convinced that if resolutions of the United Nations are approved unanimously and repeatedly they have to be upheld if we are to have a safe and stable world order. On this basis, Saddam Hussein's continuing failure to comply with them justified international action against him. The question is whether it required war in March 2003. If I am right that somewhere within the American system the truth about Iraq's lack of weapons was known, then we were not just misinformed but misled on the critical issue of WMDs. Given that Iraq had no usable chemical, biological or nuclear weapons that it could deploy and was not about to attack the coalition, then two tests of a just war were not met: war could not be justified as a last resort and invasion cannot now be seen as a proportionate response.

We know that even a just war does not necessarily deliver a just peace. When we left Iraq in 2009 it was still one country, with one government and one Parliament, but in the last few years Iraq has again been torn apart by deep sectarian divisions. There is a good reason why it was more difficult to sustain a peace than win a war. Nation-building from the outside is fine in theory but hard in practice. Not every world problem can be solved by America or, for that matter, the West. It was a lesson that was to be impressed upon us with equal force in Afghanistan.

CHAPTER 14

AFGHANISTAN: A WAR WITHOUT END?

No letter of condolence is routine. And letters to a family who have lost a loved one in war are difficult beyond imagining. As prime minister I wrote over 300 letters to parents and partners of those killed in Afghanistan and Iraq between the summer of 2007 and spring of 2010. Every letter was personally painful. By my side as I wrote, I always had four separate notes – a statement of how the soldier had died, a report from their commander on their qualities, a list of their achievements in life, and information about their family and closest relatives.

It is even harder to write about someone you know only from second-hand reports. I always knew how a letter in itself may offer little consolation at this time of most intense grief, but I thought that over time some comfort might come from knowing the esteem in which the lost soldier was held by colleagues and friends. In every letter there was an offer of further help, which was sometimes taken up. I was determined that each had to be genuinely about the individual and not impersonal. I pored over details about the dead soldier's bravery in action and their character and qualities.

In my first weeks in office, aware that my writing was at best difficult to read, I had my letters typed. But I felt the letters lacked a much-needed personal touch and quickly moved to writing in long-hand. When the *Sun* newspaper filed a story in November 2009 from one grieving mother, who complained that I had treated her son with contempt because of my bad handwriting, I was close to tears. In the letter, based on the information I had, it was simply impossible to persuade her that everything possible had been done to save her son, or to demonstrate, even when I later talked to her by phone, that my words were heartfelt. I simply hoped that in some small way the family would be strengthened in their hour of grief.

In the three years I was prime minister, I was writing such letters every few days. And, after RAF Brize Norton in Oxfordshire was closed for runway repairs in April 2007, just months before I became prime minister, almost every week the body of a soldier would be flown back to the military airbase at RAF Lyneham in Wiltshire. After the Falklands, where the majority of our war dead from that conflict remain, the practice had been established that the bodies of all those killed in combat would be repatriated for burial at home, with each death investigated by the coroner at the John Radcliffe Hospital in Oxford. After the move to RAF Lyneham, the route to the special armed forces department of pathology in Oxford was through Wootton Bassett, now Royal Wootton Bassett, a small market town to the south-west of the base, before heading east along the M4. A tradition grew that as the hearses drove along the high street, the local residents would stand in silence to honour our heroes. It was a moving ceremony, a fitting tribute to brave soldiers – and these silent processions filled our newspapers and TV screens, graphically reminding us of the losses we were incurring and adding to a growing sense that this was a war too far.

Afghanistan had not always been so deadly. In the first four years of our involvement on the ground five British soldiers were killed – only two of whom died in hostile action with the enemy. But in the year before I went to No. 10 – 2006 – thirty-nine were lost and, in the first half of 2007, just before I took over, yet another seventeen were killed. Even this rising and agonising toll of casualties was relatively small compared with what we were about to experience. From mid-2007 to mid-2010, there were 224 deaths in Afghanistan and then in the next year and a half another 109. By February 2010 we had lost more lives in Afghanistan than in the Falklands, and by the time Britain left Afghanistan in 2014–15 a total of 3,400 coalition soldiers had died; 456 – one in eight – were British.

Our armed forces suffered not just a large loss of life but also an appalling loss of limbs with soldiers experiencing life-shattering injuries that will plague them for a lifetime. I can only marvel at the way those wounded in conflict worked day after day to recover. Having met brave men and women testing themselves to the limits at their rehabilitation centre, Headley Court, I can never forget what I saw and will always regard them as heroes.

How was it that six years after the invasion, long after the Taliban had been routed from Kabul, the conflict in Afghanistan got so much worse?

We were reaping the whirlwind of a fateful decision made in mid-2005 when Britain volunteered to take responsibility for Afghanistan's most dangerous province, Helmand. Along with Kandahar, this was the spiritual home of the Taliban and the global centre for opium production. Helmand was only one of thirty-four provinces in Afghanistan but, with its land area covering 10 per cent of the country, it was the largest at 20,000 square miles, nearly three times the size of Wales. It was overwhelmingly rural – 1,000 villages with few big towns – and so depopulated that only around 900,000 people lived there, just forty-five per square mile, most of them in a relatively minor strip around the Helmand river. This vast, largely empty space was a prize the Taliban craved and the drug lords fought over. A third of the heroin produced in Afghanistan, itself responsible for 90 per cent of global supply, came from Helmand's opium poppies.

The years that followed Britain's decision to assume responsibility for Helmand were to exact the heaviest of costs – not just in money spent and public trust eroded, but most tragically in lives lost. At the peak, nearly 9,500 British troops were stationed in Helmand, most of them in Camp Bastion. From scratch, we had built a veritable city in the desert with its own airstrip, its own hospital and a twenty-five-mile perimeter fence. But to police the province, our troops had also to be spread across its unwelcoming terrain: at the height of our Helmand incursion, British soldiers were stationed at 137 bases. In brief, taking responsibility for Helmand had the effect of changing the whole basis of our presence in Afghanistan from counterterrorism to all-out war.

Ours is sometimes called the fourth Afghan war. The Anglo-Afghan wars of 1839–42, 1878–80 and 1919, fought to protect Britain's interest in north-west India from potential Russian incursions, had led historians to call Afghanistan the graveyard of British military ambitions. But as our troops landed in 2001, there was complete unity across all political parties about our objective – to destroy al-Qaeda following the terrorist attacks of 9/11, and oust the al-Qaeda-supporting Taliban. At the outset, Britain provided 4,000 troops to Afghanistan, and the first general commanding the NATO-led International Security Assistance Force (ISAF) in Afghanistan was British. By 2002, the ISAF coalition had not

only installed a new president, Hamid Karzai, but a General Assembly
of Afghan Tribes had delivered a new constitution.

Our stated aim was to start in Kabul, move north where we had
the support of the anti-Taliban Northern League, and then go west
and south, in a reverse clockwise direction. As the coalition expanded
out of Kabul into the north, the Treasury funded the first allied
Provincial Reconstruction Teams designed to extend the authority of
the central government and tackle the narco-economy; and, at the
same time, I signed off funds designed to build up a strong and efficient Afghan army and police force, that could over time empower
the country to survive on its own. At a later date, we were to be
accused of an overambitious programme of nation-building – of trying to build Switzerland in a 'medieval' country. But in practice the
allied forces went in with the support of the Northern League and
encountered little opposition. They did not attempt the same kind of
direct rule as in Iraq but quickly installed an Afghan-led government
with little more than a light footprint outside Kabul.

There was, however, certainly mission deepening, if not mission
creep, as objective was piled on top of objective – not only to destroy
the remnants of al-Qaeda and defeat the Taliban but also to create
and strengthen the Afghan police and train the army, install democracy, break the power of the drug lords, promote economic development, and bring education and healthcare to Afghan families. All the
while, the most basic objective – to protect our own troops – was
becoming even more difficult.

The early results – a growing economy, improved health and education, and then elections, tinged by corruption but still for the most
part free – seemed encouraging. But soon the Afghan government
drifted, its writ weak, its services threadbare, with corruption rife.
Obsessed with establishing a strong central government in Kabul, the
allied effort underestimated the importance of legitimacy out in the
provinces. Our light footprint was fine if the Afghan government
united the country and brought in all tribes and ethnic groups; but it
did not. By 2005 the Taliban had been rejuvenated in their home bases
of Helmand and Kandahar.

These early years from 2001 to 2005 should have been the time
when, with the Taliban in retreat, we finished the job in Afghanistan.
But Anglo-American resources and attention were concentrated on

Iraq. These were, in retrospect, wasted years. And, by 2005, with half the country viewed as 'ungoverned space', fears grew of a divided Afghanistan and the likelihood of a breakaway Pashtunistan dominated by the Taliban and other terrorist organisations. In the provinces most at risk, Helmand and Kandahar, there were only a handful of coalition troops, no more than a hundred, conducting anti-terrorist missions.

Matt Cavanagh, a strategic thinker whose family had roots in the armed forces and who was my leading defence and security adviser, has published his own study of what became the British rush into Helmand. At the point when we were asked to do more by the US, he observes, the government should have conducted an in-depth review of what could be achieved and the cases 'for' and 'against' extending our commitment when we were already overstretched in Iraq. Instead the issue was put in stark and simple terms to be decided immediately: Kandahar or Helmand? Kandahar was probably the more strategically significant province, less intractable and a more natural centre of gravity for British interests. Helmand was, however, the centre of the narco-economy and Britain was leading the anti-narcotics work across the country. But that was not the main reason why we came to locate in Helmand; or, by some accounts, let Canada choose Kandahar while we inherited Helmand by default. As Nick Beadle, one of our leading military experts with whom I worked closely, has concluded, there was 'a failure to persuade the US to support us, as against the preference of the Canadians'.

In Tony Blair's account of the war, he frames decisions about Afghanistan as part of the long struggle against Islamic extremism. And when he explains our deployment to Helmand his rationale is that having started we could not walk away or lose heart. He was instinctively in favour of the bolder course, taking on the more difficult Helmand assignment. The matter did not come to the Cabinet until very late – 29 January 2006. The minutes of the meetings running up to the decision – overseen by the Defence Secretary, John Reid – reflect an urgency to do something, that we needed to 'turn things around before it is too late'. As Matt Cavanagh records, 'there was relatively little debate at ministerial level, in the Reid group (the small ministerial team working out the tactics) or elsewhere, about the detail of the plan, including troop numbers'.

At this point Des Browne, then Chief Secretary to the Treasury, and my representative in the discussions, warned me about the open-ended nature of the commitment we were about to make. He was strongly opposed to it, but not on grounds of cost. The suggestion that the Treasury sought to impose a cap on either troop deployments or spending is just plain wrong. Our objections were similar to those of Sir Jock Stirrup, appointed Chief of the Defence Staff in April 2006, who was later to explain in graphic terms: 'We don't know much about the South, but what we do know is that it's not the North. It's real bandit country.' Like him, Des and I were sceptical of what an open-ended commitment to Helmand – still devoid of a plan for development – could achieve.

John Reid is right to remind us that he delayed any decisions until he had assurances about allied support, especially from Canada and the Netherlands; guarantees about the funding of the operation; and clarity about the role that the Department for International Development (DfID) would play in reconstruction and development. The mission was to be limited in geographical scope and strategic objectives, but the prior question remained: what could we achieve by being there in the first place?

Our efforts were designed to focus less on combat and more on reconstruction – in the terminology of the Ministry of Defence, a 'hearts and minds' operation, rather than a 'search and destroy' one. The aim was, as John told the House of Commons, 'a seamless package of democratic, political, developmental and military assistance' to slowly transform the political, social and economic fabric starting with the main population centres. In any event, preparations were short-circuited – by the end of 2005 there had been just one small intelligence reconnaissance mission – because of a deadline: Tony felt we had to announce our new stance at the London conference on Afghanistan in late January 2006. There, he not only announced our choice of Helmand but set the starting date of April 2006 for a three-year deployment.

At first, with 8,500 British troops still in Iraq, we could dispatch only a 3,300-strong brigade-level force. As our troops moved in, John Reid said: 'If we came for three years here to accomplish our mission and had not fired one shot at the end of it, we would be very happy indeed.' But what was originally a limited exercise with restricted aims would quickly escalate – and in a terrain where we knew little of the physical, human or political geography.

Our commander in Helmand, Brigadier Ed Butler, planned to concentrate our troops within a central zone, referred to as the 'lozenge of security', and around populated areas, which were called 'ink spots', in the provincial capital Lashkar Gah, Gereshk, and our base at Camp Bastion. This was not dissimilar to our counterterrorism strategy in Malaysia forty years before, during the so-called 'Confrontation' of 1963–6, but soon the ink of conflict flowed all across the province.

Within weeks Brigadier Butler was under pressure from President Karzai and the governor of Helmand, Mohammad Daoud – an anti-corruption leader we wanted to support – to deploy outwards to more far-flung towns and villages to stop them falling to the Taliban. If we did not take on the Taliban in the north, the logic went, they could then threaten us in the centre of the province. In the event, our troops on the ground – there originally to provide security in a small area – were, as a House of Commons Foreign Affairs Select Committee later described it, 'fighting for their lives no less than two months later in a series of Alamos in the north'. That summer, British troops charged up the valley in what became known as the 'platoon house' strategy: up to a hundred men, but usually around thirty to thirty-five holding outposts facing Taliban insurgents in the province's remote areas.

This was a different kind of operation from the one that had been sketched out on the drawing board. Moreover, this new strategy was being decided in a time of flux when John Reid was moving to the Home Office, Des Browne was succeeding him at the Ministry of Defence and Jock Stirrup was taking over as Chief of the Defence Staff. Without a Cabinet decision, we had moved from a peacemaking operation focused on development to all-out combat, from counterterrorism to counter-insurgency.

At first the Taliban tried to take us on in hand-to-hand fighting, but by the end of 2006, unable to defeat us in an upfront military confrontation, they mounted a guerrilla war, hiding explosive devices in the ground. And the Taliban were nothing if not patient and persistent, lying in wait – 'You have the watches, we have the time,' they said. As early as the end of 2006, it was clear that UK policy had failed to meet its stated objectives. We had been forced to increase our troop numbers to around 6,000 in the autumn, and the military situation had stabilised, but the fighting left little military capacity to establish the security conditions which would permit the planned reconstruction and development activities or elements of the anti-narcotics campaign, both essential to the delivery of our overall strategy.

In February 2007, I agreed an additional £284 million for the campaign in southern Afghanistan, though the Cabinet was warned that the UK would now be unable to mount small, short-term operations in response to new demands. Around 1,400 more troops were sent to Afghanistan in the coming months, raising our deployment to around 7,700. Total projected expenditure over the lifetime of the operation was £2.3 billion, more than double the original estimate. The armed forces would be operating at the limit of their capability.

This is the situation I found when I moved into No. 10. Without announcing a public review, I asked the new ministers – David Miliband at the Foreign Office and Douglas Alexander at DfID – to re-examine our war aims. And I also had several private discussions with Des Browne about the military strategy. Was this a war to destroy terrorists or to deter terrorists, a war to introduce democracy, a war against drugs or was it a war to transform Afghan culture and society? Was our priority to prevent Afghanistan from ever again becoming a platform for al-Qaeda, or were wider, more ambitious objectives realistic? Could we ever make Afghanistan a drugs-free country, or, more than that, a modern economy with a credible and functioning democracy? How far was it going to be possible to create powerful corruption-free institutions, and could we ever have law and order without an honest police force and armed forces who would actually fight the battles? I concluded that in our first six years in Afghanistan our emphasis had moved inconsistently between one priority and another, veering uneasily between the war against the Taliban, the war against al-Qaeda, the war against drugs, the attempt to achieve a minimum level of governance and, more recently, protecting our own troops.

And I found that our stated aims did not only always not converge but were often at odds with each other. Counter-insurgency and anti-narcotics, for example, did not fit easily together. An anti-narcotics drive could often alienate the locals and undermine our counter-insurgency work. In Helmand itself, as we discovered on entering, the governor benefited indirectly from levies on a drugs trade which employed drug runners and local farmers growing poppies. Located close to the existing US Provincial Reconstruction Team was a drugs bazaar which US forces had left undisturbed. So, when we cracked down on drug-trafficking mafias, without offering any alternative employment or source of income for the people they employed, previously loyal militias defected to the Taliban. Nothing could more vividly illustrate the dilemma of having a multiplicity of objectives that were incompatible with each other.

The way forward had to be what later became known as 'Afghanisation'. In December 2007, in a statement to the House of Commons, our government became the first in the coalition to set out how the Afghans themselves could take control of their own security. We would focus our efforts on building up the Afghan army and police, developing stronger and more effective provincial and local government, and promoting economic reconstruction, all of which was to be achieved not just by us but through greater burden-sharing with our allies.

With the change of tactics in the summer of 2006 and the Helmand intervention we had hoped to win against the insurgency militarily. Now we were trying to pursue a more nuanced counter-insurgency strategy: win the loyalty of the Afghans by securing their safety and simultaneously establish the credibility of the Afghan army and police. This became the Helmand Road Map – specific development plans for Lashkar Gah, Gereshk, Sangin and Musa Qala – which put Afghan control and economic development at the heart of our Helmand work and upgraded the status and resources for our Provincial Reconstruction Team. This was our civilian surge.

But while there was some progress – Musa Qala, which we had pulled out of before, was retaken from the Taliban at the time I outlined the new strategy in the House of Commons – 'Afghanisation' was undermined by President Karzai, who disowned an earlier agreement to work with a UN Special Representative who might coordinate the allied and Afghan civilian–military effort. And as we discovered at the 2008 NATO Bucharest summit our allies were now more reluctant to share the costs. It would not be until late 2009 that the push for increased burden-sharing would finally succeed.

As our allies stood back, our security needs grew. Before he left office, Tony had agreed an increase in British troops in Helmand. But we continued to be faced with additional demands for more troops and equipment. At every point, the story was the same: that we had 'to turn things around before it is too late', an argument that was tempting at the time but in retrospect sounds more like the rhetoric of redemption than a strategic plan.

In the two years after 2006, improvised explosive device (IED) bombings grew fourfold and then in the next two years to 2010 they doubled in number again. Nearly 80 per cent of allied attacks in Afghanistan were now in UK areas of operation. Up to 1,200 engineers in the best bomb squads in the world bravely worked to defuse and clear thousands of these devices. But with an estimated 10,000 IEDs buried in the ground in Helmand, our troops were in constant danger.

Our equipment needs clearly had to change to meet the new threats. The heavier warrior fighting vehicles were excellent, but the lighter vehicles were a problem. The Snatch Land Rovers had proved totally inadequate against IEDs in Iraq from 2005 onwards. Soon after Des Browne went to the Ministry of Defence, in July 2006, he asked me for extra money from Treasury reserves to buy new Mastiff vehicles that were specifically designed to resist IEDs – I agreed straight away – and the first Mastiffs arrived in Iraq around the end of the year. By then, though, it was becoming obvious that we would need far more of this type of vehicle for Afghanistan as well.

The Vector vehicle, which the army had earmarked for Afghanistan, was proving just as bad as the Snatch, but the MoD and the army high command seemed distracted by the long-running saga of its attempts to introduce a single generic medium-weight vehicle programme, known as FRES (future rapid effects system). Like Des, I felt the priority had to be IED-resistant vehicles in Afghanistan, and I supported him in ordering further waves of Mastiffs and similar vehicles over the next two years, with hundreds of millions of pounds coming from Treasury reserves via the Urgent Operational Requirements system. But the speed of delivery to the front line slowed down and it was not until late 2009 that we had the full range of vehicles out in Afghanistan that we needed.

Our helicopters were the vital link between the main bases and platoon houses, and later the forward operating bases. As the territory we were covering increased, along with our troop numbers, and the threat on the ground from IEDs continued to rise, the demand for helicopters grew far beyond what the MoD had planned for when the campaign began. I knew that Des was trying to address this, including by buying six new Merlin helicopters from Denmark – because the MoD told us this was the fastest way to get helicopters out to Afghanistan – and by trying to salvage the disastrous Chinook Mark 3 programme, which had left us with eight supposedly state-of-the-art helicopters that were unable to fly. The venerable Sea King helicopters were brought back from Iraq, given new blades to enable them to operate in 'hot and high' conditions, and sent out to Afghanistan; the smaller Lynx helicopters were given new engines for the same reason.

All of this took time – often it felt far too long. I told Des and his successors that I would do anything I could to speed up any of these initiatives, but they assured me that everything that could be done was being done – as did Jock Stirrup. I therefore focused on a different initiative, spending many hours phoning NATO colleagues asking them to loan us helicopters, or contribute to a pool which could be used by all NATO countries in Afghanistan. But although on paper Europe's NATO members had 1,000 helicopters, hardly any of them had the ability to operate in Afghan conditions. By the end of 2009, the Merlin fleet arrived in Afghanistan, and we had tripled the helicopter capacity in Helmand from three years earlier.

While the first years of our intervention in Afghanistan had passed without partisan controversy, after 2006 a long-running saga of accusations and counter-accusations began which would dog my time as prime minister. Debates over troop numbers drowned out the wider discussion we were having on military strategy, establishing a political settlement, weeding out Afghan corruption, and ensuring that policies for aid and economic development could make a difference. The Opposition parties and press blamed the government for the equipment problems and suggested that we were denying much-needed funds – despite the fact that spending on the Afghan campaign was rising very steeply. What had once been all-party non-partisan support descended into mud-slinging.

I bent over backwards to meet every request for new equipment that the chiefs or Defence Secretary assessed as militarily justified. While in 2007 the equipment funded from the Treasury Reserve for Afghanistan was worth £190,000 for every soldier deployed, by 2010 it was £400,000. Funding for Afghanistan from Treasury reserves had increased from £700 million a year to more than £3 billion. Indeed, Jock Stirrup explained publicly that his problem was not getting approval to buy equipment but responding to the changing tactics of the Taliban. 'Our equipment is good and improving; commanders speak of it very highly,' he said. 'But the enemy adapt their tactics and techniques to counter our capabilities, so what is "the right equipment" in a campaign changes, and often very quickly.' As the acknowledged expert on the Afghan war, Michael Clarke, has stated: 'there is no evidence to contradict the assertion of senior commanders . . . that once the operation was under way no request for equipment was ever turned down. British troops and commanders in Afghanistan . . . [were] better equipped than any force the UK has ever fielded anywhere.'

The real problem was not in the Treasury but in Helmand. What was supposed to be an intervention that began and ended with no bullets fired had descended into a day-to-day firefight simply to defend our own troops and hold their positions, and then became an attritional, asymmetric war.

By the spring of 2008 an emboldened Taliban were taking back districts, setting their sights on recapturing Lashkar Gah. In June 2008, I announced the number of British troops serving in Afghanistan would increase to 8,030 – a rise of 230.

Every advance we made against the Taliban seemed temporary: as soon as our troops moved to strengthen positions elsewhere, the Taliban returned. No one suggested that we could garrison the whole province. The strategy of 'clear, hold, build' was not working. While we could 'clear' the latest Taliban stronghold, we did not have sufficient numbers to 'hold', and DfID could therefore not 'build'. Nor did the Afghan army or police, or the Helmand governor. Repeatedly in 2008 and 2009 I phoned or met Karzai to ask him to meet his promise on Afghan troops, but too often, even when dates were given, the troops never arrived. By late 2008 and early 2009, as we prepared for the incoming Obama administration, we were going back to the fundamental questions I had asked in 2007: how could we reconcile the multiplicity of our objectives, and to what extent could a country like Afghanistan ever embrace liberal values?

Throughout 2008, the security situation in Afghanistan had deteriorated, while violent extremism in Pakistan had grown. In fact, the Joint Intelligence Committee concluded in August 2008 that the deterioration in Afghanistan was at least in part due to the situation in the border areas of Pakistan, where the writ of the Pakistani government – under a new president, Asif Ali Zardari – did not extend. Al-Qaeda, the Afghan

Taliban and the Pakistani Taliban had safe havens there, presenting risks to NATO's mission in Afghanistan, British interests in Pakistan, and the UK itself. But with a civilian government now in place in Pakistan, there seemed an opportunity to make progress: Karzai's hatred of the former Pakistan leader, General Pervez Musharraf, had previously led to fraught Afghan–Pakistani relations, but Musharraf had been forced to resign and was now in exile in London.

In mid-September 2008, President George W. Bush announced that in parallel with a drawdown of forces in Iraq, additional US military personnel would be deployed to Afghanistan in what was labelled a 'quiet surge'. But there was uncertainty until his successor, President Obama, set out his strategy. While Obama took over with a pledge to leave Iraq but secure Afghanistan, his administration was divided over the conclusions of a long-term review of policy regarding Afghanistan and Pakistan (the 'Af-Pak' strategy) led by Bruce Riedel, which reported a week before NATO's sixtieth-anniversary summit in March. One significant appointment was made by the Obama administration, though – that of Richard Holbrooke as a special adviser on Pakistan and Afghanistan. While it was said of him he was 'a bull who brings his own china shop', he was never able to bring the different parts of the American system together, nor speak with authority on Obama's behalf – and I sensed he remained frustrated up to his sad death in December 2010.

Riedel's review focused largely on building governance through political and economic means, including greater training and support for the Afghan National Security Forces, and also supported the call for the deployment of an additional 21,000 US military personnel to the country during 2009. But just as the American system was starting to implement this, it was immediately superseded by another review, by the new American commander, General Stanley McChrystal, which started in June. It was clear that McChrystal was likely to push for even more troops, but at the same time, Vice President Joe Biden was making a powerful case in the administration for troop numbers to be cut back and focus purely on counterterrorism rather than counter-insurgency.

In fact, President Obama's review created huge difficulties for us. What Obama ultimately decided was pivotal to everything we did: while Afghanistan and Pakistan represented the UK's greatest overseas commitment, our contribution was still small compared with that of America; and, ultimately, only the US had the political and military authority to broker real change. The series of reviews took the best part of 2009. For all that time, the uncertainty left me trapped between the British military's demand for more troops, which I knew could only make a difference as part of a wider American surge, and the American position, which was to wait for the results of the review and the Afghan elections. When my director of political strategy David Muir explained our frustrations to the Americans, he was told to read Gordon M. Goldstein's *Lessons in Disaster*, a recently published account of the fatal decisions around US involvement in Vietnam, 'because this is what it feels like'.

The administration was completely split down the middle. In my conversations with the new president, I stressed that we needed much stronger unity of command and purpose; and, as part of a strategy for Afghan ownership, far more detailed allied agreement on our short-term, medium-term and longer-term objectives. I was keen too to impress on the Americans the opportunities presented by Pakistan's new civilian leadership, and doubted whether US strikes in border areas would advance 'Afghanisation' – instead, it might radicalise the population against our presence and prevent Pakistan from signing up to our counterterrorism strategy.

When I met Obama at the G20 in early April he surprised us by, at the last minute, asking us to supply more troops. At the end of April, following a visit to Afghanistan and Pakistan earlier in the week, I made a House of Commons statement to mark our first strategy document focusing on Afghanistan and Pakistan together. If we were to deal with what I called the 'crucible of global terrorism', the law-less borderlands between the two countries which ultimately threatened our own security, we had to prevent young people 'falling under the sway of violent and extremist ideologies'. In Pakistan, we would want to enlist active support for counterterrorism work. In Afghanistan, the goal would be to achieve a 'district by district, province by province handover' to Afghan control. The Afghan army would grow to 134,000 by 2011, though I accepted the police were not yet seen as an 'honest and fair institution'.

At the same time, I announced 700 additional British troops to provide security during the forthcoming Afghan presidential elections, taking British forces up to 9,000. Despite pressure to do so, I did not agree to an indefinite increase in UK troop numbers. My adviser Matt Cavanagh wrote a memo at this time warning me that the 'the military will start to brief against you'. In fact, I was not against more troops: what I needed to be sure of was that, if we were to put more troops at risk, we had what I called 'a compelling strategy' and the 'sharing of tasks' in Helmand with the Americans. Yet, we had no choice but to keep waiting for the US to make their decision in order to find out what the overall strength of the allied presence in Afghanistan was going to be.

From June 2009, UK armed forces were engaged in a major offensive, Operation Panther's Claw, supported by Afghan soldiers, aimed at driving the Taliban from central Helmand, with the Americans doing similar work in the south. Having cleared the area, the question was whether we could 'hold' and 'build'. In theory the governor of Helmand, Gulab Mangal, and his district governors would follow up with plans to deliver basic services – clean water, electricity, roads, healthcare and basic justice – and then to promote economic development. But still only one part of the 'clear, hold, build' strategy was working and only then for a time: while we could 'clear' we did not have the resources to 'hold' and 'build'.

One ten-day period saw the loss of fifteen men and on my return from the G8 summit at L'Aquila in Italy – a trip that allowed us to visit the Italians made homeless by an earthquake – I went straight to Joint Command Headquarters to meet the chiefs. When I asked why the casualty figures had been so high and heard them respond that there were fewer casualties than expected – something for which we had not prepared public opinion – I knew our strategy had to change. When I raised the need for further coalition support, our chiefs, I sensed, were reluctant to concede they needed someone else's help. While I had wanted to await the outcome of the US review, I felt that the pressures our forces were under gave me no choice. So in July I announced that the 700 extra troops we had provided for the election would now stay longer – though I did not feel, not least because no decision had come out of America, that we had yet reached a tenable or lasting position. All the time I felt that there had to be greater burden-sharing if we were to reduce our losses and make headway; so when the request came for further troops in four areas – troops we needed to hold position, to deal with IEDs, to train the Afghan army and to staff our own Camp Bastion – I immediately agreed to extra troops to deal with the IED threat, but asked whether other countries could share the additional tasks with us.

As a result, over the next few months we improvised as we awaited coalition agreement on the next steps. While I had wanted to await the outcome of the Obama review, I felt that the pressures our forces were under gave me no choice but to agree to the request of Jock Stirrup and our commanders on the ground: that was why I made permanent the addition of the 700 troops that had initially been deployed as a temporary measure for the elections.

In August, with Parliament in recess, I met General Petraeus, who visited me at my home in North Queensferry. This was a good meeting at which we discussed the general shape of the next few years. But our plans, we knew, depended on the decision President Obama was yet to take. Once again as we waited we stepped up our engagement, this time with new surveillance measures to protect our anti-mine squads.

While the delay in the US decision constrained us from without, the Afghan elections, which had been postponed from August, were a major source of tension from within the coalition. My view was that President Karzai was bound to win, but our Afghan allies could not resist trying to fix the vote to ensure his victory. Worried that divisions within Afghanistan fuelled by electoral corruption would set back our core strategy for Afghan control, I asked Ban Ki-moon, the secretary general of the United Nations, that the UN do more to monitor and discourage corrupt practices. And when President Karzai topped the ballot but failed to secure an outright majority, the chairman of the US Senate Foreign Relations Committee John Kerry and I agreed that if Abdullah Abdullah, Karzai's main opponent, stood down, Karzai would have to promise far greater openness and transparency and hold to his commitment to a build-up of Afghan forces if 'Afghanisation' was going to happen.

At the start of October, I met General McChrystal in Downing Street. His report, submitted in September but the conclusions of which had been shared with us in August, had eventually come down in favour of 40,000 more US troops on top of the 68,000 already there. In fact, he had wanted 50,000 more, but he was persuaded to reduce his request. We met on the morning after he had given a controversial speech attacking Biden's preferred strategy – referred to by McChrystal as 'Chaosistan' – of relying more on drone missile strikes and special-forces operations against al-Qaeda. Tension was in the air as we met, and indeed the next day McChrystal would be summoned to a face-to-face meeting with Obama on board Air Force One on the tarmac in Copenhagen, where the president had arrived to promote Chicago's ultimately unsuccessful Olympics bid. In No. 10, McChrystal and I discussed his basic idea to embed coalition troops within the newly trained Afghan National Army. This was in line with our own thinking. As he explained, we both hoped for a 'sovereign, independent, democratic, secure and stable Afghanistan' but we would have to settle for something less than ideal.

McChrystal had divided the country into three categories: areas to focus on with more troops, those to leave entirely, and those not significant enough to reinforce but too important to leave. Sadly, I found that he had put Sangin in the third category. The fate of Sangin was a central concern for me throughout 2009: while our own generals wanted to show that we could win this part of Helmand ourselves, I was so aware of the losses we were suffering here that I wanted the Americans to bring more troops into the area and kept asking for greater burden-sharing. Generally, however, the McChrystal plan appealed to us: partnering with the Afghans and embedding our troops with them would be the shortest route to our eventual departure.

Contrary to expectations, an immediate response from the US administration to McChrystal's recommendations was not forthcoming. One possibility was that the US administration was waiting to see the benefits of the already enhanced US presence and the impact of the new 'Af-Pak' strategy before making any further deployment. Another was that the addition of troops was conditional for them on there being identifiable progress on political reform from the Afghans, in particular when it came to combating corruption. And of course the battle between proponents of a counter-insurgency strategy and a counterterrorism strategy was still unresolved. But it was clear to me that we could not wait any longer for the US to decide.

On 8 October, I asked the Cabinet to agree in principle to increase our troop numbers by a further 500 if specific conditions were met – namely that the Afghans also supplied more troops; that the right equipment was available; and that other countries also made a contribution. I had thought long and hard as to whether we should make these conditions public. Indeed, I discussed this at length during the Labour conference with Bob Ainsworth, who had taken over as Defence Secretary from Des Browne's successor, John Hutton. Making these conditions known would signal to the public that we had a plan with a chance of working. On the other hand, citing conditions did not please our military command. I decided that it would make no sense to add to our troop numbers unless we could show that with the help of further Afghan and allied troops they would make a real difference.

When the Commons returned on 14 October, I read out the name and rank of each of the thirty-seven heroes who had died that summer. I then announced our new troop total of 9,500, while stressing the importance of the three conditions. Indeed, on 16 November, because the conditions on burden-sharing and provision of Afghan National Security Forces had not yet been fulfilled, we delayed the uplift in UK numbers. At the conclusion of that meeting, I said I would try to pin down our allies over the following days.

It was only after my lobbying of fellow European leaders over the next two weeks that we did, in the end, agree to the deployment. In a visit to London on 17 November, the Slovakian prime minister announced a doubling of the country's military contribution – in southern Afghanistan – to 500 troops. The Georgians made a formal offer of an infantry company to operate alongside UK forces in Helmand. And after repeated calls to him, President Karzai reassured me that an additional 5,000 Afghan troops would partner us in Helmand. Accordingly, in a statement to the House of Commons on 30 November, I announced that with my three conditions now met we would deploy the extra 500 personnel in early December.

I then set out what I considered to be the basis for the next stage of our strategy. The nation-building of four or five years before had been superseded by a laser-like focus on the actions necessary to pass control of the country to the Afghan army, police and civilian authorities. I reminded the British public that three-quarters of terrorist attacks on British soil originated in the Afghan–Pakistan borderlands and, as Obama was to do later in his December statement, I demanded Pakistani action against the terrorist threat. Our progress was, I said, not to be measured 'in enemies killed or battles won alone': it must be measured in the progress made in improving the capability of the Afghans to protect themselves.

Training, mentoring, partnering and embedding were not the easiest or safest course, but they were the right one. Already 500 of our soldiers were mentoring Afghan forces. In operations such as Panther's Claw we and they were already operating together, and a joint Afghan and allied operational coordination centre had been set up in Lashkar Gah, which I visited that summer. 'Afghanisation' was the strategy Britain had promoted and practised in Helmand for many months, and it now needed to be the strategy of the whole coalition for all of Afghanistan: to bring the country to a point where it could control its own destiny, militarily and economically. It was vital that we improve on our past counter-insurgency strategies, and above all this meant building support from and empowering the local population.

On 1 December, President Obama raised US troop numbers to 100,000 – which meant that coalition forces would rise to 150,000. But there had to be, he rightly said, a political surge to complement his military surge. He called it an integrated civilian–military counter-insurgency campaign. The Afghan National Army was to increase in strength by 50 per cent – from 90,000 to 134,000; 10,000 of those troops were to be based in Helmand alongside 4,000 new police.

While he went further than I did by setting a deadline for departure – Obama announced July 2011 as the start of his rundown – I went further than him in detailing what had to be done if we were really serious about 'Afghanisation': alongside a stage by stage, province by province transfer of control to the Afghan authorities starting within twelve months, we offered a four-year, £500 million plan to build wealth-creating alternatives to heroin production. In our internal debates in 2009 some ministers wanted us to announce a date for departure too – a move that, they argued, would focus the Afghans on rectifying the weakness of their police and armed forces. Others wanted a build-up of forces to ensure a more limited set of objectives could be achieved. I was sure that we could not focus our decision-making narrowly through a military prism, but, in the end, there were no easy answers and I could also see that the earlier ideal of fostering a strong democracy and 'modern' society in Afghanistan was beyond our reach.

However, leaving Afghanistan as a failed state and a seedbed for renewed terrorism was unacceptable if we could possibly prevent it.

We had to achieve a sufficient degree of stability where the Afghan government would be strong enough not to be overrun by the Taliban when we left. So the British presence in Afghanistan, which was increased for the time being to 9,500 troops, would fall to 8,300 from 2010. And when we added these additional 500 troops I did so with an assurance from the Chief of the Defence Staff that I felt necessary for public confidence in our war effort: that before any left for Afghanistan he would be able to guarantee publicly that each of them was properly equipped for the tasks ahead.

But unlike President Obama, who announced that his first troop surge would be his last, I did not put an end date to our mission. For the moment, our strategy of partnering with the Afghans was not to be time-limited but task-limited.

Far later than the UK, America came to the conclusion that there was no military solution to the Afghan conflict and all that the surge could do was prepare the ground for what was ultimately needed: an Afghan government that was strong enough to deal with the Taliban. I supported Karzai's message to the insurgents: that if those now outside the entire political process were prepared to renounce violence, there was a place for them within it – though there was always a question mark over how serious Karzai was about putting this into practice. And with formal talks with the Taliban ruled out by the US, informal discussions had had to be conducted through intermediaries – provided, in the event, by Norway and later Qatar. These discussions would stretch from 2007 all the way into 2015.

For the moment, I focused on strengthening Afghan rule – first by demanding the re-elected Karzai do more to improve security, governance, anti-corruption efforts, reconciliation, economic development and engagement with Afghanistan's neighbours. In his inauguration speech he had, perhaps reluctantly, set out these objectives. When I met Ban Ki-moon at the Commonwealth conference in Trinidad and Tobago in November, we agreed to hold a London conference on Afghanistan in January 2010. When it met we were able to announce an additional 9,000 allied troops and a plan to increase the Afghan National Security Forces to over 300,000 as we transitioned to local control. The follow-up conference – agreed for Kabul in March, but which actually took place after we left office, in July – was to be the first international conference on Afghanistan in Afghanistan.

The conference I hosted in January took place in the wake of General McChrystal's announcement of a new division of responsibilities within southern Afghanistan. Adding 15,000 US troops into Helmand and Kandahar, making 50,000 in all, McChrystal had created 'Regional Command (South West)', with a headquarters in Camp Bastion, which included Helmand, Nimruz and Farah provinces, and 'Regional Command (South East)', which was headquartered at Kandahar airport. During the preliminary discussions of this, we asked ourselves if it made sense for the UK to move to Kandahar, which the Canadians were vacating and was now central to coalition plans. But Jock Stirrup, Bob Ainsworth and I felt it better to make use of the expertise we had gained on the ground in Helmand, including through our leadership of the Provincial Reconstruction Team in Lashkar Gah, and remain where we were. At the same time, though, we pressed for the US to take on the more northerly parts of Helmand – Musa Qala, Kajaki and Sangin – to allow us to focus, as we had originally planned in 2006, on the key population areas in central Helmand.

Musa Qala and Kajaki were handed over to the US in the spring of 2010, but Sangin was our biggest headache. It represented a volatile mix of the major tribal groupings, was seen by the Taliban as their safe haven, and delivered the terrorists a steady source of revenue through its narcotics trade. Sangin was generating half our casualties; indeed, at this time, they amounted to one in ten of overall losses incurred by all the allies across Afghanistan. I was not content to leave things as they were, but for months I found McChrystal reluctant to deploy extra forces there. It was eventually agreed before we left office that the US Marines would take over in Sangin and this happened just after I left. Sadly, even with their heavier presence, the Americans also suffered a high level of casualties here.

During 2009 divisions began to intensify. There was, of course, a legitimate argument to be had about equipment and troop numbers. The public were rightly shocked by a succession of losses – in one ten-day period, for example, fifteen troops died, eight of them in one bloody twenty-four hours. But while I admired him as a soldier, public criticism from July 2009 by the outgoing Chief of the General Staff, Sir Richard Dannatt, overstepped the line. When I invited him to Chequers for lunch, he was at pains to tell me that it ought to be a senior figure from the army who held the position of Chief of the

Defence Staff – Sir Jock Stirrup, who held this position, was from the RAF – and this seemed a surprising use of his time when he was publicly complaining about a lack of boots on the ground. At the Conservative Party conference that autumn, just days after retiring from the army, Dannatt was appointed as a Tory adviser. He had now fully entered party politics. When the shadow Home Secretary, Chris Grayling, heard of the move he denounced it as a 'political gimmick' – wrongly assuming that Dannatt had become an adviser to Labour rather than to his own party. A Tory attempt to install Dannatt in the Lords was blocked in the spring of 2010 on the grounds that he should wait at least a year before taking on a political role. But nothing did more to show how the war had been politicised by some of those whose job it was to be non-partisan.

Of course, our generals and serving officers have the absolute right to express their views in private – and one or two certainly did – but Sir Richard crossed a line when he publicly identified with the opposition to the government of the day. 'To abandon the principle of a non-political Civil Service would be a great mistake,' wrote a sage constitutional expert, Vernon Bogdanor, at the time. 'To abandon the principle of a non-political army would be a catastrophe.'

And Sir Richard's criticisms were belied by the the truth: 'British armed forces are better equipped today than at any time in the past forty years,' Lieutenant Colonel Nick Richardson spelt out from on the ground in Afghanistan. 'In the last two years, we have increased helicopter numbers by 60 per cent and capacity by 84 per cent.' The difficulties we faced arose not from Treasury parsimony but from the Taliban's changing tactics.

Against this difficult background – tensions within the coalition, pressures for Afghan contributions, and continuing casualties in the field – the *Sun* was running a relentless campaign during 2009 and early 2010 that accused ministers of not sending more equipment and troops and blamed me directly for the deaths in the field. The personal attacks had been ramped up in the summer of 2009 when I decided to take only one week's holiday – not leaving the country but staying at a hotel in the north of England. On the Monday, as I arrived, the *Sun* front page blared out: 'Message to politicians failing our heroes: don't you know there's a bloody war on? The *Sun* asks the government and Gordon Brown: Where is your leadership?' The paper said

I – and the Defence Secretary, Bob Ainsworth – were 'missing in action'. In the background were photographs of all 207 of our Afghan war dead, with the claim: 'To its shame, our government doesn't seem to want to face up to the fact we are in the middle of a savage conflict . . . Mr Brown has taken the country to war but is ducking responsibility for the conduct of it. The tradition of our country is that in wartime, the prime minister takes charge.'

By the autumn their campaign had intensified. In November 2007 the *Sun* had claimed I fell asleep at the Festival of Remembrance. This was, of course, not true: they used a photograph of me with my head bowed during one of the many prayers. Now in November 2009 they went one stage further – falsely alleging that I had not bowed at the Cenotaph – using a photograph of me in which I was holding my head high, just before I bowed. And, even after all the rest of the media rejected the claims from a Brighton press agency that I was indifferent to the mother of one of our war dead, the *Sun* took it up, alleging that I had misspelt the name of her son. I phoned the mother to say how sorry I was for the distress she felt. But the *Sun* secured a recording of the private telephone conversation I had with her from my desk in No. 10. Their headline was unfair and malicious, accusing me of having refused to apologise for the misspelling. Though I admit my handwriting may have been difficult to read, it was ironic that it was the *Sun* itself which had later to apologise for misspelling the surname of the mother concerned.

Because of this intensification of the *Sun*'s campaign – now covered by the BBC and the wider media – I phoned Rupert Murdoch and pointed out that his campaign criticising our conduct of the war was achieving the opposite of what he had intended. He said he wanted to strengthen the British people's resolve over Afghanistan; I presented him with our polling evidence showing the opposite had happened. In 2006 public support had been low enough – at 31 per cent – but by 2009 it stood at only 18 per cent. Ultimately, he admitted the *Sun* had gone too far and urged me to talk to his editor, Rebekah Brooks. Reluctantly I did so. But the damage was done. I followed it up with a letter explaining that his paper was criticising a Britain that was in the vanguard of the campaign.

This November conversation was the only phone call I had with Rupert Murdoch in the months before we left office. He claimed later

that I had threatened him in a phone call at the time of the Labour
Party conference in September 2009 just after the *Sun* had come out
for the Conservatives. No such conversation occurred and there was
no phone call of any kind between us in September or October. In
fact, I had decided that I would make no complaint to the Murdoch
papers or Murdoch himself over their endorsement of the Conservative Party.

Afghanistan was now, however, thoroughly at the centre of domestic politics. The *Sun* and the Conservatives wanted people to believe
that lives were being lost not just because of alleged mismanagement
of the war but because we did not care. It revealed to me just how
much newspapers had changed. No longer the first port of call for
up-to-the-minute news, with TV and social media operating on a 24/7,
minute-to-minute cycle, newspapers needed another unique selling
point – hence their rising trade in sensationalism. It was not enough
for the *Sun* to allege that I had made a mistake; it felt compelled to
report an ulterior motive. So it crafted and maintained a narrative
that I didn't care about what happened to the troops. On Afghanistan,
they claimed not only that our policy was suspect but that our motives
were too. We were not just misguided but malevolent. A newspaper
that always claimed it was defending the armed forces – running events
in praise of them – ended up using the war and the troops for their
own political and commercial purposes. With the Conservative Party
now working hand in glove with the *Sun* – and promising new laws
to neuter Ofcom and undermine the BBC – we were under attack
every day. And with the *Telegraph*, the *Mail* and the *Express* as anti-
Labour as ever, we faced an uphill fight in getting our message across.

I was saddened and angered at the breach of the all-party consensus
on Afghanistan and felt party interest had been put before national
interest; indeed, when they came into government, both the
Conservatives and Liberal Democrats did not change course and followed in most respects what we had done.

But the debates we were now engaged in were a sign of something
more profound: a war-weariness after eight years of conflict, during
which we had been fighting on two fronts, not just in Afghanistan but
also in Iraq. Ultimately, an insoluble problem lay at the heart of the
British intervention. I had a clear view of the limits of what we could
do – a handover to Afghan control – and recognised that we were not

good at the business of state-building. It was simply too late to persuade the Afghan people that we were liberator not occupier.

By 2010, the allies had spent $1 trillion in Afghanistan: dollar for dollar, in today's prices, vastly more than on the whole Marshall Plan for Europe after the Second World War. Yet the coalition never properly sequenced its multiple objectives nor even how they fitted together; and so every problem seemed to lead to one reflexive answer: a bigger build-up of troops – in 2005, 2006, 2007, 2008, 2009 and even later. But no military or financial resources would ever be sufficient to pacify such a large and ungovernable terrain, which had defied everyone from Alexander the Great to the Soviet Union in the 1980s. One observer has argued that over-optimism, even hubris, led Britain to assume that too few troops could do too much. Others suggest that, in a multinational US-dominated operation, Britain was free to make only the tactical judgements, not the strategic decisions. My own conclusion is that even with more limited objectives and a far greater commitment of troops than we or our allies were prepared to make, our success still depended on a cooperation that was not forthcoming, neither from a local and fractured population nor, in any material sense, from the Afghan or Pakistani governments.

In conception, the nation-building (or, more accurately, state-building) we were attempting – based on the use of armed forces to underpin the construction from outside of state institutions and the fabric of the country's economy – was very much in tune with the western notion of promoting liberal ideals. Even though ultimately it was born out of the colonial enterprises of the nineteenth and twentieth centuries, it seemed to fit the new thinking contained in the UN's 'responsibility to protect', agreed by all its member states in 2005. It also drew inspiration from what we saw on the ground in Afghanistan – a weak civil society and broken governmental institutions – and an understanding that we could not just kill or capture our way to a lasting victory. For this reason, the received wisdom was that military operations should be used to support the development of the economy and apparatus of state. In the American parlance, 'stability operations' offered a direct civilian complement to 'military operations'. This was also sometimes known as 'muddy-boots diplomacy' and on occasion as 'three cups of tea'.

Sadly no one found the best way of delivering development. Some had favoured handing this task to the military or to private contractors, as had been done in Iraq, others argued for a DIY approach, giving such responsibility to the Afghans wholesale, but we never had sufficient personnel working on development and reconstruction on the ground to achieve this end ourselves.

Yet, whatever model is chosen, if reconstruction – delivering infrastructure and services – is at the expense of building local capacity, it can be the enemy of development, and the more we intervened in the domestic affairs of Afghanistan, the more we looked like an occupier and lacked the cultural understanding, local knowledge and even essential language skills needed. When we tried to encourage local initiatives free from dependence on outside aid, we found feeble local institutions, widespread corruption, and tribal loyalties more important than loyalty to the government.

Nation-building failed not just because it required almost limitless funds at a time when budgets were strained, nor because it was difficult to find the greater number of trained civilians and military experts we needed long-term on the ground: it failed because converting one of the world's least developed and most ungovernable countries into a modern functioning society in one short decade was an unrealisable goal. And when it came to the crunch, even more basic aims had to take second place to our first duty: protecting our own troops.

Yet, during our time in Afghanistan, 6 million children who had been denied education – including 2 million girls – went to school, and we ensured that 80 per cent of the population had healthcare. All this was only possible because of the bravery and dedication of our troops – rightly regarded as the best armed forces in the world – and some of the most dedicated aid workers.

But these undoubted gains never gathered momentum and they now seem at risk. As I write, the Taliban controls half of Afghanistan and, according to claims from American military intelligence, it is now being armed by Russia. Although massively weakened by drone attacks, al-Qaeda still hides in the mountains. Two ISIS groups and the Haqqani network are now mounting regular bombings and attacks. Pakistan remains weak and at the epicentre of terrorism. The reflex response is as before – Washington sending in more troops. But if we did not succeed with 150,000 men and women under more favourable conditions than we now face, it is right to ask how much can be achieved today with a fraction of that number.

Nation-building did work in post-war Germany and Japan, in Cold War Greece and Turkey, in Korea and more recently in the Balkans. But it has failed again and again – in Vietnam, despite the presence at once stage of more than 500,000 US troops; in Iraq with 200,000 troops; and in Afghanistan. Nation-building will not succeed where there has never been a complete surrender of enemy forces or where a large proportion of the people are not on your side. Afghanistan suffered from levels of development not seen in Europe since the medieval era. Perhaps even more importantly, the Afghan state has never exercised effective control across a land mass in which a province such as Helmand hosts a kaleidoscopic population, subdivided into a multiplicity of tribes, mini-tribes and extended families, often with competing interests and loyalties, often at odds with each other. The overall campaign for Afghanistan could have been lost in Helmand, but never won there.

Now, with so many recent terrorist attacks in Britain, led by militants born here, it is harder to say we are fighting 'over there' to prevent violence 'over here'. It will take time and perspective to gauge the ultimate impact of the Afghan war. Today many will ask the question first posed by General David Petraeus about Iraq in 2003: 'Tell me how this ends.'

CHAPTER 15

THE BANKING COLLAPSE THAT SHOOK THE WORLD

'No one should panic.'

With these words, the BBC's business editor Robert Peston signed off his broadcast on the evening of Thursday 13 September 2007, having broken the news to the world of the Bank of England's rescue plan for the Newcastle-based ailing bank Northern Rock.

The words might just as well have been spoken by the hapless Corporal Jones in *Dad's Army* – for, like Jones's famous catchphrase, they had the precise opposite of their intended effect. The public panicked.

The next morning, I was holding my normal meetings in 10 Downing Street when I was told I should turn on the television. All across the world, pictures were being broadcast of ordinary savers, now terrified they might lose everything, queuing outside branches of Northern Rock in Newcastle, Sheffield, Surrey and north London, in such large numbers that police officers were deployed for crowd control. Nothing like this had happened to a British bank since Overend Gurney & Company collapsed in 1866.

In fact, on the day that Peston delivered his scoop, the bank's fortunes were looking better than they had in weeks. At the end of June 2007, Northern Rock had issued a profit warning in advance of poor results. Little public comment followed, but intensive and very private discussions were held during August and early September with the financial authorities about the state of the bank's balance sheet. As the Treasury and Bank of England worked with Northern Rock on a rescue plan, the news leaked to the BBC and the rest is history. The next day Alistair Darling formally announced liquidity support. The Bank of England was clear in its judgement that Northern Rock was solvent. But none of these reassurances stopped the queues lengthening. I believed that the Bank of England needed to do far more to guarantee all Northern Rock deposits and, if necessary, those of other banks that could be imperilled by a run. That we did by Monday.

At first, I was determined to avoid nationalising Northern Rock. We did not want a bank on our hands. We knew that at some time it would have to be sold back to the private sector and we would be faced with a dilemma of whether to sell it back at a loss or to try to hold on to it to recoup our investment. We looked at all the options, including an auction to find a private buyer, but outside interest was conditional on the government assuming all the firm's debts. Ten private companies expressed an interest in buying the bank at bargain-basement prices. In every case we were being asked to take on all the firm's risks without receiving any of the benefits: in short, to nationalise the losses and privatise the gains.

When Northern Rock announced that all of those offers were below its stock exchange value, its share price dropped a further 20 per cent in November. By mid-February 2008 only two bidders remained: Virgin and the Northern Rock board. Alistair and I met to discuss both offers. Each bid would cost the government dearly: Virgin's was conditional on three more years of liquidity support. I phoned a very unhappy Richard Branson to tell him his bid was far costlier to the taxpayer than state control. At 4 p.m. on 17 February, we announced that Northern Rock would be nationalised and managed at arm's length as a commercial entity. When the Conservative–Liberal Democrat government later sold Branson the bank on what seemed to be similar terms to the ones he had been proposing in 2008, the British taxpayer was the loser. Our estimate had been that Virgin stood to make a quick £1.2 billion out of the deal.

It is true we were not prepared for what was happening – or for what was going to happen in the coming months. No one was. But we had not been passive. In 2006–7, Ed Balls, then Economic Secretary to the Treasury, had led the Treasury, the Bank of England and the FSA in a simulation exercise, a kind of 'war game' to model what might happen in the event of a bank failure. Would the fall of a bank or a building society spread contagion and raise systemic issues? If it did, at what point would we have to intervene? And what risk did Britain and indeed many other economies face from the increasingly global operations of financial conglomerates based beyond our shores?

I had approached Hank Paulson, the US Treasury Secretary, and he readily agreed to participate in a transatlantic simulation. Normally, the only such exercises that the UK conducts with the United States are military ones. As far as I know this was the first joint 'war game' focused on finance. Besides Hank, we brought together by video conference Ben Bernanke, chairman of the Federal Reserve, and the main regulatory bodies in the States, including the Securities and Exchange Commission and the New York Fed, as well as Callum McCarthy, chairman of the FSA, and Mervyn King, the governor of the Bank of England.

I suspect that most of the assembled group started out with the conventional view that the moral hazard of rescuing a bankrupt institution was so great that it was wiser to let it go under: if a bank thought it would be rescued, it could take undue risk. Yet after playing out various scenarios, everyone moved to accept, albeit reluctantly, that there were circumstances in which a rescue would be unavoidable.

Had it been known we were conducting such simulations, the markets might have panicked, so no private sector participants were in the room. In hindsight, we might have been better prepared for what was to come if we had simulated potential private sector responses, for the question that our simulation could not definitively answer was whether the private sector would be prepared to be part of the rescue.

More importantly, the exercise was not designed to explore what might happen in the case of a succession of failures around the world. Nor did it include enough detailed discussion of the increased entanglement of financial institutions with each other, the possible effect of a 'shadow banking system' hidden from view, and what might happen if we suddenly had to account for a mountain of debt that had never been included on the official balance sheet. But this was the scenario that lay ahead of us.

Capitalism needs credit to flourish. Of course, we knew of the historical tendency of markets to go too far, to generate unsustainable credit booms and so-called 'overleveraging'. We also knew that at the peak of a cycle, when lending is at its greatest, the risk to the system is greatest too, and so extra capital is needed to maintain confidence and prevent collapse. But we could never obtain international agreement on the kind of global financial regulation I had championed since the Asian crisis: namely on transparency, capital requirements and cross-border supervision. The general feeling was that globalisation – sourcing capital from all over the world – had spread the risk and, by diversifying it across many institutions and through many instruments, had reduced the risk too.

In fact, as we were about to discover, these supposed safeguards would become the driving force for disastrous contagion. We were to find that banks everywhere were so entangled that, when one of them had too little capital to cover its positions, the whole market seized up; so when the crisis really hit, the system would be too highly leveraged to cope with the fallout from the collapse in American sub-prime investments. To keep the economy moving, governments would simply have to intervene.

Given Mervyn King's participation in the war game, I was surprised when in mid-September 2007 he spoke out publicly on the moral hazard of intervening to save banks. By now, the banking failures were moving beyond Northern Rock. In October 2007, UBS and Citigroup each announced losses of over $3 billion from sub-prime related investments. At the end of the month, the CEO of Merrill Lynch had resigned after reporting an exposure to nearly $8 billion of bad debt. By December 2007 all of this was having a major impact on the banks' willingness to lend to each other, and central banks were now coordinating billions in loans in order to get money flowing.

At Christmas 2007, while busy planning our new initiatives on the NHS and public sector reform, I also spoke regularly with Shriti Vadera, a former investment banker whom I now moved from her role as a minister in the Department for International Development to the Department for Business, Enterprise and Regulatory Reform. Shriti had been monitoring events. The freezing up of lending, she said, seemed to reflect a growing recognition that banks' balance sheets were riddled with toxic assets.

The practices that had led to this would have appalled the ordinary depositor. The banks' books no longer held the loans they had made to their customers, even though customers had been repaying them for the last fifteen or twenty years: instead the banks had parcelled up those loans, sold them on, and used them as collateral for further borrowing. By late 2007, although we did not know this at the time, 50 per cent of Britain's outstanding mortgages had been sold off and were held in so-called 'securitisation vehicles'. This meant they had been bundled together along with trillions of dollars' worth of other new mortgages of variable quality from across the world, which had been given the most secure, reliable and, in many cases, thoroughly misleading of debt ratings – 'Triple A' – and then sold on and on and on in a speculative spiral that had become a rich source of income for many Wall Street and City firms.

In Northern Rock's case, just 20 per cent of its loans were covered by retail deposits and mortgage payments. No other bank relied so much on short-term borrowing – often overnight lending – from the marketplace and at the same time paying low interest rates to fund long-term mortgages, so much so that their very survival depended on it. They had no plan B if the short-term financial markets dried up. Indeed, their strategy was so aggressive that it was but a short step from criminality: when they issued figures for mortgage debts in the months before the bank's collapse, they had failed to disclose the arrears of hundreds of mortgages. The FSA later reported that the staff felt 'under pressure' to produce attractive figures. The true repossession figures were, in fact, 300 per cent higher than those reported. This was an offence – they were later fined – but the sanctions of the law should have been stronger, and should have led to prison sentences.

However, while Northern Rock was proven to be an outlier in the extent of its unorthodox financing, its practices were not unique: right across the system, particularly in the USA, even the most prestigious institutions were discovering the toxicity of their holdings. I now found to my horror a vast shadow banking system made up of banking affiliates that were not bound by the rules that applied to the banks themselves but which acted like banks – trading in dubious financial instruments and offering nearly twice as much credit as that interme-diated by traditional banks.

The sheer size and pervasiveness of these instruments – free from regulation but also free of any government guarantees – formed the breeding ground for everything that subsequently went wrong. We now know that during 2008 an astonishing $50 trillion – more than the entire annual income of everyone in the world – was pledged across financial companies, all of it done without ever being properly declared. One company, AIG, had signed $1 trillion worth of insurance contracts without the resources to cover them. Even as the music stopped, extravagance and excessive risk-taking continued.

This shadow banking system had proliferated without politicians realising it, and with no one ever reporting the huge risks inherent in their practices. It was now so extensive and so far beyond the reach of the supervisory authorities that if it was not addressed, it was bound to be an ever-present threat to stability. But it was also clear to me that this gathering storm was not something Britain could deal with on its own. It was a global phenomenon flowing out of America and in all directions – indeed, I later discovered that half the US sub-prime debt was, by then, owned in Europe. As we returned in the New Year I drafted an article for the *Financial Times* under the title 'Ways to Fix the World's Financial System'. It was, I said, an underpricing of risk and a deficit of transparency that now had to be addressed by regulators and by firms themselves. That was the message I carried to the annual World Economic Forum in Davos, Switzerland, and was encouraged to do so by its energetic and path-breaking leader, Klaus Schwab.

For years Davos has been a celebration of globalisation. I had attended regularly since the 1990s. This time I warned that the sheer size of banks' losses, unless addressed, could bring the threat of a global recession. New, more stringent, national and international rules for banking were urgently needed along with monetary and fiscal support to prevent a serious economic downturn.

At the end of January 2008, the US Fed revealed the scale of their concerns with two successive interest-rates cuts within a week. On 29 January, I brought European leaders Nicolas Sarkozy, Angela Merkel, Romano Prodi and José Manuel Barroso to discussions in London. We started off in the Cabinet Room and then, after an hour, moved to a small dining room on the first floor of Downing Street. In a relatively informal atmosphere we would be freer to say candidly where each of us stood.

None of us believed the banks when they said they had cleaned up their balance sheets. Our starting point was that they had first to rid themselves of their impaired assets. I suggested that, to restore confidence, we then had to set a timeline and standards of transparency for a clean-up. We all agreed that we had to ratchet up pressure on the banks but there was a sense around the table that this was America's problem and that the UK was caught up in it because, unlike mainland Europe, we were much more closely tied to Wall Street.

In the easy atmosphere of a small dinner party, everyone agreed that the current G8 – which included the advanced economies of Europe, America and Japan, as well as Russia, but which excluded major economies like China and India – could no longer be the sole vehicle for economic coordination. Suggestions ranged from a G8 plus five or six countries to an even wider group – a debate that was to continue right up until September.

On 6 February, I talked at length to President Bush about developing a joint plan to reduce the uncertainty gripping the markets. This led to a unanimous call from the G7 finance ministers in Tokyo for the prompt disclosure of banks' losses. Over the next few weeks I had a videoconference with Chancellor Merkel and further meetings with President Sarkozy and Prime Minister Zapatero of Spain – and each conversation increased my certainty that we had to do more than just push for a declaration of losses. That was a first step towards restoring confidence, but it was certainly not enough. Slowly but surely I was coming to see that the assets of some of our biggest banks were so impaired that they did not have nearly enough capital to cover their liabilities.

The thunderclap that signalled massive underlying vulnerabilities across Wall Street was the demise of Bear Stearns in March 2008. A year earlier, it had been valued at $18 billion. Now JP Morgan Chase bought it for $240 million. When I met President Sarkozy at No. 10 on 27 March we issued a joint public statement calling for the first time for the immediate write-offs of toxic debts and the reform of the IMF so that, in concert with the Financial Stability Forum, we might at last have an authoritative early warning system.

On 8 April, the IMF confirmed that losses were spreading from sub-prime mortgage assets to commercial property, consumer credit and company debt. Those additional losses neared $1 trillion, as Ben Bernanke confirmed at the G7 meeting a few days later when he estimated US write-downs alone at $250 billion. It was becoming clear that even if the banks issued new shares to raise more capital, they would not have sufficient resources to lend to businesses and thus keep our economies moving. This was starkly demonstrated when the Royal Bank of Scotland and HBOS issued shares worth £16 billion while Barclays, supported by Qatar and the UAE, issued shares worth £4 billion. Even the biggest rights issues in British history, together worth £20 billion of capital, were simply not big enough to keep them liquid.

On 15 April, as these events were unfolding, I invited British bank leaders to No. 10. All the banks but one – HSBC – were keen for the Bank of England to provide more liquidity; but even if that happened, they seemed unprepared to raise the amount of lending in the economy. They were thinking of their own survival, not of the needs of the wider economy. So, after the banks left, I summoned an impromptu meeting with Yvette Cooper, then Chief Secretary to the Treasury, representing Alistair who was in Washington with the G7 finance ministers, and Shriti Vadera, the permanent secretary to No. 10 Jeremy Heywood, the senior Treasury official Tom Scholar, and the Cabinet Secretary Gus O'Donnell. We approved the terms of a new Special Liquidity Scheme that would provide cash flow to ensure business lending would resume. This allowed banks and building societies to swap some of their illiquid assets, including mortgage debts, for UK Treasury bills for up to three years.

Later that day I flew to the USA to give a lecture at the Kennedy Library. Before travelling to Boston, I invited leading American bankers to sit down with me in New York and quizzed them, without great success, on what measures would be necessary to return lending to the economy. In Boston, I repeated John F. Kennedy's famous call for a 'declaration of interdependence among the nations of the world'. It was now more urgent than ever in a globalised world: only on an international basis would we be able to deal properly with the fallout from bank failures and the contagion of recessions spreading from one country to another.

The next day, in Washington, I explored this issue further with Alan Greenspan, the former chairman of the Fed, then with the three leading presidential candidates – Barack Obama, Hillary Clinton and John McCain – and finally that evening with President Bush himself, first in the Oval Office, and again later when our wives joined us for dinner. The next morning I saw Ben Bernanke. Everyone seemed to know there was an impending crisis but there was no consensus on what to do. I flew home to London convinced that Britain had to act right away.

To my disappointment, the Bank of England had been slow to cut interest rates and, even when it did, reduced them only marginally, despite the fact that we were already experiencing a credit crunch and that the funding available for mortgages was now half what it had been. By Easter 2008, confidence in the UK housing market had reached its lowest point in thirty years. America was already in an even worse position: by July the Bush administration had to step in to prevent the collapse of America's two largest lenders, Fannie Mae and Freddie Mac, who were owners or guarantors of $5 trillion worth of home loans, nearly half of the outstanding mortgages in the US.

Although we could not solve the underlying problem – which had originated in Wall Street – on a purely national basis, we had to try to limit its impact on Britain. The Special Liquidity Scheme now ran to £100 billion. Recalling the damage that had been done to home-owners by the Tories in the previous recession of the 1990s, we also set aside money to help mortgage-holders. But it was not just the mortgage market that was freezing up. I now worried about the entire economy: 850 companies had gone into administration in the first quarter of the year, 54 per cent up on the previous year – with retail and construction the worst affected. The FTSE 100 stock index was already down 20 per cent and the British Chambers of Commerce survey was predicting recession. In fact, between April and July 2008, as the Office of National Statistics would later confirm, the UK econ-omy was at a standstill and we were about to face declines in national economic output in the next two quarters. A recession that had started in summer 2008 would be declared official in January 2009.

The global economy was under stress in other ways too. One of the great ironies of 2008 was that even as the western economy was slowing and faced collapse, oil prices were still rocketing because of high levels of demand from Asia. I spent an inordinate amount of time trying to help prices to fall. It may have been a detour from the bigger business of the day – preventing a world depression – but it mattered. We called in experts from the industry and beyond and carried out an examination of all obstacles to supply that, if alleviated, could bring the oil price down. Then, on my initiative, the king of Saudi Arabia called the Jeddah oil summit where it was agreed that they would pump more oil. As a result, oil prices peaked at $148 a barrel and two weeks later began to fall. Soon they were to collapse as world economic activity ground to a halt. By December they were down by 75 per cent.

Throughout the early months of 2008 we struggled to persuade the banks that their problems demanded radical surgery. Bankers kept telling me that their problem was one of liquidity, but it was becoming clear that the real issue was solvency. When HBOS had issued shares to raise capital, they had failed to sell two-thirds of them: the markets were telling HBOS to come clean on the toxicity of its assets. Even Barclays faced a similar problem before they were rescued by cash injections from the Qatari government.

The collapse in credit and its consequences for the global economy were the questions on my mind throughout the short holiday I took that summer. As always, it was great to spend some private time with Sarah and the boys. Sarah had chosen Suffolk so that our children could spend time playing with some of their friends who would also be there that summer. I took some time out to get fit. The personal trainer I hired locally would come to regret taking on a client who brought with him such press attention, which swiftly turned its focus on her colourful private life: yet another individual was to learn a lesson about the pitfalls of entering the political orbit. And of course the usual summer political gossip started up when David Miliband wrote an article hinting he was ready for a leadership coup.

As usual I tried to use the holidays to read widely in a way that wasn't possible when faced with a daily diary of back-to-back meetings. I picked up Ben Bernanke's essays on the Great Depression. I could see the parallels: the swift withdrawal of credit worldwide could drag Britain into recession or even depression. I also invited Shriti to join us. We talked about Bernanke's ideas for quantitative easing and I made a mental note to talk to Gavyn Davies when we were all back in London. In fact, Gavyn was the first to suggest to me that the Bank should buy bonds outright and that it should finance part of the budget deficit by expanding the monetary base. I then talked to Mervyn King, who in January was to announce the Bank's Asset Purchase Facility and then in March the Bank's first purchase – £75 billion of assets.

In 2008, we had started thinking the previously unthinkable. Quantitative easing would be £200 billion by November 2009. It was to be a central element of the recovery programme in 2009 and, after the 2010 election, the only element of the recovery programme. A further £175 billion would be added by the coalition government after November 2011 – required to compensate for austerity and the loss of the fiscal stimulus.

That summer, however, our primary focus was on the banks. We studied Japan's experience with what were now called 'zombie' banks – those that had no actual worth but continued to operate because they were propped up by the government. Shriti, who always thought far into the future, gave me her bleak assessment: poisoned by bad sub-prime assets, some banks might now fail. If they were to stay afloat, then an even bigger injection of capital would be needed than the one provided by their recent share issues. Where would it come from? Might sovereign wealth funds step in? Might there be other sources of private capital around the world? Could we in Britain do what the US had done in the case of JP Morgan and Bear Stearns, with the stronger banks taking over the weaker? Or would governments have to step in?

Jeremy Heywood arrived in Suffolk to discuss these crucial questions and we agreed that a Civil Service team would explore both how banks might be incentivised to resume lending, and how they might be recapitalised if this was deemed necessary. Shriti sent me a long set of email exchanges in which she had been exploring the options ahead with a group of hand-picked experts: they were bluntly entitled 'is it capital?' And the more I explored the lessons of the past and applied them to the data of the present, the more it became clear that a massive amount of capital was indeed needed to strengthen the banks, but that even then both additional government spending (a fiscal stimulus) and lowering interest rates or printing money (a monetary boost) were essential to restore the economy to decent levels of growth. It was also clear to me that all of this would work best if the rest of the world joined in. Indeed, when I started to examine the cumulative benefit that would come from all countries taking similar action along these lines, I quickly found that joint action would achieve twice the impact.

Alistair too saw problems ahead: in an interview with the *Guardian* from his holiday cottage in the Outer Hebrides, under the headline 'Storm Warning', he said the economic times would be the worst for sixty years. He was absolutely right, but it wrong-footed us because he was interpreted as singling out a peculiarly British problem. When we later talked by the phone, he and I were agreed that we had to emphasise the reality that the roots and failures were worldwide.

By now the Treasury was acting – and intervening – far faster than the Bank of England. Alistair announced a temporary boost to the housing market – exempting stamp duty on purchases at £175,000 or below. But I found it difficult to understand the Bank of England decision to keep interest rates at 5 per cent. Even though all the signs were there that the economy was now entering recession – later confirmed by the official statistics – the Bank was holding back on the monetary stimulus the economy clearly needed and maintaining its position that intervening to save distressed banks should be resisted because of the moral hazard involved. Rates would still be at 4.5 per cent at the start of October 2008 – a whole year after the Federal Reserve had cut rates from 5 per cent to 1.25 per cent. They would come down to 1.5 per cent only in January 2009 and then to 1 per cent in February, four months after the Fed cut rates to 1.25 per cent and two months after reducing them to 0.5 per cent. I was right not to criticise the Bank publicly for keeping rates high for so long – that would have reopened the whole question of Bank independence – but it is obvious now that we needed far earlier and far more proactive monetary intervention.

Things had to change. If the Bank was going slow, governments had to do more in Britain and Europe. But even then, we already knew it would not be enough. America – where the problems had started – had to act. I talked to President Bush by phone on 11 September. Four days earlier Fannie Mae and Freddie Mac had been nationalised, and after posting a three-month loss of $3.9 billion, Lehman Brothers was on its deathbed. A later report showed that Lehman had removed liabilities from its balance sheet to create a materially misleading picture of its financial position. By now Hank Paulson was in touch asking for British support for a rescue operation. He enquired if Barclays could buy Lehman's US operations – something Barclays, keen to become a global bank with a strong investment banking arm, were interested in. But the US conditions attached were impossible: Hank wanted to transfer to Britain the responsibility for providing Lehman with liquidity, and he wanted Barclays to be able to ignore the legal requirement to put the acquisition to their shareholders for approval. So, the deal would have left the UK taxpayer footing the bill for the collapse. We could not offer such an open-ended guarantee. There was another issue. By the Sunday when we rejected the proposal it was becoming clear that despite their ambitions to enter the top tier of investment banking, Barclays did not have the funds to mount the Lehman rescue.

The next day, 15 September, Lehman filed for bankruptcy, and a Wall Street institution that had survived two world wars and the Great Depression was no more. Previously there were four big independent Wall Street firms; by that Monday morning, there were two. That same day the Fed bailed out AIG to the tune of an astonishing $85 billion.

Barclays were saved from themselves when we blocked their Lehman deal – they would have taken over $60 billion of losses – and were now able to pick up Lehman's US investment banking and trading assets for $2.5 billion. To cover their outlay, they successfully placed 750 million shares for £700 million and raised the capital necessary for the acquisition.

HBOS appeared to be the bank in most trouble. Fortunately, one of our options, a private sector solution, seemed doable. Lloyds had been interested in acquiring HBOS for many years, but competition issues had blocked any merger. When each of them made separate approaches to us, asking for a waiver, we agreed. I talked directly to Victor Blank, then Lloyds chairman, who was to be unfairly criticised for his role in the Lloyds–HBOS link-up, mainly by Lloyds shareholders who would have to endure hefty losses. I found him straightforward, a man of integrity, and in my view he behaved in a way that was beyond reproach.

By now the chaos in the United States was at the forefront of everyone's minds. In Downing Street, we were all watching the markets anxiously, and around me I could feel the growing tension in the air. Every time Jeremy Heywood said he wanted to update me on something, I expected another banking collapse.

The Lehman bankruptcy marked a turning point; from then on not just mortgage markets but all markets froze across the world. The Lehman case revealed that right at the heart of the world's banking system, which prided itself on and indeed advertised its prudence, there had been a reckless culture of excessive risk-taking. For a century and more Lehman had been a brokerage firm. For the most part, it did not use its balance sheets to acquire assets to make its own investments. But in 2005 it made a strategic shift: it was risking money it did not have to speculate in commercial real estate through leveraged lending and private equity. It was a change in business model that had now had devastating consequences.

The Royal Bank of Scotland had made similar mistakes. On paper, it had been making huge profits, paying high dividends, acquiring new assets and, as one of the first banks to enter China, seemed to be on its way to becoming the world's biggest bank. To the public in Britain it was a dynamic retail and commercial bank with branches all over the country, backed by some of Britain's most famous names. At least that was how RBS presented itself on advertising boards round the country.

I had known the bank from my early days as an MP. The Fife constituency I served was just across the Forth from the bank's headquarters in Edinburgh, and I remember visiting their new offices before they were officially opened. Their plush £350 million headquarters, which were opened by the Queen, were the size of a small village, with shops, cafés, auditoriums, a swimming pool and even space at the rear for a proposed golf course.

The RBS chief executive, Fred Goodwin, was a self-made man. I first came across him as one of the accountants involved in privatising Rosyth Dockyard. Over the years I saw him change. By the time the bank collapsed he had from his company a private suite in the Savoy costing £700,000 a year, a fleet of twelve chauffeur-driven Mercedes limousines with RBS emblazoned all over them, and regularly used a private jet at the weekend – whether for hunting in Spain or following the glamorous F1 circuit around the world. Every year £1 million was paid out to each of RBS's 'global ambassadors', including Sir Jackie Stewart, Jack Nicklaus (whose image was on one of the bank's commemorative £5 notes), and Andy Murray (who, to his credit, would volunteer a cut in his payment) as part of an estimated £200 million sponsorship budget. Large five-year contracts, including for cricketer Sachin Tendulkar, were to be signed just weeks before the bank crashed. Millions of pounds were simply wasted.

Fred and I spoke only rarely, but I do recall one conversation with him. While I was still chancellor I met Fred at his Edinburgh office and asked about what were called 'orphan assets'. These were assets held on banks' balance sheets belonging to customers who had died without leaving any instruction as to where the money should go. In some cases, these customers had passed away a century ago or more, but their savings were still held by the bank and accruing interest. The banks estimated them at £400 million. We thought they were in excess of £1 billion. Once the unclaimed assets of insurance companies were added, the figure exceeded £2 billion. I told him that this was money that the institutions did not own and that, according to a plan drawn up by the Commission on Unclaimed Assets – led by the philanthropic venture capitalist Sir Ronald Cohen, who proved masterful in raising money for social purposes – it should be put to community uses. One was building new youth centres, another was funding education in financial literacy. I was planning to introduce a policy that would bring this plan into effect, and in my discussions with other banks had found them, if not overjoyed, at least receptive. Goodwin was resistant, the odd man out, and for reasons that at the time I couldn't work out. I can only now imagine how delicate his bank's position must have been.

RBS did indeed have an unusually low capital base, but we did not know quite how vulnerable it was. And when RBS proceeded in 2007 with a leveraged and risk-laden $60 billion bid to take over the Dutch bank ABN Amro, they did not do the checks necessary to discover it was riddled with sub-prime and impaired assets. The information made available to RBS by ABN Amro in April 2007, the FSA later reported, amounted to 'two lever arch folders and a CD'. I was later told of the crucial email that gave the order to go ahead: they would deal with the assets and liabilities later.

In just over a year, from mid-2007 to late 2008, Fred Goodwin had doubled the bank's debt and inter-bank borrowings to £500 billion, suffered a £2 billion write-off in Germany, and amassed further losses in American and eastern Europe. And, with too little capital in the first place, funding was about to dry up. Yet at no point did I ever hear Fred Goodwin express real contrition to me – or to anyone else – for his role in the bank's collapse.

HBOS had fallen too, but for a different reason. It had staked everything on rising prices in the property market. When the new finance officer of the merged Lloyds–HBOS gave a slide presentation in New York entitled 'Understanding the HBOS Loan Book', he revealed an astonishing figure: 40 per cent of HBOS's £432 billion loan book was what he called 'outside Lloyds' appetite'. It was a curious phrase, but it meant that these loans should never have been taken on. His conclusions about the biggest loans on their books – £116 billion of corporate lending – were as brutal. Two-thirds – that is, over

£70 billion – should never have been agreed, he said. The bank's business model enjoyed the innocuous label 'integrated finance' but it was little more than a cover for speculative property deals funded for a group of privileged customers by an undercapitalised bank: deals which, worryingly, were ramped up in number and cost even as the bank approached the precipice of financial ruin. When added to its exposure to billions of dollars' worth of toxic sub-prime debts, which were only finally revealed at the time of the Lloyds merger, HBOS was, to all intents and purposes, bust.

Well into the crisis, in late 2008, I had a conversation with one of the country's leading bankers who told me all I needed to know about the gulf between his profession and the rest of society. He admitted that he himself was only beginning to understand the risks that his bank had been taking. I questioned the justification for continuing to pay bankers huge bonuses even as the consequences of their poor judgements were coming to light. 'But they'll leave the country,' he responded. I refrained from offering him the response that ordinary members of the public would have given him. The very fact that the government was forced to step in at all exposed the bankers' rationalisation of their big bonuses – that they bore the risks they took on their own shoulders and that they paid the price when things went wrong – as utterly illusory and self-serving.

Why did we not spot these problems much earlier? I had spoken often before this point of the hazards of an interconnected global financial system, but despite the fact that I and others had pressed for years for some sort of early warning system, no one anywhere had the detailed information we needed to comprehend the extent of these global entanglements and liabilities. And although in retrospect I hear many players claiming that they had warned us of the risks we faced, no one had presented to me or to international organisations any concrete picture of the extent of those risks within the system, nor of the scale of the shadow banking operations that operated at its fringes.

Although the crisis exploded out of America, British regulation was deficient too. We had created what I still believe is the right framework – a tripartite group of Bank, regulator and government as our early warning system – but from the start the FSA had been in a territorial tug of war with the Bank of England and, as I look back on their minutes, none of the three partners gave the tripartite system the time, input and commitment that was needed. What's more, the FSA did not probe the shadow banking system, which effectively existed beyond the regulator's reach. Even in the formal sector, the assessments of the FSA depended less on in-depth examinations by investigators than on bland assurances from the investigated – all this a product of the neoliberal culture of the time that talked about better regulation but in fact favoured even more deregulation.

On 18 September 2008, we banned one of the practices that seemed to have got out of hand: short selling, which is the business of betting on, and profiting by, a fall in a share's value. This brought only temporary respite, as did Warren Buffett's $5 billion investment in Goldman Sachs. He warned that without a $700 billion federal bailout of US banks, America faced an 'economic Pearl Harbor'. The US administration then announced their plan to end the crisis: the Troubled Asset Relief Program, whereby they would pick up the banks' diseased assets and place them in a separate fund. But when the bailout bill – commonly known as TARP – initially failed to pass through Congress, markets around the world collapsed further.

To its credit, TARP attempted to provide a comprehensive resolution to the crisis. But for me TARP promised too little too late. No longer was it going to be enough to carve out the banks' bad assets. Even with the rotten assets stripped out, the banks would remain too weak and too overleveraged to recover. What was needed was a bolder plan – to recapitalise the banks. Shriti, I and others were turning the question Hank Paulson was trying to answer on its head. Instead of buying up diseased assets that in any case could not be quantified or even properly priced for sale – leaving people in doubt as to whether the bad assets had been removed – why not strengthen the banks, deleverage them and enable them to clean up their act? Of course, I was not prepared to subsidise banks that did not reform. Instead our proposal would inject new capital into the banks subject to their cleaning up their books and, if necessary, through public ownership.

What was happening was unthinkable, but we had to think it through. When I spoke to the Labour Party conference on 23 September, I said the crisis was a defining moment for us – a test not just of our judgement but of our values. My speech at the conference was high-pressure and high-stakes, not just because of the economic challenges but because from August onwards David Miliband was reported to be contemplating a leadership challenge. When I said of the young Tory leaders, David Cameron and George Osborne, 'this is no time for a novice', it was generally taken as referring to David too. He backed away.

As the conference came to a close I boarded a plane for New York to attend the UN General Assembly on 25 September. The minute I arrived I brought together at short notice some of the best economists in the world, including two Nobel Prize-winners. There was complete consensus on the need for massive fiscal stimulus and growing support for bank recapitalisation. When later that day Shriti and I met with American investors, I couldn't let them know we were looking at recapitalisation – that would have set off a round of market speculation – but Shriti teased out of them what we needed to know: that even they, the beneficiaries of TARP, did not see TARP as the solution. And when I met with Tim Geithner, who was then president of the New York Fed, he conceded that within the TARP legislation, there would be a provision that would enable the government to purchase bank shares. I was encouraged. A recapitalisation in the US might not yet be probable, but it was possible. Buoyed by that additional information, I called Alistair and asked him to speak to Hank Paulson about recapitalisation. Alistair came back reporting that Hank was not giving much away. We still had a long way to go.

After my conversation with Alistair, I told Tom Fletcher, my private secretary for foreign and security matters, to arrange an appointment with President Bush for the next day, 26 September, and announced to my long-suffering events team, led by the ever-diligent Barbara Burke, that there had been a change of plan: we would have to shorten our stay in New York and fly to Washington. Before departing, however, I convened an impromptu gathering of the main heads of government who were still in New York for the UN General Assembly. The purpose of this meeting – described fully in the next chapter – was to put forward my proposal for an international forum with which to tackle the causes and consequences of the crisis over the longer term, plans that I would put to President Bush the following day.

I landed in Washington around 3.45 p.m. on Friday 26 September and reached the White House at about 4.15 p.m. President Bush, who always had a ready joke, was in remarkably good spirits. He told me he knew how the Republicans could defeat Barack Obama and was frustrated by their failure to label him an 'elitist' who had derided ordinary people for clinging to their religion and their guns. 'He's a Harvard elitist,' said President Bush, who had himself gone to Yale.

When I turned to the matter of the banks I expressed my view that Hank Paulson's toxic-assets plan, which was on that very day embroiled in congressional controversy, was a start but provided only half the answer. I suggested there was a more direct approach: taking equity in the banks. The crisis had moved, I said, from appearing to be a liquidity problem to what it now clearly was, a solvency problem, and that nobody believed the protestations of the banks any more. He said that this was a matter for Hank and that he would speak to him, but at this stage the priority was to get TARP through Congress.

As the meeting in the Oval Office finished, a fax came through from No. 10, and a request for an urgent call with Alistair. I went into an anteroom to talk to him. He reported that Bradford & Bingley was going under, and we agreed that there was no alternative but nationalisation. I then I picked up the document that had been sent by fax, which contained the figures I had requested from the Treasury: our estimates of bank losses and what it would cost if we decided on recapitalisation. The figures I now had showed we were only days away from a complete banking collapse – of companies unable to pay creditors, workers left unpaid and ATMs without cash to dispense.

It was while I was flying back across the Atlantic that I resolved what we as a government had to do regardless of the Americans' decisions. As has been my habit for decades, I was writing notes – action points and reflections – on the back of the faxes I had been sent. I was particularly drawn to the question Shriti had been asking for some weeks now in her email exchanges: 'is it capital?' Only one possible course of action remained. I wrote it on a piece of paper, in the thick black felt-tip pens I've used since that childhood sporting accident affected my eyesight. For good measure, I underlined it twice. It said simply: RECAPITALISE NOW.

The banks were sure to resist; after all, we would be asking some of Britain's proudest businesses to submit to semi-nationalisation, and we would be asking others who had said they did not need capital to go out and get it, a move that could dilute shareholder equity and so perhaps threaten the position of the executives. But they still needed the government to provide liquidity or they could no longer function as banks. So we had a bargaining position. I wrote it out with my felt-tip pen: NO LIQUIDITY WITHOUT RECAPITALISATION.

It didn't have the elegance of 'No taxation without representation', but it would do. As our plane crossed the night sky, I did not have any doubt – and I certainly could not afford to show any – about the decision I was making, even as I churned over the difficulties ahead.

No one in our media travelling pack was aware of what we were planning. I asked Mike Ellam, the Downing Street director of communications, what story the press were filing from the back of the plane. We joked that they were probably weighing up whether the meeting with the president was short enough for them to get away with calling it a snub. My team, who had gathered around my seat, laughed, and I went back to work.

Once we had touched down in London, we talked the proposal through with Alistair, Shriti and Treasury officials, who started work on a comprehensive plan – to be published within days – that would turn the orthodoxy of the past thirty years on its head.

Events moved quickly. On 4 October, there was a mini-summit in Paris with President Sarkozy, Chancellor Merkel, Prime Minister Berlusconi, President Barroso, and the prime minister of Luxembourg, Jean-Claude Juncker, who was then also president of the Eurogroup (the finance ministers of Eurozone nations). Most of Europe still considered the problem an essentially American one, but the Belgian banks Fortis and Dexia had just had to be rescued, Dresdner Bank had just been merged with Commerzbank in Germany, and generally European banks were more highly leveraged than US banks.

In the next few days, confusion reigned over European policy to guarantee bank deposits. Chancellor Merkel first offered to guarantee them, then redefined the offer not as a cash guarantee but rather a political guarantee to reassure markets; the Danish prime minister Anders Rasmussen announced a day later that he would bail out the banks; and there followed an EU Finance Ministers' Declaration of minimum Europe-wide guarantees for bank deposits.

But on Tuesday 7 October share prices fell across the world, by nearly 10 per cent in some places, and governors of central banks were forced into a coordinated move on interest rates, to be announced the next day. Not only were financial markets frozen but the world economy looked as if it was going into cardiac arrest. Ben Bernanke later reported that he feared for the survival of twelve of the USA's thirteen biggest financial institutions. I could envisage in a few days' time the cash machines simply not dispensing money in the morning.

At least we were now in the final stages of preparations for implementing our recapitalisation plan. Privately Mervyn King, Alistair, Shriti and I discussed what conditions we would lay down. I had two red lines: I had determined that there would be no recapitalisation without changes in remuneration and bonus payments, and without the resignation of executives at the centre of the crisis.

As matter of courtesy I phoned President Bush to inform him of the announcement we would be making the next day. There was as yet no sign of the Americans adopting our approach. Alistair, who had gone to meet the chief executives of the banks to go over the final details of our plan, rang me to report that the banks were incredibly unhappy and resistant. The truth is that despite the chaos around them they had not yet recognised the scale of the problems they had created and now faced. Even the most vulnerable banks were saying they did not need the capital, nor did they want it. They thought that to accept it would publicly signal their weakness. We thought that to refuse it would bring them down, and were in no mood to compromise.

But irrespective of whether some banks needed public capital or not, we needed a united front from the banks on the need for rescue measures. Alistair asked if I would speak to Stephen Green, head of HSBC. Green gave me all the assurances I wanted: that he would raise a token amount of private capital and would support the plan.

Late in the day Tom McKillop, the chairman of RBS, phoned me. He explained his problem was cash flow. All he needed, he said, was 'overnight finance'. A few days later his bank collapsed with the biggest losses in banking history. RBS's problems were not simply about liquidity, and additional cash flow could not have helped for more than a day or two. The problems were structural. The bank owned assets of unimaginable toxicity and had too little capital to cover their losses.

Finally, that evening, bank CEOs came to the Treasury to hear the details of the plan. They were shocked by the amount of capital we said they needed – £50 billion – and tried to halve it. Alistair and I rejected the compromise and told them the deal on offer was final.

I went to bed at midnight on Tuesday 7 October, with my mobile phone next to me in case of any further disasters. Alistair and I had decided to announce the plan at 7 a.m. the following day, and that we would phone other national leaders and finance ministers immediately beforehand and afterwards.

When I got up the next morning I told Sarah that she would have to be ready to pack our things for a sudden move out of Downing Street. If what I was about to do failed, with markets collapsing further and confidence ebbing from Britain, I would have no choice but to resign. As I walked into the office, I didn't know if I'd still be there at the end of the day.

Before the markets opened Alistair announced the government-led recapitalisation plan to buy up to £50 billion of bank capital and equity, together with a £250 billion credit guarantee for banks issuing debt and £200 billion of extra liquidity. We had insisted that in return for making capital available the banks had to lend to get the economy moving.

At 9 a.m. Alistair and I held a joint press conference to answer questions from journalists who were still trying to get their heads around the scale of the measures. I phoned Sarkozy, Merkel and Berlusconi to ask them to consider recapitalisation too. Then I went over to the House of Commons, as I did each Wednesday, for Prime Minister's Questions.

Adding a further twist to a day of high pressure, twenty minutes before I got to my feet in the Commons Mervyn King called me to confirm that at midday, precisely when PMQs would start, the Bank of England would announce what had already been leaked: an interest-rate cut to 4.5 per cent as part of globally coordinated action by the central banks.

We now had to agree how much capital each bank would receive. Fred Goodwin had changed his tune. Having previously denied the need for any capital, he was now telling Shriti that taking some capital would be prudent. He said he didn't want to shock anyone but that his needs might be as high as £5 billion or even £10 billion. When she recounted the call to me she told me her reply: 'I am shocked – not by how high your estimates are, but by how low.'

When HBOS realised that RBS would be taking up the offer, they too came on board and their new partner Lloyds also joined them. That weekend, bank by bank, we hammered out the numbers and the terms of the government's stake in the failing institutions.

Barclays stood aloof. Earlier in the summer it had gone for help to the governments and sovereign wealth funds of Qatar and UAE. Indeed, only 19 per cent of its first rights issue in July had been taken up before Qatar and other sovereign wealth funds came in. Now, according to our calculations, Barclays had to find £13 billion from share issues or sales by June 2009. A deadline was imposed by the Bank of England and the FSA but institutional investors shied away and a further rights issue was deemed impossible. Now needing to devise a debt instrument that would convert to equity, Barclays turned again to Qatar and UAE. In the deal they then brokered, Qatar would raise their stake in the bank to 12.7 per cent and UAE would go even higher to 16 per cent. Qatar's 12.7 per cent stake would turn out to be temporary: in the autumn of 2009 Qatar were to sell off a 3.5 per cent stake and in November 2012 they sold off more. But what Barclays executives and its board now did, to escape British government control, was in my view unconscionable. They paid the sovereign funds a service fee – in Qatar's case, £300 million – that they never disclosed. Because of this they have been warned they may well be subject to a Financial Conduct Authority (FCA) fine for handing over money they did not properly declare. However, the FCA probe had to be temporarily suspended to give way to a Serious Fraud Office investigation into a £3 billion loan subsequently given by Barclays to Qatar.

If Barclays found money elsewhere in a legitimate way there could be no objection, but I was always suspicious of the bank's lack of openness with their shareholders – and the public – about the deal it did with the Gulf states. And I was always unhappy that Barclays chose to use their deal to make a political statement: denouncing our state recapitalisation of the banks. The fact that it was state money – from Qatar and UAE – that bailed them out did not discourage them from trying to score cheap political points and build a myth about the awfulness of state interventions. In doing so, they made it far more difficult to explain to the British public that this was a widespread banking crisis and not just an emergency faced by one or two banks and, by not telling the full truth, they hampered our ability to persuade legislators around the world of the need for far-reaching reform.

Their unwillingness to be open about their own problems was brought home when, during our recapitalisation negotiations, Barclays asked if they could buy RBS. If we had allowed that – and no doubt some other governments in the same position might have tried to promote this – then an even larger part of the British banking system would have collapsed.

Now we had acted, the question was what would the rest of the world do. During that flight back to London from the USA, I remember asking, 'If we go out on our own, how does that solve it?' and then answering my own question with another: 'But do we really have a choice?' If the alternative was a succession of bank collapses that triggered a depression, we had to act. But still there were risks from acting alone: a Britain-only recapitalisation might not be enough to gain the confidence of the markets and it might put even the UK's own credit worthiness at risk. Although the Americans were still focused on buying up their banks' diseased assets, there was still a chance of persuading the rest of Europe that they had to recapitalise the banks as well.

While Alistair attended the annual meetings of the World Bank and IMF, on Sunday 12 October I made my second trip to Paris in the space of a week. I had been asked by President Sarkozy to attend an extraordinary meeting of the Eurogroup. The meeting was special for two reasons: first, the Eurogroup was properly a meeting only of Eurozone finance ministers, who jealously guarded their control over policy for the euro member countries. This was the first time since the birth of the euro nine years previously that policy would be discussed at the level of heads of government. The second reason was that Britain was not, of course, a member of the Eurozone. I know that some of President Sarkozy's colleagues complained bitterly about the British presence. He took a personal risk in forcing my involvement on them. We both believed that the urgency of the task meant we had to dispense with protocol.

Prior to the larger euro meeting I met privately with Sarkozy, President Barroso, Chairman Jean-Claude Trichet of the European Central Bank, and Prime Minister Juncker of Luxembourg. I told them I now believed European banks held around $2 trillion of US-originated assets, of which around $400 billion were toxic – with probably a similar amount in the shadow banking system. I repeated that European banks were now more highly leveraged than American banks. When the full Eurogroup met, I presented these same figures again to show why the problem was lack of capital, and why Europe should not confuse the origins of the crisis – which came out of

America – with its severity and its still-multiplying consequences. It was now undeniably a European crisis as well.

Since I was not a member, I left the meeting once I had spoken, but I was to find that my words did have an effect: in the next few days, one by one, countries in the Eurozone decided to recapitalise their banks, and they would design common European rules for a credit-guarantee scheme like ours. But as I had told the Europeans, the world would be safe only if America acted too.

By this stage, the Bush administration had finally won congressional approval for TARP. By Hank Paulson's own account, the administration had now also come to accept that buying up toxic assets would not in itself resolve the crisis. 'Here we were,' he wrote in his diary, 'worse off than ever.' And, as I had already sensed from my meeting over a fortnight before with Tim Geithner, the Americans were moving towards recapitalisation. Hank and President Bush had had a telephone call to prepare for the G7 and G20 meetings that weekend in which they talked about recapitalisation. As Paulson records, 'He [the president] pressed me about the capital program and asked, "Is this what it's going to take to end this thing?" "I don't know, sir," I admitted, "but I hope it's the dynamite we've been looking for."'

As chairman of the Fed, Alan Greenspan had been quick to understand the impact on our lives of new technology, of the changes in the energy markets, and of globalisation. It is to his credit that he now spoke openly about mistakes made and the failings of the US financial system. That weekend he spoke out about the inadequacy of the banks' capital and explained that the capital-requirement models of the banks were deficient. 'Had the models instead been fitted more appropriately to historic periods of stress, capital requirements would have been much higher and the financial world would be in a far better shape today in my judgement.' It was exactly what we had been saying in Britain. The United States was at last changing tack.

By Friday, Hank was offering us more hope that there could be a coordinated approach. He had already approved a paper for the G7 hinting at recapitalisation and he now went further: as long as it did not mean nationalisation, he would support capitalisation. Thanks to Alistair's deft handling, the final G7 agreement did not rule out public stakes in our banks. It spoke of the need for 'capital from public as well as private sources'.

That weekend US officials worked to get a US capitalisation plan into shape. On Sunday 12 October and in great secrecy Paulson, Bernanke and Geithner agreed its terms. As we now know from his account, Hank then personally called all the major bank executives and asked them to meet him in the Treasury at 3 p.m. On that Sunday evening, as I returned from the Paris meeting, President Bush phoned to tell me that they would formally announce on Tuesday that TARP funds would be used for recapitalisation of their banks.

While America prepared to announce its decision in principle, we had to move forward on the practical detail of our own and announce it before the markets opened the following morning, but with our figures being revised and reviewed every hour, this was proving difficult. Having travelled back from Paris, I had got to bed at 1 a.m. At 5 a.m. I was suddenly woken by a noise at the door of our bedroom. I thought it was our young son, John, who often woke up and came through to our room, and I heard Sarah say, 'John, seriously, not tonight, you need to go back to bed and let Dad sleep.' The reply was a whispered, 'Sorry, Sarah, it's Shriti.' And then she added something that jolted me fully awake: 'The Treasury have come up with new numbers which Alistair wants Gordon to see.'

Overnight the Treasury had agreed the final offers we would make to the banks. That had led them to important conclusions which Alistair wanted me to approve: RBS's needs were so extensive that to make recapitalisation work we would own a majority of RBS shares. While Lloyds and HBOS would merge, we would initially also have a majority stake in HBOS. I had been well prepared by Shriti for that probability. Before the markets opened we announced a £37 billion recapitalisation of RBS, Lloyds and HBOS resulting in a 57 per cent stake in RBS (later to rise with a further capital injection above 70 per cent) and a 58 per cent stake in HBOS, with a percentage stake in Lloyds subject to their mergers. Other banks would increase their capital from private sources. To get lending to business and homeowners moving again, the recapitalisation was matched by the biggest credit-guarantee scheme Britain had ever announced: £250 billion.

Throughout the crisis I had felt that we were dealing with more than a financial failure: this was the fallout from years of greed. Andrew Haldane, who would later become the chief economist of the Bank of England, has calculated that if dividend payments had been reduced by a third during the period 2000–7 then £20 billion of extra capital would have been available to the banks. If the banks had restricted dividends in years when they made annual losses, £15 billion more would have been available. And if they had paid themselves just one-tenth less, then another £50 billion could have been used to bolster the banks' positions. As he puts it: 'Three modest changes in payout behaviour would have generated more capital than was supplied by the UK government during the crisis.' So, for me, an indispensable part of our announcement of recapitalisation was that there would now be tight conditions attached to bonuses and pay: remuneration was cut back, dividends were cancelled, the chief executive and the chair of RBS both tendered their resignations, and the CEO of HBOS would also leave.

On 13 October, Germany announced €400 billion in guarantees and €100 billion in capitalisation; France €320 billion in guarantees of medium-term debt and €40 billion for capitalisation; Italy €40 billion in capitalisation and 'as much as necessary' in guarantees; the Netherlands added €200 billion in guarantees; and Spain and Austria €100 billion each. Our diagnosis – that banks were dangerously low on capital – had prevailed, despite being the opposite of what most bankers had been saying for much of the last year. That day also saw a 10 per cent rise in the European stock exchange – its biggest rise ever.

At no point in history have governments injected so much money into buying up assets in the banking system and guarantees. In the coming year, governments around the world would provide a total of $15 trillion in bailouts, guarantees of bank liabilities and special central-bank liquidity. When officials gave me a list of all the countries that had followed Britain's lead – Germany, France, Spain, Denmark, Portugal, the Netherlands, Austria, Switzerland and America – I knew that the world was finding our way forward. The patient was out of the emergency room and into intensive care. The banks had been saved; now could we prevent a global recession becoming a depression?

CHAPTER 16

PREVENTING A GREAT DEPRESSION

'$1 trillion?'

Shriti Vadera left this note on my desk on Monday 30 March 2009, three days before the G20 summit that would be held in London later that week. It was her estimate of how much the G20 could make available through all of its various instruments – trade credits, International Monetary Fund and World Bank crisis support, extra development aid – as part of a global recovery plan. Earlier figures had come to $850 million, but by Thursday 2 April, the day of the summit, Shriti had filled in the blanks, confirming that the total figure for stimulus, having added in further trade credits and more generous development aid, would in fact be $1.1 trillion. This made it the largest publicly funded injection of resources the world had ever promised.

It was a repudiation of the do-nothing response to the economic crash of 1929, which had brought the long Global Depression of the 1930s, and contributed to the failure in international cooperation when the London Monetary and Economic Conference of 1933, organised by the League of Nations, had collapsed without agreement.

Needless to say the significance of the 2009 package came more from the confidence it generated than the money it offered – and indeed much of the money was never called upon. In the three months that followed the G20 summit, the world economy recovered fast as a result of it. So, how did we secure such an unprecedented degree of international cooperation? And why did this cooperation dissipate quickly when it came to dealing with climate change, global banking reform and weak economic growth?

The international community had never been good at preventing or dealing with financial crises. Since the onset of the latest wave of globalisation in the 1980s, banking crises – a hundred in all – have been twice as common as at the turn of the last century. But none of these more limited, mainly national, crashes prepared us for the first truly global crisis of the modern era. All countries were slow to see the looming storm and to understand the need for major reforms in the world financial system.

While I had talked to European leaders about a global leaders' economic forum since January 2008, it was not until the UN meetings in New York in September that I laid down a concrete plan for what would become the leaders' G20 economic summit. This I did at the impromptu gathering I had convened of the main heads of government who were still in New York for the UN General Assembly.

We met in an out-of-the-way, poorly furnished room at the UN – chosen because it was far from the places where the press were lying in wait. It was almost certainly the dingiest room ever chosen for a historic meeting attended by such distinguished company. Going around the table in New York, President Lula of Brazil – who held the chair of the finance ministers' G20 at that time – was the first to say he was on board. He was seconded by José Manuel Barroso, president of the European Commission, and prime ministers Zapatero, Socrates, Balkenende, Rasmussen, Stoltenberg and Rudd from Spain, Portugal, the Netherlands, Denmark, Norway and Australia respectively. I had invited President Jakaya Kikwete of Tanzania, the retiring president of the African Union, to our meeting – and he was enthusiastic about the proposal. When Prime Minister Meles Zenawi of Ethiopia arrived in New York, he joined the consensus.

As we concluded, President Lula made a magnanimous offer: to pass the chairmanship of the finance ministers' G20 from Brazil to Britain with immediate effect, three and a half months ahead of the scheduled date. With general agreement that Britain was now at the helm, I contacted Chancellor Merkel of Germany, Premier Wen Jiabao of China, and Prime Minister Manmohan Singh of India. They too were supportive.

The next day, addressing first the United Nations and then the Clinton Global Initiative, I laid out publicly for the first time the arguments for a common approach to the crisis. In both speeches, I recalled that the institutions of the global economy had been created for a different world – of sheltered and separate economies – and had to be adapted to a new era. All through the day I was still going over the previous night's conversation in my mind. I knew that the consensus we had reached was useful; but I also knew that without American buy-in it would be difficult to get it off the ground.

It had been agreed the night before in New York that I would pitch the idea at my meeting with the president in Washington the following day, and that Nicolas Sarkozy would follow up. When I sat down with George Bush in the Oval Office, as well as discussing the matter of the banks I also raised with him for the first time the possibility of a leaders' meeting, and told him that if he supported the idea I would take responsibility for knocking heads together to secure an agreed agenda and communiqué. He agreed in principle to a meeting while still wanting to consult over its composition, but he had one other stipulation: during the final weeks of the presidential election and ensuing handover, he would not travel abroad, so if any meeting was to take place before the end of the year it would have to be in Washington.

It was not just monetary and fiscal coordination that the world economy now needed, I said to him, but also a new World Trade Agreement that would halt the growing resort to protectionism, which had killed hopes of a strong world recovery in the 1930s. The lengthy round of trade negotiations that had begun in 2001 – the so-called Doha Round – were currently stalled all these years later because of a disagreement between America and India. I informed him of assurances I had sought and received from Prime Minister Singh: India was prepared to move from its entrenched position that it would cut off food imports if they rose unacceptably high. But when the president called his trade adviser into the meeting it became clear to me that even if we could do a deal with India, America was still reluctant to move forward. His adviser was more worried about jobs lost because of cotton imports to America than jobs gained from food exports to India.

From then on, getting the leaders' forum up and running became a central preoccupation. There ensued a period of telephone diplomacy – of almost daily calls, backwards and forwards, between the Americans and others, in order to agree both the date of the first meeting – it was to be 14 and 15 November – and what kind of membership this group of government leaders would have. But by the time we had agreed on that date, the time available to plan and prepare the meeting was so attenuated that when we met as a group we did little more than agree to fight protectionism and coordinate our domestic responses. The meeting's main decision was to hold another meeting. But where? There we faced a battle too. The Japanese were keen that the leaders come to Tokyo. The Australians proposed that we travel down under. But in the end, everyone came round to London as the right venue and 2 April 2009 as the right date.

In sorting out the London attendees, we had two problems. The Netherlands and Spain were not part of the G20 of finance ministers but their economies were important and their prime ministers were anxious to be a part of the new forum. We found a compromise. President Sarkozy would vacate his seat as president of the EU and attend as president as France. The prime minister of Spain would take Sarkozy's seat, and the prime minister of the Netherlands would sit beside him as if his adviser. The G20 was already in practice the G22.

Africa presented a bigger headache. The African Union's 2009 chair was Colonel Gaddafi and I dreaded the prospect of him pitching his tent in Whitehall. On the pretext of the G20 being an economic rather than a political forum, I turned instead to the head of the New Economic Partnership for Africa's Development, Prime Minister Meles Zenawi of Ethiopia, and he agreed to attend as Africa's representative.

In the run-up to April I visited as many of the G20 countries as I could. In March, I was the first European leader to visit the newly installed President Obama at the White House. I did so amidst the now predictable attempts by our right-wing media to demonstrate that the special relationship was being downgraded. In fact the press pack objected to not being accorded the official press conference they had expected – Barack and I did an impromptu media briefing from the Oval Office – and spent more time complaining about delays in being let in to the White House. When the *Daily Mail* later wrote that Obama's gift to me of a set of DVDs of twenty-five US films was 'as exciting as a pair of socks', I did not tell them that the DVDs were coded for the US and unreadable by any UK DVD player. The new president was, however, shocked at the treatment meted out by the UK press. In a private call I took from him on our plane just after I flew out of Washington, he said he could not understand the British media pack. They were just 'hound dogs', he said.

During my visit I had also delivered an address to a joint meeting of the US Congress and Senate. I spoke of how in fighting the economic crisis, Europe and America had renewed our 'partnership of purpose'. My theme was that 'an economic hurricane has swept the world', bringing us to a point where 'change is essential'. The very financial institutions designed to diversify risk across the banking system had spread contagion right around the globe. In the depths of the Depression of the 1930s, Roosevelt had battled with fear itself: the agenda I now set out for the G20 would build a new confidence in the future. Once again the media focused less on my words and more on the USA's supposedly cool reaction to them, but as I received nineteen standing ovations over the course of the speech from the attending congressmen and senators, the media's preferred story soon died.

By now I was engaged in telephone diplomacy around the clock, often calling Kevin Rudd in Australia first thing in the morning and ending with calls to North and South America in the evening.

When I spoke to the European Parliament in the last week of March I said that the banks had created 'risk without responsibility'. Despite repeated interruptions from Nigel Farage and the Eurosceptic Tory MEP Daniel Hannan, I appealed to Europe to lead a bold plan for world recovery – the biggest interest-rate cut, the biggest fiscal injection, and the biggest reform in our international institutions that the world had ever seen.

I flew from Strasbourg via New York to Brazil, where President Lula made headlines by blaming the crisis on 'the irrational behaviour of some people that are white, blue-eyed' at our joint press conference. I knew instantly that his remarks would be reported all around the world, but joked with him that they would be unlikely to strengthen my case for global unity.

The next stop was Chile. Peter Mandelson and Douglas Alexander came with me to address the Third Way Conference, convened by President Michelle Bachelet. As we stepped out of the aircraft and down the steps, we were greeted by a Chilean officer who said, 'Welcome to Chile on behalf of President Pinochet,' quickly correcting himself with the words 'President Bachelet'. The two could not have been more different, and when she greeted me at the presidential office she showed where President Allende had died. The Chilean visit was the best preparation for the G20: with Joe Biden, the new US vice president, and two G20 leaders – Zapatero of Spain and Kirchner of Argentina – we were already planning an ambitious communiqué.

Back in Britain, three days before the summit, my preparations were completed with a long call with Prime Minister Shinzo Abe of Japan and a meeting with Mexico's President Felipe Calderón, who was already in London on a state visit and staying with the Queen. As the rest of the G20 members arrived in London, I hosted individual meetings with the presidents of China, Russia, Indonesia and South Korea to make sure they were on board for the decisive action we planned. America – still in the eye of the financial storm – remained the key.

The day before the plenary, I had breakfast in the Cabinet Room with Barack Obama. Only three months into his presidency, he had already announced a fiscal stimulus for the US economy. There was, however, one rather awkward moment. There is a tradition that the prime minister makes a gift to the new US president. Tony's gift to President Bush – a bust of Churchill – had now been removed from its place in the Oval Office, much to the criticism of the British press, so on this, his first official visit to London, I offered Obama a gift from Britain that drew on his own life. It was the loan of the famous nineteenth-century painting by George Frederic Watts called *Hope* which the president had referred to in his book, *The Audacity of Hope*. In fact, Watts had painted the same scene twice, so while one original was in the Victoria & Albert Museum, the other was gathering dust in a vault in the Government Art Collection.

But I had not realised when I made the offer to Barack that the painting had become more a source of embarrassment than a memento to be cherished. He had been introduced to both the painting and the phrase 'audacity of hope' by his one-time pastor Jeremiah Wright, whose incendiary comments had been a source of controversy for him during the 2008 election campaign. I should have taken more time to inform myself of the circumstances around the Wright controversy and, had I done so, would not have made the offer. I understand now why, sitting across from me in the Cabinet Room, Barack politely declined.

I would later offer another gift instead that was Sue Nye's inspired suggestion: a pen holder made from the same wood as the renowned 'Resolute Desk' used by the president in the Oval Office and which had been gifted by the British in the nineteenth century and later rescued from a storeroom in the White House basement by President Kennedy. This sequel was not entirely pleasant either. When the White House later issued their list of gifts received – alongside valuations – the pen holder (together with some world-history books by my friend Sir Martin Gilbert) was estimated to be worth $16,500. Understandably I was then asked by the press why the prime minister should be spending so much public money during the recession to, as they put it, ingratiate himself with the US president. I had a choice: to live with the criticism or to reveal that the pen holder had actually cost £260. I chose to live with the accusation of being overgenerous.

Following our breakfast that morning, Barack and I walked out of No. 10, across the street and into the far more luxurious surroundings of the Locarno Suite in the Foreign Office for our joint press conference. I started by reminding the assembled international TV crews and journalists of how slow we had been to respond to the Great Depression of the 1930s and that it was not until 1945 that the world came together to reshape the world economy. Without revealing the precise details of the next day's communiqué, Barack and I previewed our joint proposals for cleaning up the banks, strengthening international institutions and kick-starting global growth.

At the press conference, Obama did everything he needed to do to reassure the British press that when his officials had talked of a 'special partnership', rather than a 'special relationship', they were not downgrading the British–American link; Britain and America would always be linked by a 'kinship of ideals', he declared. We had granted the British and American press three questions each, but when I decided to admit a fourth British question, the Sun's political editor brushed aside any of his readers' concerns about the economy and asked President Obama if he, having won a landslide, had any advice that would turn around my poor poll numbers. Good policy was good politics, he countered, and praised me for showing integrity. The morning that Barack and I met and gave the press conference, Sarah introduced Michelle Obama to London, including a visit to Maggie's Cancer Caring Centre at Charing Cross Hospital.

Elsewhere there was tension in the air. Arriving in London, Nicolas Sarkozy and Angela Merkel made what the press reported as a provocative joint appearance when they argued not just for tougher global rules on tax havens but also the regulation of financial markets. 'The crisis didn't actually spontaneously erupt in Europe, did it?' Nicolas opined. It was a direct challenge to America from a French president who, as he told me, felt that his major overtures to the USA – including returning France to the inner counsels of NATO, which had been abandoned forty years previously in protest at American domination – had not been taken seriously enough. Barack had already tried to deflect this European finger-pointing when he said, 'Some are to blame but all are responsible.' That same day Sarkozy's foreign minister warned that tomorrow's summit would be 'rather difficult' because it would involve a confrontation between 'two worlds'. But while American relations with France remained frosty, America and Russia appeared to be moving closer together: at Barack's London meeting with his Russian counterpart Dmitry Medvedev, they announced a reduction in their nuclear arsenals. At least one form of international cooperation was moving forward.

I had asked the Queen to host an early evening reception for all the G20 members, and before that she offered the Obamas their first audience. The pictures of a young US president meeting the longest-serving monarch in the world were to go around the globe. Michelle Obama was criticised for touching the Queen's back in breach of royal protocol. And once again the gift the Obamas gave the Queen – an iPod preloaded with photos from the president's inauguration and audio files of his speeches – came under press criticism. But Barack's words in praise of the Queen were well tuned to both British and American audiences: before, he said, he had known her only from stamps and documentaries; now he could attest to her 'decency and civility'.

Even the reception at Buckingham Palace did not pass without incident. As all the leaders sat in rows for the standard 'family' photograph, with the Queen at the centre, she was far from impressed with Silvio Berlusconi who, seeing the new US president for the first time, loudly yelled out 'Obama' and delayed the photograph. Not for the first time was the Italian prime minister at the sharp end of a reprimanding look.

But not even the Obama love-fest could prevent a wave of anti-globalisation protests in the streets of London, during which a news-paper vendor, Ian Tomlinson, tragically died near the Bank of England after he was struck by a police officer as he walked home through the protests.

Harriet rightly wanted us to focus on the global recession's impact on women round the world – and in discussions with other countries she led a review which did exactly that. I could not invite her to a dinner that was solely for the G20 presidents and prime ministers and the UN, World Bank and IMF leaders. Indeed, I had to tell my friend Ngozi Okonjo-Iweala, with whom I had worked for years and was chief executive of the World Bank, that I could not invite her either as the World Bank president was attending. Sarah organised an event for the women present in London from the rest of the world – leaders like Ngozi and the partners of the G20 leaders, who were all making a difference in their own countries. At this event, designed to celebrate the contribution women were making in all areas of our lives, from politics and business to the arts, sports and fashion, prominent British women – including J. K. Rowling; the activist against honour killings, Jasvinder Sanghera; and Paralympic champion Tanni Grey-Thompson – were present at tables chaired by Harriet and the Leader of the Lords Jan Royall.

The model Naomi Campbell, well known for supporting emergency humanitarian causes with her Fashion for Relief, arrived fashionably late, creeping in the side door, but confessed she had wanted to walk through the door of No. 10 as the world leaders had done. Sarah quickly arranged it for her, and she popped out the side door again and then walked down Downing Street to arrive at the famous black door.

My dinner for the leaders did not start on time. This was partly due to an elaborate process whereby each of the leaders arrived separately at five-minute intervals, the later times being accorded to those who had served longest in office. On that basis, Barack Obama was among the first to arrive in a car that I was informed was so big there was concern about how to get it down the street. Nicolas Sarkozy should have come next. Instead he had instructed his driver to take him from the reception at Buckingham Palace back to his hotel rather than straight to Downing Street, and so he arrived last, in the most senior slot.

I started our dinner conversation by urging that we do better than our predecessors had done in the 1930s and recalled Churchill's words

that in that decade, too many leaders had been 'resolved to be irreso-
lute, adamant for drift, solid for fluidity, all-powerful to be impotent'.
I then invited the other leaders to speak, starting with Barack. When
Nicolas Sarkozy spoke he warned that the world economy was in
meltdown, and in frustration he challenged the leaders. But when he
said that 'none of us have a plan', Barack jumped in helpfully and
said, 'Gordon has a plan.'

The UN secretary general rounded off the dinner with a plea that
special measures for the poorest in the world, particularly the poor
of Africa, should be part of the communiqué that we produced at
the summit, in which the intentions and resolutions of the G20 would
be formally broadcast to the world.

During the dinner President Lula and Prime Minister Zapatero
asked the No. 10 staff for regular updates – not of the latest economic
data, but the goal alerts from that evening's World Cup qualifiers. I
did not read out the football results to the assembled leaders, but
Spain and later Brazil won – as fortunately did Scotland, England and
Northern Ireland, while to British disappointment and Angela Merkel's
delight Germany beat Wales 2–0.

As our dinner ended, we joined the guests from the other dinner
for coffee. Silvio Berlusconi could not stop himself from asking for
Naomi Campbell's phone number. I moved to the sitting room of No.
11 to work with Shriti and Jon Cunliffe, who had brilliantly led our
official preparatory work, to finalise the $1.1 trillion reflationary meas-
ures, around which we believed there could be a consensus the following day.

At 6.30 a.m. I arrived at the ExCel Exhibition Centre where the
summit was being held to greet world leaders as they arrived for
breakfast and to review the draft communiqué that officials had been
working on overnight. One item still in dispute was the target I wanted
to set for the growth of the world economy. We could not persuade
Germany, whose experience of hyperinflation in the 1920s had ever
since led it to focus rigidly on price stability above all else. There was
deadlock and I had briefly fallen out with Angela Merkel when I had
asked her to unblock Germany's opposition. As she and I took the
lift up to the first floor that morning, I pressed her personally, pointing to the uniqueness of the challenge we faced. I argued that
inflation would remain low for some time and if we could collectively

pursue something like a 5 per cent global growth target then we could raise confidence, create jobs and speed recovery. I could not persuade her. Although it was the right time to act, I had to back off for the moment.

The ExCel Centre in east London had been chosen not just because it could accommodate such a large gathering at short notice but also because it was to be one of our Olympic venues, and we wanted to publicise the very extensive Olympic preparations that we were making. But when I arrived at the centre I was shocked by the seating plans for our plenary sessions. I had hoped for the kind of informality that allowed a free and frank exchange of ideas. I now saw that each leader would be surrounded by their large entourages and be positioned so far away from other leaders that the informality I sought would give way to a very formal process – long statements being read out and little interaction between leaders. This would make it impossible to go round the table negotiating line by line the final details of the communiqué. I made a quick decision: I told staff that most of the work would now be done during the leaders' lunch, at which only leaders would be present. We started lunch as early as possible, and until I had an agreement on the issues that mattered, I refused to let the lunch finish.

So anxious was I to get the business done that our No. 10 staff stood guarding the door preventing leaders' advisers from entering, and refusing even to allow any of the serving staff in to clear the plates from the table. The advisers were furious. Their staffers tried to pass notes into their bosses but No. 10 officials kept saying that the leaders' lunch was not finished and could not be interrupted. So angry was the Argentinian president that she pushed Tom Fletcher up against the wall, demanding her adviser be let in. She was right to be angry. We were in effect holding world leaders hostage until the communiqué was agreed. But in the informality of a lunch of twenty-four around one relatively small table, I could work the room, suggest compromise wordings and push through the deal. Sometimes we would break off for a minute or two while I left my chair and talked to the one leader who, on the agenda item under discussion, was still holding out. Barack quickly realised what was going on, and he – and then Kevin Rudd and Angela Merkel – had a quiet word in the ears of leaders in need of persuasion.

The speed at which we were moving became, understandably, a source of complaint from those for whom English was not their first language. Nicolas Sarkozy was determined to wring out concessions on economic reforms and I was as determined to support him. Cross that most of the discussions were being conducted in English, he insisted on his interpreter being at his side. To get the Chinese on board I also agreed that their number two, their expert on tax, now came into the room – and fortunately no one else noticed (or if they did, they did not complain).

Readers might be surprised to learn that the single greatest controversy was not over spending $1 trillion; after all the spadework done in advance, that went through without objection. Instead our talks faced a threatened walkout over tax havens, what the French call *paradis fiscaux*. Our proposal was to name and shame those countries who refused to take immediate action against tax evasion. Before us was a list of offenders, which included China's Macau. The Chinese complained that tax was no issue for the G20. This was not the only point of contention between them and the French president: in Poland the previous December, Nicolas had met the Dalai Lama, whom the Chinese consider a dissident separatist.

I had tried to fend off the tax-haven dispute in a series of phone calls to the leaders in advance of the summit, but with no success. Even an attempt the night before at last-minute talks between the French and Chinese at Sarkozy's hotel – helpfully called the Mandarin – failed. The Chinese had refused to turn up until the French issued a joint diplomatic statement moderating their position on Tibet. No agreement could be reached and the next morning, as the G20 got under way, Sarkozy repeated his threat that he would walk out if the communiqué did not include a declaration on tax clampdowns. The Chinese refused to sign such a communiqué. All morning, we laboured on a compromise; it was to no avail. So too was an eloquent plea from President Obama that at this decisive moment in world history, we could not fail to find a way forward. 'Let's get this all in some kind of perspective guys,' Obama said at one point.

As chairman of the meeting, I was being sent regular notes saying that Premier Wen would not budge and President Sarkozy was indeed serious about walking out. During the lunch the tension between the French and Chinese presidents grew. We needed to think laterally.

I phoned the secretary general of the Organisation for Economic Cooperation and Development (OECD), Angel Gurría, to put a proposal to him in advance of the second session, which was just about to begin. I proposed that that the OECD issue a statement pledging the very action on tax havens the Chinese were refusing to accept. Fortunately, the secretary general was up for this. I then put to the G20 a proposal that the OECD would take all the action necessary on tax havens. The Chinese got their way; there was no declaration at the G20. The French had got their way; there was a tax declaration. To Sarkozy's satisfaction, the declaration was issued from Paris, where the OECD was located. A press statement would be released there to coincide with our communiqué.

We managed to complete our full discussions by 3 p.m., and had there been more photocopying machines to print sufficient copies of the communiqué we could have held our press conference earlier. In the event, our press conference was at 4 p.m., with individual press conferences from other leaders choreographed to follow. The day had been harder than expected, and for reasons we had not anticipated, but the outcome was historic. The communiqué spoke of 'the largest fiscal and monetary stimulus and the most comprehensive support programme for the financial sector in modern times'. As I told the press conference, our agreement showed that in a global economy, prosperity was indivisible and that to be sustained it had to be shared. We trebled the resources countries made available to the IMF to $750 billion, with the IMF itself adding a further $250 billion to that figure in so-called Special Drawing Rights – a tool for increasing liquidity in a country's currency reserves – and $100 billion was set aside by the Multilateral Development Banks to invest in low-income countries. With $250 billion of trade credits, we did everything in our power to avoid what had bedevilled world recovery in the 1930s: protectionism. Following this, central banks rapidly cut interest rates, bringing them close to zero, and increased the purchase of assets to prop up a frail banking sector and incentivise lending and growth. What I had called for – a worldwide fiscal stimulus – was implemented in both advanced and emerging economies: in 2009 and 2010, the injection of new spending and tax cuts averaged almost 2 per cent of national incomes.

Before the G20, world trade, global industrial production and stock market valuations had all declined faster than during the onset of the 1930s Great Depression, and we had been heading for a repeat. After the G20 there was a sharp turnaround: the world economy grew 4.5 per cent during the second half of the year, and 5 per cent in 2010. Why? Because, as Christina Romer, the chair of the US Council of Economic Advisers, explained: 'While the economic downturn of 2008–9 was directly comparable to the 1930s, the policy responses have been vastly different.' In the 1930s, it took six years for world output to return to previous levels; but acting together, we had achieved the turnaround within one. I felt reassured by the World Bank's verdict that the London summit had 'broken the fall' of the global economy. It is likely to go down in history as the moment when the international community united to stop a slide into a depression.

Over the summer, as I worked on the G20 Global Action Plan which would be announced in September, I again met Barack Obama at the UN in New York and then in Pittsburgh. Once again the media was primarily interested in how much time he allocated to me. It did not seem to matter to them that throughout the entire first day at the UN I was sitting next to him and we were in continuous conversation. Out of New York, the BBC's coverage of our attempts to revive the world economy was reduced to a ridiculous story that I had been snubbed by him. When we got to the Pittsburgh G20, the normally placid Obama was calling the British press 'savages'. His chief of staff remonstrated to his good friend and my adviser David Muir: 'You have to get your press pack under control. They are a f***ing disgrace.'

The Pittsburgh G20 approved what was now called a 'growth compact' to be driven by what was termed the IMF's 'mutual assessment process', or MAP. MAP examined the growth and employment potential of individual economies and the world economy as a whole. In their first report the IMF demonstrated that over the next four years global coordination could achieve 5.75 per cent higher global growth, create up to 50 million additional jobs and take 90 million out of poverty. But despite the scale of our ambition, the momentum for joint action we had fashioned in April 2009 was already flagging. For want of such coordination, growth turned out to be 3 per cent lower than it might have been, and those 50 million extra jobs did not materialise. A bold South Korean-led initiative of 2010, in which China and America would limit each other's trade deficits and surpluses to 4 per cent, was stillborn. So too was every effort to secure a world trade agreement and to reverse the rising tide of protectionism.

Buoyed by our April success, I thought we could deliver the first global climate change treaty. Already global emissions of carbon dioxide in 2009 were almost 50 per cent above their 1990 level. Millions of hectares of forest were being lost every year, renewable water resources becoming scarcer, and small countries at risk of evacuation from coastal erosion. I was the first head of government to announce that I would attend the Copenhagen Climate Change Conference called for December 2009. Slowly but surely we managed to persuade other leaders to attend too, including Barack Obama. By the time we reached Copenhagen and with help from Hillary Clinton, the Americans had come on board for our proposed financial package that would offer up to $100 billion to crisis-hit countries to pay for mitigation and adaptation. But the format of the conference defied any reasonable chance of agreement. All 192 countries met in one session with no drafting committee or executive body. We should have seen the writing on the wall when, at the outset, the Chinese delegate challenged the right of the host, the Danish prime minister, who had invited us there, to chair the gathering.

The only procedure we were all agreed upon was that each leader would make a set speech to the conference. In mine I emphasised that scientific truths know no boundaries of ideology or politics and that I was not asking any country to suspend their national interest but to advance it more intelligently. And I called for common action: 'not one block against another, not north against south, not rich against poor, but the first global alliance of 192 countries, a new alliance for the preservation of our planet'.

An event made up of 192 speeches was, as my friend Kevin Rudd, the Australian prime minister, put it, 'floating in space' – that is, going nowhere – so I proposed there and then that a smaller group of the more powerful countries meet as a G20-style executive, this time with far stronger representation than at a formal G20 from the poorest countries hit the hardest by climate change. Unhappy with what he saw as undue pressure on China to come to an agreement, the Chinese prime minister never attended this thirty-strong gathering, and when Angela Merkel proposed that the richest economies signal their own commitment to halving carbon usage by 2050, the Chinese delegate objected. His country was entitled to veto this, he said, because China by 2050 would also be a high-income country. At that point, we had to prevent him and Kevin Rudd coming to blows.

The G20-style format gave way to a series of separate discussions. President Obama went to see the Chinese premier at his hotel. Unannounced, President Lula of Brazil, Prime Minister Singh of India and President Zuma of South Africa turned up in support of China. A patchwork of an agreement was hammered out. All countries would agree to report each year on how they were meeting their climate change targets. So the Copenhagen Accord was born. It instituted national carbon reduction plans, transparent reporting, some immediate help for poorer countries to adapt to and mitigate climate damage, and it agreed the need for further work, which I took forward, on a $100 billion plan to help the island states and other states facing drought and floods.

But Copenhagen's stated objective had not been achieved: we could not agree on a legally binding treaty, nor even an overall framework that would give the world confidence that all countries would reduce their emissions. While in the early months of 2010 Angela Merkel and I tried to revive the climate change discussions, it was to no avail. It was to take until 2015 in Paris – and a deal between President Xi Jinping of China and Barack Obama – to secure a climate change agreement. Countries now have to show they are meeting their emissions target in a more transparent way, but the $100 billion a year promised to the crisis-hit countries for mitigation and adaptation has yet to materialise.

Global poverty – like growth and climate change – was a challenge that now required but did not receive the global coordination that had been so effective in preventing a world depression. Throughout the crisis I positioned Britain as a leader in global aid, because I believed that we should shine a light on the needs of the poor and inspire other advanced economies to do more to help poor countries vanquish poverty, illiteracy and disease. While most states cut their aid budgets in the wake of the crisis, I announced that Britain would honour in full its commitment to raising aid from the 0.26 per cent of national income that we inherited to 0.7 per cent. In the year we left office, we passed 0.6 per cent and were on track to achieve 0.7 per cent in 2013.

And yet there was still one major task – agreed at the April G20 in London – which would require collective global action too and which was essential if our work was to go beyond a rescue operation and make the global economy secure in the future.

Because the crisis had revealed so much of what was wrong with our financial system – its brittle structure, its excessive rewards, its lack of transparency – I wanted the post-2008 period to be as energetic a time for rebuilding and reform as the post-1945 period, which had produced the IMF, the World Bank, the Marshall Plan and the United Nations. These international institutions, which had been built in the 1940s for the era of separate national economies, were now out of line with the needs of an interdependent global economy where financial institutions worked across borders and were so internationally interconnected. At the suggestion of the Indian prime minister, the April summit agreed that I would head a review of the structure and role of the international institutions. I wanted the outdated Washington Consensus – which had become synonymous with neoliberalism – replaced by what I sometimes called a new London consensus, in which we explicitly abandoned the mindset of deregulation, privatisation and liberalisation at the core of economic policy in favour of a more balanced approach.

At London and then Pittsburgh we agreed, on paper at least, common global financial standards for bank capital and liquidity, including basic leverage ratios to prevent banks from risking their savers' money in the absurd lending and trading practices that had been revealed by the crash. But I wanted to go further and create a global banking constitution that would set standards across the system to be applied in every financial centre in the world. I wanted an international early warning system to identify and head off future crises. I wanted a global growth strategy driven forward by a reformed IMF and World Bank, and the G20 bolstered with the staffing and representative membership necessary to make it what it said it was: the premier forum for economic cooperation.

In the end, delivering these proposals meant overcoming more obstacles than I had time left in government to surmount. And, just at the time I argued for enhanced cooperation, I found resistance to change was growing. The backlash from the banks came as early as November 2009 when in Britain we introduced a one-time levy on bank bonuses and it spread round the world.

The arguments for such a levy were compelling: banks had raised dividends, salaries and bonuses to jaw-dropping levels in the pre-crisis years. I recalled the Bank of England calculation that if British bankers had paid themselves 10 per cent less each year between 2000 and 2007, they would have had some £50 billion more capital to help them withstand the crisis – precisely the amount stumped up by British taxpayers for the emergency stabilisation of our banking system. Excesses in remuneration are not cost-free. We knew that we had to act before the bonus season early in 2010, and we had a special responsibility for banks funded by the taxpayer. In some instances, we were legally bound to meet contractual obligations on bonuses, but we had other means at our disposal than non-payment. In December 2009, Alistair Darling bravely demanded a 50 per cent tax on bank bonuses.

Of course, we were prepared for the familiar counter-argument to restricting bonuses: that, if Britain brought down remuneration while other countries did not, then whole companies would relocate. Switzerland became a much-quoted option and, as the Swiss told me, there were no plans there for changes in its remuneration rules. Prior to Alistair's announcement I was reassured by one chief executive who told me that making money was his business but taxation was solely a matter for government. They would accept what government did. This position was maintained only until we announced the tax, at which point that bank, with others, threatened to leave the country.

We were under daily pressure to modify the tax, and to his credit Alistair refused to backdown. We were right to press on, and the eventual gain to the public purse from the tax was £1.2 billion. However, in this form, it had to be no more than a one-time boon as the banks swiftly restructured their remuneration packages, some converting bonuses into salaries, in order to avoid having to pay a similarly constructed tax in future.

There was a prize waiting to be grasped that I was still pursuing in the final weeks before I left office: a globally coordinated levy on the banking sector. Andrew Haldane of the Bank of England has estimated that in the three years after the crisis the largest UK lenders alone enjoyed a taxpayer subsidy worth £55 billion each year. It was only right that banks should play their part in insuring against future failures. At the G20 finance ministers' meeting in November at St Andrews, I said that there were a number of ways we could protect taxpayers against the cost of a future banking crisis. The banks could be charged an insurance premium. We could require them to set aside so-called 'contingent capital'. We could simply make provision for a better mechanism for resolving any crisis that would set out in advance their responsibilities for compensating the taxpayer. There could be a levy, either on transactions, assets or revenues. But any measure had to be universal: it could not work unless all the major financial centres imposed it.

While I had raised all the options, my own thinking on this revolved around a levy on banking assets. I privately estimated that Britain alone could raise £25 billion through this measure. But just the mention of a levy sparked a firestorm. Critics rushed to judgement assuming, wrongly, that I was proposing a levy on all financial transactions, the so-called Tobin tax (named after the American economist James Tobin). The US Treasury Secretary, Tim Geithner, immediately announced that he opposed a transactions tax. The initial response from Europe was equally discouraging. I had gone into the lion's den and been mauled.

I could see a rocky time ahead as we continued to promote the global assets levy, but I was in no mood to give up. Over the next day or two, I telephoned all who had publicly criticised the proposal and asked them to look again in the cold light of day at all the options I had put forward. I left them in no doubt that I would be stepping up my campaign and would seek to win public support for the levy. We could not stand still, act as if nothing had happened, and leave the banks to pick off governments one by one, with the inevitable result that no action would follow.

By the beginning of 2010 what had been dismissed as a wayward idea started to gain traction. Tim Geithner telephoned me to say the Americans were considering a proposal that the banks contribute to an insurance scheme. This, as President Obama later proposed, would recoup the costs of the Federal government's TARP programme.

President Sarkozy had always been a strong supporter of a banking levy. Chancellor Merkel also saw the logic of global action. Because of the amount of state banking in Germany, much of the levy would involve a transfer within the public sector, but she confirmed that Germany would move in line with an agreed proposal. And with the support of President Barroso and Prime Minister Zapatero, who was now president of the European Council, we had a shared European position. It was suggested that Europe could move ahead on its own with an all-European banking tax. But, in my view, we needed the US.

In March, I conferred privately with Larry Summers, then Obama's director of the National Economic Council. We agreed on the shape of a tax that would be applied in an equivalent way in the main financial centres, and we even talked about the level at which it would be set. After this meeting, I phoned President Obama. I told him that Europe was ready to move in concert with America. In April, the IMF put forward the option of a levy in a form which I found easy to support – a Financial Activities Tax, to be levied on the profits and remuneration of financial institutions and paid into national budgets. It would sit alongside a Financial Stability Contribution, which all financial institutions would pay and which would be used to cover the cost of any future financial sector bailouts.

With the British general election looming, it was a race against time. We were caught between our desire to announce the policy before election day, showing the progress we had made, and the complicated process of working out and agreeing details with the rest of the world. In the end Barack told me that there was no chance of Congress passing it at this stage. I replied that he had European support and it would be enough for him to say that he planned to deliver the policy in his second term. In the event, it was the election here in Britain that proved fatal. The new Conservative–Liberal Democrat coalition elected in 2010 were so dead set against such a levy that even as Chancellor Merkel and President Sarkozy continued to support it – and it remains even now on European Union policy agenda – any chance of international cooperation had passed. It is, however, an idea whose time will come.

It is remarkable how little has changed since the promise in 2009 that we bring finance to heel. As I write today, the banks that were deemed 'too big to fail' are now even bigger than they were. Similarly, with inadequate oversight of shadow banking, with exotic new financial instruments like collaterised loan obligations and without, as yet, a proper early warning system, some regulators freely confess that risks have morphed and migrated out of the formal banking system, and if the next crisis came they would still not know what is owed and by whom and to whom. 2009 has proved to be the turning point at which history failed to turn.

Dividends and bankers' pay today represent almost exactly the same share of banks' revenues as before the crisis hit. While bonuses have fallen from their £19 billion high in 2007–8 to around £14 billion last year, the financial sector has paid out a total of £128 billion in bonuses since 2008 – enough to recapitalise our banks. Moreover, the fall in bonus payments does not mean bankers are being paid less. After the European Union capped bonuses at a maximum of 200 per cent of salary – a move fiercely opposed by the coalition government, who excluded asset managers from the cap – the banks circumvented it by introducing a new category of remuneration called 'fixed pay monthly allowances' and raising salaries. The typical senior banker earns £1.3 million and Britain has three-quarters – more than 4,000 – of Europe's €1 million bankers, a figure that has risen 50 per cent since the crisis. Even at RBS, which has had £58 billion of accumulated losses and is guaranteed by the taxpayer, the number of bank employees earning more than €1 million has barely changed – 121 down from 131. We still do not have the right balance between the capital that banks need, the dividends they pay, the remuneration they give employees, and the contribution they make to the public for the social costs of their risk-taking.

One of the arguments for high pay in the banking sector – that they take risk – has not survived the crash. With many banks back-stopped by the taxpayers, they make their profits at least in part because of the government guarantee. The risks they are taking are often not with their money but with ours. And often bankers are not being compensated for risk but rewarded for failure. It cannot be right that Fred Goodwin walked away with all of his past bonuses untouched, a reported tax-free lump sum of £5 million, and even after he agreed to halve his pension it still amounted to £350,009 a year.

If bankers' conduct was dishonest by the ordinary standards of what is reasonable and honest, should there not have been prosecutions in the UK as we have seen in Ireland, Iceland, Spain and Portugal? While the new criminal offence of reckless misconduct in the management of financial institutions is intended to deter irresponsible management decision-making within banks and building societies, defendants will likely argue that their institution was in difficulty more because of fluctuations in interest rates or exchange rates, inter-bank illiquidity, or even regulatory changes imposed by government, rather than their own conduct. The Fraud Act 2006, which criminalises fraud by false representation, failing to disclose information and abuse of position, may be more relevant. If bankers who act fraudulently in this way are not put in prison with their bonuses returned, assets confiscated and banned from future practice, we will only give a green light to similar risk-laden behaviour in new forms.

The crisis not only exposed the flaws of neoliberalism but reinforced my view of the need to change the way our international institutions operate. If the roots of the recession lay in global imbalances between producer economies with high levels of savings, such as China's, and consumer economies, like those of the US and the UK, weakened by high levels of personal borrowing that arose in the wake of stagnant wages and rising inequality, then we needed – and still need – better management of the global economy to address these underlying problems. Supra-national bodies like the IMF, the World Trade Organization and the Global Stability Forum have a larger role to play but, dominated by unelected experts, their detachment and distance from national electorates and civil society is no unalloyed virtue. One way we can combine the need for expertise, for accountability and for decisive economic leadership that can deliver is a better organised and broader G20. It should not have to take yet another crisis for this to happen.

The London G20 drew a line in the sand. The leaders of the world agreed on concerted action that may have saved the world from a second great depression. We forged unprecedented global cooperation, which is what I had been fighting for all along. We understood that each country's national interest could best be protected and advanced by cooperation between all countries. We could have done more – growth and prosperity since 2010 has been much lower than it might have been – and still can. But while the crisis brought about international cooperation, this has since waned as countries have retreated into their national silos. Even so, I think of what was achieved: we found a way through a global crisis. It was not what I had envisioned spending my time on when I became prime minister, but any leader must be prepared to deal with unpredicted and potentially shattering events. More than this, we would leave behind a model, a way of working together, that could shape global financial cooperation to prevent and deal with crises in the future, and we had shown that, even though nothing in global cooperation will ever run smoothly and no outcome is ever guaranteed, it is possible to create a worldwide coalition for change. In the spirit of my old school motto, I had done my best.

CHAPTER 17

FIGHTING OUR WAY OUT OF RECESSION

Buried away in the library of the Treasury was a forgotten memo-randum that I discovered. It was written in the 1920s by the world-renowned economist John Maynard Keynes – and in it I found a note inscribed on its first facing page. The words had been scribbled on the document by one former permanent secretary about proposals from a far greater economic mind on how to tackle the recession of the day. When, long before his *General Theory* of 1936, Keynes had proposed public works, fiscal expansion and short-term deficit financing to lift the economy out of a downturn, the permanent secretary of the day dismissed him in three words scrawled across the page: 'Inflation. Extravagance. Bankruptcy.'

Understandably the 2008 global financial storm dominated the mod-ern Treasury's thinking in a way no other issue ever would, and what to do about deficits again became a burning question eighty years on. Would we learn anything from the 1920s and 30s? Would the ortho-doxy of balanced budgets and aversion to debt have too strong a hold on public opinion? Would the same official mantra rejecting public works and temporary deficit financing as 'inflation, extravagance and bankruptcy' hold? Given an embedded mythology hostile to debt and deficits, could I ever do enough to convince the general public to trust us to get it right in a crisis?

By the autumn of 2008 it was clear to me that monetary policy by itself was insufficient to counter a fast-worsening downturn and clear too that we had to act quickly. I knew from history that once recession took hold and gripped our economy, it could not be readily reversed; and I was well aware of the evidence that our economy would suc-cumb to what economists called 'hysteresis' – low levels of demand that eventually destroy supply and turns cyclical unemployment into structural unemployment as more and more of the unemployed see their skills atrophy, and a future recovery moves further out of our reach.

The answer, as Keynes had taught us, was to increase spending, reduce taxes and run a deficit: higher levels of government spending directly increase overall demand, while lower taxes increase the after-tax incomes of households, enabling them to spend more and add to that demand. And if monetary policy has exhausted its potential to stimulate growth, and if there is no inflationary risk alongside mass unused capacity which might be permanently lost, then there is no reasonable argument against the principle of a counter-cyclical fiscal stimulus. This was, indeed, a circular process. Getting the economy back to growth was itself vital to cutting the deficit. Indeed, the Office for Budget Responsibility has recently suggested that the long-term growth rate of the economy is the single most important determinant to the health of the public finances.

Britain was, in fact, the first of the recession-hit countries to act – in the autumn of 2008, when in an emergency Budget in all but name, Alistair Darling introduced a Small Business Finance Scheme to support up to £1 billion of bank lending; a £145 income tax cut for 22 million basic-rate taxpayers; a year-long VAT reduction from 17.5 per cent to 15 per cent; a £3 billion capital spending programme for transport, housing, the NHS and education; and brought forward increases in the old-age pension, child benefit and the child tax credit.

I knew that, as the economy crashed, mothers and fathers were sitting at their kitchen tables in the evenings worried sick as to whether they would lose their jobs; and, if they did, whether they would then lose their homes. So, mindful that homeowners had been hardest hit in previous recessions, those who lost their jobs or saw wages fall would now have the right to defer unpayable mortgage interest for up to two years. We gave guarantees to Britain's main mortgage lenders that protected those with home loans up to £400,000 from repossession even if six months in arrears. None of this could prevent a 60 per cent slump in mortgage lending over the next few months; but, fortunately, the number of homeowners who held mortgages – 11.8 million in 2007 – kept relatively steady at 11.4 million.

Of course, people do not think back to what might have happened and how repossessions which at one point seemed inevitable – and hit America and countries like Spain much harder – were avoided in

Britain. But in the most difficult year, 2009, the homes of only 0.42 per cent of mortgage holders were repossessed, a rate just under half that in the 1990s recession.

Banks would not lend to small businesses. Shriti Vadera and later Peter Mandelson – and I – spent more hours cajoling banks to lend than on almost anything else. Both the Treasury and Bank have since had to radically extend the range of assistance they offer, but then by trial and error we moved from credit guarantees to the working capital guarantee to tax deferrals. And while America lost 170,000 small businesses in just two years, 160,000 British businesses were shored up by delaying £4 billion in tax payments. As a result the rate of company liquidations was just 0.9 per cent in 2009, and compulsory corporate insolvencies ran at half the rate of the 1990s recession.

Alongside generous new allowances for new investment, £750 million was spent underpinning the sectors we knew were vital to our recovery: the car industry, house-building and low-carbon technology.

Paying people to scrap their old car and buy a new one may have sounded like a gimmick. When I first looked at it I thought so myself. But when I saw the facts I quickly changed my mind. Vehicle production in the UK had collapsed – falling by over 50 per cent between the start of 2008 and early 2009. The fate of some of our best-known car producers – even that of Ratan Tata's Jaguar, rebuilt by this very modest man with extraordinary skill – appeared to be hanging in the balance. The car scrappage scheme, which lasted from July 2009 until Easter 2010, offered car owners a £2,000 incentive, half of it paid for by the government, to give up their car and buy a new one. It was boosted by lower VAT until January 2010. At a cost of £400 million it generated nearly 400,000 new car purchases at a time when the auto market most needed assistance. One in five of all new cars registered in the UK – smaller cars and the most environmentally efficient ones being most popular – came through the scheme. One report suggested that as the average emissions of new cars was 25 per cent lower than those of the old that the car scrappage scheme had done more for a cleaner environment than any previous measure.

Our initiatives, not least the cut in VAT, were designed not just to save individual businesses from collapse but to increase overall demand in the economy. However, while we argued that a time-limited but unexpected cut in VAT, like temporary increases in government spending, would provide an effective stimulus to aggregate demand, we were initially condemned by Germany and France – before they later moved in a similar direction.

In the end, almost every country went for large-scale stimulus – Germany's stimulus package was €59 billion, France's €26 billion, with the EU as a whole committed to €200 billion. In turn, India committed $38 billion to fiscal expansion, Russia $53 billion, Japan $298 billion, China $585 and America $787 billion.

The post-2010 rewriting of history – to forget that deficit financing was critical to emergence from the crisis – is to deny that alongside quantitative easing our concerted fiscal stimulus drove the economic recovery. A British recovery that started from spring 2009 speeded up with 0.4 per cent growth by the fourth quarter of that year, leading to even faster growth by mid-2010 than in 2007. But this was then killed off by austerity.

Well aware that good employment news tended to lag behind other economic indicators we spent a total of £5 billion on jobs. Summer school-leavers and then all long-term unemployed under-twenty-fives were guaranteed training or jobs. While unemployment did rise – from a pre-recession 5.2 per cent to, very briefly, 8 per cent at its pre-election peak – it never approached the levels of 10 per cent and over in the Eurozone and America. And, in a far deeper recession, jobs losses were a fraction of the 1.5 million jobs lost in the 1980s and 90s. It was a costly irony that the high point of British unemployment – 8.4 per cent – came more than a year later at the end of 2011 after Labour's stimulus had been replaced by coalition austerity.

My whole childhood experience, witnessing the damage unemployment could do, strengthened my resolve to act – and to fend off criticism about the fiscal cost of doing so. I did not want ever again to see another lost generation permanently shut out of opportunity or families forced to leave their own homes. Doing what was right carried a heavy political price, but as I told Sarah: 'If the choice is between doing what is popular and what is right, I will do what is right.'

In the worst global recession in eighty years the rates of redundancies, repossessions and bankruptcies in Britain were about half of what were suffered in the previous two recessions. But as we paid out more to prevent unemployment, bankruptcies and repossessions, falling output meant less in revenues – less VAT receipts as people bought fewer goods and services, less income tax as employment fell and earnings stalled, less stamp duty as the housing market slumped, and less corporate taxes as businesses retrenched. In the 2007 Budget, I had projected tax receipts would rise over the following three years to an estimated £616 billion by 2009–10. In total, we received £164 billion less than expected. And while some outlays were recouped with a new payroll tax on the banks, which raised £3.5 billion, and later the introduction of a new top rate of tax of 50 per cent for those earning over £150,000, public sector net debt increased from 35.5 per cent of GDP in 2007–8 to 64.8 per cent in 2009–10.

I take some pride that we did more than any other government to cushion the shock and pain of the economic downturn. Without this the recession could have descended into a depression. Action was even more urgent in Britain because we have historically depended more on the sectors which collapsed: UK economic activity is far more heavily dependent on trade than other countries, like the United States, while financial services represent around 8 per cent of our national income.

Because we had cut debt as a percentage of our national income between 1997 and 2007, keeping it below 40 per cent throughout and repaying debt in four successive years around the turn of the century, it had not been an issue of much public concern for ten years. But as an issue it had never gone away. Our fiscal rules demonstrated that, under all normal circumstances, when the economy was growing, we would not rely on borrowing to finance current expenditure. We had recognised the popular aversion to debt by paying for our NHS improvements with a tax rise, when we had taken time to explain what a National Insurance increase would achieve for the health service. I hoped the public would trust us to get things right.

After 2005 we announced that the catch-up period in public spending – the time when we dealt with the historic and chronic underinvestment in public services – was at an end. Furthermore, in the Comprehensive Spending Review published in February 2007, just before I became prime minister, we halved the growth of public spending from the 4 per cent a year of the previous eight years to 2.1 per cent per year for 2008–9 to 2010–11. Public spending would now grow more slowly than the expected growth rate of the economy.

In a presentation given to Cabinet in 2005, I also called on the pay-review bodies to deliver lower settlements. A new rule was laid down that no significant public sector pay rises could be approved without Treasury agreement. Having achieved greater efficiency in the use of resources, we had also started to cut the public sector workforce from 2006. While the government pay bill had grown after 2000, this period of catch-up was followed by a sharp fall in the growth of staff costs between 2006 and 2009. In real terms, compared with CPI inflation, general government staff costs increased by just over 6 per cent a year during the period of catch-up in 2000–6, but growth fell to just 0.2 per cent a year between 2006 and 2009.

Since we had consistently paid for the expansion of public services not by amassing debt but from the proceeds of growth and tax rises, revenues were not falling before the crisis but rising – from 34.1 per cent of national income when we came to power to 36.4 per cent in 2007–8. And while up to 2003 the tax share from business had been falling, it had been rising from then onwards. Indeed, as the Institute for Fiscal Studies reported, revenues from 2005 to 2008 were 'growing more quickly than spending' with the result that public sector net borrowing fell from 2.9 per cent to 2.4 per cent of GDP between 2005 and 2007, while debt at 35.5 per cent of GDP in 2007–8 was lower than what we inherited. Public spending at 38.6 per cent of GDP was lower than it had been for most of Mrs Thatcher's time in government.

The Treasury had maintained its control of the public purse. We entered the global financial crisis with debt and deficits low by historical standards. There was no profligate pre-crisis spending spree. Indeed, in September 2007, the Conservative shadow chancellor George Osborne had explicitly declared that he would match Labour's spending promises; and the Tory policy of combining the annual spending increases we proposed with tax cuts meant they proposed a far larger deficit and debt.

But if I had a problem in convincing the public, I had – just as Keynes did – as big a problem in persuading the permanent secretary of the Treasury. As the recession started to bite, I could sense from my new vantage point in No. 10 that there was a change in the air at the Treasury.

By moving to the forefront of its role promoting industry, productivity, science, healthcare and poverty alleviation, the Treasury was praised and criticised in equal measure as it bestrode Whitehall between

1997 and 2007. From 1997 I had worked closely with my Treasury team, cooperating day after day, valuing each other's advice and perspectives – we had grown together. Despite opposition from his peers, I had promoted Nick Macpherson from private secretary to managing director, when he ably masterminded the introduction of tax credits, and then to permanent secretary. He had smoothed our first difficult days when we made the Bank of England independent, effectively led welfare reform and became a popular leader of a department that was often thought of as difficult to lead, despite (or perhaps because of) having some of the best brains in the country.

But as I surveyed the response to the recession, I was alarmed. Was I now witnessing this once powerful institution retreating into a shell? Was it shifting away from being the activist department that said 'yes' to innovation and reform and reverting to its traditional role as the finance department that specialised in saying 'no'?

When the recession started to engulf us, I could see the need for far more effective coordination across government. I thought of changes that would have put Gus O'Donnell, who had experience in both the Treasury and the Cabinet Office, in charge of a joint operation, with Nick becoming secretary to the Cabinet. When I told Gus very confidentially what I was considering, and simply asked him for his personal and private view, he broke my confidence by telling Nick, who clearly – and wrongly – regarded it as a demotion. Between them they scuppered the plan; from that time I could sense my relationship with Nick would never be the same again. While I felt we needed to see greater flexibility and innovation within government, we struggled to tackle new problems within an old and ostensibly tired machine.

I'm told that Nick proudly displayed in his office a statue of Philip Snowden, the parsimonious chancellor of the 1920s and 30s, who had left Labour to join a coalition government committed to austerity; and who, in his enthusiasm for Treasury orthodoxy, had been compared to 'the High Priest entering the sanctuary'. Perhaps it was there more in jest or even as a warning about the 1930s. Nick worked night and day to help us achieve the bank recapitalisation and was later to repudiate the main Tory argument about Labour profligacy, and state, correctly, that there was no substantive fiscal problem in advance of the crisis. But, as he himself acknowledged in a *Financial Times* article of 2017, he considered everyone far too soft on the deficit and debt.

Britain, he wrote in 2017, 'never experienced austerity' in the way Ireland did and 'there was a case for going further faster'.

It is well known that in the spring of 2009 I discussed with Alistair Darling his role. When he was appointed chancellor, I had been upfront with him: I would want to make a change in the not too distant future. I explained that because I was older than the rest of the Cabinet, I would want us to go into the next general election with a younger, rejuvenated team. In the June 2009 reshuffle, I offered Alistair the choice of the other top jobs. He refused to move, and when Ed Balls then made it clear to me that he did not want to move either, I relented. In the shadow of the resignation of James Purnell – and an attempt to dislodge me – I accepted that the reshuffle had to be limited.

What of the Bank of England? Labour governments traditionally had difficult relations with the Bank. Not just in the 1920s, under the austere governor of the day, Montagu Norman, who had taken us on and then back off the gold standard, but also under Harold Wilson. In 1964 Lord Cromer, the then governor, had told Wilson to stop building hospitals, axe the school-building programme and slash public spending, in an attempt to secure a balance of payments surplus and restore confidence in sterling. There ensued a very public row: Wilson complained about the 'Gnomes of Zurich', who, like Lord Cromer, were, he said, thwarting the will of the people expressed through the elected government.

So, it did not bode well when Mervyn King went before the Treasury Select Committee in March 2009, just before the G20 which was planning a coordinated fiscal stimulus, to volunteer his objections to our stance. When in 2003, after the retirement of Eddie George, I sought continuity by promoting Mervyn from deputy governor to governor, it was a bold appointment because, unlike Eddie, he was not a 'markets man' but an academic. And when, in the early stages of the crisis, Mervyn argued against intervening to support the banks, before turning full circle and submitting to me a paper calling for outright nationalisation, I did not agree with him. But I accepted this advice was well within his remit as governor. However, was it right for Mervyn to decide to move outside his remit and become a public commentator, siding with our critics without even informing us beforehand?

I did not do a Harold Wilson and publicly criticise Mervyn, even when on further occasions he volunteered advice on our fiscal policy without telling anyone in the Treasury or No. 10 in advance. Instead, after his intervention in March, I asked to see him in private. I reminded him that his predecessor and I had a firm understanding: I would not comment on monetary policy and he would refrain from weighing in on fiscal policy. Could independence work, I asked him, if a central bank charged with one responsibility started pontificating on another? Mervyn promised not to intervene again. But just three months later, not long after Alistair had announced a deficit reduction plan, Mervyn now called for 'a credible' reduction path to deal with the 'truly extraordinary' deficit. This was a direct attack on our policy. I write in more detail of the events of May 2010 in the next chapter, but we now know that Mervyn insisted that month's inflation report call for 'significant fiscal consolidation' and a more 'demanding path' than had been set out in the Budget. We also know there was unhappiness within the Bank of England itself over what one member of the Monetary Policy Committee called 'excessively political' statements 'in the context of the election'.

During a revealing press conference in May 2010, Mervyn claimed it was his right as governor to comment publicly on the overall fiscal position because of its impact on monetary policy. Ironically that should have led him to my position, not his. Mervyn could have come to us with private advice that monetary activism alone could not achieve the growth and employment he was charged to help deliver, nor the 2 per cent inflation target. But that would have meant him conceding that a fiscal stimulus, not austerity, was the only way forward. He might even have argued, as some did at the time, that the Bank should create 'helicopter' money to pay for a stimulus that did not entail additional public debt. Instead he gave the opposite advice: to end the stimulus and reduce the deficit as quickly as possible. The chairman of the US Federal Reserve, Ben Bernanke, has consistently argued that Congress's failure to deliver a temporary fiscal stimulus made his task harder – Mervyn took the opposite view.

I make this point to emphasise that Mervyn was thinking less about his remit as governor than his own personal attitude to debt. There are, as we proved, great benefits in having non-partisan experts setting interest rates, but it is a fundamental part of our constitution that the elected government of the day make decisions on tax and spending. If this was abandoned, in favour of an unelected Bank of England holding court on tax-and-spend and publicly trying to pressure the government, then there would be a popular reaction against elites that were out of touch. The constitutional position is that there should be 'no taxation without representation' – not 'no taxation without the Bank of England's say-so'.

By the summer of 2009, Mervyn was echoing the relentless opposition cry – backed up by the right-wing media – that our primary concern should not be growth or jobs but the debt and the deficit. While we were solving one problem, we were being blamed for another.

Of course, as our deficit reduction plan acknowledged, large budget deficits cannot go on forever. But it is counterproductive to withdraw fiscal support too soon. During these months when we were under pressure to withdraw the stimulus, I read two books, one given to me by our chief strategist in No. 10, David Muir: *FDR: The First Hundred Days* by Anthony Badger, and *FDR* by Jean Edward Smith, which showed that in tackling the Great Depression, Franklin Roosevelt's mistake was to try to retrench prematurely. Too-rapid deficit reduction would undermine growth and ultimately result in a bigger debt – which is what happened after 2010.

Our approach was to get the deficit down by bringing the economy back to growth without jeopardising essential public services. In that we benefited from low interest rates, while debt interest payments, at 2 per cent of GDP, were around half the level of the 1980s recession. Only when the recovery was secured did we plan to raise taxes – National Insurance by 1p in the pound in 2011 – and in a fair way: no one earning under £20,000, or any pensioner, would have paid more tax. Our Fiscal Responsibility Act, which came into force in February 2010, mandated that the Treasury must ensure that for each of the financial years ending in 2011 to 2016, public sector net borrowing expressed as a percentage of national income was less than it was for the preceding financial year. Under Labour's plans, cyclically adjusted public sector net borrowing would fall from 8.4 per cent of GDP in 2009–10 to 3.1 per cent in 2013–14 – halving the fiscal deficit over the next four years. While higher than in recent decades, public sector net debt would be lower than for much of the last century.

The economics journalist William Keegan – whom, long before I did, my father read in the *Observer* – has remarked: 'There is an impressive weight of evidence that recovery had begun in 2010, thanks to the collective impact of fiscal and monetary measures known as "the stimulus", but the recovery was aborted by the premature abandonment of the fiscal side of the stimulus.'

It was to be an irony that by our prompt actions we lifted the country out of recession quickly, but many gave us no credit for it. Still, no previous British government facing recession had ever faced the popularising of counter-cyclical fiscal strategy as 'driving the economy over a cliff' with 'money they didn't have'. But this was the basis of the Conservatives' argument that the only route to recovery was austerity.

There are important economic and political lessons to be learned from what we did. The austerity argument, in the end, is founded on an orthodoxy that deficits and debt are always bad. The myth of good fiscal housekeeping is that each budget should balance. The comparison is drawn with families 'living within their means', ignoring the fact that most borrow to buy a home. The same is said of businesses, though they too borrow to invest. Britain has run a surplus in just seven years since 1970, four of them – 1998, 1999, 2000 and 2001 – when I was chancellor. In the same period, the annual average budget deficit has been 3.1 per cent of national income.

The facts were on our side. I had also spent years in opposition and then government establishing our credentials for prudence. During our first two years, I had frozen public expenditure. Then I had taxed rather than borrowed to pay for NHS investment. I halved the growth rate of public spending after 2005. Going into the financial crisis we had lower debt than any other major country. In 2007, debt was 77 per cent of GDP in the United States, 68 per cent in Germany, 77 per cent in France, 115 per cent in Italy, and 174 per cent in Japan. In Britain, it was 51 per cent. Indeed the current balance deficit was 0.5 per cent and 0.6 per cent of GDP in both 2006–7 and 2007–8 respectively – hardly a large number.

For a time, we had all-party support for our measures. In September 2008, the Conservatives signalled they would back the government's policies to tackle the crisis: David Cameron phoned me from his party conference to say that he was about to announce they would back an all-party consensus. However, a few weeks later, George Osborne changed tack and suddenly compared the fiscal stimulus he had recently endorsed to 'a cruise missile aimed at the heart of the recovery'. In the end, false and widely reported rhetoric about Britain going the way of Greece came on top of general distaste for debt.

The Conservatives alleged that Britain was suffering less from a global financial crisis that started in Wall Street than from a national debt crisis caused by Labour profligacy in Downing Street. As the economic historian Robert Skidelsky has observed, the Conservatives 'constructed a consummate political narrative that linked folklore economics ("the government can't spend money it hasn't got") to the politics of blame ("cleaning up the mess left by Labour") to the politics of fear ("the Greek bogey") to grand economic strategy ("reducing the deficit is a necessary condition for sustained recovery")'. It was all wrong and, once the Conservatives were in government, would be proved wrong.

Previously the Conservatives had not only backed our spending plans but made additional proposals on tax that would have entailed an even higher deficit, so their new stance was quite clearly opportunistic. More importantly, given what happened to Britain's economy after they took power in 2010, it was bad economics. Deficit spending, as Robert Skidelsky reminded us, is like pumping air into a deflated economy. Just as in the 1930s, extra government spending was urgently needed to bring idle resources back into use – this is how we propelled the economy back to growth by 2010 – and by increasing employment and growth, would pay for itself. But after the Tories took power, it would take nearly another six years for our economy to recover its pre-recession levels of output, a process that took only four years in the 1930s. The next seven years of austerity were ultimately to cost households £4,000 each and in some cases as much as £13,000. 'One cannot stress how dreadful that is – more than a decade without real earnings growth,' wrote the director of the Institute for Fiscal Studies, Paul Johnson. 'We have certainly not seen a period remotely like it in the last seventy years.'

The Conservatives needed a narrative that would justify austerity in spite of the lessons of history. So even while it was the crisis that had caused the deficit, the truth was inverted: it was the deficit that had caused the crisis, they claimed. Labour, it was now alleged, had created 'a structural deficit' as a result of persistent overspending. It had come about in part, they said, because we had underestimated the 'output gap', the difference between the actual output of the economy and its potential output. If an economy is growing faster than it ought to be, then higher than expected tax revenues – from, for example, City earnings and bonuses – reflect no more than a temporary and passing advantage and should be discounted. Our mistake, it was argued, was not to have realised that our revenue growth was only transient, and thus in failing to discount such revenues when planning the public finances we had overestimated the sustainability of our revenues. In short it was, they claimed, our reckless overconfidence in the economy's health, rooted in a desire to spend more and more, that had precipitated the crisis.

Two years after we left office, the IMF and the OECD calculated with the benefit of hindsight that the entire global economy in 2007 had been growing above its sustainable trend rate of growth. In our case, they determined that the output gap had been 4 per cent – double the size that it had been calculated to be at the time by the Office of Budget Responsibility. This revision was used by the Conservatives to bolster their arguments and justify the ruthless surgery that would be required to deliver the long-term reduction in the public sector to which they had always been committed.

But in the pre-crisis years just about everyone, including the IMF, had assumed not only the British economy's but the entire Western economy's potential for sustained growth, and its underlying productivity levels, to have been higher. Indeed, the Conservatives themselves had gone further than we did, claiming that the economy could afford not only our public spending programme but a programme of tax cuts too. In truth, the proper charge against us was not that we chose to spend too much in defiance of the evidence but that, like everyone else, we had failed to anticipate such a profound global recession, a failure not of profligacy but of prophecy. As the respected Oxford economist Simon Wren-Lewis has concluded, 'It would be foolish to use the latest estimates of cyclically adjudged budget deficits to criticise policy at the time. It is equivalent to saying . . . [they] should have foreseen . . . the financial crisis itself.'

Other equally contentious claims were also used to justify austerity: that even in the depths of a recession, government spending crowded out private investment and put upward pressure on interest rates; that a national debt beyond 90 per cent of the economy's size could cut – even halve – the rate of growth; that deficit financing itself destroyed confidence. Yet in 2009 none of the anti-stimulus arguments the Conservatives deployed made much economic sense. In fact, despite initially criticising us, the IMF later found that deficit financing in a recession was sound and that the impact of fiscal stimulus on restoring growth was much bigger than previously thought. They had underestimated what they called the 'multiplier effect'.

To those who alleged we should have put the country in a stronger fiscal position before the crash, I answer that we had low debt by historical and international standards; that there was fiscal tightening from 2005 to 2007; and that, while we had made major improvements in health, schools and policing, public spending's share of national income – and thus the size of the state – was smaller than it had been for most of the Thatcher period. This was hardly proof of profligacy.

There are, of course, legitimate questions. Should we have had fiscal rules set not over the cycle but over, say, five years? Should we have aimed for a declining debt ratio rather than a simple target of keeping it below 40 per cent? Should we have focused as much on the flow of debt than on its stock? But these questions, in effect, are different ways of asking the same thing: should we have anticipated a global recession as deep as the one the world suffered?

'All economies recover in the end,' Skidelsky writes, 'the question is how fast and how far.' The fact is we recovered under Labour and then growth stalled under the Conservatives. Current estimates suggest that the UK pulled out of recession in late 2009, and contracted in two quarters after 2010: both in 2012. Following 2010, GDP growth slowed considerably. Osborne's austerity brought weaker growth and by the end of 2011 unemployment rose to 2.68 million and 8.4 per cent. The current budget deficit actually increased by £8 billion between 2011 and 2012, while net borrowing increased by £14 billion over the same period. The Office of Budget Responsibility has calculated that austerity reduced GDP growth by 1 per cent in each of these two years.

In July 2012 the IMF, which had initially criticised us, came out in our favour, suggesting that 'more expansionary demand policies would close the output gap faster'. Their economists have now moved to the view that contractionary policies were not the way to deal with the post-2008 crisis, and proactive fiscal policy had to be pursued alongside monetary policy to facilitate and assure a strong recovery. I put the point more starkly: had we not acted as we did there would have been around a million more job losses; thousands of businesses – whose tax payments we deferred – would have gone under; and hundreds of thousands of homeowners, who faced negative equity, might have had their homes repossessed. And the 2008 recession would have lasted longer.

As it happened, we quickly brought the economy back into growth. Then a year later the Tories undermined recovery – not because their brand of austerity was the only possible option but because they seized on the crisis and made an ideological choice. However, Keynes was right and they were wrong. In normal circumstances, demand management could be left mainly to interest rates, but the highly unusual slump conditions of 2008–9 made fiscal measures an essential component of any recovery. Keynesianism may not have been right for every season, but it was right for this one.

The Conservatives would decry our policy as 'imprudence'. But our policy to run a deficit was for a purpose: it was the right thing economically and morally not just to cushion the shock but to propel recovery – it was, I believe, the only prudent course.

In a crisis, you tend to focus on getting the policy right and at times neglect getting the message across. Under intense pressures, finding solutions becomes all-consuming. I knew that if we had any chance of succeeding we had to make what might seem like detail – our mortgage support, car scrappage scheme, tax holiday to save businesses – the essential building blocks of a comprehensive national mission to help each other. I also understood we had to explain why deficits were not inimical to responsible economics but the essential means of dealing with a global crisis as deep and wide as we faced. Nevertheless, I also recognised that what is essentially a counterfactual – the jobs, homes and businesses that were not lost – would struggle to be heard above the Conservatives' propaganda that even new-born children were being burdened with unpayable debt. As David Muir warned me: the very mention of debt sends shivers down people's spines; just like 'incest', he said, it has no positive connotation and is something to be abhorred.

The power of myth in politics can be stronger than reality. It is far easier to dramatise and exaggerate the horrors of debt than to convey complex arguments about automatic stabilisers and pro-cyclical investment. Deficits and why they are wrong are easier to explain than deficit financing and why it is right. Even now the fiction that any deficit, at any time, under any circumstances is unacceptable still has a stranglehold on the public mind.

On the rightness of running a deficit to stimulate a failing economy back to growth, we did not prevail in the battle for public opinion. I have to accept that our attempts at explaining what we were doing fell short. We fought the battle too little and too late. One reason was our unrelenting focus on wave upon wave of policy issues crashing around us. The financial situation was then so grave, the challenges so urgent and the stakes so high that my colleagues and I had a driving conviction that we had to get the policy responses right. And so, in a seemingly never-ending cycle of Cabinet and Cabinet subcommittees that I chaired – on housing, jobs, business rescues, bank support and so on – we were racing against the economic tides as we introduced measures to minimise unemployment, bankruptcies and repossessions. I believe that by 2010 we could demonstrate more success than any other recession-hit country including America. And as, day by day, we worked through the solutions and almost every waking hour was taken up thinking through the steps to recovery, the public knew little of the lengths to which we were going to protect their savings, their homes and their jobs.

In more ordinary times I could have been excused, perhaps, for focusing on the policy and not the explanation and presentation of it. But this was a national crisis. In a crisis, a progressive politician who advocates change and reform cannot sit tight but has to mobilise support.

I could and should have engaged in a continuous national conversation with the British people. I should have been out in the country every second day explaining how the crisis had happened, why we urgently needed the extraordinary expansionary measures we were enacting – why in the short-term the deficit would rise as revenues from taxation fell and we used the spending power of the Treasury to rescue the economy. I should have explained more clearly to the public, and over and over, that we were confronting a national peace-time emergency that required unprecedented interventions. But how?

With its focus on the cut and thrust of partisan debate, and with its aversion to the kind of set speeches favoured in America, the House of Commons can never be the arena for winning the battle for public opinion in economic matters. Parliament is a very different place than it was when Churchill, in a time of united resolve, rallied the country from the Dispatch Box. On any occasion in recent times when I, or for that matter anyone else, tried to speak directly to the nation at the Dispatch Box, such speeches have failed to break through. Any attempt to raise people's hopes and their confidence will be drowned out in a cacophony which, sadly, thrives on petty point-scoring.

At one time speeches , whether in or out of the Commons, mattered – and were widely reported – but today almost any major set speech will swiftly fade in the ceaseless churn of the news cycle. So opposed anyway were most of the press to our party and therefore our policy that I had scant if any hope the print media would help me put the case.

In the interwar years radio was at its peak, and reassuring words broadcast to the nation could make a difference. Throughout the post-war years politicians competed for attention on peak-time TV and by the turn of the millennium it was usually six-second, eighteen-word sound bites that they relied on to make them household names. All the more reason that I should have taken any and every oppor-tunity to deliver the message directly on TV and radio.

I thought of how, in the Great Depression of the 1930s, Franklin Roosevelt reached beyond the press barons who editorially assailed his New Deal and persuaded a commanding majority to welcome his great national endeavour of reconstruction. He is remembered for his 'fireside chats', broadcast at peak time on national radio and reaching 80 per cent of the radio-listening public, in which he countered pre-vailing fears by explaining in accessible language what he was doing and why. But by 2009 perhaps no politician, even ones far more skilled than me, could have successfully competed for a peak-time audience with soaps, sitcoms and game shows.

And as I tried to get our message across I found just how much the world of communications had changed – even in the ten years since 1997. Not only had newspaper readerships halved but television news was barely watched by young people.

No longer, as I discovered in 2009, is there what could be called a single national conversation. In a very real sense, everyone has a plat-form and with so many social-media outlets on the one hand and so many voices competing for attention on the other, mobilising national opinion is far harder than before.

In fact, Twitter and Facebook were turning the tables on TV.

TV, it was said, allowed someone into your front room whom you'd never invite in through your front door. But you sat passively in front of the screen. Social media, at least in theory, puts the citizen in the driving seat – it allows you to say harsher things about people online than you ever would if you were face-to-face. In this new multimedia world, people using Twitter can effectively sometimes have a bigger megaphone than a prime minister. Indeed, by the time we left Downing Street, Sarah had more Twitter followers – 1.2 million – than I could ever dream of.

I desperately wanted to show what we could achieve as a country working together and perhaps some of our initiatives – on jobs for the young and the car scrappage scheme – did seep through into public consciousness for a time. But I never persuaded the country that we were part of a great national endeavour. I was not alone. No European leader or finance minister other than Angela Merkel and Wolfgang Schäuble (who became German finance minister in 2009) survived the financial crisis. In 2009 even Barack Obama found it difficult to get his message across. The popular mobilisation he had built to secure election in 2008 could not be so easily sustained out in the country as he faced the economic crisis and healthcare challenges of 2009 and 2010.

I held a series of public meetings, many question-and-answer sessions with business and did a host of regional visits, like the ones in May 2009 that I described in the Introduction. But by then even the BBC's coverage of politics was now leading on debt and deficits – the Tory agenda – and not jobs; ignoring the reality that without government spending we could not haul our economy back to life.

There was another reason why we failed to communicate our message: I think, in retrospect, that I was too ready to assume – wrongly as it turned out – that we had done enough in the previous ten years to be trusted by the public to make the right economic choices. I felt that after a decade of managing the economy prudently, the public would, at the least, give us the benefit of the doubt. This assumption was instinctive on my part, an almost unquestioned political miscalculation.

So, in these crisis years we may have won the fight against recession; but even as we did so, we lost the battle for public opinion.

It was said of an early hero of mine, James Maxton, that he had every quality except one: the gift of knowing how to succeed. Strangely,

perhaps, I felt up to all the demands of the day – for technical competence, command of detail and substance, managing and motivating
a committed team, and most of all seeing the bigger picture – and
felt undaunted by any of them. Indeed, I warmed to all these tasks.
As I tackled the crisis, I felt that Downing Street was now seeing the
real me, but the country was not. Despite all the experience I had
built up working inside the media – writing, reporting and
broadcasting – I found that no matter what I did to get my message
across I often fell short. It was a tide that though taken at the flood
did not lead to fortune.

In short, I believe that I failed to convince the public not because
the policy was poor but because the communications were poor. I
felt I had shown the courage to take difficult decisions and learn from
adversity. But I should have gone out on the front foot to show why
it was not imprudent to run a deficit in a recession. I write this not
as an excuse, but to emphasise what I now know better than ever
before and should have realised after our earlier and successful strategy building support for a tax rise for the NHS: the challenge is not
just to do the right thing, but to bring people along. This is vital, and
never more so than in a crisis. Even when 'there is . . . vision [you
can] perish' if you do not instil confidence and hope in your plan. It
is a lesson for anyone in a position of leadership in times to come.

CHAPTER 18

2010: LOSING AND LEAVING

Perhaps I am alone in thinking that the most remarkable aspect of the general election result in 2010 was that only 10 million people voted for Tory austerity, whereas more than 15 million voted for parties with policies to keep the economy growing.

The election was to deliver the first hung parliament since 1974 – the Tories winning 306 seats, Labour 258, the Lib Dems fifty-seven and the first coalition government since the Second World War, but it will go down in history for ushering in the austerity years, which turned into a lost decade for Britain.

Most readers will be able to recall the Liberal Democrats' subsequent breaking of their promise to abolish tuition fees. What is now forgotten is what lay behind it: that the Lib Dems stood in 2010 on a platform that demanded reflation and public spending – and then unceremoniously ditched that position. In their election manifesto, they had solemnly promised there would be no spending cuts in their first year in office and had even sought a slower deficit-reduction path than our Labour government. It was only in the aftermath that, in forming a coalition with the Conservatives, they sacrificed growth for austerity.

It was because we appeared to share a similar approach to growth and employment that it made sense to aim for a post-election deal with the Liberal Democrats, even though it was a long shot. I knew the difficulties of attempting such a course and some might even say that we were attempting the impossible. I would have not done so but for one reason: a commitment to completing the economic recovery spurred me on. In retrospect, it might have been better for the Liberal Democrats to have paid more attention to Labour: their failure to do so decimated them in the elections of 2015 and 2017. But that is not the most important point: what happened during the days of negotiations following the general election reveals weaknesses in our constitution that I feel merit attention.

For a long time, I had sensed how difficult it would be to win outright. Indeed, well before Tony Blair left office, public support had generally been moving away from us.

In 2010, the issue that was most important in the 2005 election – Iraq – had not been forgotten, but we also faced the fallout from the recession. As the previous chapter records, an unrelenting message from the Tories and the newspapers about debt and deficits had not fallen on deaf ears. I also had to contend with a general sense that, after thirteen years in power, both the government and Labour Party looked tired.

Worse was the fallout from the MPs' expenses scandal, which had filled the news for weeks from May 2009 onwards. This cast a long shadow. Even MPs whose behaviour put them beyond suspicion felt the heat from an angry electorate. It was the shape of things to come, not only in the UK but across the West: political elites were increasingly seen as out of touch, living well and governing badly within their own self-contained bubble. Over Iraq, MPs had been accused of lying. Over expenses, MPs were accused of cheating. And as allegations about 'lying' and 'cheating' became the order of the day, it was the government of the day who, perhaps understandably, got the blame. The Conservatives calculated that it was in their interests to do nothing to resolve the expenses crisis: even though it was a matter for all parties and the whole of Parliament to address, they rightly gauged that the question people would ask was: 'What is the government doing to sort this out?' Even if public feeling about politicians was 'they're all the same', the blame did not fall equally and the answer was to throw out those in power. The full force of this anti-establishment revolt would be felt in the European Union referendum of 2016.

Perhaps surprisingly, even as we were weighed down by these multiple crises, we found that our poll numbers went up as well as down – up significantly in the run-up to and during the G20 as Britain led the world in responding to the recession, and then dramatically down in April when Damian McBride had to resign, and then yet further down after the MPs' expenses crisis. But even then the polls recovered a little: the Tories were not trusted, especially on the health service. As our chief strategist David Muir observed at the outset of the election campaign, against the more pessimistic forecasts of those around him, Labour could still end up the biggest party.

I believed we also had a strong record in government. The minimum wage, which for one hundred years had been an undelivered promise, became the law of the land. Nursery education – a lottery for under-fives when we came to office – became a right. As I said at the Labour conference before the election:

> If anyone says that to fight doesn't get you anywhere, that politics can't make a difference, that all parties are the same, then look what we've achieved together since 1997: the winter fuel allowance, the shortest waiting times in history, crime down by a third, the creation of Sure Start, the Cancer Guarantee, record results in schools, more students than ever, the Disability Discrimination Act, devolution, civil partnerships, peace in Northern Ireland, the social chapter, half a million children out of poverty, maternity pay, paternity leave, child benefit at record levels, the minimum wage, the ban on cluster bombs, the cancelling of debt, the trebling of aid, the first ever Climate Change Act; that's the Britain we've been building together, that's the change we choose.

At the start of 2010, only three months before the declaration of the general election, almost all my waking hours had been taken up not with campaign planning but with another Northern Ireland crisis: deadlock around the same contentious issues was again threatening to bring down the Assembly, force the reinstatement of direct rule from London and herald a return to sectarian violence. We tried everything to find a resolution of the key issue: who was to be justice minister. Despite interventions from me, Taoiseach Brian Cowen as well as Bill and Hillary Clinton, by the end of January there seemed no alternative but for Brian and me to decamp to Belfast in the hope that each of the many blockages to a deal could be removed.

After two days and nights of constant talks, both sides were as far apart as ever. Brian and I then took the decision to leave – risking a complete breakdown but hoping that this would make the parties realise they could not hold out indefinitely. This worked. Ten days later, Brian and I flew to Stormont and sealed a comprehensive arrangement. Ten years on from the Good Friday Agreement, we had now completed the devolution process. Paying tribute to Tony Blair, the Irish government and the people of Northern Ireland, I spoke of a 'momentous journey, from division to dialogue, from conflict to cooperation . . . after decades of violence, years of talks, weeks of stalemate, this is the day we have secured the future'.

I was then, and still am, clear how we finally got a deal. When trouble flares up in Northern Ireland, I always remind myself of two basic preconditions that we forget at our peril if we are to maintain the peace: the UK as an honest broker, and having the Irish government as a partner. When the 2010 election came around, however, a new fuse had been lit which eventually undermined hopes of continued power-sharing between Northern Ireland's opposed factions. The Conservatives and Ulster Unionists entered a pact to stand in Northern Irish seats as 'the Ulster Conservatives and Unionists – New Force', at a stroke ending the long-standing neutrality that ensured both the main UK parties could be honest brokers in Northern Ireland disputes. If Theresa May was later to mortgage that neutrality in a deal with the Democratic Unionist Party, David Cameron had already breached it with this pact.

Should I have handed over power in the months before the election to a new leader? I did think of this, in particular over Christmas 2009, and I would have stepped down had it not been that I had set myself a clear target of building a better post-recession economy. I felt that the work I had started was not yet done. Given what we had been through to bring the economy back to life, I felt it would be a dereliction of duty not to complete the job.

But that is not how the press saw it. We know now from the private correspondence of Aidan Barclay, the chairman of the Telegraph Media Group, that David Cameron was offered the opportunity to speak to the *Daily Telegraph* editor every day of the campaign, to make sure the paper's headlines helped him. The *Express* was as anti-Labour as it always had been. Paul Dacre made no secret of the fact that he ran the *Mail* as a Tory paper. But it was the Murdoch media, in alliance with the Conservatives, that sought to damage me most. In 2007 the *Sun* agreed to help David Cameron by pulling away from their petition for a referendum on the Lisbon Treaty. They ran campaigns on crime and Afghanistan that could not have been better written by Conservative Central Office. Not that the Murdoch empire got nothing in return. The Conservatives now promised Murdoch new broadcasting laws to neuter the regulator, Ofcom, to undermine the BBC – its licence fee, its Internet presence, its commercial activities, its stake in sporting events – and even hinted they would advantage Sky by breaking up British Telecom. Now during election year – as Leveson would reveal – they were in day-to-day communication. Later I could only laugh as I read of the constant texts exchanged by David Cameron and Rebekah Brooks; but no one should be in any doubt that the *Sun* and the Conservative Party were on a joint enterprise in the year to May 2010.

While my predecessors suffered from this, in one way at least I was in a more disadvantageous position. The Tory-supporting papers – *The Times*, the *Mail*, the *Sun*, the *Telegraph*, the *Express* – represented 70 per cent of newspaper readers. Adding in the *Independent* which wanted a Liberal–Labour coalition and the *Guardian*, who declared for the Lib Dems, newspapers which accounted for 90 per cent of all readers opposed Labour. That would matter more in the 2010 election than in 2017. Not, in fact, because the *Guardian* and *Independent* editorial line swayed their own readers, as a bigger share of their readership voted Labour in 2010 than in 2005, but because of the right-wing press. Half the *Sun*'s readers had voted Labour in 1997 and 2001. Now, in 2010, just over a quarter – 28 per cent – did. Seven years later the *Sun*'s sales had halved – and with Twitter, Facebook, YouTube and social media, new and pervasive sources of information were available. A relentless drumbeat of criticism, distortion and falsehood unfairly directed against Jeremy Corbyn had far less impact than the press barons counted on. There is a dark side to this, in that social-media sites can spread a contagion of falsehood within a matter of minutes. But they do provide a platform for leaders to communicate directly with the public and for supporters to organise and interact with each other. I do not think the influence the tabloids had in 2010 is ever likely to be as significant again.

Up against all of this, some in Labour felt a spell in opposition might be beneficial. You could not say that of Peter Mandelson and Douglas Alexander, who were coordinating our election strategy and working all hours running our day-to-day campaign. But many Labour MPs, fearing they would lose, stood down and gave their Conservative challengers, many of whom had been in the field for some years, a clear run against a hitherto unknown Labour candidate. Not only did we lose the benefit of incumbency in many marginal seats, we undoubtedly lost seats in London because of our principled stand in favour of the expansion of Heathrow airport. The Conservatives exploited local resistance to a project that I believed was in the national interest. As a result, the eventual Heathrow expansion would be delayed for at least ten years.

For months we had been working flat out to handle the financial crisis. The election campaign ratcheted up the pace even further: I was now moving from place to place, staying in a succession of hotels, unable to operate to a fixed routine. This was compounded by the novelty of three televised leaders' debates that demanded time for preparation – time that I did not really have when constantly touring the country and still running the government, including making difficult decisions on Afghanistan.

Time was not the only resource we sorely lacked. The party's debt, which was being reduced at the rate of £3 million a year, still stood at £20 million. So even after securing a higher level of donations than in 2005 we could afford to spend only £33.8 million in 2010 compared with £49.8 million in 2005. In fact our direct campaign expenditure in 2010 was only £8 million, down from almost £18 million in 2005. In 2010 the Tories outspent us two to one.

While it is no excuse for losing – at all times I have taken personal responsibility for the defeat – this meant we could not afford the posters, billboards and newspaper adverts that the Tories were spending millions on. Money did make a real difference: while we were forced to reduce our advertising spend to a few hundred thousand pounds, the Tories spent almost £8 million on that alone. Moreover, at a time when it was becoming increasingly important, we could not afford the social-media campaign we needed. Douglas Alexander and David Muir were being asked to do more with less. We were not so much out-campaigned by the Tories as outspent.

This made the televised debates more appealing. I agreed to them because I thought it right that the country hear the arguments debated through TV questioning. And, of course, without them our underspend on advertising would have been even more exposed. The debates created a more level playing field that disguised how limited our resources were, offering us free advertising at a time when we could not afford paid advertising. But, weighed down in the autumn and early spring by responding to the recession, I had not given enough attention to the downsides of TV debates. They tend to favour opposition leaders, untainted by any record in office, as President Obama discovered in his first 2012 presidential debate against Mitt Romney. In Britain in 2010, they also gave the third party the same platform as the two main leaders. Both factors helped Nick Clegg, who did very well and was able to give the impression of offering a fresh start as a new kid on the block.

What's more, the once-a-week debates did suck the oxygen out of the campaign on the ground. In the weeks that the debates took place, on Monday, Tuesday and Wednesday there was understandable media speculation about what would happen in the debate on Thursday, while on Friday, Saturday and Sunday the issue was the fallout. Speeches were drowned out. I remember the preparations for the second debate, which would be about foreign affairs, being especially rigorous as we anticipated a difficult time over Iraq and Afghanistan. As for the final debate, I went very hard on David Cameron over the threat to tax credits. Working women in particular feared their loss under a Conservative government – and from that point we put the Tories' proposals under much more scrutiny.

Only when the debates were over did any of my speeches gain traction. Even so, I am still in favour of TV debates, though it is important they are staged in such a way that they do not wholly overshadow what happens on the doorstep, at rallies and in visits meeting people on the ground. I cannot see how leaders hoping to govern the country can justify avoiding a direct encounter with each other – and the electorate – on the most visible of platforms.

Not all face-to-face encounters end well. On the day before the last leaders' debate at Birmingham University, as I was being driven from one stop to another, I blurted out a private remark in an unguarded moment about Gillian Duffy, a voter whom I had met in Rochdale. I was in the north-west to focus on the increased police numbers that were helping us tackle crime. Mrs Duffy, however, wanted to talk about something else – immigration. And as a media scrum built up around us, I signalled to the staff who were with me that it was time to migrate to the next stop.

Normally as I got into the car, someone travelling with me would remove the mic from my lapel. And, of course, usually the broadcaster who had pinned it would have turned the feed off from their studio. The previous week Sarah had been with me and always removed it. But on this occasion, with the microphone still on and my words being transmitted to Sky TV, I made the mistake of describing Mrs Duffy as a 'sort of bigoted woman'. It was a remark born of frustration that the next day's media coverage would not be about our policing policies but immigration. Now instead it would be about my insulting a voter, which no amount of apologising could prevent.

To make matters worse, when I entered a BBC studio for a radio interview with Jeremy Vine an hour later, I did not even know that the remark had been overheard and was now becoming public property. Without warning, they played my own words back to me. And when I put my head in my hands, I had no idea that the interview was also being filmed. One mistake had led to two more.

Even on air it seemed obvious to me what I had to do: my instinctive response was to say, 'I apologise if I have said anything like that. What I think she was raising with me was an issue of immigration and saying that there were too many people from eastern Europe in the country. I do apologise if I have said anything that has been hurtful, and I will apologise to her personally.' And when asked who I blamed, I replied: 'I'm blaming myself. I blame myself for what is done.'

I went to the home of Mrs Duffy to apologise in person. She kindly allowed me to explain to her what had happened. I tried to limit the damage with a statement saying: 'I'm mortified by what's happened. I've given her my sincere apologies. I misunderstood what she said, and she has accepted there was a misunderstanding . . . If you like, I'm a penitent sinner.' But it was to no avail; the damage had been done.

I did not relax my campaigning efforts, though. On the Saturday before the vote I travelled to Newcastle and Sunderland and made speeches in both cities before visiting Tynemouth. On the Sunday, I did a full tour round London seats – starting with Eltham, Peckham and then Streatham for a service at the Church of the New Testament, then touring Dulwich, Tooting, Hammersmith and Harrow before finishing off with a visit to campaign in Hampstead with Glenda Jackson.

On the Monday, I visited a number of south-east seats and then

Lowestoft and Great Yarmouth on the coast of Suffolk and Norfolk, before the Citizens UK Rally in London. On Tuesday and Wednesday, I took in the Midlands and Yorkshire, staying in Leeds overnight and speaking in Bradford. And then in the final hours I travelled to Liverpool and the north-west before driving north to Carlisle, where I met staff at the haulage company Eddie Stobart, doing a live interview from there for the BBC *Six O'Clock News*. There was no let-up as our car then drove across the border to Dumfries and Galloway to visit this marginal Scottish seat. In the car, my special adviser Kirsty McNeill and I were furiously writing my last major speech, a plea to Labour voters to 'come home'. I spoke at 9 p.m. and was back in my bed in Fife by midnight.

By the time the polls opened on election day, I had slept only a few hours. I went with Sarah to cast our votes around 11 a.m. I spent the rest of election day preparing for every possible eventuality. The Conservatives clearly expected an overall majority. The Liberal Democrats were anticipating they would move into second place. I thought both were wrong.

When the results began to come in, it was clear that Labour were going to lose seats, but it was equally obvious that the Tories would not make the gains they needed for a majority. Sunderland Central, a new seat far more marginal than its predecessor, revealed a nominal swing to the Conservatives far below the 5 per cent required. Labour held Gedling, Telford and then Tooting in London, all seats the Tories had targeted. In fact, with the exception of the constituencies affected by Heathrow's expansion, we mostly held our own in London. It was also clear we were doing well in Scotland and Wales. One of our impressive young ministers, Gareth Thomas, narrowly held on to Harrow West despite a swing to the Conservative challenger. And then across the country we won in areas where we were expected to lose, such as Birmingham Edgbaston, Plymouth Moor View and Exeter. They had one thing in common: good candidates who had stayed the course.

On Friday morning, our flight left Scotland at 3 a.m., touched down in Stansted at 4 a.m., and I arrived at Labour Party HQ in Victoria Street around 5 a.m. After thanking the loyal but weary staff I returned to Downing Street. It was a strange No. 10. The offices had already been reconfigured. We could not log onto the No. 10 computer system. Email accounts had been deleted. Clearly someone had expected us never to return. Somehow, though, we plugged in a laptop and some printers. When I went up to our flat, I was pleased to see that at least the beds were still there. Having enjoyed another short bout of sleep – around three hours – I went to work at 10 a.m. I had my energy back.

By this time, with 615 constituency results declared, a hung parliament was a certainty. The senior civil servants at the Cabinet Office, primed for this situation and armed with their *Cabinet Manual*, now moved into action to host what they knew would follow – inter-party negotiations. This was something I had anticipated before the election, and now authorised.

When I heard Nick Clegg's statement half an hour later that he would first talk to the Tories – and that David Cameron would soon issue a statement of his own – I decided we could not sit still but had to act quickly.

I had already conferred with the then Transport Secretary, Andrew Adonis, our best go-between with the Liberal Democrats, on the morning of polling day. I was conscious of what had happened in Scotland in 2007 when the SNP had not won a majority but seized victory by claiming it. The Labour–Liberal Democrat coalition in Scotland could have made a compelling case for staying in power, but the SNP leader Alex Salmond simply went to the Scottish Parliament and announced he would form a government – a gesture which destroyed any residual self-confidence the Scottish Lib Dems had about renewing a coalition with us. My moves on the Friday morning were designed to avoid any Salmond-style declaration by David Cameron.

We reminded the media of the constitutional position – that the incumbent government stays until someone else can produce a majority. I talked to Cabinet members, senior party figures and trade union leaders, telling them that we were considering talks with the Liberal Democrats. I was never one to exaggerate the likelihood of securing a deal, but the numbers showed we could construct a governing coalition. Taken together, Labour and Lib Dem seats amounted to 315, outnumbering the Tories' 306; both of us were short of an outright majority. But we needed only eleven more votes – or even fewer as Sinn Féin never voted – for a majority in the House of Commons. Because the nationalist parties in Wales and Scotland had to consider their own elections in 2011, I knew that they would not dare to bring down a progressive coalition for fear of alienating the progressive vote in both countries. While the Ulster Unionist Party and the Conservatives had stood under the same banner in Northern Ireland, neither had gained any seats in Northern Ireland. I believed that if we remained neutral towards all the Northern Irish parties they would not vote us out. The figures showed clearly that with Lib Dem support we could govern.

But that is not how Nick Clegg saw it. Before the election, Clegg had said he would talk first to the biggest party. He maintained this was what the constitution mandated. In 2010, this appeared to be the Cabinet Secretary Gus O'Donnell's view too (he included a reference to it in a new edition of his *Cabinet Manuel* in 2010), although he has since qualified it. I did not object at the time – Nick Clegg was, of course, entitled to talk to anyone he wanted – but few constitutional observers agree that he was following any clear principle. Others had done it differently in the past. It was, rather, his personal preference.

It should have been inconceivable that the Liberal Democrats would prop up an austerity regime. It went against every economic position they had adopted during the campaign. While the Tories had fought on a programme of spending cuts, the Lib Dems had pledged an extra £5 billion of expenditure a year. 'If spending is cut too soon,' their manifesto said, 'it would undermine the much-needed recovery and cost jobs.' This was a stark rejection of austerity. Their manifesto also explicitly rejected immediate expenditure cuts for the first year after the election. The Lib Dems had a similar commitment to Labour's to prioritise growth and a similar target to ours for borrowing in each year – in all of these areas their manifesto placed them a million miles away from the Conservatives. I thought that in any coalition negotiations it would not be difficult to reach agreement with the Lib Dems on the economy.

They also had more in common with us than the Conservatives on what they proclaimed to be their make-or-break constitutional issue – voting reform. I had come out for an alternative vote system and could provide assurances of good faith. They wanted Lords reform and I was committed to that. They wanted a climate change policy that could reopen the drive for a global treaty, despite the breakdown of talks in Copenhagen, something I was campaigning for too.

The other main issue was Europe. The Conservatives had promised to tear up EU social and employment legislation and their campaign had strong anti-European rhetoric. Once again, on a defining issue, the Lib Dems and Tories were entirely at odds with each other.

It was clear that across the whole field of government policy there was potential for agreement between Labour and Liberal Democrats on a progressive programme. However, we had to reckon with a party that was bruised from a result that fell far short of their expectations. At 23 per cent of the vote – about the same as in 2005 – the Lib Dems had failed to make the breakthrough they had confidently assumed. They were down five seats on their 2005 performance, when they had won sixty-two. For every five seats held by Labour, the Lib Dems held only one. Their campaign manager Danny Alexander, who spoke to Andrew Adonis on the morning after the election, confirmed that they were licking their wounds.

On election night, many believed that the Liberal Democrats were about to be installed as the second party in British politics. But the next morning they were 200 seats short of that dream. When the next day I spoke to Alan Rusbridger, the editor of the *Guardian*, who had supported the Lib Dems, I urged upon him the logic of supporting a progressive coalition. However, it soon became obvious that Nick Clegg had only one real objective in mind: forming a coalition with David Cameron. A good indication of this came when Paddy Ashdown, who seemed to be at the centre of every manoeuvre, cancelled a meeting that Andrew Adonis had previously arranged with him for Friday morning.

At 1.45 p.m. on Friday, before David Cameron was due to speak, I made my statement. I had consulted as many members of the Cabinet as I could beforehand – while at the same time trying to contact some of our candidates who had sadly lost their seats to thank them for their efforts and commiserate. There was an attempt to ban me from speaking from outside No. 10. I replied that this was both my home and my office. As a compromise, I made a statement at a modest distance from the black door of No. 10. I was told a suitable lectern – one without the government crest – could not be found, which meant I had to speak from a rickety one that had been located somewhere in the basement.

'For my part,' I said, 'I should make it clear that I would be willing to see any of the party leaders.' I then emphasised that we needed 'strong, stable and principled government'. The word 'principled' was carefully chosen to highlight the decisive questions. Would the Lib

A photograph with HM Queen Elizabeth II taken at Buckingham Palace at the time of the G20 London Summit, April 2009.

In discussion with 44th US President Barack Obama at the London G20.

Above: Delivering a speech to a joint meeting of both houses of the United States Congress, February 2009

Left: Talking to Nancy Pelosi, then Leader of the House of Representatives

The Chequers staff including Head Chef Alan Lavender (far left), who had served four consecutive prime ministers, on the occasion of Lady Thatcher's visit.

My speech after the 2010 election
outside 10 Downing Street
on 7 May – taken by Sarah
from the No. 11 flat.

Leaving as a family – our
official moment of departure
from Downing Street
after thirteen years.

Final words inside Downing Street before departing for the last time, 11 May 2010.
Left to right: Sarah, John, me, Fraser, Justin Forsyth, Douglas Alexander,
Joe Irvin, Ed Miliband, Ed Balls, Peter Mandelson, Alastair Campbell,
Leeanne Johnston, Gavin Kelly, Kirsty McNeill.

Back home in Fife with Sarah by the famous Forth Bridge after leaving government.

The eve-of-poll speech (one of around 200 delivered during the Scottish referendum campaign) given at Maryhill, Glasgow. Eddie Izzard looks on.

In front of Coventry Cathedral about to make a People's IN campaign film ahead of the European Referendum. It attracted more than 5.5 million views on Facebook.

As the United Nations Special Envoy for Global Education with former UN Secretary General Ban Ki-moon and UNESCO Director Irina Bokova visiting East Timor in 2012.

Joining Sarah and Education Commission Director Justin van Fleet and young campaigner Alberto Verrilli on the Avaaz climate change march in New York City, in September 2015.

On stage with pop superstar Shakira and Norwegian Prime Minister Erna Solberg at a G20 2017 concert in Hamburg to speak up together for a new education financing vehicle.

The first meeting of the Commission for Financing Global Education Opportunity. Left to right: Aliko Dangote, Justin van Fleet, Amel Karboul, Yuriko Koike, Jakaya Kikwete, Kristin Clemet, Lubna Khalid Al Qasimi, Tarald Brautaset, José Manuel Barroso, Felipe Calderón, me, Strive Masiyiwa, Jack Ma, Helle Thorning-Schmidt, Baela Jamil, Teopista Birungi Mayanja, Julia Gillard, Theo Sowa, Ju-Ho Lee, Patricio Meller, Anant Agarwal, Tony Lake, Liesbet Steer.

With Canada's Prime Minister Justin Trudeau talking about education financing at the World Economic Forum, Davos.

With former president of Tanzania Jakaya Kikwete, African lead on the Education Commission.

With France's President Emmanuel Macron.

Campaigning for global education, global security and global growth
with UN Secretary General António Guterres.

Dems join in government with a party that was so virulently anti-European? Would they sacrifice voting reform for a hollow Conservative promise? Most of all, would the Lib Dems hold to the principled commitment in their election manifesto to oppose austerity? I was sending an unmistakable message about the incompatibility between the Lib Dems' pledges and the Conservatives' programme.

When he spoke forty-five minutes later, David Cameron offered Clegg a full coalition. This too represented an opening for us: by accepting the need for coalition negotiations, he had declined to claim a right to govern, legitimising the entire process of talks and by implication our involvement in them. But, of course, all depended on the Liberal Democrats. Their decisions over the next few days were to have historic significance for progressive politics.

At 5 p.m. on Friday, I spoke to Nick Clegg, congratulated him on his campaign and told him there was genuine common ground on which we might forge an agreement. To show our good faith, I said I would share a policy paper with him – one we had prepared for internal consumption – and proposed that we meet soon.

The next day at noon I attended a ceremony at the Cenotaph to commemorate the sixty-fifth anniversary of VE Day. Rather unusually, at Gus O'Donnell's insistence, David Cameron and Nick Clegg were given equal billing with the sitting prime minister. This incident and the *Sun*'s front-page headline that morning – 'Squatter holed up in No. 10' – brought home how easily it might appear I was clinging on to power. Being alert to this possibility, I had already decided on Friday to leave London for Scotland. Early on the Saturday afternoon, Sarah and I left to fly home to my constituency.

Back in Scotland, I again talked to Clegg by phone. My message to him was that David Cameron could not deflect his party from its anti-European stance, even if he wanted to. If they reached agreement with the Tories, the Liberal Democrats would be going into coalition with a party that held exactly the opposite view to them. I re-emphasised that the Lib Dems and Tories had irreconcilable policies on the economy as well. But when it came to the crunch, as I found, even the rancid anti-Europeanism of the Tories did not deter him. In all our private talks, I felt that I was far more concerned than he was about the UK becoming isolated in Europe. To me, he gave the impression that he had hardly thought about this.

That same day, Nick Clegg had been approached by some leading Lib Dems asking him to reconsider his attitude to Labour and to seriously contemplate a Labour–Liberal coalition. There was certainly scope for agreement. Andrew Adonis, who has chronicled the events of these few days, concludes that 'there could have been a radically different dynamic, leading to a Lib-Lab coalition, had Clegg instead said the day after the election that the key issue had been economic policy'. So why did the Liberal Democrats go into the election on an anti-austerity manifesto but into a coalition government on an austerity platform? Why did they U-turn on their earlier commitment to forswear cuts before mid-2011?

Such an arrangement would have been all but unthinkable until Nick Clegg became leader of the Liberal Democrats. I believe he was personally more comfortable with Conservatives. In the event, the assurances he secured from them were paper-thin: the Conservatives gave him his referendum on changing the voting system but then sabotaged it – and, in the end, it was Tory votes in Parliament that killed off Lords reform. Nick Clegg's later rationalisation that the Lib Dems moderated right-wing policies by entering a coalition with the Conservatives is an early example of fake news: if Labour and the Liberal Democrats had gone into coalition together there would have been no shift to the right in the first place.

But the ultimate rationalisation for a Tory-led coalition – which turned the Lib Dems' own self-declared policies and progressive principles upside down – was a convenient post-election conversion to austerity. The Liberal Democrats signed up to Tory economics and their later fiasco over tuition fees was the inevitable outcome of their surrender.

David Laws, one of the leaders of the Lib Dems' negotiating team, was far more upfront than Clegg on this matter. Published in 2004, Laws' work *The Orange Book* had been a thinly veiled attempt to shift the party to neoliberal economics. But Clegg and Laws were given cover. As Vince Cable has written, the Lib Dems found themselves under pressure from more than just the Tories to adopt their plan to reduce spending by £6 billion. He explained the pressures: 'This sense of urgency and importance was enhanced by the personal briefings I and others received by phone during the coalition negotiations from the Cabinet Secretary [Gus O'Donnell] and the permanent secretary to the Treasury [Nick Macpherson], reflecting, at one removed, the views of the governor of the Bank of England [Mervyn King].' And he went on: 'The formation of the coalition coincided with the first major crisis of confidence in Greek government bonds and the euro. The government's top officials expressed the fear that, as the country most exposed to a banking crisis and with the largest fiscal deficit of any major country, the "contagion" could easily spread to the UK.'

This was thorough nonsense. There was no chance of the UK going the same way as Greece. Our deficit was lower than that of the USA, our debt at around the same level as Germany's and lower than our major competitors. It was simply wrong to say the deficit could not be funded. The argument that it would be difficult to sell British government bonds would prove to be completely incorrect.

On Friday 7 May, in his discussions with the Liberal Democrats, George Osborne now claimed that the Bank of England and the Treasury shared the position that £6 billion of immediate spending cuts were needed to send a powerful message to the markets. Laws records Osborne saying that Mervyn King and Nick Macpherson were 'very supportive of what we want to do'. The draft Tory–Liberal Democrat agreement, prepared on 8 May by the Conservatives, laid bare what was happening: 'The Conservatives explained our [i.e. the Conservatives' and the Liberal Democrats'] belief that the achievement of a further spending reduction of £6bn in 2010 would be regarded by the financial markets as a test of whether a Conservative–Liberal Democrat government was capable of carrying through the necessary deficit reduction plan. This view is shared by the Treasury and the Bank of England.'

These statements of official support were never corrected; indeed, Laws also reports that William Hague and George Osborne, two of the lead Tory negotiators, claimed authority from Nick Macpherson and Mervyn King to offer meetings with them during the negotiating period.

The newspapers contained reports that the Bank and Civil Service had endorsed the Tory austerity plan. There was even a report that there would be a meltdown on Monday unless austerity was agreed. Back in London on the Sunday, I called Mervyn King at around 7.15 p.m. He was evasive; it was clear, though, that his views had been communicated to the other parties. This all suited Nick Clegg's position. It is important to remember that the Lib Dems needed the consent of a three-quarters' majority of their party group and a conference vote to enter a coalition government. It was thus to Clegg's advantage to create the illusion of a national economic emergency to persuade his party that they must accept austerity in the national interest.

On Sunday, Vernon Bogdanor, our leading constitutional scholar, reminded me that under the constitution I had the right to present a Queen's Speech – and in the *New Statesman* later that week he proposed a progressive alliance. After having fought so hard to achieve economic recovery and sensing it was in danger, I decided to make one last effort. I considered a public appeal. With help from Kirsty McNeill, who was writing speeches of the highest quality, I planned to say that 'last Thursday, 15 million people voted for progressive parties – and it will be to my lasting regret that I could not win enough of them for Labour'. I then would have gone on to say: 'The British people cast their ballots for progressive commitments on public services, the economy and the environment . . . [this] is now an urgent dividing line in our public life.'

But I settled for the more mundane. I met Nick Clegg at 4.15 p.m. in the Foreign Office after an elaborate series of walks in underground tunnels to prevent the press knowing of our meeting. Before that I talked to Vince Cable by phone. While more favourable to Labour, Cable spoke as though he had been excluded from the main Lib Dem team and seemed unable to influence events. My exchange of views with Clegg was entirely amicable. I told him that to expedite a deal I was prepared to stand down as prime minister; moreover, before I did so, I would throw the Labour Party's weight not just behind a referendum on the alternative voting system but behind a 'yes' vote. But there was not much good faith around: while I had offered to leave as Labour leader, the Lib Dems briefed that I had said the opposite.

I followed up the Clegg meeting with further calls to Vince Cable and Menzies Campbell. In a letter sent to Clegg – prefaced by a phone call on Monday morning around 8.15 a.m. – I said we needed a clear statement of principles and a governing philosophy. I told him we could sign up to a new democratic and constitutional settlement and to far-reaching changes to our economy and banking system. I ended by saying that all the decisions the new government made would be taken on the basis of a pro-European agenda.

At 10.45 a.m., I then met Nick Clegg in the House of Commons, with Peter Mandelson and Danny Alexander present. It soon became apparent that the talks between Labour and Liberal Democrats had yielded little. But there was an air of unreality about the encounter: Danny Alexander seemed to think he was there to be the 'hard man' and quickly demanded that I resign immediately. I repeated that I was leaving but that I needed to get the coalition agreement through the Labour Party and that we had to create momentum within it to win a referendum on voting reform. This, I reminded him, would not happen without backing from the top. If I resigned immediately, the Queen would have no choice but to ask the Conservatives to form a government. It was becoming abundantly clear to me that Nick Clegg was using the meeting for ammunition to strengthen his negotiating position with the Conservatives.

Following this, at 5 p.m., I made a statement saying I had asked the Labour Party to begin a leadership selection process in which I would take no part. My intention would be to step down by September. I had no desire to stay in my position longer than was needed. However, I made clear that it was in the 'interests of the whole country to form a progressive coalition government', leaving open the prospect of Labour–Liberal coalition, following further formal discussions with Clegg.

All the time I was having to talk to MPs, party officials and Cabinet ministers, explaining that we had put to the Lib Dems a progressive agenda for government. When the Cabinet met after my public statement – the first time since the election and the last time it would come together – there was some pushback from one or two ministers who thought it best to rebuild Labour from the Opposition benches – and some criticism of who was in and out of our negotiating team. But the Cabinet gave me a free hand to reach a conclusion.

By Tuesday morning, I had made up my mind that, unless the Lib Dems were genuinely interested in reaching an agreement with us, I would hand in my resignation as prime minister that day. I had one last meeting with Nick Clegg at 1 p.m., talked to Paddy Ashdown, Menzies Campbell and Vince Cable, when I kept emphasising to them that a pact with the Conservatives would legitimise the austerity agenda and anti-Europeanism of the Tory Party – both of which they had opposed vehemently during the election. But when at 3 p.m. I met with our own negotiating team – Ed Balls, Ed Miliband, Peter Mandelson, Harriet Harman and Andrew Adonis – it was clear that the Liberal Democrats were unprepared to enter into meaningful negotiations. I then talked separately with Harriet and gave her an assurance that I would resign as leader with immediate effect and that she could take over as acting leader. Following this, I signalled to Sarah that we would be leaving for good within an hour or two. All the time, Kirsty McNeill and I were working on the resignation speech to be given from outside No. 10.

At 6.50 p.m., I phoned Nick Clegg to tell him I was stepping down. He asked for a few minutes to consult, but it was clear to me the extra time he wanted was only to wring some concessions out of the Tories. Anyway, I wanted to leave Downing Street as prime minister for the last time in the light of day. I informed him in a phone call at 7 p.m. that I would be handing in my resignation within the hour. Again, he asked for more time. I refused: I told him the time for talking was over and wished him well. However, I clearly remember warning him of two things as we conducted these conversations: the Tories will destroy you, I said, and they will pull us all apart on Europe.

I had already arranged to go to the Palace before I went out to make my public statement. Before leaving, I thanked the staff at Downing Street for their professionalism and total commitment to public service. And then at 7.15 p.m., while it was still light, I made a public statement outside No. 10 with Sarah and our two boys by our side.

Sarah wanted all four of us to leave Downing Street together as a family. As I have written, we had never wanted the boys to be in the public eye; we wanted them to have lives that were as normal as possible. But for this one occasion we decided that all four of us should walk out the door of No. 10 together and then walk side by side down the street. John and Fraser had to know that something was changing in their lives and they would never live there again. They needed to know there was a reason they were leaving the only rooms and beds they could remember. In a youthful assertion of independence, John was insistent he would not wear a shirt and tie but a favourite T-shirt; after he and Fraser had been told of their roles, both behaved as if out for a normal evening walk.

I had always known that Downing Street was never more than a temporary home for us. Most of all it was a place of work. I was departing because the work I had been doing had come to an end. But I felt that in losing I had let millions of people down. And I was determined to display the dignity that I had always expected and demanded of Labour MPs and ministers. My remarks were direct and to the point:

As you know, the general election left no party able to command a majority in the House of Commons. I said I would do all that I could to ensure a strong, stable and principled government was formed, able to tackle Britain's economic and political challenges effectively. My constitutional duty is to make sure that a government can be formed following last Thursday's general election. I have informed the Queen's private secretary that it is my intention to tender my resignation to the Queen. In the event that the Queen accepts, I shall advise her to invite the leader of the Opposition to form a government.

I wish the next prime minister well as he makes the important choices for the future. Only those that have held the office of prime minister can understand the full weight of its responsibilities and its great capacity for good. I have been privileged to learn much about the very best in human nature and a fair amount too about its frailties, including my own. It was a privilege to serve. And yes, I loved the job not for its prestige, its titles and its ceremony – which I do not love at all. No, I loved the job for its potential to make this country I love fairer, more tolerant, more green, more democratic, more prosperous and more just – truly a greater Britain. In the face of many challenges in a few short years, challenges up to and including the global financial meltdown, I have always strived to serve, to do my best in the interest of Britain, its values and its people.

And let me add one thing also. I will always admire the courage I have seen in our armed forces. And now that the political season is over, let me stress that having shaken their hands and looked into their eyes, our troops represent all that is best in our country and I will never forget all those who have died in honour and whose families today live in grief.

My resignation as leader of the Labour Party will take effect immediately. And in this hour, I want to thank all my colleagues, ministers, Members of Parliament. And I want to thank above all my staff, who have been friends as well as brilliant servants of the country.

Above all, I want to thank Sarah for her unwavering support as well as her love, and for her own service to our country.

I thank my sons John and Fraser for the love and joy they bring to our lives.

And as I leave the second most important job I could ever hold, I cherish even more the first – as a husband and father.

Thank you and goodbye.

Sarah, John, Fraser and I then left quietly, hand in hand. We walked into the suddenly gathering twilight and took our leave of Downing Street for the last time.

There remained one official duty still to perform: going to the Palace. The traditional departure from government does not involve, as some people believe, the prime minister handing over seals of office, or anything formal like that. It is simply saying goodbye to the Queen – and thanking her. As usual, she was charming and the occasion itself was relaxed. I think the Queen would not object to me recounting what happened. She had kindly invited John and Fraser to be present at this last official event and wanted to give us a personal gift, an inscribed photograph of herself. Fraser was just four, and when he looked at the photo he said, 'That's the Queen!' – as if it was of someone other than the person who had just handed it to him. Queen Elizabeth, startled by his response, replied: 'But I'm the Queen, I'm the Queen.' We laughed, and then we left. And so ended three years of regular audiences – more than a hundred – at Buckingham Palace.

The boys drove off from the Palace to prepare for school the next day. I went to Labour Party headquarters to give a speech to the staff and thank them for the work they had done. I was leaving London for good; Sarah and I flew back to Scotland, arriving in Fife around 10 p.m. For the next month, we were split as a family. I was mainly in Scotland and Sarah down in London as the boys finished their school term. I visited as regularly as I could without wanting to intrude on the Westminster scene.

Since 2010, I have often been asked whether I was too eager to form a coalition with the Liberal Democrats. Many Labour MPs, including some members of the Cabinet, did not want one; this was not for the most part because of a belief that it would entail a surrender of principles, but because they felt that in opposition we could rebuild quickly. Their calculation was that we would be back in power within five years. I thought this was foolhardy: in my view letting the Conservatives in the door would help a previously unelectable party manoeuvre itself into the mainstream. So, indeed, it came to pass.

Why do I tell the story of May 2010 in such detail? I do not do so because I believe I or my party had any special right to stay in power. I knew from the outset that we would almost certainly have to leave, and I do not complain that we had to go. But how it happened raises important issues, for at least some of what transpired is an object lesson in how not to do things. Britain has no written constitution, no formal rules or procedures to follow in the case of a hung parliament, and no clear guidelines for civil servants or other unelected public officials which prohibit interference. The advantage here is flexibility; the disadvantage is that non-elected officials may have the power to do more than is reasonable in a democracy. As I have argued, not least on fiscal policy, Mervyn King failed to understand the limits of his unelected position.

I had anticipated that the Civil Service would convene discussions with Opposition parties: indeed, I approved them. It was only right that the Civil Service made talks possible. But I did not think, as I now do, that it was necessary to stipulate the limits of its role.

The first set of talks between the Tories and Liberal Democrats was convened in the Cabinet Office, into which they were welcomed by Gus O'Donnell, on 8 May. And it was, of course, right that all factual information requested from the Civil Service was provided. In 2015, the Constitution Unit at King's College London described the Civil Service's role in coalition discussions as 'to be available to offer information, but not advice'. But was advice not given in 2010? How do we explain the statements from key participants in the Conservative and Lib Dem negotiating teams that were never contradicted: George Osborne's assertion that when it came to a £6 billion deficit reduction plan this view was 'shared by the Treasury and the Bank of England'; David Laws' statement that civil servant heads were 'very supportive' of the policy; and Vince Cable's statement that 'the government's top officials expressed the fear that . . . "contagion" could easily spread to the UK'?

A seasoned observer whose opinions carry weight, Peter Riddell, has written that there is a balance 'between factual advice and that which might be seen as implying a preference for one course of action over another'. The danger in 2010, Riddell writes, was 'that the Civil Service itself would become the heart of the controversy, endangering its impartiality'. In a thoughtful survey of lessons learned from the 2010 election, the Institute for Government highlights 'the difficult balancing act that the Civil Service had to play in all this: between factual advice and that which might be seen as implying a preference for one course of action over another'. 'The Civil Service was not in the negotiating room in May 2010 but its advice was,' the Institute observes, pointing out: 'The distinction between factual advice and advice on what you should do can easily be blurred: for instance, in providing analysis of the feasibility of "in-year" spending cuts (that is in the 2010–11 financial year), the advice would be seen to have played one way – particularly with the governor of the Bank of England seen as operating outside the Whitehall rules.' Its conclusion is that: 'Parties involved in negotiations should be able to consult the Civil Service on costings of pledges and policies but this should not stray into policy advice.'

The *Cabinet Manual* is silent on where the provision of information ends and the provision of advice starts. The problem, the Institute for Government says, is a lack of clarity in wording on the type of 'support' that can be offered. In any event, it is clear that the current *Cabinet Manual* is inadequate, an unacceptable halfway house between an unwritten constitution and a constitutional document. The Institute recommends that in future the Cabinet Secretary should be cautious about their level of involvement.

Prime ministers leaving government will in future find it impossible to play any sensible part in the House of Commons. If you speak out, then you are accused of trying to upstage your new leader. If you don't speak regularly in debates, then you're accused of being someone who is moping or bitter. In 2016 David Cameron would come to the same decision as Tony Blair to leave quickly. In a previous era, Churchill decided to stay in Parliament for nearly ten years. Edward Health was an MP for twenty-five years after he lost office and was declared 'a great sulk'. I met Jim Callaghan and talked to him in the years from 1983 to 1987 when he was still in the Commons on the back benches. But the twenty-four-hour news cycle and wall-to-wall TV coverage of the Commons make it increasingly unrealistic to do anything other than step down as an MP when you leave Downing Street.

As happens so often, one event encapsulates what is happening in your life. A few days out of No. 10, I was back in London for a day, taking my younger son Fraser to nursery. As parents do, I was asking him what job he wanted to do when he grew up. 'A teacher, a builder . . . and a dad,' he replied. Beaming with delight that he thought being a father mattered so much, I turned towards him as he said: 'But you're only a dad.'

CHAPTER 19

BATTLES FOR BRITAIN

I had no desire to return to front-line politics after 2010. When I spoke at public meetings after leaving office, I often joked I was too old to be the comeback kid and too young to be an elder statesman. It was true: I was, at fifty-nine, almost certainly the wrong age to launch a wholly new career, and writing any memoirs was years away. I was at a stage in life where the over-exuberance of youth had subsided but I had no intention of slowing down. I had plenty of energy left. Since my schooldays, I had dreamed of what I could contribute in any way, however small, to creating a world free of poverty. This is the mission that has come to preoccupy me.

Against Sarah's better judgement and the advice of Sue Nye, I had volunteered to take full personal responsibility for the defeat in 2010. While there were many reasons for us losing – the MPs' expenses crisis, Iraq, the fallout from the recession and the simple fact that Labour had been in power for thirteen years – I felt that the party needed someone to blame.

On the Tuesday after he became leader, Ed Miliband apologised for the mistakes we had made in government over Iraq. Although it was not intended as such, this came to be seen as a renunciation of our entire record. Privately I called it the 'year zero' approach. The upshot was that no one defended our record. By airbrushing our past and appearing to denigrate our own achievements, we made it difficult for people to feel proud of Labour again. Not wishing to rock the boat, I decided it was best to keep silent and stand aside. I knew from experience that the media would seize on any comments from a past leader in order to embarrass the present leader. My advice to my successor, I joked, was not to take my advice.

A few days after the 2010 election I made it clear that I would focus as an MP on work in my own constituency and attend Westminster only for vital votes. I chose to speak in a few debates – on constituency issues, in a tribute to Nelson Mandela, on Scotland, and on events in Nigeria, Syria, Iraq and elsewhere where children were being denied their basic rights. I continued the work I had started in government to help Britain's child migrants, many of whom I now found had been abused when they were forcibly removed from Britain and sent to countries in the Commonwealth.

My remaining time I devoted fully to various other community-based and charitable activities with which I was involved. I attended to my duties as chancellor of the Adam Smith College and president of Fife Society for the Blind. I helped Sarah with the Jennifer Brown Research Laboratory – which has, in its first fifteen years, conducted path-breaking research into saving premature babies. I am privileged to be patron of The Cottage, Kirkcaldy's family centre. I was proud to be involved also in the first stages of setting up Kirkcaldy's food bank. A close family friend, Marilyn Livingstone – whose husband Peter was at school with me and whom I have known since the age of ten – talked with me about creating a foundation based in Kirkcaldy to help rejuvenate the area. She suggested setting it up in my name but I proposed that she call it the Adam Smith Global Foundation. Leading public figures have subsequently delivered an annual Adam Smith lecture there at her invitation, including Michael Sandel, Amartya Sen, Emma Rothschild, Jim Wolfensohn and most recently Ed Balls, almost every one of whom chose to address the theme of globalisation.

In the past two decades, the world has seen great initiatives that have transformed the lives of millions, some of which were started under the inspired leadership of valued friends of mine, Kofi Annan and Jim Wolfensohn, such as the Global AIDS and Health Fund and the Global Alliance for Vaccines and Immunization, which have prevented 100 million child deaths; debt relief, which wiped off $100 billion of the unpayable debts of the world's thirty-six poorest countries; the doubling of aid to Africa; and, most recently, the historic 2015 climate change agreement from which Donald Trump may be walking away, although at least he is walking alone. For too long, though, global education has been neglected. Its share of aid has fallen from 13 per cent in 2000 to 10 per cent today, with the result that half of the world's children – 800 million – are forced out of education before their time, mainly through poverty, and lack even the basic skills necessary for the jobs of the future, a figure which will worsen by 2030 if we do not act now.

In the 1960s, a civil-rights struggle starting in America swept the world. In the 1970s and 80s, people came together to boycott a South African regime and end the oppressive forces of apartheid. And in the last two decades, guarantees for the rights of women, people with disabilities and LGBT persons have started to emerge. But the cause of children's rights is too often unrecognised, unfulfilled and met with indifference. Even when armed with the knowledge that the best antidote to the great evils of child marriage, child labour and child trafficking is an education, we still fail to deliver on that most fundamental promise of a quality and inclusive education for all – and not just some – children. That is why I believe fulfilling this promise – particularly with respect to girls' education – is the civil-rights struggle of our time.

I see Britain's commitment to universal education – guaranteeing schooling to the poorest and most vulnerable children in the least promising corners of the world – as the British people demonstrating our internationalism in practice and cajoling other nations to do likewise. I want our internationalism to be akin to a bright beacon on a mountaintop, radiating enough energy to enlist the generosity of others and give hope to desolate and despairing children everywhere. Of course in practice our internationalism will often seem no more than a small flame flickering dimly amidst the strong countervailing winds of nationalism and narrow self-interest. But as long as millions of parents believe investment in education is a path out of poverty, and desire for all children what they seek for their own, then that flame can never be extinguished. And it is, of course, education that also unlocks our other great development goals: gender equality, improved girls' health, better employment prospects, a higher quality of life, and a more enlightened attitude to coexistence between the religions of the world.

In 2011, I authored a report with Kevin Watkins, now head of Save the Children UK, showing that education aid was less than $10 per child per year – barely enough to buy one second-hand school textbook. While global health, I argued, had a regiment of patrons across the world – from governments in Norway and the US to institutions like the Gates Foundation and the Global Fund – there was, at that time, no government championing global education (though Norway soon came on board) and no philanthropic equivalent to Bill Gates. That year, Ban Ki-moon, whom I knew from before he became UN secretary general, asked me to serve as the UN special envoy for global education. It is a role I have continued to hold under the new secretary general, another friend, António Guterres.

To fulfil my duties as special envoy I employed a small team, led by the highly qualified education expert and tireless campaigner Dr Justin van Fleet, and funded by the proceeds of any speeches and writing work I did, all of which were donated to this and other public service and charity work. In this role, I have since travelled to meet children in countries where millions are not at school – Pakistan, India, East Timor, South Sudan, Uganda, Nigeria, Ethiopia, Tanzania, South Africa – and in countries with large refugee populations from the conflicts in Iraq and Syria – Jordan, Lebanon and Turkey. I took up the cases of the Chibok girls who had been kidnapped from their school in Nigeria, of girls fighting child marriage, and of Malala Yousafzai and her two friends, Shazia and Kainat, who had been shot by the Taliban in October 2012 simply because they were girls daring to go to school. I visited Malala in hospital a few days after her shooting, ran an event to mark her sixteenth birthday at which she addressed the UN, and Sarah and I were among those who helped Shazia and Kainat through their schooling in Britain.

As UN special envoy I also helped raise money to offer 250,000 children in Lebanon education in 'double-shift schools', where the same classrooms in which local children are taught in the morning are used to teach refugees from bordering Syria in the afternoon, and fought for a new fund – Education Cannot Wait – to pay for education for the world's 30 million displaced children.

Thanks to the Norwegian government, in 2015 the International Commission on Financing Global Education Opportunity brought together a groundbreaking team – composed of presidents and prime ministers to Nobel Laureates, NGO leaders and young people – to plan the future of global education. I was privileged to chair the commission, which produced an ambitious yet credible road map to make ours the first generation in history where every child is in school and learning. After demonstrating that no ordinary initiative could ever fill the $90 billion a year aid funding gap, we proposed an International Finance Facility for Education – underpinned by guarantees from donor nations – that will raise $10 billion a year for developing countries, virtually doubling annual education aid. With the help of Shakira – a global superstar and champion of girls' education whom I first met in London in 2005 – the proposed Finance Facility was endorsed by the 2017 G20 in Hamburg. Today, there are still 260 million boys and girls who will never receive any schooling and another 400 million who will exit schooling far too early at the age of ten or eleven and, in turn, miss out on a secondary education. By putting education on the agenda and agreeing to marshal the vital funds necessary to launch the International Finance Facility for Education, the G20 of 2018, to be hosted by Argentina, can mark a turning point for global education in the same way that the G8 of 2005 turned the corner on debt relief.

But even with these new public responsibilities I had no desire to be back in the limelight. I had been on the public stage only because of the job I did. In the seven years since my time in government, I have re-entered the public square only if I thought I could make a difference. But in 2010 and 2011 I was to find that while I was out of government, I was not out of the Murdoch empire's range of fire.

While relations with Murdoch's editors were never good, nothing had properly prepared me for the treatment meted out to my younger son Fraser, which came to a head in 2011 when I gave evidence to Lord Leveson's inquiry about the *Sun*'s intrusion into Fraser's life. As I explained then, Sarah and I had kept our counsel when in 2006 the *Sun* had exposed Fraser's cystic fibrosis. So unconcerned were they about Fraser's condition that when they first phoned to say they intended to run a story about him, they claimed he had cerebral palsy. At any rate, they had secured the story in an underhand way, paying the husband of an NHS midwife for the information. When in 2011 the *Guardian* published an article headlined 'News International papers targeted Gordon Brown', emails circulating at the *Sun* at the time admitted: 'We're f***ed.' Another stated: 'And so it begins . . .' – a reference to the revelations that had brought down the *News of the World.*

But instead of admitting they had breached the confidentiality of NHS information, they commissioned and paid for a video from the husband of their source accusing me of being a liar. Their stablemate *The Times* was enlisted to discredit me and later had to apologise for this. Rebekah Brooks, meanwhile, told the Leveson Inquiry that Sarah and I had actually asked her to report my son's condition. This was completely untrue. In his report, Lord Leveson responded: 'The claim that the Browns were "absolutely committed to making this public" frankly defies belief . . . one hardly needs Mr Brown himself to point out that no parent in the land would have wanted information of this nature to be blazoned across the front page of a national newspaper . . . As a whole, the experience of the Browns provides a fine example of a number of aspects of unsatisfactory and/or unethical press practices.' It is not clear that since Leveson anything has really changed.

Leveson aside, however, I remained out of the limelight, busily engaged in my international and constituency work when, in 2013, I found myself drawn reluctantly back into British politics at a national level – by the referendum on Scottish independence.

One of the threads woven through my forty years in public life, a theme that runs across all my speeches past and present, is my commitment to the unity and integrity of Britain. From the perspective of 2017, I call the effort a modern 'Battle for Britain'.

When I was young, no one thought Britain would ever break up. When Churchill died in January 1965 I still vividly remember taking part in a special memorial service in a packed church in Kirkcaldy on a Sunday afternoon. All the uniformed youth organisations – from the Life Boys, the Boys' Brigade, the Scouts, to the Brownies and the Girl Guides – stood to attention in a display of British patriotism. The Royal British Legion in Scotland was there in uniform displaying their war medals. The Union Jack was unfurled. The national anthem and 'Land of Hope and Glory' were sung. Churchill's state funeral, entitled 'Operation Hope Not', had been organised years before he died. And while the service itself was one of the most elaborate ever seen, including the voyage of his coffin up the Thames with Dockland cranes lowering to honour him, there was added significance in the countless memorial services held in towns and cities all across the country. This was an all-British commemoration that now feels like something from another age. I cannot imagine a similar outpouring of distinctly British unity for anyone other than Queen Elizabeth II in the foreseeable future.

In the 1950s, 60s and 70s institutions such as British Steel, British Airways, British Leyland, British Telecom and British Home Stores were part of everyday life and language. Many, of course, still exist, but in modern discourse the word 'British' has all but gone, replaced now with initials. Our mid-century years, as the sociologist David McCrone observes, 'were the high point of Britishness in Scotland as well as being a turning point'. Since then there has been a distinct shift: English people now identify themselves as more English than British, the Scots more as Scots, and the Welsh more as Welsh. In Scotland, the sense of belonging to Britain has declined fastest. While many Scots say they feel equally Scottish and British, there are now far more who feel more Scottish than British or not British at all – two thirds in total. Indeed, if asked to make a choice between being Scottish and British, only 18 per cent of Scots identify as British first. 'An emphasis on our Britishness in the years after the war,' McCrone argues, 'has given way to a more recent emphasis on Scottishness.'

Of course, in the global era, identities are likely to be multiple. I myself am at once a Fifer, Scottish, British and European. But if Britain is to survive and flourish in the future we will need something more than simplistic superficialities – like New Britain or Young Britain or Cool Britannia – to hold the country together.

Historically, countries like America and France have found common ground by consciously affirming shared ideals. Britain, especially England, has never felt the need to do the same. Partly because it has not been invaded, defeated in war or suffered a constitutional breakdown for three and a half centuries, it has never engaged in recent years in the kind of constitutional debates that could define the character of the country and bring people together as one. Unlike the French or Americans, Britain as a whole has shied away from a story we can tell about ourselves, a narrative that draws strength from our past, makes sense of our present and offers hope for the future.

Over the last fifty years the unity of Britain has frayed for want of such a narrative precisely because we have failed to recognise that what binds us is not our institutions, which change over time, or our ethnicity – after all, we are four nations – but our values and the way they shape our society: a commitment to tolerance, liberty, fair play and social responsibility.

I saw some of the difficulties of achieving this as chancellor and prime minister. In an effort to strengthen our sense of Britishness, I made speeches, held conferences, wrote articles, proposed an Institute for Britishness and indeed in 2008 encouraged a book, *Being British: The Search for the Values That Bind the Nation*, edited by the journalist Matthew d'Ancona. For purely partisan reasons, however, the Conservative Party were determined to prevent Labour from being identified with patriotic British values. In 2009, the Conservative MP Michael Gove, himself a Scot now ensconced in a southern English constituency, accepted an invitation to contribute to the collection and then penned an extraordinary attack against me, charging that 'the very political reason for his frequently trumped-up interest in the question of British nationality is that he is acutely aware that his position as an MP from a Scottish constituency places him in a difficult position now Scotland has its own Parliament'. I was, he alleged, making the case for Britishness 'for reasons of career self-defence' and attempting to 'flatten Britain's past into just one way of looking at the world which is poor history and partisan politics'. A few years later, Gove, as education minister, would himself be talking of 'British values' in an attempt to rescue his failing curriculum reforms.

I faced similar problems – outside the party political arena – when I tried to break the deadlock that prevented full participation of all the home nations in an all-British football team in the London Olympics. I sought to overcome the veto of the Scottish Football Association, which was worried that they would lose their status as a single nation within world footballing bodies. On a number of occasions, I talked to Sebastian Coe, president of the Organising Committee for the 2012 Games, about this. I thought the most famous Scottish manager, Sir Alex Ferguson, should be invited to lead the British team to bring Scotland on board. When I raised this with Alex himself in 2009 and 2010, he was positive, albeit with one caveat: he did not know what post he would be in come 2012. I then persuaded the then president of FIFA Sepp Blatter and in turn the FIFA board to sign a waiver, ensuring that Scottish participation in the Olympics football team would never be used as a pretext for Scotland losing its separate status in international football. But still the Scottish Football Association were reluctant. Eventually, my proposal was kicked into the long grass: we did have a British team but without Scottish participation and, sadly, without Alex Ferguson as manager. The team failed to get beyond the quarter-final. I had found it impossible to bring the four nations together.

The failure to forge a unifying purpose has been compounded by our failure to recognise and deal with the emergence of Scottish nationalism, Welsh nationalism and now English nationalism through greater local empowerment at every level.

From the 1970s, before the mainstream of my party came around to it, a few of us put the case for devolution and the creation of what became the Scottish Parliament as part of a new constitutional settlement for the United Kingdom. After 1997, when colleagues argued we had killed nationalism stone dead, I continued to call for further devolution. Even at the height of the financial crisis, I tried to find a way to enable Scotland to feel more comfortable inside the UK.

All my life I have been a fervent Scottish patriot. Never have I tried to hide my love for Scotland nor my Scottish roots. But I have also never seen any contradiction between my patriotism and my belief in the unity of the United Kingdom. Scotland's greatest strength has come, in my view, not just from its own devolved Parliament but from the leadership role we can play in the UK. I worked alongside my fellow Scottish Labour politicians John Smith, Donald Dewar and Robin Cook as they tried to forge a modern role for Scotland inside the Union and show the influence Scots could exert in advancing an agenda that favoured social justice. They were well served by Murray Elder, who was at the Bank of England, when I recommended him as an adviser to Denis Healey and John Smith. He soon became John's chief of staff and then later Donald's right-hand man. It was because of them that Labour championed a Scottish Constitutional Convention in the late 1980s and early 1990s that was to pave the way for a Scottish Parliament.

I was delighted when Donald became Scotland's inaugural First Minister in 1999. But one of my saddest moments was to see him laid low by ill health, coming back to full-time work too soon after heart surgery and falling, suffering a brain haemorrhage and then tragically dying. I spoke at Donald's funeral: it was one of the most difficult hours I have lived through. But for his commitment to an egalitarian Scotland that tackled poverty he might have stood down after his momentous achievement in delivering devolution. For Donald, though, the work was not yet done: he wanted a Scotland free from unemployment and deprivation. He saw that standing up for the Scottish people and social justice went hand in hand.

For the first decade of Scottish devolution, the SNP found it impossible to drive a wedge between Labour and Scotland. But in 2007, it found its opportunity to do so. The 2007 Scottish Parliament election came just six weeks before the transfer of prime-ministerial power from Tony to me in late June. For purely Scottish reasons, if I'm honest, I asked Tony to consider the changeover a few weeks earlier, believing that the simple fact of there being a Scottish prime minister would help us win power in Scotland. The contest, as it transpired, went down to the wire. With sixty-two Liberal Democrat and Labour MSPs, as against the SNP's forty-seven – and with the Conservative Party hardly likely to want to see the SNP run the show – another Labour–Liberal government was possible. I tried to persuade the leader of the Lib Dems, Menzies Campbell, that instead of walking away they join with Labour to re-form our coalition, but the Liberals seemed traumatised – they had lost only one seat yet their vote had collapsed – and would not come to the table. This loss of nerve allowed Alex Salmond to capitalise and opened the door for the SNP to form a minority administration.

The economic roots of Scottish nationalism lay in the same long-term trends – industrial decline, insecurity and the squeezed middle class – that have bred anti-establishment rebellions across the West. In the 1950s, 40 per cent of our workforce were in manufacturing or mining, but by the second decade of the new century only 7 per cent were. A million skilled jobs had been lost in coal, textiles, steel and shipbuilding, and with them many people's standard of living, status and prospects. When the British state looked less able to reverse these trends, 'London mismanagement' became a constant refrain of the nationalists, and 'Westminster' an all-purpose adjective to sustain grudges, both real and imagined.

The SNP sought to distance Labour from Scotland and identify it with London. I was referred to as a London and Westminster politician, despite the fact my home was in Scotland, my children were born in Scotland and I returned to Scotland weekend after weekend. This angered and saddened me.

There were cultural forces at work too: traditional Scottish institutions had ceased to be vehicles through which people could express their Scottishness in an apolitical way. The Church of Scotland itself had lost a million members since the 1950s and voluntary organisations no longer exerted the influence they once had. People were looking for new ways to express and assert their identity. With their 'Scotland first' slogans – 'it's Scotland's oil' being the prime example – the SNP were well placed to step into this vacuum.

In December 2007 the challenge of reviving Labour in Scotland was taken up, enthusiastically and professionally, by a dynamic new leader, Wendy Alexander, part of a remarkable family that included her brother Douglas, MP for Paisley and Renfrewshire South. With my support, Wendy secured the Scottish Parliament's endorsement for a new Commission on Scottish Devolution, under the chairmanship of Sir Kenneth Calman, to report to both the UK Parliament and the Scottish Parliament. With the help of a highly experienced and far-sighted civil servant, Jim Gallagher, who served as secretary to the commission and was later to be an influential pro-devolution writer and campaigner, the Calman commission's final report of June 2009 recommended new tax-raising powers and more economic devolution for Scotland within a UK securely grounded in the pooling and sharing of resources. Overshadowed by the global financial crisis, the report never got the attention or support it deserved.

Even so, at the 2010 general election, Labour more than held its own in Scotland, regaining the two seats we had lost in by-elections. Overall, Labour won forty-one out of Scotland's fifty-nine seats, outpacing the SNP in vote share by two to one, an increase of 2.5 per cent. Over the next four years I saw Labour's fortunes in Scotland wax and wane as Scottish leaders came and went, but despite a disastrous loss to the SNP in 2011, Labour enjoyed a revival in the local elections in 2012 and then an even bigger swing to it when my election agent, Alex Rowley, was elected to the Scottish Parliament in a by-election in my own constituency.

And yet, by 2015 the Labour Party had haemorrhaged so much support in Scotland that we won only one Scottish seat in the election of that year, and since the election of 2017 now hold only seven. None of this was, in my view, inevitable; nor is it irreversible. I fear it was political mistakes we made that let the SNP overtake us as Scotland's most popular political party – and threaten our very existence to this day. The key was what went wrong during the referendum.

The SNP had been elected in 2011 on a mandate to hold a

referendum on Scottish independence. During the course of 2012, negotiations between the SNP and the UK government took place over the nature and timing of the referendum, which was eventually scheduled for 18 September 2014. As the campaign on Scottish independence got under way in 2013, I had no desire to be centre stage. I was happy when Ed Miliband and the Scottish Labour leader, Johann Lamont, nominated Alistair Darling and Blair McDougall to be the lead Labour voices at the heart of the pro-union campaign Better Together. I was also encouraged by the first video issued by that campaign – a plea to patriotic Scots to think of a proud Scotland with both a strong Scottish Parliament and an influential place in the UK. At this point, support for independence was at around 30 per cent; and, even two years after Alex Salmond's victory in the Scottish Parliament elections of 2011, half of SNP voters were doubtful about independence. How, then, did support for independence move up from 30 per cent to a near majority?

The Better Together campaign was right to argue that an independent Scotland would be worse off economically but should not have allowed its opponents, Yes Scotland*, to define its entire campaign as 'Project Fear'. Inadvertently, the No campaign allowed it to be thought that it was talking Scotland down, suggesting it was too poor, too weak, too dependent and too fragile to be independent. The SNP, in turn, portrayed Better Together as speaking not for Scotland but for Britain; and in doing so effectively depicted themselves as the only genuine party of Scotland. Better Together was an umbrella under which Labour cohabited with the Conservatives, but while Labour people did their best, the 'no' message that came through was a Tory defence of the status quo.

Concerned that unless Labour fought its own corner we would be viewed as an appendage to a Tory government campaign, I met with David Cameron and George Osborne in the prime minister's office in the House of Commons on 20 March 2012. I told them directly that the old argument – that Scots saw themselves as equally Scottish and British – had run its course. They now felt more Scottish than British, and any successful referendum campaign had to recognise this.

---

* 'Yes' because the referendum question was 'Should Scotland be an independent country?'

Under the right circumstances, however, most Scots could still be convinced of the benefits of combining a strong Scottish Parliament with being part of the UK. My proposal was simple: the only way a referendum could be won convincingly was if Labour ran its own strong campaign, calling for a greater degree of autonomy for Scotland and reaching its own supporters with a Labour case for staying in Britain. I made the point that while Labour's vote was still solid in Scotland, it was also the most vulnerable to the nationalist message that independence was preferable to living under a Conservative government. I urged that half the funds raised by Better Together be allocated to a distinctive Labour campaign, and that some funders should be encouraged to support this distinctive campaign alongside Better Together.

Cameron and Osborne were receptive to this proposal. But when Labour in Scotland shied away from this option, we lost the one chance we had of fully financing a Labour campaign wholly directed at Labour voters.

Having thought through an argument that was, I felt, radical, progressive and compelling, I decided that the only way I could get my views across was to write a book. I spent December 2013 and the early months of 2014 writing furiously. I could not have done any of this without excellent work directing the project by Andrew Hilland, who gave up a prestigious job as a lawyer in New York to return to Scotland to fight the referendum and who subsequently came very close in the 2017 election to defeating the SNP in his home constituency of Lanark and Hamilton East. Kirsty McNeill edited the book, and Rachael Thomas and Ross Fulton undertook the research. The book, *My Scotland, Our Britain*, argued that Scotland was a natural leader of a UK that pooled and shared its resources to deliver the objectives of full employment, free healthcare and a welfare state. It traced the origins of modern social provision to Scotland's demands for the abolition of the Scottish Poor Law and its replacement by a British welfare state. Sharing across the United Kingdom was, I argued, not an English imposition but a Scottish invention. I also tried to show that, far from this being a hangover from the twentieth century, cooperation between nations was the way of the future for our increasingly interdependent world. The challenge was to build a modern constitution with as much autonomy as the Scottish people sought – through a strengthened

402 MY LIFE, OUR TIMES

Scottish Parliament – and as much cooperation as we needed to sustain our economy and public services.

Fortunately, in March 2014, Scottish Labour under Johann Lamont – drawing on the expert work of Jim Gallagher and a highly intelligent and perceptive policy head, Ross Christie – committed itself to an enhanced Scottish Parliament. As the campaign heated up and the margin between Yes and No narrowed, I suggested to Johann that we counter the rising momentum of the SNP's big rallies with our own distinctive Labour events, separate from Better Together. At the first of these, at Glasgow Fruitmarket, Johann and I addressed around 1,000 people.

Yet our message was not getting through. With all the headlines focusing on the negative back-and-forth, the No campaign was increasingly viewed as Cameron and Osborne speaking for the United Kingdom, allowing the SNP to claim it was not for Scotland but anti-Scottish. What *was* getting through, loud and clear, was that the people of Scotland wanted change. And here there was an irony: each pro-union party had a strong devolution programme, with detailed proposals about additional powers for the Scottish Parliament over taxation, employment, social policy and welfare. The problem was that nobody had heard about the proposals or had any idea that if they voted No, new powers would be delivered.

Privately, in fact, I had favoured a third option on the ballot paper, one that offered a more powerful Scottish Parliament as a positive alternative to both independence and the status quo. Later I was advised by the respected Edinburgh University academics David McCrone and Frank Bechhofer that had there been such an option, support for it could have been around 78 per cent and support for independence would have been much lower. In hindsight, it would have been far better if the campaign had relentlessly counterposed independence with a powerful Scottish Parliament playing a bigger part in running its own affairs. As the campaign went on, it became increasingly clear to me that we needed that kind of forward-looking offer.

Better Together regained some ground when Alistair Darling won the first TV debate against Alex Salmond at the beginning of August 2014, but by the end of the month it was on the back foot again. People continued to think that the alternative to Scottish independence was the status quo. I believed that the answer was to set a timetable, showing how the new powers supported by the different pro-union political parties could be brought in expeditiously.

Having talked to Johann Lamont, Ed Miliband and David Cameron, I decided to move things forward by publishing my own timetable in the hope that all the parties would follow it up. Two Mondays before the referendum and the day after a poll that suggested we would lose, I spoke in Midlothian and called for legislation within a year: I said that proposals should be agreed by St Andrew's Day in November and legislation drafted and published by Burns Night in January. With all pro-Union parties agreeing to this timetable, it set in train events that led to the Smith Commission on further powers for the Scottish Parliament and the Scotland Act 2016. The SNP came back with the argument that this was tinkering and technical and unlikely to be delivered. They were wrong, but we still had to do more to convince people that change was on its way.

What the Scottish people needed to know was not so much the detail of the individual powers but that the main United Kingdom parties were wholeheartedly and irrevocably committed to – and would deliver – what we called 'faster, fairer, safer and better change' than the nationalists could offer. In conversation with Bruce Waddell, the former award-winning editor of the *Daily Record*, Murray Foote the current editor, and Alan Rennie the managing director, the considerable weight of the *Record* was put behind what they called the Vow: an iron-tight commitment to be signed by all UK party leaders in support of more devolution on the timetable I had previously outlined. To get the leaders on board, I spoke to David Cameron, who agreed to approach Nick Clegg, and to Ed Miliband and Douglas Alexander. They agreed with me that the Vow, while signed by UK leaders, had to be an initiative that was not imposed by London but initiated from Scotland. Originally the Vow was to appear on Monday 15 September, three days before the referendum, but because of the tragic murder of David Haines, a Scottish aid worker in Syria, we postponed it until Tuesday.

Over the course of the final months of the campaign, I had joined Labour and Better Together leaders in addressing nearly a hundred meetings and rallies in cities, towns and villages across Scotland. I particularly enjoyed one aspect of the campaign: speaking at meetings alongside an old friend, Shirley Williams, whom I admired greatly from across party lines. I worked with her before and after I became prime minister on issues from disarmament to Europe, and to be honest, tried to persuade her on a number of occasions to rejoin Labour. I spoke in schools and at pensioner forums, to the Royal British Legion and Carmelite nuns, in almost all of Scotland's great universities and at a joint meeting in Glasgow, the largest meeting of all, comprising members of the Hindu, Christian, Sikh, Muslim and Jewish communities. I had come a long way from my initial reticence on re-entering the political fray. But the referendum was unlike an ordinary election: we were making an irreversible decision that would have consequences for every Scottish family for generations to come.

Arriving outside Maryhill Community Hall for my final speech of the campaign just twenty-four hours before the poll, I was instantly struck by the number of Yes posters on shop and flat windows on the building opposite. Inside, there was an altogether different atmosphere. The hall was packed to the rafters with noisy supporters of Better Together and the walls were adorned with the slogan 'Love Scotland, Vote No'. It was the most positive poster message I had seen throughout the whole campaign. As I sat quietly in the corner of the upstairs green room, word came back of camera crews and journalists squeezed together, upstairs and downstairs, that it was hot, and that there was a real air of anticipation in the hall.

The Maryhill speech had been organised by Better Together at short notice and would have to be word-perfect. While the stump speech that I had delivered to audiences across the country ran to forty-five minutes, this was to be just thirteen minutes. Kirsty McNeill had come over to my house the evening before to help me develop my ideas. Valuable advice also flowed in from Douglas Alexander – who had relocated to Better Together headquarters and was making some telling interventions in defence of the Union – as well as from Bruce Waddell and Andrew Hilland. I was convinced that in addition to focusing on the benefits of the Union and on exposing the economic risks of independence, we also had to make people feel proud about voting No.

I had been ushered to a corridor and was ready to be introduced to the audience when, thirty seconds before I was about to enter the auditorium, someone whispered loudly in my ear: 'Your right shoe is covered in mud!' It was suddenly a frantic race between Labour's tireless and always helpful organiser Annmarie Whyte, clawing the mud off my shoe with a paper towel, and Eddie Izzard, who was wrapping up his introduction of me from the stage. I would call it a dead heat.

Fortunately, I had been listening to what was happening inside the hall, and having heard the speeches that preceded mine – spirited and eloquent testimonies from members of the public drawing on their personal experiences of the NHS, the shipbuilding industry, our education system and pensions – I was able to walk on stage and begin spontaneously: 'At last, the world is hearing the voices of the real people of Scotland. The silent majority will be silent no more.'

As I spoke about the benefits of sharing and cooperating across the United Kingdom, I reminded people that we had fought two world wars together. When young men were injured in the trenches they did not look to each other and ask whether they were Scots or English – they came to each other's aid because we were part of a common cause. I then sought to counter the claim made by some nationalists that No voters were less than patriotic Scots. Scotland was not owned by the SNP, the Yes campaign or any politician, I argued: our country belonged to everyone. You could be as proud and patriotic a Scot by voting No as you could by voting Yes. I implored the public to 'tell them this is our Scotland'.

I hope that what I said in that speech accorded with what the majority of Scots felt. While I had seen – and indeed predicted to friends – the dangerous decline in support for the No campaign as polling day drew closer, I never believed that we would lose. So, on the night of the referendum I was nervous only about how narrow the majority for No might be, but once I had heard the first result – a clear No in Scotland's smallest local authority area, Clackmannanshire – I felt able to go to bed and fell soundly asleep at the end of an intensive few days campaigning across the country. I woke up at around 6 a.m. on Friday 19 September, just as the nationalist leaders conceded defeat.

What determined the final referendum result? Alex Salmond had chosen the referendum question and the timing so it would occur just after Scotland's Commonwealth Games and in the year of the 700th anniversary of the Battle of Bannockburn, when Robert the Bruce defeated the forces of England's Edward II. This had little effect. But he himself has said that the Vow threw the SNP off course: it upended their presumption that the closing ten days of the campaign would be a cavalcade towards independence. However, the Vow worked only in the context of a more patriotic case put squarely to the public. While economic arguments mattered, the Scottish people could not bear to think of themselves as unpatriotic.

I saw immediately that while we had won the vote, the SNP would assert they had won the argument and claim the moral high ground. Two days after the referendum, in a speech in my constituency, I appealed for the country to unite around an agenda for social justice which could be realised through a stronger Scottish Parliament. A month later l led a House of Commons debate demanding that the Vow be kept. The Scotland Act that followed gave substantial new powers to the Scottish Parliament. However, unable to shake off the accusation that Labour had aligned with the Tories to deliver a negative message and could no longer speak for Scotland, we were virtually wiped out in the 2015 general election in Scotland, holding on to only one seat – Edinburgh South, a constituency I knew well, having fought it in 1979 and which Ian Murray did brilliantly to retain. It was to take until June 2017 for the party to mount the first stages of a recovery under Jeremy Corbyn and Kezia Dugdale.

At root the still unanswered question, which will decide the long-term future of Scotland, was whether any strong sense of Britishness could flourish in the years to come or whether we would see the country fragment into mutually suspicious enclaves. On the day after the 2014 referendum, David Cameron called for 'English votes for English laws' – arguing that English MPs should meet as an English Parliament for England-only decisions. Immediately after he had done so, at around 8 a.m. I telephoned the Cabinet Secretary Jeremy Heywood and told him that Cameron had made a disastrous and sectarian decision that would only increase support for the SNP. Alistair Darling relayed the same message. When the prime minister wrote to thank me for my work in the referendum, I replied in blunt terms, warning him that 'English votes for English laws' would allow the constitutional reform package to be traduced as an insult in Scotland. The SNP would now say that he had misled the Scottish voting public by cynically waiting until after the referendum to tell them that restrictions would be placed on the right of Scottish MPs to vote on the UK Budget.

I now worried that Scottish nationalism was being matched by the rise of a knee-jerk English nationalism. Then, in the 2015 general election, as the Tories fell behind, they pivoted strategically and played the 'English card' again, publishing posters and newspaper adverts featuring Ed Miliband and Alex Salmond, asserting that any Labour government would be in the pocket of the SNP. It was a conscious attempt to whip up English fears and resentment against the Scots. It worked.

The same global economic forces that gave rise to Scottish nationalism were now giving rise to profound insecurities in England, with UKIP whipping up populist support for another referendum – this time on our membership of the European Union. David Cameron's decision to placate his restless right wing in the face of UKIP's rise with his now notorious undertaking to hold an in/out referendum was shown, of course, to be a terrible misjudgement. I suspect he calculated he would never have to follow through on it because he anticipated another coalition with the Liberal Democrats, who would oppose such a move.

Perhaps because of my perspective on the Scottish referendum, and how easy it was to incite an anti-establishment protest, I always believed that Britain might vote to leave. Indeed, a referendum on EU membership in many European countries in 2016 would have been a close-run thing. The European Union seemed to many to be governed by precisely the out-of-touch and technocratic elite that anti-globalisation protestors had identified as the enemy. What's more, the Eurozone crisis had not united Europe as it sought to manage the fallout from an American-led recession. Instead it had divided the continent – with the north telling the south to accept austerity. In the process, the idealism which bound Europe together – the sense that the EU embodied decency, solidarity and social democracy – was tarnished, as bail-outs for bankers, privatisation and the dismantling of social and labour protections confirmed the inequalities and insecurities of globalisation, rather than correcting them. The harsh reality was that a European Union that was created in order to make nationalism disappear had become the umbrella under which nationalist parties across the continent were making their claims for greater self-government.

Britain, of course, had its own very particular objection to the direction of Europe: most people bought the idea that the EU was moving inexorably towards becoming a federal superstate. Despite the fact that the high tide of European integrationist ambitions had been reached at the beginning of the century and had since been receding, Leave campaigners seized on this popular misconception, arguing that by voting Remain, the UK would be forced to accept greater economic and political integration against its will, hence the populist slogan 'Take Back Control'. The parallels with the SNP's campaign were plain to see.

I felt I had an argument that could win people round. For me, just as in the Scottish referendum, the starting point was not what we thought of Europe but the needs and aspirations of the British people – and what was in our patriotic interest as a country that had always been open, outward-looking and internationally minded.

One of the keys to Scotland's vote to remain part of the British Union was that under a more radical devolution settlement Scotland could have a strengthened Scottish Parliament while continuing to share resources with the rest of the United Kingdom. In the same way, we could argue in the EU referendum that Britain could have a balance between the national autonomy it desired and the international cooperation it needed.

Before 2010 I had secured a European agreement that there would be no more of what I privately termed 'empire building' for ten years: no new federal-style constitutional initiatives. I had persuaded finance ministers to reject tax harmonisation in favour of a simple exchange of tax information, and I envisaged a European Union that also downgraded automatic standardisation of rules and integration in favour of mutual recognition of each country's standards and thus subsidiarity. I still see Europe as a multi-speed and often multi-need and multi-directional union that should accommodate varying degrees of integration across different spheres of policy and between different countries. Yet, in their six years in power, the Conservatives had done nothing to persuade the public that their previous claim – that the EU was on the road to a federal superstate – was more myth than reality.

Years later people still remember Mrs Thatcher thumping the table to secure a UK budget rebate from Europe, but not one of the concessions negotiated by David Cameron in the run-up to the EU referendum are remembered – and but for a few positive column inches at the time the referendum date was announced, they featured little in the ensuing debates. His was a botched renegotiation that did not even bring the paper-thin but at least tangible results yielded by Harold Wilson's renegotiation after 1974.

David Cameron was the wrong man in the wrong place with the wrong argument at the wrong time. His campaign playbook was simply the same script he and George Osborne had used in the elections against Labour in 2010 and 2015, and what he still thought had been the winning card in the Scottish referendum – fear. A day away from an economic fear story was, for David Cameron's team, a day lost. Yet they found it impossible to keep immigration and issues of national identity off the agenda, while at the same time George Osborne's fear stories crowded out any positive appeals that might have been made, and hardly ever did any Labour voice hold centre stage in any news cycle.

At the end of April 2016, I asked for a phone call with David Cameron to warn him that he was facing a perfect storm on immigration, terrorism and a fragile economy. I said that the Remain campaign's message was getting through to Tory voters who were financially secure and worried that Brexit might make them insecure, but it was not having an effect on Labour voters who were financially insecure and did not think that leaving Europe would make things any worse. I argued that we needed 'horses for courses', including a positive message targeted towards Labour voters that would show how membership of the EU could improve their lives. The last thing Labour voters needed was another round of Project Fear.

To show what I meant I released a video, shot at Coventry Cathedral by two very talented film-makers, Eddie Morgan and Mark Lucas, in which I made the case for a Remain vote. The video began with a shot of the ruins of Coventry Cathedral, bathed in morning sunlight. Bombed and destroyed by the Nazis in the Second World War, I pointed out that these ruins had been painstakingly and lovingly maintained as a monument to the wars we had left behind and to the sanctity of peace. 'What message would we send to the rest of the world,' I asked, 'if we the British people – the most internationally minded of all – were to walk away from our nearest neighbours?' It was an appeal to people's emotions and their patriotism. To my great surprise, the film received 5.5 million views on Facebook.

I also wrote a book, *Leading, not Leaving*, which attempted to put the positive case for Remain. I tried to show not only that Britain's best interests were served within Europe on everything from the economy and employment to the environment and security, but that because of our quite unique outward-looking and engaged approach to the wider world, Britain was capable not just of trading with Europe but of leading it. My first national speech of the campaign – hosted at the London School of Economics on 11 May – coincided with the book's publication. There I argued that the Remain campaign should stress to working people the benefits of EU membership on pay, working conditions and employment rights. Despite the speech being covered by the BBC and ITV, its message was drowned out by a political comic opera that dominated the week's news – first, a gaffe in which Cameron called Nigeria and Afghanistan 'possibly two of the most corrupt countries in the world', remarks picked up by a stray microphone; then a speech in which he implied that if we left the EU, the Third World War might break out. Project Fear was becoming Project Apocalypse.

The following weekend I spoke to a large pro-European audience at the Fabian Society Summer Conference, articulating the Labour reasons to 'vote Remain rather than remain at home'. I argued that being part of Europe could deliver positive, practical and progressive benefits for Britain over the next decade – new jobs, energy-bill cuts, enhanced security, tax fairness and the protection of workers' rights. I had been assured that no other Remain politician would be competing for the headlines that day. But that morning, George Osborne entered the fray from the G7 finance ministers' meeting in Sendai, Japan, with another scare story – this time that the value of houses in the UK would fall by as much as 18 per cent following a Brexit vote. This preoccupied the broadcast media all day and the only question I was met with in my post-speech interviews was how I could defend such an indefensible claim. At each point, I tried to turn back to an affirmative message but we had again lost the opportunity to put it across. Over and over the 'blue versus blue' debate – Tories such as George Osborne and Boris Johnson fighting each other – drowned out any attempt to get through to Labour voters, whose alienation by it all would only fuel the urge to vote Leave.

A few days before the referendum, David Cameron phoned me and we spoke for a second time. The call started well. He said he wanted my advice on how to win. I replied that we had to appeal to British patriotism – by showing that Britain could lead in Europe. I suggested to him that he put British leadership at the heart of the campaign by publishing and setting out the practical benefits we could secure from an EU reform agenda, including half a million new British jobs through reforms to the European single market; European financial assistance for hard-pressed steel, coal and other industrial communities hit by closures and restructuring; and funding from Europe to pay to reduce the pressures from migration on our NHS, schools and housing. This would appeal to Labour voters, many of whom felt they had nothing to lose.

Cameron responded that he had already produced his own reform proposals after negotiations in Brussels and would be criticised for reopening the issue without European support. I countered that we should present this as the agenda for our presidency of the EU that was scheduled to begin later that year and that I had already gathered support for it from the president of the European Parliament, Martin Schulz, and was in touch with the Social Democrats in Italy, the Netherlands, France and Germany who were all anxious for Britain to remain.

Cameron then made the request I had been anticipating. He wanted all three ex-prime ministers – Tony Blair, John Major and me – to stand alongside him outside No. 10, each in front of lecterns, to make the case for staying in Europe. I said there would be no greater signal of an establishment stitch-up than four prime ministers of opposing parties appearing together to make the case for a Remain vote. I had no doubt the ploy would garner column inches, but it would be perceived as the agenda of the elites and would not win over Labour voters. Just as David Cameron and his Conservative colleagues were the only ones who could get through to the Tory vote – only 43 per cent of whom would, in the end, vote Remain – only Labour leaders had the best chance of getting through to the Labour base. In the end, the prime minister had little influence over Labour voters just as I would have had little influence with Tory supporters.

I offered a different proposal: a rally attended by past and present Labour leaders from Neil Kinnock and Tony Blair to Ed Miliband and, critically, Jeremy Corbyn, with all of us affirming without reservation that we wanted Britain in Europe. It was better, I thought, than Cameron's idea, and he liked it too. Through the shadow chancellor John McDonnell – who shared my concerns about the erosion of support for Europe among Labour voters in the north – the message from Jeremy's office came back: he would not appear on the same platform with Tony. I countered with a compromise: what about Jeremy in London, Tony in Belfast, Neil in Cardiff, and Ed in Yorkshire? Margaret Beckett could appear in the East Midlands and Harriet Harman in the south-east. I would speak in Glasgow. Again, Jeremy said no. All he did agree was that on the same day the following week, each of us would make pro-Europe appeals. In the event, for very understandable reasons, Tony could not appear – his mother-in-law's funeral was that day – but he wrote an article published that morning. While the initiative went ahead, it was never going to have the impact of a joint appearance.

Everything I had worried would happen was now coming to pass. Weeks before the referendum campaign launched in earnest, I had sent a note to the Labour peer and party-funder David Sainsbury – who did more than any other single individual to support Remain – as well as to other Labour colleagues, warning that the Leave slogan 'Take Back Control' would resonate with Labour voters. I argued that we could not leave the field open to their campaign that played on the loss of manufacturing, a lack of decent jobs, our country not being what it once was, the prospects for our children being poor, other countries doing better than us, and Britain being stronger when it stood alone. The lesson of the Scottish referendum was that we had to demonstrate in concrete terms not only how Labour supporters would be hurt by leaving the EU – but also how they could benefit by remaining.

The campaign led by Cameron and Osborne could only mobilise voters in the shires and cities who wanted nothing to threaten their already comfortable lives. Yet Britain was becoming two countries economically – and to secure a majority for Remain we had to recognise and respond to that. Cameron and Osborne had argued in the 2015 general election that a Labour government would put prosperity at risk; in the Brexit campaign, they reprised this familiar line, but now the enemy was not Labour but Brexit. The Remain pollsters had identified two groups who had to be hauled back: those who were torn between heart and mind – emotionally they wanted to vote Leave but intellectually they had to be convinced that it was in their interests – and 'the disengaged middle' who, the campaign calculated, would be won over because of economic risk. Cameron and Osborne were insistent that a firm focus on risk could blunt cultural concerns, not least over immigration. And so while I wanted to reassure voters worried about immigration by pointing to the new immigration fund I had proposed to Cameron, No. 10 was terrified of us even mentioning the word.

Both Ed Balls and Yvette Cooper also urged a change of stance on free movement of workers. But when, with ten days to go, Peter Mandelson called for a positive Remain initiative on migration, and Will Straw, the director of the official campaign Britain Stronger In Europe, suggested a major speech at Dover to confront the issue, Osborne reportedly responded that 'we just need to stick to the economy'. The chancellor's view was that while everyone criticised negative campaigning, it was the only message that was working. This strategy culminated in a ludicrous 'shadow Budget', which asserted on the basis of patently contrived figures that the costs of leaving the EU would mean slashing funding for the NHS. This transparently cynical ploy was rightly condemned across the political spectrum as a low point in British politics.

Tragedy then struck. On Thursday 16 June, a week before the referendum, my friend Jo Cox, the Labour MP for Batley and Spen in West Yorkshire, was brutally murdered. For days I grieved, our family grieved and the whole country grieved. Sarah and I had been privileged to work with Jo and her husband Brendan over many years and in her tireless efforts on behalf of poor and desolate children and mothers. She went to some of the most dangerous places in the world to do so. The last place she should have been in danger was in her home town.

There was now little time left before polling day and when I agreed to speak at the eve-of-poll rally in Birmingham, I did so with the specific intention of getting through to Labour voters in danger of defecting to Leave with a positive case based on better jobs, stronger workers' rights and – perhaps more important – taking the unusual step of citing Orwell, Churchill and Shakespeare as I tried to encourage patriotic pride in our long history of engagement with Europe and the world. But the speech had little impact. Indeed, most of the speech that I composed was never delivered. The meeting at Birmingham University was supposed to have been in a large auditorium that would offer a platform for final appeals to the British people, but the event turned out to be nothing more than a small gathering outside, mainly Tory staffers assembled to greet David Cameron as he descended from the Remain tour bus – and the twenty-minute speech I had planned had to be condensed into less than five minutes.

The turnout on 23 June was greater than in any general election since 1992, and I was not surprised when the northern towns voted Leave. They had not even been visited or canvassed. In the same way that Hillary Clinton would mistakenly take much of the rust belt for granted in the US election later that year, the Remain campaign neglected the old industrial towns, almost all of which voted to leave by two to one. Many working class parts of the cities, including poorer communities in London, also voted for Brexit. The middle-class Labour vote turned out heavily for Remain but, in total, 3 million Labour voters were for Leave.

Lord North is remembered as the prime minister who lost America at the end of the eighteenth century. David Cameron may be remembered as the one who lost Europe at the beginning of the twenty-first – and who in the process plunged a three-centuries-old United Kingdom into even greater danger. What the Brexit-voting public rejected was not just the Cameron advice but the combined and concerted view of the financial, industrial and cultural elites. In this sense, the result of the EU referendum was more than a confirmation of the limits of one-dimensional, negative campaigning, it was the biggest rebellion the country has ever seen against its political establishment, perhaps the most remarkable moment in British politics since Churchill was deposed by Attlee in 1945. There have been moments in our history when pressure from below forces change in the political system: the popular unrest that culminated in the Peterloo Massacre of 1819, the riots demanding voting reform in 1832, the Chartist demands of 1848, the industrial agitation in the aftermath of the Second World War, and after 1979. In 2016 there was an earthquake that was as close to a revolution as modern Britain has ever come.

Behind the disaffection that spiralled upwards in the EU referendum are the same basic concerns that also lay behind the drive for Scottish independence and the dramatic chastening of the Tories in the 2017 general election: growing insecurities over jobs, livelihoods and futures, all of which seem to be endangered by tidal waves of global change. People sense that globalisation permeates every aspect of our lives, but because it is leaderless and lacks a human face it presents itself as a conspiracy of the powerful that the majority are powerless to resist – almost like a lottery that is forever loaded against them. This perception is confirmed and exacerbated by structural inequalities that divide the north from the south and decouple the former industrial towns from the global hub that is London, a separation every bit as profound as the ones between England and its Scottish and Welsh neighbours.

Part of the solution, therefore, has to be more balanced regional economic development to secure additional and better jobs and rising living standards. This is in the interests not just of the north, Scotland and Wales, but of London and the whole country. While the northern regions face high structural unemployment and even forced emigration, a London-centric view of the United Kingdom no longer works even for London – a capital city rife with congestion, overcrowding, overheating of its economy and high house prices. In this sense, the so-called Great Repeal Bill, transferring powers from Brussels to Westminster, has got it wrong: wherever it is possible, following Brexit, the powers repatriated from the European Union – including agriculture and fisheries, regional policy, social policy and employment rights – should not be automatically transferred back to Whitehall, which would reinforce the over-centralisation of power but, in the spirit of devolution, to the Scottish Parliament, the Welsh and Northern Ireland Assemblies, the new city mayors and, in my opinion, to newly established and enfranchised Councils of the North and Midlands and other English regions. Indeed, there is a case for even broader and more profound change: a People's Constitutional Convention, modelled on the successful Scottish Convention, could test the case for a more federal approach to governing the UK, and for the end of the House of Lords and its replacement by an elected Senate of the Nations and Regions.

If one set of divisions is economic, the other is cultural. In government we were right to demand that immigrants speak English and learn about our history, and we were justified in emphasising the importance of integration. But we did not encourage and foster enough contact between communities or talk enough about what unites us across the different religions and ethnic divides and thus build sufficient common ground. Of course, community has to mean more than 'integrating' minorities or immigrants: it is about discovering and acting upon what we all have in common. And national unity is not possible if we allow patriotism to become appropriated by those who think of themselves as the only 'real' or 'true' carriers of our national identity. But where there is day-to-day contact between people of different faiths, ethnicities and classes – as is the everyday experience in London and some of the other cities – the views we have of each other, and the contribution we feel each makes, become far more positive. It is in areas where immigration is lowest that UKIP and others can do most to fuel prejudices. One lesson of the referendum is that we have to work harder to forge a shared British citizenship and a shared sense of destiny – a matter I shall address more fully in the remaining chapters.

Scotland will also require a settlement more ambitious than any so far enacted. In the 2014 referendum I put the argument for a strong Scottish Parliament within a United Kingdom built on the pooling and sharing of risks and resources. Since then we have seen, in turn, Scotland and England diverge over support for the EU; the Supreme Court brushing aside the Sewel Convention – the devolved institutions' right to consultation in matters that affect them; the Great Repeal Bill which will automatically repatriate all Brussels powers to Westminster; and the creation of a new UK fund which will amass at a UK-level what were previously our contributions to the European budget. All of these developments will make the Scottish people less willing to believe that English sentiment favours sharing.

The Scottish Parliament should now, I suggest, have new guarantees that powers over agriculture, fisheries, regional policy and the environment – not held in Brussels – will be transferred directly to it; guarantees that the £800 million or so of money now spent by Europe on Scotland's behalf will be for the Scottish Parliament to control and spend; guarantees of consultation and co-decision-making in areas where it matters; guarantees about the Scottish Parliament's power to sign treaties with Europe on devolved matters; and guarantees of powers to top up benefits and decide on taxation that will never allow it to say it cannot pursue an agenda for social justice.

Shared sentiment, unwritten conventions and wishful thinking will not now be enough to hold the Union together. What is needed is a Guarantee of Right – one step on from the Claim of Right with which the Scots began the process of devolution in 1989 – which enshrines in law all of these guarantees in a new Scottish covenant with the UK.

As for Britain, a game-changing offer by those of us who support Remain is also needed if we are to stay in the European Union. 'Leave' seems unable to deliver its promise of British control of our borders, laws, money and trade. But if any alternative is to succeed we have to persuade millions of Leave voters that there is an alternative that offers something new which justifies a change of mind. It will have to answer the questions that the Conservative leadership failed to address in the referendum: specifically, concerns expressed by the British people about how we can manage migration, respect the authority of British courts, secure value for money for our budget contributions and demonstrate that Britain's desire to build better trading relationships with the rest of the world need not be incompatible with membership of the EU Customs Union. Above all, such an offer has to make the patriotic case for a Britain proud to be outward-looking and, through maintaining close links with Europe, fully engaged with the world beyond our shores. Such an offer has to secure the right balance for the modern world between the national autonomy nations desire and the international cooperation they need for both security and prosperity.

My proposals suggest that the old answers will no longer hold water and that we need new approaches for new times. But forging new relationships between the north and the south, between England and Scotland, and between Britain and the EU will only take us so far. To tackle the two fundamental issues, economic and cultural, raised by these two referendums, we must find a way to talk meaningfully about the values that unite us and we must find a programme for managing the global economy in a way that maximises life chances and minimises insecurities. It is to these challenges that I will turn in the final two chapters.

CHAPTER 20

FAITH IN THE PUBLIC SQUARE?

From the outside, No. 10 Downing Street appears both imposing and forbidding. But while life behind the famous black door can be both exhilarating and daunting, the place itself offers the prime minister of the day practical benefits. You have quite spacious living accommodation, dedicated and hard-working secretaries, clerks, messengers, custodians, porters, IT specialists and telephonists, and a support system on hand that helps you get through a busy day, as well as an advantage that few, especially in London, enjoy: you can walk to work.

For a parent of young children it offers the greatest advantage of all: it allowed Sarah and me to see our children between meetings and, in fact, at any time we had a spare minute during the working day. Even while doing one of the busiest jobs around, you need not miss out on seeing your child take their first steps or speak their first words or prepare for their first day at school.

There are, of course, the predictable downsides from living above the shop: you are always on duty. What's more, with over a hundred staff working behind that black door from desks or sometimes just chairs in corridors, basements and lofts, the building is full up – literally to the rafters. Ministers, civil servants and advisers are falling over each other. And after a century of neglect, what is now a run-down building is in desperate need of top-to-bottom renovation – something that no PM will contemplate despite each of us being presented on appointment with detailed information of its parlous condition. For the few years that you hold the office no prime minister wants to be holed up in Admiralty House or to be greeting foreign dignitaries at the door of some anonymous office block.

Living in Downing Street has one other downside: you are never out of the public eye and, although the chancellor has a Downing

Street flat that comes with the job, I did not initially warm to living there when chancellor. I felt Downing Street was Tony's home and place of work and it was right that the best and biggest flat in the building – the chancellor's flat at No. 11 – was available to Tony and Cherie's growing family. So for the first eight of my ten years as chancellor I lived in the small flat of my own in the shadow of the House of Commons. Only in 2005, when John was two and just before Fraser was born, did Sarah and I move into the No. 10 flat. We were advised to do so in the wake of a security review after 2005's 7/7 attacks, but the timing was right too: I could spend more time with the children as they grew up.

Naturally, things can go awry when a toddler is at loose in the corridors of the main decision-making centre in the country. Intrigued by the controls of the intercom system, Fraser seized them one day and in his first act of Downing Street defiance broadcast to the staff that they could now all leave for home. It was 3 p.m. On another occasion, John surprised one of America's top military commanders General David Petraeus by asking him to teach him how to march. And he astounded Rev. Ian Paisley when on a later date he blurted out: 'Show me your marching.'

But if Downing Street is an office and a home it is, rightly, also something else: a small but vital and globally recognised centre of Britain's public square. Downing Street is a public building – but with little public access. Sadly, its unwelcoming gates and tight security make it look more like a walled private compound. And so just as Tony and Cherie had done – and their predecessors before them – and with the help of an amazingly public-spirited staff who wanted to let the public see in, we opened up Downing Street for public events as often as possible – sometimes half a dozen in a week at lunchtimes and in the evenings. We held receptions to celebrate Diwali, Eid, Chanukah, Christmas and other special religious seasons, even including the Humanists for good measure; commemorations of special days that give pause for thought – like Armistice Day – and adding Holocaust Memorial Day, International Women's Day, World Aids Day and World Autism Day; celebrations for the emergency services, the military and, in particular, the NHS on its sixtieth anniversary, when Lesley Garrett delighted the assembled doctors, nurses, midwives and catering and cleaning staff with 'The Impossible Dream', her tribute – as an NHS user but also as a GP's wife – to a service achieving what was once thought unattainable.

Sarah and I had an idea of what the twenty-first-century public square could look like and how Downing Street could play a part in shining a spotlight on our modern, diverse and creative Britain. We wanted to encourage and help build a far more inclusive public square filled with men, women and children from all our nations and regions and our ethnic and religious communities – giving proper place to people who devoted their lives to public service. In particular, we invited in and encouraged people who were championing innovative community projects and who had hitherto enjoyed little of the recognition they deserved.

No. 11's main room was probably the best place for receptions – with its small outdoor balcony overlooking the gardens and Horse Guards Parade. (It would perhaps have been better known as the 'smoking gallery': when I first arrived I found it full of ashtrays and cigarette ends left behind by my predecessor Ken Clarke.) This room was also ideal for the children's Christmas party which each year highlighted the work of a children's charity. Traditionally the chancellor had played Santa Claus, but I knew I would not be very good at swapping my navy-blue suit for a red and white one, so I recruited Lord Richard Attenborough, who reprised his role as the 'real' Santa Claus in *Miracle on 34th Street*, and later Robbie Coltrane, then at the height of his fame as Hagrid in the Harry Potter films. At another children's party, my team hauled me back from a photo with Basil Brush, the famous fox puppet, worried that his 'Boom Boom' repertoire would make for an embarrassing media story.

The Downing Street events cycle allowed me to pursue my interest in the environment – many green charities came to Downing Street for the first time – and my passion for all sports, with receptions for our Olympic heroes and, of course, for national successes in cricket, rugby and football – including the Scotland football team. At one of them I introduced the then Liverpool player Michael Owen to Sir Alex Ferguson, who later signed him for Manchester United. And I remember arranging for Rebecca Adlington, our top Olympic swimmer, to be driven at speed from an Olympic reception at Downing Street to King's Cross station so she could make the last train back to Yorkshire for her training session at dawn the next day. No. 10 also hosted the

London Fashion Week reception, with Sarah heading off – successfully, as it happened – an unwelcome bid by New York to steal London's annual slot. I recall Ozwald Boateng adjusting my tie to smarten me up before I entered the room to speak.

Most of all we promoted new and often unsung charities – breaking new ground, for example, to launch a children's bedtime storybook to raise money for St George's Hospital's baby unit with a pyjama party, and hosting one party with just four days' notice to give the new Hibbs Lupus Trust a chance to launch in style when a last-minute slot came up. While No. 10 does not have its own cinema, unlike the White House, we hosted two British film premieres, one – on religious repression – smuggled out of Burma, and another on the perils of overfishing and emptying our oceans.

And we celebrated each National Poetry Day, and usually World Book Day and Children's Reading Day, with events featuring our best authors and illustrators. Poets, it is often said, are the unacknowledged legislators of the world, and writers and artists are an under-acknowledged part of our public square – despite the fact that out of the diversity of their work, which provides such a sharp and welcome contrast to the often mechanical and introverted world of politics, comes our common culture. I am proud that our government did more to fund the arts – including free entry to galleries – than any in living memory. Many of our leading authors did events. I remember in particular supporting Carol Ann Duffy's poetry-reading fundraiser that she organised at short notice for the Haiti floods disaster appeal of 2009. I said then that if politicians understood poetry the world would be a better place, and that 200 years from now our age will be remembered more for its works of art than for the work of any politician.

Our public outreach had a much wider purpose than supporting charity or campaign work. Just as I became prime minister, inspired by the work of three very innovative charity campaigners – M. T. Rainey, Jane Tewson and David Robinson – I had published a book called *Britain's Everyday Heroes*. Its purpose was to honour community campaigners and philanthropic citizens who showed us how everyday acts of generosity and kindness turn desolation into hope and build strong communities. I had wanted to follow this up as prime minister by focusing one of the 2008 Queen's honours lists exclusively on community service at home and abroad. Of course, for very good reasons, such a list is no longer decided by politicians; the compromise reached – which sadly did not survive long – was that in all future lists, often in preference to celebrities or government officials, around half the recipients would be local heroes who had improved their communities. Behind all of these initiatives was an attempt to summon a new generation to a new season of service. I learned a lot when Sarah and I used one week of our 2009 summer – our last summer in government – to volunteer in the local hospice in Kirkcaldy. I found men and women facing death were grateful for very small acts of kindness. It was a humbling experience.

One of the great questions that I faced as prime minister and that we face as a society is: what role should ethics and moral values play in day-to-day discussions of policymaking and the larger task of setting a vision before the nation? If you start from the view eloquently expressed by Rowan Williams in his book *Faith in the Public Square*, that they are an inescapable part of public life, then one of the great challenges is how to involve ethics and morality in public discourse at a time when the common framework and language for doing so – the one previously provided by religion – is no longer universally shared and when some argue that we should banish religious arguments from the public square altogether. To lose the moral energy that comes from the motivation of people with strong religious convictions would, in his and my view, diminish our civic life. But our contention that there are shared principles which create mutual obligations for each other's welfare was soon to be tested.

For our public discourse could never be the same again after the dramatic events of 2008, which raised in my mind important ethical questions and also alerted me to the problems associated with attempts to answer them. Right from its start, I had no doubt that the financial crisis was also a moral crisis – and not just for our country but for the entire western world. Its roots lay in risk-laden, speculative and often dubious financial transactions in what was an unsupervised and shadow banking system. Put in more biblical language, the world had worshipped at the altar of wealth and greed, and forgotten that a successful economy needed to be built on trust and fairness. Bankers and boardrooms had awarded themselves bonuses they did not need for work they had not done and for risks they had taken at the expense of those who went without. The phrases 'globalisation', 'free-market

economics' and 'efficient markets' had been invoked as a heedless
mantra to justify these activities, with no account given to the pain
and loss of those who suffered the consequences.

Led by Wall Street, the world had stopped listening to the lesson
Adam Smith had taught when he wrote *The Theory of Moral Sentiments*,
a book that he said was far more significant than his more famous *The
Wealth of Nations*. There he had argued that the market economy had
to be underpinned by the right ethics. The helping hand of compassion was to him more vital than the 'invisible hand' of the market.

On the eve of the G20 in London at the beginning of April 2009,
I tried to inject an ethical dimension into the debate about the causes
and consequences of the crisis, asking St Paul's Cathedral to host a
day of debate led by speeches from Kevin Rudd, the Australian prime
minister, and me. In a note he had kindly prepared for me, the chief
rabbi Jonathan Sacks cautioned against the outsourcing of morals to
markets. People, he said, were buying things they did not need with
money they didn't have for a happiness that would not last. The chief
rabbi reminded me that the word credit comes from the Latin *credere*,
which means 'to believe', and that confidence, that prerequisite of
growth, was derived from the Latin *confidere* meaning 'to have full
trust'. A good economy is based not just on balancing supply and
demand but on honouring contracts and showing respect. A country
that elevates its material comforts over and above its principles can
end up sacrificing both.

The aim of the debate at St Paul's was to underpin the resolutions
of the next day's summit with a call for more ethical behaviour from
our financial institutions and a fairer distribution of wealth across
society. At the same time, I was aware of the dangers of appearing
sanctimonious or moralising. In the words of the trade union leader
and post-war Labour minister Ernest Bevin, there was a risk of 'hawk-
ing your conscience round the country'. Mrs Thatcher had been praised
and blamed in equal measure for lecturing the people of Scotland on
the morality of wealth creation in a speech to the Church of Scotland
General Assembly, and was widely criticised when she said that the
Good Samaritan behaved virtuously not just because he had compassionate intentions but also because he had the money to do so.

Perhaps I should not have worried so much. Try as I did, I failed
to alter the terms of the debate, not because I lost the argument but

because we never really had it. Of course the bankers were under fire, but in the public's mind protecting their own savings and jobs understandably took precedence over any dissection of the roots of the crisis or any search for meaning from it.

Spring 2009 was not the first and certainly not the only time that I tried to engage the faith communities in a national debate. For over ten years their representatives had regularly joined me at No. 11 Downing Street, often monthly, for meetings as we were planning debt forgiveness and increased aid for the world's poorest countries. Later in 2005 I persuaded all the faith leaders to come together in support of a nationwide effort to reduce child poverty. And after a year as prime minister, I had decided to make a bold proposal to our faith leaders: one by one I invited them to join a non-partisan debate about British values, and as part of this to discuss our core identity as a country and where we were heading.

I hoped to start this dialogue outside London and suggested Liverpool because I knew of the ecumenism there which had been led by a hero of mine, Bishop David Sheppard. I thought we needed to talk about what we meant by community and how we could strengthen it. Could we revitalise and bring into the public square and expose to rational debate the beliefs and values that are common to all religions and many secular ideologies too? I had in mind the values referred to in the preceding chapter: our commitment to liberty and tolerance, to civic duty and strong communities, and to fairness or, as Churchill put it, 'fair play' – in other words, a civic humanism that had originated from religious beliefs but was justified on ethical and rational grounds.

I did not explain my proposal very well. Our religious leaders were understandably wary of being accused of entering the political arena. All that did emerge from our discussions was the book of essays also mentioned in the previous chapter, *Being British*, to which almost all our well-known church leaders contributed.

Not that I was by any means an uncritical supporter of the views of my own church or any of the churches. From the 1980s onwards, I came under sustained criticism from a small group of anti-abortion activists in my own constituency. I felt for the many women who were in agony about what to do when faced with a dangerous or unwanted pregnancy. While everyone had to work within an agreed set of laws,

I had no right, I told them, to tell young women faced with the most difficult of choices and who, if abortion was illegal, might have to resort to a backstreet abortionist, what to do. We should respect their own judgements, and they should not be ostracised, repudiated or rejected, nor denied the right to make their own choices.

I disagreed too with the more traditional religious hostility to research into the human embryo. I accepted there were different views and religious traditions when it came to the moral status of the embryo and its stages of development. But genetic conditions like the cystic fibrosis my younger son suffered from could be prevented by modifying the genes: was it not unthinkable to deny ourselves the scientific and medical capacity to do so?

I took a different line too on organ donation. Although most church denominations support organ donation, there was resistance among some of them to proposed new laws that assumed you would donate unless you had opted out. Shocked by the numbers dying on waiting lists for transplants, I had also seen at first hand a friend come perilously close to death before organs became available, so I supported the legislation. Of course, Labour held to the tradition that on an issue like this MPs could not be mandated to vote a particular way by anyone, neither our party nor even our constituents. To them we owed, in Burke's words, 'our judgement not our slavish obedience'. While at that time I could not take all the denominations with me, there is fortunately growing support for this option.

Appalled by the blatant discrimination against homosexuality legalised by Section 28, I am proud that our government, against religious opposition, created civil partnerships. From the Treasury I insisted on creating an equal right of civil partners to inherit and to share pensions and social security payments, and as PM I extended these rights by removing 'the need for a father' clause when considering whether to allow in-vitro fertilisation. While there were few areas where my successor David Cameron and I found common ground, I salute him for pushing through marriage equality for same-sex couples despite the fierce opposition of some on his back benches. In my time at No. 10, I actively pressed countries like Uganda to revoke prejudicial laws against gay rights, and remembering the millions of gay men and women who had been traduced I apologised for the horrible mistreatment of the mathematician Alan Turing, who helped us win the

Second World War and was then prosecuted and driven to suicide simply for being gay. The Queen was right to issue a royal pardon. But we have yet to do justice to all those whose lives were menaced by this discrimination.

One new issue forced itself to the forefront of debate in my years as prime minister: assisted suicide. Here I instinctively agreed with the weight of religious opinion that it should not be legalised. The real question was whether we could get beyond two encamped and embattled positions: that a God-given life must not be taken away and that a good life means the avoidance of unnecessary pain; once again, a predominantly religious view fighting a predominantly humanist one. I turned to my university friend for advice, Dr Colin Currie, a consultant geriatrician and clinical academic and researcher, who had taken up a part-time post in No. 10 as an adviser on the care of older people, as well as contributing to speech-writing. With his help I penned an article in *The Times* suggesting that assisted dying changed the very nature of the doctor–patient relationship. Of course, I could see the logic of allowing a dying person to end their life at a time of their choice, but could we avoid the charge that, even with checks and precautions built in, such provision could be abused and misused to permit assisted suicide on a whim or in a moment of desolation or during a prolonged period of depression? While public opinion has shifted almost overnight to favour assisted dying, I still believe there is a better way forward under which what we value – the avoidance of undignified suffering – can be upheld by the quality of end-of-life care. Thus, even when I agreed with the religious view, I did not couch my arguments in religious terms.

This was quite different from the way predecessors of mine put their case. In the 1930s Stanley Baldwin drafted most of his speeches by hand before sending them to his office staff, and would regularly inscribe on the margins of the page the phrase 'refer to A.G.'. Upon seeing these notations, conscientious civil servants duly sought the advice of the Attorney General about the legal propriety of the relevant language. Invariably the Attorney General replied that he had nothing to add. Only after many months did the civil servants realise that Baldwin was leaving an aide-memoire for himself that, as he gave the speech, he should, with great regularity, invoke as inspiration and sustenance for his argument 'A.G.' – meaning Almighty God.

Baldwin assumed he could win support by calling Almighty God in aid. Today, far from Baldwin's times, even the act of continually referring to God would be dismissed as smug, sanctimonious and out of place. When Alastair Campbell famously said 'We don't do God', he was implicitly acknowledging the fact that Britain has become a predominantly secular nation.

Historians will look back at the period from the 1950s until the early twenty-first century and be astounded by the scale and speed of the collapse in religious adherence. When I was growing up the majority of Scots were church or faith-group members. Today the figure is less than 10 per cent, with attendance perhaps closer to 5 per cent. In his book *A Secular Age*, the Canadian philosopher Charles Taylor charts the story of how in 1500 it was 'virtually impossible not to believe in God', whereas 500 years later 'faith, even for the staunchest believer, is one human possibility among others'. The majority of young children will now never attend a church, synagogue or mosque unless through school services.

I don't think these new trends in churchgoing represent an angry or bitter rejection of religion. Indeed, all too often when religious arguments are introduced into a debate there is a refusal to take sides for fear of being accused of being judgemental. Rather, I would characterise it as more of a detached indifference. I have noticed that after a death or violent incident, TV cameras often still head for the nearest church and report 'prayers were said'. It suggests a common view, that religion's main role today is to provide comfort when things go wrong without any further explanation of why.

No one can any longer assume, like Baldwin did, that the public would warm to religious assertions as justifications for action. In a more secular West, finding and uniting around a shared language and ethic to talk about what we have in common – and indeed what matters most – is ever more difficult. Without such a national conversation it is difficult in turn to find a solid basis for national unity. As the philosopher Jürgen Habermas has argued, our whole society is enfeebled without the motivation religion once inspired. I have often asked myself: in the absence of references to our religion and religious tradition – and the language we have inherited from it that infuses our debates – in what terms can a political leader or any public figure today make reference to shared moral values? Some who fear religious dogmatism would exclude all religious arguments from the public square, but might the better way forward not be, as Rowan Williams suggests, greater clarity about their proper place? For are we not impoverished as a society if the public square is emptied of such a discourse that insists on a generosity of spirit and our mutual obligations for each other's welfare?

More personally, how can a public figure who holds convictions that are religious in origin be authentic if we do not state what influences what we say and where we are coming from? A religious conviction cannot be equated with a private preference, such as a liking for sports or a taste in food or music: it is something that shapes your life, public as well as private. The public demands authenticity from our politicians – for us to reveal who we are and what makes us tick. No political leader can survive for long if people think of him or her as false, as a PR creation, as an invention of a focus group. To expect those of us with strong beliefs to leave them at the door of the House of Commons or No. 10 is to require us to bring an incomplete version of ourselves into the public arena. If the values that matter most to me are the values that I speak about least, then I am, at least in part, in denial of who I really am. This was, to my regret, a problem that I never really resolved. I suspect I was thought of as more like a technician lacking solid convictions. And despite my strong personal religious beliefs, I never really countered that impression. Instead of defining myself, I gave my opponents room to define me.

Of course, there are limits to the role of religious arguments in the public square. We should not forget the lessons of history: in the name of religion and out of a dogmatic insistence that a theocratic view must prevail, bombs have been dropped; wars have been waged; human beings have been despised, humiliated and tortured; blacks, women and LGBT people have been reviled, ostracised and persecuted – and still are. Today the greatest theocratic threat we face in the West is not that one faith group might dominate the organs of the state, but that anyone in a position of power might claim divine authorisation for their decisions, imply moral superiority, attempt to turn God into a party-political figure and circumvent rational deliberation in the name of an assertive faith. Being religious – or being from 'our' religious tradition – should not give any politician a privileged position or a get-out clause that allows them to ignore the accepted bases of authority: logic, scientific fact, experimental test, critical evaluation and an appeal to values we share in common. Indeed, people of faith have a duty to use the same tools of reasoning that a person of no faith would use, and to invoke reasons that can be understood and explained at the bar of public opinion, framing their arguments about values in such a way as to include rather than alienate those who do not share their position.

This is what the philosopher John Rawls meant when he said that in an argument it is right to weigh only those reasons that are part of 'an overlapping consensus' of 'what reasonable people could be reasonably expected' to endorse. In our public debates we should, he said, appeal not to comprehensive doctrines but to general principles around which there is a possibility of agreement. No matter how strongly felt your religious beliefs, you cannot justify your case for action purely on grounds of faith, and you have to accept that your views are more likely to command authority in the eyes of non-believers because they are supported by logic, evidence and an appeal to shared values, than because they have a religious basis. You have to argue your case in the public square, submit to scrutiny, acknowledge alternative points of view – and live with the outcome even if your point of view loses out. And that is in line with modern theological thinking: our faith obliges us to use reason, and it is an act of worship to use the brain you have.

Indeed, any public figure who introduces faith into debate must be sure they are not exploiting it for partisan reasons: deploying dogma to short-circuit democratic debate. To invoke God as if He favoured one side over the other, or to suggest your interpretation of faith must be the last word, or to play religion as some sort of trump card, to use religion cynically for political gain, is to make a mockery of the very idea of God and religion. So I would repudiate both those who say 'Do this because my religion demands it' and those who say 'Vote for me because I'm a Christian'. We must never make God a partisan figure, never claim that theology is the beginning and end of any debate, never act as if any kind of theocracy overrules democracy, and have the humility that Abraham Lincoln had: not to claim that God is on our side but to hope, as he did, that we are on God's side.

But while religious engagement within the public square must accommodate itself to public reason, public reason must also be willing to accommodate itself to religious engagement. A liberal state is not truly liberal unless it makes room for a conversation amongst believers and between them and non-believers. The question is: what are the shared terms and common ground that will allow for this?

In the wake of two of the bloodiest world wars in history, in the face of the horrors of the Holocaust and then Hiroshima, many of the world's most famous thinkers and artists rejected the very idea of a moral compass. But while religion in Europe has seen a dramatic post-war decline, that kind of nihilism has not taken over. 'Didn't we get it all wrong when we said there were no such things as moral values?' one of those thinkers, Albert Camus, is reported to have pleaded with his existentialist friends. If, he said, they were to acknowledge such things as moral values, 'that would be the beginning of hope'.

And that is where I think most of us stand. It may be, as the eminent American philosopher Michael Sandel told me, that it is now almost impossible to persuade people to think of our society as 'a moral community'; but most people would agree that in public debate moral views do matter and there can and must be a dimension to the public square that allows for ethical arguments to play their part. When in our everyday conversations we talk approvingly of decency, honour, duty and character, and value loyalty and compassion for others, we are talking about qualities that are indisputably moral.

The roots of our motivations are not exhausted in the sum total of what is called reasoning. As I understand it, morality – promoting and pursuing good human relationships – is the effort that flows from our reasoning, from what we sometimes call our moral sense and from advice we absorb that is tested in a never-ending public dialogue and confirmed in our day-to-day experiences.

Adam Smith has often been accused of saying there was no morality in markets, but as Professor Craig Calhoun, who has written widely and persuasively about the origins, role and impact of social movements, has pointed out, Smith was happy to emphasise the qualities, such as thrift, honesty and duty, that facilitated a good economy and underpinned a good society. As Craig remarks, Smith and his fellow Scottish Enlightenment writers who wrote approvingly of our 'moral sentiments' were not called the Scottish moralists for nothing.

Indeed, my reading of history suggests to me that all great social movements – from the anti-slavery crusades to the struggles for civil rights and for the renunciation of Third World debt – have been built from the ground up on the foundation of guiding ideals shared by countless, often unrecognised, men and women imbued with moral purpose.

And what is truly remarkable is that over the last fifty years the scope of what we call our 'moral sense' has expanded. When we talk disapprovingly of malice, selfishness, envy, hypocrisy and indifference, we are making moral judgements that are not now seen as specific to one culture, one religion or one continent but are universally applied and understood. It may be that centuries of civilisation have not made us, as individuals, any kinder, any more altruistic or any more dutiful, but over time the arena in which we exercise our moral sense has continued to expand. Millions have come to feel sympathy towards men and women outside their family or immediate circle and have been prepared to stand up against discrimination no matter where it is found.

In recent years, national constitutions that uphold human decency have been complemented by universal declarations of human rights that outlaw crimes against humanity, wherever they happen, and uphold the rights of women, children, the disabled, refugees and other minorities everywhere. And the main pressure to extend and update these conventions has come not from governments but from men and women with strong moral convictions.

The Iraq War that I discussed earlier raises important ethical questions about war and peace, and whether on occasions the victory of might can be a violation and not a vindication of right. And whether abroad or at home, we cannot, in my view, deal with matters of poverty and social justice without at least considering the ethical basis of our actions. Budgets, as the Rev. Jim Wallis once told me, are statements which have an ethical dimension because they tell people what we value. We might claim, as Martin Luther King did, that the Good Samaritan could have done more by dealing with the causes of the poor man's poverty, but most of us can identify with the Samaritan's good intentions and agree with some version of the 'golden rule' on which all religions are ultimately based: that we have an obligation to look out for others as we would look out for ourselves and, more than that, to act with integrity, to treat people fairly and to always show them respect.

And I have come to the view that politicians do have a role in encouraging the cooperative and altruistic instincts that are part of our moral sense, in discouraging the competitive and appetitive parts when they can damage our communities, and in demonstrating that the rights we have and the responsibilities we owe each other go hand in hand.

This is not to say that politicians should moralise, hector or sanctimoniously lecture people. It is arrogant for politicians to presume some superior moral authority that allows them to tell people what their morality should be. However, there is a big difference between foisting your moral stance on others even when they do not agree with it and appealing to an agreed morality that underpins our society.

But perhaps I did not get it quite right in repeating as a politician a phrase that my father had often used as a church minister – the need for a 'moral compass'. I was most definitely not seeking to claim a role for myself as an ethical arbiter: I was simply arguing the case for the role of ethics in politics. The distinction I should have made more clearly is between patently dogmatic attempts to impose your will on others – which are wrong – and focusing public attention on values we share.

Of course, the public square today is mediated not just by print and TV journalism, but also by Twitter, Facebook, Instagram and the explosion of social media. In both traditional and digital media, we have seen in my view a coarsening of public debate. All too often, the public square resounds with voices that are harsh and discordant, frivolous, or at times even menacing.

But while all my experience tells me that we have to be careful when we carry religious or even moral arguments into public decision-making, I believe, as I look back at the debates we had when I was an MP, chancellor and prime minister, that I should have been more open about my beliefs, more upfront in dealing with the difficulties of doing so, and more willing to take potential criticisms head-on. In the end, the choices in our public square should not be reduced to a theocratic and unacceptable dogmatism on the one hand and a joyless and barren secularism on the other. A more ethical politics can introduce an essential moral dimension into the biggest of issues, make for a far healthier and more robust national conversation, and help build what I think millions today yearn for – a better, fairer and more compassionate Britain truer to its best hopes and ideals.

CHAPTER 21

MY LIFE WITH LABOUR

This book has been the story of my life with Labour. It has also been a morality tale showing how the fortunes of a progressive party can rise and fall.

For more than a century the Labour Party has been the indispensable agent of economic progress and social justice in Britain. If a Labour Party did not exist, I believe it would have to be created if the needs and aspirations of the people are to be properly represented. Perhaps this is why for most of its members and its leaders, from Keir Hardie to Jeremy Corbyn and all those in between, Labour is not simply a party nor even a movement for change, but a cause.

Indeed, throughout my life with Labour I have borne witness to the dedicated work of committed men and women who get up in the morning thinking how to achieve a better, fairer world. They work through the day, whether as councillors or MPs or citizens in their own communities, testing themselves, their actions and their decisions against their progressive ideals. For it is the mark of being Labour to believe that people are not just competitive and appetitive by nature but cooperative and altruistic. It comes down to what you believe and what makes you tick.

Before 1997, Labour had been in power for less than a year in 1924, for two years between 1929 and 1931, and for no longer than six consecutive years in the governments of 1945-51, 1964–70 and 1974–9. And on those occasions when Labour's time in power went beyond the length of a single parliament, in the early 1950s and late 1960s, the party was already looking exhausted and beset by seemingly insoluble problems by the time it left office. So winning and holding power for thirteen years was a unique and momentous passage in Labour history.

In telling the story of these years I have tried to focus not just on the comings and goings of politicians and personalities – important and, at times, dramatic as they are – but on the movements and ideas that have shaped our times. And in this final chapter, as I have tried to do throughout the book, I write not just to review the past but to contribute to the debates ahead. In politics, nostalgia is a self-indulgent exercise. Looking back is only worthwhile if lessons from the past can influence the future.

For forty years I have fought against the assertion that prosperity will simply trickle down to those in need and that the best government can do is get out of the way. There are, of course, many obstacles to a better life that we can surmount either on our own or within our families, but government exists because there are some challenges that we cannot meet and master unless we do so together. When failures arise in the operation of markets and powerful private interests – whether banks and utilities or, as now, IT and big data companies accumulate too much power, exploit that advantage and hold people back – it is, as I have suggested earlier, Labour's historic role to call them to account and rein them in. It has been done before. It can and must be done again.

Of course, the Labour Party of the 1980s had to break with the idea of command-and-control statist socialism, the illusion that everything could be taken to and run from the centre. I remember being horrified and amused in equal measure when in the 1980s one of President Gorbachev's right-hand men visited London from the Soviet Union and, seeing that food was in plentiful supply in the shops but being unable to conceive that this might be due to the successful operation of a market in which supply matched demand, he asked to meet the controller of London's food distribution. For me it conjured up the pioneering sociologist Beatrice Webb's observation that in 1930s Russia there was no problem that an extra 300,000 junior-grade civil servants could not solve. The alternative that I favour – decentralised decision-making wherever possible – is what Labour's post-war health minister Aneurin Bevan eloquently called 'taking power to give it away'.

The aim of progressives today is the same as it has been for one hundred years: running a full-employment economy and treating people fairly. To pursue this aim since the latter half of the twentieth century, we have had to battle with an ideology at the other end of the spectrum: neoliberalism. At a private meeting in the House of Lords the last time I saw him, J. K. Galbraith recounted to me a speech he had given in Vienna City Hall to celebrate the fortieth anniversary of the Austrian Republic. In the front row were Friedrich Hayek and other Austrian neoliberal economists who had emigrated to America and won fame and status by rejecting the very notion that governments should pursue policies that advanced economic efficiency and social justice together. Galbraith started by thanking them for their contribution to Austria's development for, as he put it, if they hadn't left Austria, the country could never have enjoyed the social progress it had achieved in the forty years since 1945. With typical wit, Galbraith was exposing as an illusion the idea that social justice and economic prosperity were incompatible.

But at every point in our history, the question that arises is the same one we faced when I was starting out as a young party member: is the Labour Party in its current form the right vehicle to deliver the change our country needs?

The only way a progressive party can succeed is by being both radical and credible. It can be radical without being credible, but it will never be a successful party of power. It can also be credible without being radical, but it will no longer be progressive. In neither condition will it achieve anything truly worthwhile.

We need to be credible radicals not only in the policies we adopt but in the way we behave as a party. Political parties are communities in which, in Michael Ignatieff's words, strangers come together to defend what they hold in common. And here is the tension: between the activist impulse to pursue ideals on the one hand, and the representational responsibility to articulate and aggregate the views of the general public – and thus speak up for the needs and aspirations of the population as a whole – on the other.

In forty years of attending Labour conferences I have seen this tension at first hand. Nuclear disarmament, renationalisation, unrealisable spending pledges that defy fiscal gravity – examples abound of motions that would often be passed in the most general of forms in order to express a broad statement of objectives but which, by their very nature, glossed over the difficulties of implementation, prioritisation and funding. These motions would be passed to cheering crowds and, when the leadership failed to deliver, were inevitably followed by cries of betrayal.

I remember the bitter battles Neil Kinnock fought in order to make us credible radicals – against those who wanted telecom renationalisation, unilateral nuclear disarmament, no council-house sales and nothing to do with the private sector. Eventually most members came to accept that we could, at one and the same time, respect public opinion and honour our values. We need not be swayed by purely sectional interests. We could be the party that stood for fiscal realism and not just for more and more spending irrespective of whether it delivered better outcomes.

But it took time to persuade even the best-informed commentators of our prudence. Indeed there was a long period right up to 1997 – and even after – when each time I went on the BBC's *Today* programme the only question that the interviewer thought worth asking was 'How much will your programme cost and how much will you have to raise taxes in order to pay for it?' The Labour Party had to counter this caricature, and so we did: through the sterling efforts of Neil Kinnock, then John Smith, and then Tony Blair.

But by the mid-1990s we had to offer something more. The left's traditional answers – to pull the levers of state power through nationalisation, currency and capital controls, and restrictions on imports – had failed to recognise the new reality: that national economies were interconnected in a global economy and that money and goods now moved freely across borders irrespective of national decisions. The prevailing neoliberal orthodoxy offered a simple but dishonest framework within which to understand globalisation. In response to a fast-changing world that had moved on from the 1980s, what approach would we propose instead? Voters knew what we were against; now they had to know what we were for.

Tony and I both wanted to build the widest possible base of support for our new approach, and I supported the lengths he travelled, geographically and rhetorically, to deal with the *Sun*, *The Times* and other newspapers which had so unfairly undermined Neil Kinnock. But the question was: would New Labour take on not just the obsolete shibboleths of the left but also the prevailing dogma of the right? Would we cave in to the new neoliberal orthodoxy, fall in line with the privatisers, deregulators and liberalisers, and ignore what was becoming a defining issue – inequality – or would we take that orthodoxy on?

I was in no doubt where New Labour had to stand. We supported markets but resisted the automatic equation of markets with the public interest, so there were limits to the sale of nationally owned services that were often referred to as 'the family silver'. We supported fiscal realism but rejected the myth that national finances were the same as household budgets albeit on a larger scale, and with it the inflexible neoliberal insistence on a 'balanced budget', and so our fiscal rules would allow us to borrow in order to invest. We wanted to reward hard work, merit and the contribution citizens made to the strength of our communities, but we were not prepared to overlook the gross and glaring inequalities of income and wealth in our country. At the same time, while we stipulated that certain services – defence, law and order, health and education – could not be run on purely market principles, we needed to ensure that, within the public sector, all services were run efficiently and accountably.

As trade and industry spokesman before 1992 and shadow chancellor thereafter, I left my colleagues in no doubt that we had to embrace markets, competition and the essential role of the private sector in achieving economic growth. But we would not accept a private sector free-for-all. Competition was usually in the public interest – hence our support for new businesses joining the marketplace – but competition also required there to be laws that would challenge the power of monopolies and cartels as well, now, as the excesses of the privatised utilities. Liberalisation had a public purpose, but in areas like health and safety, environmental protection and conditions in the workplace, it was often regulation, not deregulation, that would best serve the public interest. New Labour did not mean ditching our principles but, as John Prescott was right to keep reminding us, implementing our enduring values in a modern setting.

The successful changes we delivered in our first term in government arose from that approach – the New Deal for employment paid for by a windfall tax on privatised utilities; Bank of England independence and tougher financial regulation; the minimum wage and tax credits for working families; a focus on reforms and resourcing that would put 'schools and hospitals first'. We were updating the Attlee government's post-war social contract, providing twenty-first-century answers to twenty-first-century problems. And under Labour, the public sector was in turn supporting science, innovation and a major drive to improve public and private sector productivity, and thus higher levels of economic growth.

I have described the internal battles that took place within Labour over foundation hospitals, tuition fees and deregulation, and the changed mood I sensed in No. 10 after the election victory of 2001. I recall how at one point we had to counter the suggestion from one health minister that there were no limits to the private sector's role in our NHS and, at another, having to respond to Tony's own proposals for unwarranted deregulation of the City of London and for splitting up the Treasury. I was, as always, up for modernisation, but I was never up for a narrow interpretation of it that made the only measure of being a moderniser the size of one's appetite for privatisation and liberalisation and the degree to which I could remain agnostic on reducing inequality.

I did promote some difficult privatisations – air traffic control was especially controversial – and the Treasury moved ahead in the face of internal party opposition not just with more public-private partnerships but with a new Enterprise Act that encouraged competition, with cuts to corporation tax and capital gains tax targeted at small business, as well as with the major initiatives I have described aimed at making the public sector more efficient and instituting a better system of regulation. Before and after I became prime minister I encouraged Labour to endorse the use of private providers not as an alternative to the NHS but in addition to it in order to meet our targets. So where I thought competition, liberalisation, privatisation or tax incentives to be in the public interest, I would be not just supportive but leading the charge.

However, I drew a line between modernisation that was progressive – where it could advance economic prosperity and social justice together – and the kind of modernisation that all too readily assumed that private was invariably better than public, that business interests and the public interest were always as one, and that inequality was not a pressing concern – a view of modernisation that could so easily have been mistaken for neoliberalism in disguise.

When Peter Mandelson famously said that Labour had nothing against people being 'filthy rich as long as they pay their taxes', he thought he was striking a blow in favour of modernisation. Peter did not, I am sure, mean to suggest there should be no limits on inequality, but that was how his remarks were interpreted. Yet when I said that the levels of inequality in our country were a problem – and if asked, 1 always did – or that I wanted to tackle tax avoidance, that was often depicted as the Old Labour desire to tax for its own sake.

Much of this debate was driven by the media, whose test of how far we would modernise was simpler still: 'How far would Labour move to the right?' If I wanted to attack the far left or the unions for refusing to modernise, I could get good coverage, but when I raised concerns about inequality, market failures or greed, this was considered either boring – peremptorily written off as the traditional Labour obsession with fairness – or, more likely, dismissed as anti-modernisation. When I resisted tuition fees and then even more controversially expressed concern about the exclusion of working-class students from Oxbridge and Britain's unacceptably low levels of social mobility, my proposals were branded as either the politics of envy or an attempt to dumb down at the expense of excellence. Even when I was able to prove that, without sensible controls over their borrowing, foundation hospitals would likely run up deficits which the taxpayer would have to guarantee and fund, this was branded as 'Old Labour'. For a time, 'Old Labour' and 'New Labour', 'consolidators' and 'modernisers', were thrown around as shorthand in order to isolate and dismiss party opponents, which had the counterproductive effect of obstructing rational discussion of policy. This became an increasing source of contention – and, if I'm honest, irritation – within the government.

But politics is invariably about choosing your priorities, and in government that often means sidestepping the barriers in your way by concentrating your attention where you think you can make the most difference. At the Treasury after 1997, I focused on tackling Britain's age-old problem of low productivity, on fighting poverty through welfare reform and tax credits, and on preparing the ground for refinancing the NHS. In the period after 2001, I kept reminding myself that the one way to hold the show together – and to avoid conflict – was to focus on areas of policy that did not cut across No. 10's interests. For example, I fought hard in Cabinet – and even more so behind the scenes – for educational maintenance allowances to prevent early school-leaving, additional funding for disadvantaged schoolchildren in the poorest areas, and the suite of measures to help infants in poorer communities known as Sure Start – all initiatives to promote greater equality. Where I felt honour-bound to put my alternative view – as on tuition fees – I eventually yielded to Tony's judgement. At that time, I also focused my attention on the Treasury's international development priorities, where we were able to work closely with our international development ministers and delivered not just on our government's shared objective – more aid and more effective aid targeted on the very poorest countries – but also broke new ground with our innovative plans for financing 100 per cent debt relief and global education and health.

Later on, the financial crisis frustrated the more progressive agenda that ministers had started to advance on affordable housing, access to education, the integration of social care with the NHS and the eradication of entrenched inequalities. I had, for example, been fascinated by John Prescott's proposal for building new affordable homes to be sold for £60,000, and until the crisis stalled our progress we were planning a new set of mini-towns, the release of more land for building, and measures that would open up the house-building industry to a wider range of companies and investors. After 2007 we did legislate the Child Poverty Act, start to implement new employment rights for temporary, part-time and zero-hour contract workers, and, with Harriet Harman in the lead, pioneered a radical new Equalities Act. But in the worst days of the recession, we had no choice but to concentrate our energies on stopping redundancies, bankruptcies and home repossessions. Had we been returned to government in the election of 2010, there was a comprehensive agenda to integrate health and social care, to reform tuition fees, to tackle discrimination and inequality – and, of course, to restructure the post-crisis financial sector and industrial economy – that I wanted to pursue.

With progress in these areas, and in the NHS and public services too, either halted or reversed in the Conservative years, there is so much more for the next generation of Labour to do. And although I am no longer a candidate for office, I write as a Labour Party voter and member whose thoughts are focused not on the day-to-day Westminster infighting but on the longer term: the world of 2025 when my sons will be eighteen and twenty-one years old.

Parties that lose tend, understandably, to return to first principles. It is right to ask what we are for, but soon we have to answer people's questions about what programme we propose and then persuade them of its benefits if we are to be elected again. So we cannot ignore these second and third stages: devising a credible programme of government that is sufficiently thought-through to stand up to scrutiny, and then developing a credible plan for popularising it. In recent years, though, Labour has got stuck in the first phase of its renewal – and while our leaders have announced many good and successful policy initiatives, many of which have captured the public imagination, we will ultimately be judged on how beneficial and credible our overall programme is when measured against the demands of a dramatically changed and rapidly changing new era.

My years as prime minister came at a turning point between what some have called the Age of Moderation, a time when economies and politics were relatively stable, and what I call the Age of Instability, in which economies and politics both seem more volatile than ever. If any policy is to make sense for this new age, it needs to be born out of an understanding of the current and future causes of this volatility, which are: new waves of globalisation, vast and rapid technological advances, and climate change. As I hope to show in these final pages, each of these factors leads to the inescapable question of what to do about inequality and requires of us a policy programme not of restoration – reversing the damage since 2010 – but of transformation. We need to build anew.

Climate change and our response to it will dramatically impact on the coming generations' quality of life and indeed, in some threatened island states, their very chances of survival. It is therefore impossible in the twenty-first century to talk about social justice and economic prosperity without including a third urgent imperative: environmental stewardship. Any progressive agenda must give a proper place to global carbon trading, alternative energy sources such as wind, wave and solar power, and to enforceable limits of emissions. I have described my push for a global climate change treaty that would, for the first time, oblige every state to honour its emission targets, but while the Paris agreement of 2015 has moved the world forwards, the treaty that still eludes us is more necessary than ever. Having commissioned as Chancellor the pioneering Stern Review of 2006, I believe it is now time for a sequel that maps out how investing in renewables, green technologies, carbon trading and green activism can deliver good jobs and sustainable prosperity.

While physics and chemistry were the key to technological progress in the twentieth century, in the twenty-first century genetics and biotechnology, information technology and artificial intelligence are shaping a new era of economic change that is faster and more profound than any we have previously seen. But while this technology is opening up vast new opportunities, it is also creating vast new inequalities.

Writing in the 1930s Keynes prophesied that by now technological progress would have satisfied all of our material needs, that we would all work less – as little as five or ten hours a week – and spend our many remaining hours of leisure time enjoying art, sports and culture. That transformation has not happened. As Robert and Edward Skidelsky point out in their book *How Much is Enough?*, Keynes got it wrong because new products – from washing machines and televisions to iPads and driverless cars – don't just satisfy needs, they create new ones, or at least new desires. There is, as the American historian Christopher Lasch has written, a ceaseless transformation of luxuries into necessities. And while technology has put a billion people on Facebook, it has not yet been able to take a billion people out of poverty. Across our world there are still poor people in rich countries, and there are entire societies and even continents that remain disfigured by extreme poverty.

Some are pessimistic about what lies ahead and predict that the rate of technological innovation will now decline, leading to slower or even stagnant growth in advanced economies (known as 'secular stagnation') and what they call 'premature deindustrialisation' in emerging ones: the loss of jobs to automation before the traditional rewards of wide-scale industrialisation – a broad workforce and shared prosperity – are felt. In my view, the rate of technological progress will speed up in years to come but the consequences may be no better. For all the breathtaking new possibilities brought about by technology for longer, healthier, more prosperous and more meaningful lives, it seems likely to me that only a minority will benefit from them. Some predict high levels of unemployment as new technologies replace people. I predict that levels of employment may not change dramatically but the kind of work available will: higher-paying, higher-skilled jobs in manufacturing will disappear and be replaced by low-paying, less-skilled, precarious employment in personal services – such as cleaning, gardening, cooking, childcare and care for the elderly – that will aggravate the divide between rich and poor.

This divide will be further magnified by the next wave of globalisation.

When I was growing up, most of the clothes, fridges, washing machines, cookers, radios, TVs and furniture that were sold in our local high street were manufactured by British companies in Britain. Fifty years on, trace the production of any number of high-street goods, from a T-shirt to an iPhone, and they will be found to originate in Asia. What is more, you will find that the worker sewing the designer T-shirt that sells here for anything between £10 and £50 earns less than 1p per T-shirt. The worker making £500 mobile phones, meanwhile, earns not much more than £1 an hour. Fifty years ago, even twenty-five years ago, Asian workers laboured on old-fashioned machines – usually ramshackle cast-offs from western firms – without access to the most up-to-date technology. Today, Asian workers are not only vastly cheaper to employ than western workers but they use manufacturing technology every bit as modern as our own. The effect of this – a global supply chain starting with poverty pay in Asia – is a constant downward pressure on western pay, and thus the benefits of globalisation flow disproportionately to company boardrooms and shareholders.

Some claim we have reached 'peak globalisation' and that there will now be movement in the opposite direction through 're-shoring' and the emergence of local and regional supply chains. Yet the latest research suggests that over the next decade business transacted through global supply chains will not slow but double to $190 trillion a year by 2030.

Equally concerning is the fact that global supply chains allow companies to sidestep tougher environmental laws in one country by moving their production to another. At the same time, simply by threatening to move elsewhere, taking their jobs and tax contributions with them, companies are able to pressurise governments into providing them with low tax rates. And by sheltering their profits in tax havens, they deprive nation states of revenues desperately needed for education, health, poverty reduction and economic infrastructure.

In this way, globalisation challenges social democracy at its very foundation. Deprived of their tax base, national welfare states and the publicly provided services of the past are now said to be unaffordable. Without coordinated intergovernmental action to reform the supply chain – and to set labour, environmental and taxation rules and standards – the price of our open global economy will inevitably be economic and social insecurity for millions. Combined with the further destabilising effect of technological advances on employment, the polarisation of the workforce between elites and the rest of us, the anxiety caused by migration around not just what we have but who we are, and more and more people will suffer from insecurity.

It will take many forms: an even more strongly felt sense of powerlessness; easily manipulated anxieties about crime, terrorism and migration; hard-to-answer worries about the cost of growing old; anger at jobs churned, traditional skills lost, precarious employment; young people angry that their prospects today are far inferior to those of their parents' generation, what some call the 'youthquake'. This widespread disenchantment means that running an open economy on an engine of inequality and insecurity is increasingly incompatible with stability, and it is the reason that political parties around the world, under pressure from these global realities and unable to conjure up the old nation-state solutions, are now fighting for their very survival.

After the 2010 election delivered a hung parliament, commentators were predicting the end of the two-party system in Britain. The 2017 election might have suggested a reinstatement of two-party dominance, at least outside Scotland, but whatever the current composition of the House of Commons I do not think this reflects any deeply embedded sentiment on the part of the public. For when I look more closely at the distribution of votes and the evidence of polls, I do not detect a new stability. Instead I see a new volatility that reflects a country more divided than ever – economically, socially, geographically and ideologically – between Remainers and Leavers, globalists and anti-immigrant nationalists, the socially conservative and the socially liberal.

The evidence is stark and compelling. According to a Natcen poll in 2017, nearly 60 per cent of British people considered themselves 'politically homeless', a sentiment strongest among the young, those who rent rather than own their homes, those on low incomes, and working women. The more fearful you are about the future, the more willing you are, it seems, to move from party to party searching for answers. This political homelessness – a weakening of long-term loyalties to a single party side by side with heightened partisanship over individual causes such as Europe, the NHS or immigration – may explain why the 2017 election campaign saw the biggest ever shift of support between the start of the campaign and the end: from a twenty-point lead to just 2 per cent support for the Tories, confounding the standard view that campaigns do not matter and that people do not shift their views much in the heat of a contest.

A major shift may be under way. Fifty years ago, in 1966, only 13 per cent of voters changed their minds between one election and the next. In 2015, 38 per cent of voters changed their minds. And more seemed to have done so in 2017: 35 per cent of Conservative voters and 40 per cent of Labour voters did not vote in 2015 for the parties they chose only two years later. For a hundred years social class has been the best predictor of political affiliation. But perhaps neither that, nor where you live, what age you are or what education you have can adequately account for the vast switches in preferences we are witnessing now. By election day in 2017 the state of the NHS and stagnating living standards – and Europe – had come to the fore as concerns influencing the Labour vote. Yet millions were not voting primarily for a government but were, to borrow an American phrase, 'sending a message', opting for the party that at that moment offered the most striking rebuke to the status quo. Finding someone to articulate your anger at what is happening in your life, punishing elites who are in power for not 'delivering', or just registering your protest may now explain why millions have been moving from one party to another in a sometimes futile cycle of searching for fundamental change that never happens. This anti-politics, anti-establishment mood is borne out by evidence from one post-election study of 2017: nearly three in every five voters think politicians will always let them down. Indeed, the majority think both business and politicians could never speak for them.

For some years I have been involved in helping the volunteers and care workers who run The Cottage, Kirkcaldy's innovative family centre. In 2011 it was providing Christmas toys for a hundred poor children. In 2016 there were now 800 children in need not just of Christmas presents but the basics, food and clothing. Through involvement there I meet mothers and fathers who tell me of the pressures they are under and the downward slope they feel their family finances are on, with housing, child care and social care unaffordable, schools and the NHS underfinanced, and savings in such short supply that in or out of jobs they are vulnerable to the most minor economic downturn.

Such insecurity is no longer limited to poor families on low pay but now also extends to millions in temporary or 'gig' jobs bypassed by growth, and millions more of our middle class whose wages have stagnated and who also feel that the recession has never ended. Since the 1980s Britain's middle-income earners – families with incomes 25 per cent below or above the median – have shrunk from 40 per cent to 33 per cent of the working population. Even Britain's middle class have seen a winner-take-all culture erode their pension rights, their workplace protections and their (and their children's) opportunities to do better.

Britain's workforce will never again, of course, take the cohesive form of the poorly housed, urban factory workers of the nineteenth century, nor the organised manufacturing class of the twentieth. But insecurities felt right up the income scale are now such that men and women in work – and those looking for work – are starting to appreciate that their everyday economic difficulties are not theirs alone; that the economic anxieties they live with spring from common roots; and that others like them are starting to share a similar perspective on what needs to change. Their own experience tells them that all of us go through periods in our lives – as children, as young parents, in our old age and if we are sick, lose our job or become disabled – when we are vulnerable, and that it makes sense for people across Britain to come together to pool resources and share these risks. Even before the elites have cottoned on, the public sense the urgent need to make the economy work for them. This is the message I take from the outcomes of the Scottish and European referendums and from the general elections of 2010, 2015 and 2017.

Some argue differently, that the real divide is between liberalism and illiberalism and that it is now impossible for Labour to win both the liberal, educated middle class and the more traditional, more socially conservative working class. More polemically they talk of a divide between 'open' and 'closed' minds, and by implication between an openness of outlook that supposedly follows from a good education and the greater insularity of view that supposedly comes from a lack of it. I find that patronising. It suggests that voters are suffering from some kind of false consciousness, that somehow they do not know where their real interests lie. On the contrary, as they lose out in wave after crushing wave of change, they sense all too well that our political system is failing to respond – and they are right.

The pressures that have brought this rising insecurity are so profound that, now and in the future, we cannot afford to return to past conflicts, whether between New Labour and Old Labour or between any other polarised positions. To fulfil our enduring mission, we must transcend these differences. In Abraham Lincoln's phrase, we must disenthrall ourselves and think anew to act anew. Just as climate change, technology and globalisation are changing our world, so Labour's response has to change too. Once again, we have to enact our lasting values in a new setting with new approaches. So, what might those approaches look like?

At one extreme, there is the neo-liberal or laissez-faire approach to managing our future. The economy, it is argued, works best with the least government; as long as our policies never stray from this tenet, everything else will follow. But such a free-for-all can offer no way of tackling rising insecurities and the widening divide between the very wealthy and the vast majority. Indeed, it is important to note that after reviewing the polices they pursued in the recession, international institutions such as the International Monetary Fund have had to accept that free trade and open capital markets make for losers as well as winners; that greater social equality is not the enemy but the ally of economic growth; that fiscal activism is a necessary element of anti-recession economics and should include more redistribution; in short, that their previous way of thinking, the Washington Consensus, is wrong and that we need to change the way we manage the global economy and move away from a neoliberal approach and closer to what I and others were advocating. A new consensus is forming that endorses this view.

At the opposite extreme are those who are militantly anti-globalisation, who think of globalisation as synonymous with a new stage of free-for-all capitalism. Yet adherents to this view have no answer to the question of how we manage global flows of capital and the global supply chains other than denouncing their very existence. While there may be a moral high ground to be claimed in opposing globalisation, there is no road to the future through the command-and-control economics of the twentieth-century nation state.

At the same time, we cannot afford to ignore real and understandable fears about the erosion of national identity and traditional culture, which the neoliberal view tends to ignore, and genuine concerns about security and order that have given birth to the 'take back control' movements. We can debate whether it is economic insecurity or a concern about identity that does most to fuel these fears, but either way we must address the concerns of voters who may be demanding greater equality on economic issues but who are traditionalist on social issues, demanding greater order and social cohesion.

A progressive Labour must therefore move forward on two fronts that are inextricably linked: internationally, with an agenda for international cooperation to tame the excesses of globalisation, and domestically, with an agenda that offers economic security and social justice – and with environmental progress integral to both. What unites them is an egalitarian vision: of a Britain fair to all or, to employ a phrase I used for years in opposition and government which is now back in vogue, a Britain for the many and not just the few.

But when we talk of equality, we must be precise. As my friend the Nobel Prize-winning economist Amartya Sen asks: equality of what?

In 1997, in the springtime of the Labour government, Tony Blair wrote to the iconic philosopher Isaiah Berlin, famous for his *Two Concepts of Liberty*, to ask him why we can only advance what Berlin termed 'negative' freedoms – the freedom from coercion – and not 'positive' freedoms – the freedom to pursue goals like equality – as well. Because of his experience of Nazism and Soviet Communism, Berlin had spent a whole life attempting to caution against the over-excited passions that led to intolerance and extremism, which flowed, he felt, from demands for positive freedoms. But Tony was right: our generation can do better than the last. Championing negative liberty is not enough if, in the world of 2017 and beyond, we are to uphold the dignity of every individual.

At its most basic, positive liberty is about ensuring that a child born into poverty will have every chance to fulfil their potential and every obstacle in their way removed. This is what I mean by equality. The neoliberal may call for opportunity for all, but such a demand is insincere rhetoric if we do not address the very injustices that put genuine equality of opportunity beyond reach. This narrow version of equality of opportunity is, in effect, the opportunity to be unequal.

Anti-globalisation protestors, on the other hand, would erect self-defeating protectionist barriers to the outside world, which in the end would impede growth, diminish our economy and leave us all worse off. By favouring equality of outcome, which cannot be achieved without unacceptable restrictions on individual freedom, they would deny recognition for hard work, initiative and merit. For me, the progressive challenge is to find a modern balance between the competing claims of equality and liberty to ensure we treat every citizen with dignity.

So, how might this be done?

I saw at first hand in 2008 during the global financial crisis that we cannot fully succeed in delivering national prosperity without concerted international action. As I have argued at several points in this book, international cooperation is therefore a prerequisite if we are to reform the global financial system and the European Union and ensure that, in a reformed global supply chain, companies do not pollute, syphon money into tax shelters or exploit their workforces. I saw also how difficult it is to persuade the general public that remedies for problems faced at home – job losses and stagnant wages – actually lie abroad and cannot be delivered solely by action within or by Britain. When I talked of global problems and how they needed global solutions, it was mendacious but all too easy for my Conservative opponents to claim that I was simply trying to shift the blame. But if we do not explain that we need international as well as national remedies to the insecurities that are intrinsic to today's economy, we are failing in our duties as politicians.

Just as our shared planet makes the need for international coordination on climate change intuitively obvious, so our global economy means that any standards we set for our own financial institutions – to cap and tax bankers' bonuses, for example – must be globally coordinated. Low-taxed and unregulated financial centres are already well positioned to steal business and deprive Britain of tax revenues. A Labour government can, of course, raise the minimum wage and introduce wage subsidies like tax credits, and trade unions are more necessary than ever to fight for justice in our workplace, but jobs are already being lost to companies and countries that offer the commercial advantages of low environmental, tax and safety standards. If nothing is done to end the exploitation of workers in other parts of the global supply chain, then wages in Britain will continue to stagnate and we too will suffer the fallout from a race to the bottom.

At a national level, meanwhile, our task is to destroy, systematically and aggressively, all impediments to a fair start in life and a fair share of globalisation's benefits. Of course it would be naïve not to recognise the reality that children start from different family advantages, will possess different talents and have differing ambitions but, in my view, equality does not ever mean everyone being the same. Rather, equality is about everyone having the best chance to make the most of who they are.

I often tell the story of the surgeon who saved Ronald Reagan's life when he was shot just after becoming president in 1981. As he was being wheeled into the operating room Reagan quipped that he hoped the doctors were all Republicans. Shortly after his recovery he made a speech thanking Joseph Giordano, the Italian-American surgeon who had led the medical team, praising him as someone who had started with nothing, worked his way up, paid his own way through university and was a living example of the American dream. In response, the surgeon penned an article for the *LA Times* that corrected Reagan's account. Yes, he had worked hard, but he had been given a scholarship for college and national funding to take him through his postgraduate degree in medicine. He owed everything, he wrote, to the support he had received from the community. Individual initiative by itself would not have been enough: his whole future was made possible by public investment in education.

There should be no cap on the ambition of a child who is poor, as this surgeon-to-be once was; no ceiling, glass or otherwise, to thwart aspiration; no barriers that prevent her or anyone else achieving their potential. To achieve this, we require nothing short of an educational revolution: to improve teacher quality, empower school heads, develop relevant curricula, offer lifelong access to educational opportunities and use the latest technology to transform the learning environment.

In the years I have served as UN special envoy for global education, I have seen how education holds the key not just to a fairer society but also to a stronger economy. Despite the growing use of robots and AI, it is human capital – our ability to innovate, acquire new skills and be entrepreneurial – that is the crucial determinant of a company's success and a country's progress. Investing in education is the starting point for re-establishing the link between high productivity and jobs with good pay. Alongside this, though, we must remind ourselves of the work that matters most and value it accordingly. This means valuing more highly – and paying more for – currently low-paid but highly responsible jobs in the personal services like nursing and caring.

We must also ensure that workers benefit from a more equitable sharing of corporate profits that are currently reserved for a small elite of executives and shareholders. It is only fair that all employees should benefit from the successes they help create. Global corporations resist paying higher wages arguing that doing so in advanced economies will render them uncompetitive. One answer is profit-sharing, which is not an obstacle to competitiveness but a spur to it: while it spreads the benefits of success from the few to the many, it also incentivises employees, thereby increasing productivity overall.

One of globalisation's most persuasive historians, Branco Milanovic, has observed that redistribution of wealth and income has rarely been achieved outside of war, revolution or the collapse of a state. In Britain today, however, the chief executives of the biggest companies now earn on average 386 times more than workers on the national living wage, demonstrating that the biggest divide in income is between the top 1 per cent, who now amass 16 per cent of all income, and the rest. Such disparities of income and wealth have become so entrenched that they should offend even those who support mild forms of equality of opportunity, as inequality of outcome in one generation is creating what some now call a 'hereditary meritocracy' and destroying the possibility of equality of opportunity in the next.

I believe that it is not anti-wealth to say that both within companies and across the country the wealthy should do more to help those who are not so wealthy. Between 1997 and 2010 we tried to create a far fairer tax system, not just through tax credits but also through tax rises at the top – by twice raising the National Insurance ceiling, by increasing rates of stamp duty on expensive properties, by clamping down on tax avoidance and then, in 2009, by introducing a higher rate of income tax. Once we include tax credits, the share of tax paid by the top 10 per cent rose from 34 per cent of all taxes in 1997 to 43 per cent in 2010. Now, under the Conservatives, the share has started to fall again, making Britain more unequal. In fact, the top 20 per cent, who accounted for 53 per cent of taxes in 1997 and saw their share rise as high as 65 per cent after Labour's top-rate rises went through, now account for 62 per cent of taxes.

The Conservatives under David Cameron and George Osborne wanted to cut the top rate of income tax from 50 per cent to 40 per cent, but they cannot now risk the wrath of the electorate by lowering the highest tax rate – for those earning above £150,000 – below 45 per cent. Now that vast inequalities of income and large-scale tax avoidance have been exposed, the right is on the defensive. But there is more we can do. Ownership of capital is far more unequally distributed than income, and while living standards are, of course, raised by measures such as increasing the living wage, widening access to capital is one sure way of raising those standards further. Responding to this, the Child Trust Fund that we introduced in 2005 gave every child for the first time a share of the nation's wealth. It entitled all children to an endowment at birth, and at seven and eleven, and allocated more to those who were least well off. Through its reinstatement, as well as through profit-sharing, employee ownership and fair taxation, we must widen the ownership of wealth. Today a windfall tax on the IT and big data giants is as justified as were past windfall levies on the utilities. And as I have argued earlier, a global levy on our banks is now an essential element of any modern economic policy, if only to insure ourselves against the need for a future bank bailout.

Growing up in Kirkcaldy I hoped that the grinding poverty I saw around me could be eradicated in my lifetime. And yet it is a sad fact that even though child poverty fell during our government, more children – 4 million of them – are in poverty today than in 1965 when the Child Poverty Action Group was founded to deal with a poverty emergency. On current trends by 2022, 5 million children – one child in every three – will be consigned to poverty, more than at any time in the Thatcher–Major years. No child should be brought up in damp, substandard homes, and there is for this reason if no other a need to return to John Prescott's original plan to build affordable houses. Nor should any child grow up ill-clad, undernourished, with basic needs neglected and basic chances denied. We must try once more to popularise the single most effective measure of ending child poverty, superior to raising tax thresholds, introducing a citizens' income or even raising child benefit: tax credits.

Taken together, these proposals and those I have made earlier in the book for reinvigorated public services can unite all the nations and regions of Britain in a proud and shared endeavour. Such a project represents a demand for equality not for its own sake but for liberty's sake: to give every British family the best chance to make the most of their lives. In response to those who criticise this as a move to the centre, I would reply that we will be moving the centre towards the progressive cause.

Of course, issues of identity and culture matter as well as economics. Some will conclude that no single party can be broad enough to bridge the divide between so-called 'globalists' and 'nativists', 'cosmopolitans' and 'communitarians', 'anywheres' and 'somewheres', or hold together the socially conservative 'settlers', the swing-voting 'prospectors' and the socially liberal 'pioneers'. It is true that there are many who think of themselves as somehow being more British than others and try to make patriotism their exclusive preserve. And we have yet to convince others, many of them potential Labour supporters, that immigration, if managed well, will not weaken our country's sense of national identity or undermine social cohesion.

I would argue that we can address these concerns and enhance cohesion by matching today's celebrations of diversity – and of a Britain 'safe for diversity' – with the recognition and celebration of the common bonds that bind us together. Separate national, regional and ethnic loyalties are now well established across a United Kingdom that has lived with diversity as long as it has existed. But by putting more emphasis on what we hold in common, we can marginalise the intolerance that preys on difference.

To sum up, we can approach the future in two ways, both of which lead us to similar conclusions: we can start, as I have in this chapter, from the massive insecurities and inequalities that twenty-first century globalisation now generates, and build for new times a fresh paradigm, based on the liberation of human potential, within which we deliver modern policies that create a fairer, more prosperous and more cohesive country; or we can start, as I did in the previous two chapters, by identifying the enduring British values that most of us share, and by coming together in support of them and by applying them in updated policies for new times, we can meet and master the challenges that lie ahead.

What is clear is that the Britain of 2017 needs – even more urgently than the Britain I led ten years ago – a single national conversation that can engage the whole country, and which can take us beyond today's entrenched, tribal divisions – between those who are for and those who are against Brexit, immigration, nationalism, capitalism and globalisation – a British Tower of Babel with factions ensconced in their own silos, using social media to talk at and across one another rather than to and with each other.

We have to recognise the very real barriers to such a conversation: that in a multi-national state such as ours, there is no shared basis for a nationwide dialogue that appeals to common ethnicity; that popular trust in, and support for, national institutions like Parliament to lead such a conversation cannot be taken for granted; and that in a secular age, appeals to shared religious traditions have far less resonance than ever before. So, as I have suggested, we need to rediscover a common language that speaks to, and values, our traditions of tolerance and our love of liberty, and in particular gives voice to the British peoples' strong sense of social responsibility, civic duty and our instinct for fairness – what we often call 'fair play'. These enduring values, in support of which millions of our fellow citizens can find common cause, are the golden threads that tie the Britain of the past to the Britain of today and tomorrow. As an expression of what our country is about, they stand alongside, while constituting a uniquely distinctive British alternative to, France's 'liberty, equality and fraternity' and America's claim to be the 'land of opportunity'.

Such a conversation would thus expose as out of date and out of character the two ideological extremes that have never commanded much support in our country: a very un-British selfish individualism that runs counter to our long-standing commitment, as reflected in the NHS, to an equitable pooling and sharing of resources and risks across our country; and an equally un-British over-centralisation of state power that would stifle both individual initiative and Edmund Burke's 'little platoons' of public-spirited citizens whose voluntary service makes for strong communities and reflects our need 'to belong'.

Upon this foundation, rooted in a modern articulation of lasting values, and rejecting the ahistorical notion that Britain is at its best when it chooses to stand apart and alone, we can debate, agree and unite around a credible and radical vision for the future of a United Kingdom founded on liberty and built around fairness – one that commits us to minimising the insecurities that globalisation has created and to maximising the opportunities young people should and can have.

What is certain is that we cannot chart a path ahead by reverting to the policies of the 1940s, the 1970s, or even those of the years after 1997. The test now is to live and lead not through attempts to re-live these years but in the world that is ours now, and the world that is to be. I said in the Introduction that there are cycles in politics: eras of collectivism and then of individualism; periods of rapid change that yield to times of consolidation; demands for a new stability that then give way to an impatience for something new. I am convinced that Britain is once again a country ready to move forward: a Britain tired of adversarial extremes, exhausted old ideologies and politicians with nothing to offer beyond themselves – and tired also of its inability to move our national conversation beyond all this. The British people are yearning for something different. There is an impatience for change. A new generation has a right to dream and to hope – and we have a responsibility to respond.

AFTERWORD: OUR TIMES

Modern leadership offers huge opportunities and makes huge demands: the pace and unpredictability of Macmillan's 'events' is just a starting point. The 24/7 news cycle – avid for coverage and comment – adds an urgency that is often disproportionate to a story's relevance beyond that news cycle. Headlines about crises, splits, anger, fury and horror – not always justified by the details that follow – compete round the clock for the attention of readers, listeners and viewers.

As a result, leadership is sometimes left with too little time to think, to sift and absorb information, to plan, to persuade and deliver. And yet the challenges we confront are greater than ever. In this book, I have set out the four strands that in my view have defined our times and formed the backdrop to my life in politics – globalisation as an unstoppable economic force, neoliberalism as a long prevailing but failing economic theory, the sometime perilous condition of the Labour Party and the fate of Britain itself. Each of these has been a source of mounting pressures during the forty years I have been in politics.

I came into politics with a conviction reinforced again and again across the years: to lead is to champion a hopeful vision of the kind of country most of us believe in. Ideally, perhaps, the top job would be best delivered by someone with a range of qualities from the analytic to the interpersonal, preferably at the highest level. I have found that in politics no one person can offer all the qualities, all the time or even some of it, that modern leadership requires – the problem-solving skills associated with the engineer, the spirit of enquiry of the scientist, the mastery of fine detail of the mathematician, the command of substance of the teacher, the ability to communicate of the writer, all preferably combined with the compassion of the finest examples of the caring professions, and the patience of a saint too. And whether someone like that could rise to lead a major political party is another question. But while most leaders can survive without some of these gifts, they are totally lost without a sense of the bigger picture – a clear vision of what you want to achieve matched by the willpower to look beyond the preoccupations of the day and never lose sight of your goals.

Leadership, I have also observed in these pages, can flourish only with effective teamwork, and it requires a talent for being ahead of events, though not too far ahead.

Making people feel part of a common mission was exactly what Field Marshal Montgomery did addressing his troops the night before battle. Having asked them what was the most important thing as they prepared for combat, he heard answers like 'air support', 'the quality of our tanks' and 'the sophistication of our weapons'. He begged to disagree. He told them 'the most important thing you have is you' – in other words, the strength and unity they had built together, the sense they had that together they were part of a bigger mission.

At the Treasury I brought together a team of civil servants and advisers who grew in government and learned together. As prime minister, I found that after the great collective efforts to surmount the initial crises of my first months in No. 10 – from the terrorist attack to foot and mouth and Northern Rock – engendering the same kind of team spirit we had in the Treasury was more difficult. In part, it was because after ten years in power Labour was running out of steam. In part, it was the modern nature of prime-ministerial politics, having to handle a multiplicity of crises in a twenty-four-hour cycle. In part, it was the difficulties in creating the right balance between ministers, officials and advisers, which meant I found myself with too little time to focus on longer-term strategic issues where I think I had most to offer and where my input might have made more of a differ-ence. I did not fully resolve this until preparing for the G20 in the wake of the financial crisis. Then, an already highly talented group of people rose to the occasion with tireless commitment and dedica-tion built around a shared sense of purpose.

I wrote in the Introduction about the importance of turning points – and of course, no leader will foresee every high noon. But despite the turning points I missed, I believe it is fair to say I spotted and took in hand one or two. In 2002, I thought the time was right after careful preparation to persuade people to pay more in tax to renew the NHS. In 2003, I thought the time was wrong to join the euro, and despite my colleagues' initial enthusiasm for the common currency, I was able to convince them how difficult it would be for Britain. It is, however, no comfort to me as we deal with the impact of Scottish, Welsh and English nationalism that I feel ahead of my time in warning that we have to find a shared sense of purpose for a United Kingdom that otherwise would be united in name only.

I am often asked what we can learn from Britain's most famous political leader, Winston Churchill. If Barack Obama wrote of the audacity of hope, Winston Churchill taught us the necessity of hope. He is remembered precisely because he, more than anyone else, understood the importance in our country's darkest moment of conveying a message of hope. Indeed, I suspect that when Churchill famously rejected the portrait of him at eighty years old by the artist Graham Sutherland, it was precisely because he saw himself depicted as old, austere and withdrawn – and not the inspirational figure of hope he knew a leader had to be. No leader, now or in the future, can afford to ignore that lesson of history.

I write of lesser tests, smaller peacetime tests, but in the biggest test that I faced – the gravest financial crisis of our lifetimes – our country desperately needed a message of hope.

While I did not predict the recession that exploded out of America and infected the world, I did immediately grasp the need to act with unprecedented speed and our government was the first to push for cooperation among all the leading economies: first to avert a Great Depression, and second, to deliver far-reaching reforms of the financial sector to prevent a future collapse. The former succeeded, but not the latter. Unlike the leaders whom I most admire, I fell short in communicating my ideas. I failed to rally the nation. We won the battle – to escape recession – but we lost the war – to build something better. Banking should have been transformed, our international institutions refashioned, inequality radically reversed – and if we are to be properly equipped to face the next crisis this is still the agenda we must pursue. It saddens me that our economy succumbed to a lost decade of austerity, division, protectionism and now isolation.

Through thirteen years in office, we did, as I have recounted, take big decisions in other areas that reshaped our own economy and society, and I believe these decisions will stand the test of time and changing political tides. I look back with pride on path-breaking reforms which could never have happened without a Labour government – Britain's first legal national minimum wage, tax credits to tackle child and pensioner poverty, repairing a nearly broken NHS, Sure Start to give the youngest children better chances, international debt relief and the trebling of aid for schools and hospitals in the poorest countries.

The mission I felt – and feel – most strongly about is championing the cause of children, not just in Britain but also in the most difficult and most desolate places in the world. Since my schooldays, I had dreamed of what I could contribute in any way, however small, to creating a world free of poverty. When in 1980 Edward Kennedy famously spoke of 'the dream [that] shall never die', he was challenging millions like me. And for me, the dream does not fade. It is as real today as ever it was, part of who I am, what I have become and what continues to drive me on.

I am forever awestruck by the men and women of goodwill in charities, philanthropy and non-governmental organisations who do so much for so many every day. I have explained in an earlier chapter why I believe that encouraging and energising what is best in our moral sense is an indispensable element of good leadership.

I remain convinced that no matter what men and women of compassion accomplish through individual efforts, those who dismiss the power of collective action – nationally or internationally – are seriously mistaken. The advancements that bend the arc of history come from steps that are never taken alone.

Indeed, most people I know who undertake public service say they do so because they want to 'make a difference'. Their dedication and daily achievement – at times against the odds – and their self-sacrifice, confound the reactionary and self-serving myth that the best government is the one that does the least. In fact, the only governments that really count are those with a cause.

I often tell the story of David, the eleven-year-old football-loving boy who wanted to be a doctor and loved making people laugh – and whose short life is memoralised in the children's room of the Rwanda Museum. He was brutally murdered in the genocide of 1994 and his death was all the more tragic because he died just after telling his mother, who died alongside him, that the United Nations was coming to save them. In his idealism, that young boy believed that political leaders can act to save and lift up lives.

When politics fails, people go hungry and suffer. They cannot triumph over disease, are left without the light of learning, and they lose hope. But when politics succeeds, people live and are more secure; the young are educated; the sick are cared for; and people are empowered to make the most of their talents. And politics can offer not just words of hope but the resources to make that hope real – to help bridge the gap between what millions of people are and what they have it in themselves to become.

Often change is slow, sporadic and undramatic. But sometimes an idea can change the world and the impact can be as dramatic as a train that starts slowly, suddenly and unmistakably picks up speed, then roars ahead and becomes unstoppable.

I do not miss the trappings of office, but there is a frustration. It can literally take years to do what you might have been able to accomplish in a few minutes as prime minister or as chancellor. Not to say even that is easy. In politics, you must decide and then you have to persuade – and you have to overcome the political tendency to think too much of the short term. Through thick and thin, amid the clamour of the days, you have to stay true to the dream. That I hope I did most of the time.

ACKNOWLEDGEMENTS

Writing about things past, and especially about one's own life, did not come easily to me, and the reader may have noticed how much I have tried to infuse my reflections on the past with thoughts about the future.

While in the nineteenth century most interactions were by letter and thus recorded, in the twentieth century most of the important conversations were by telephone with little recording of them. I was the first prime minister to use emails regularly, and this – and, of course, access to Cabinet and Treasury papers – has allowed me to chart my day-to-day interactions with my staff, my colleagues and world leaders.

And so, for his endless enthusiasm for retrieving, analysing and checking information and sources, I am grateful to Ross Christie, who headed the research effort and whose encyclopedic knowledge of just about every relevant place and event has informed my writing greatly to its benefit.

Andrew Hilland edited this draft and, as he has done with recent books on Scotland and Europe, advised on the whole manuscript from start to finish – and did so while at the same time distinguishing himself as a Labour candidate for Lanark and Hamilton East in the 2017 general election.

Bob Shrum is a long-time friend, himself the author of a highly readable and eloquent memoir of his life, and sacrificed some of his well-earned holidays to mentor me.

For nearly half a century – on numerous projects and now on this project too – I have been fortunate to draw on Dr Colin Currie's wise and measured advice.

As I have written this book, Kirsty McNeill has shared with me her love of Scotland and her passion for international development, and she did so while, as always, working night and day for the causes she believes in.

I have benefited hugely from Bruce Waddell's broad knowledge of the ups and downs of Scottish life and politics gained over many years as a highly successful editor of the *Daily Record*.

I have also been grateful for suggestions from Michael Wills, now Lord Wills, with whom I served in government and whose contribution I mention earlier in this book; from David Muir whose strategic advice I have always valued; from Professor Craig Calhoun who understands globalisation in all its different manifestations better than anyone I know; and from Cormac Hollingsworth who combines an intellectual acumen with his active campaigning for social justice.

This draft has also been read and commented on by Alistair Moffat, whom I have known and worked with for forty years as a writer, broadcaster and family friend, and by two long-time friends, Murray Elder, mentioned earlier, and Wilf Stevenson, whom I first met at Edinburgh University and who has, in turn, run the BFI and the (John) Smith Institute, been a senior adviser in No. 10, and a valued member of the House of Lords. All have helped me recall and write of events that, in some cases, I might have preferred to forget.

I am grateful also to Gavyn Davies, Shriti Vadera, Ed Balls, Sue Nye, Nick Butler, Matt Cavanagh, Nick Catsaras, Tom Fletcher, Robert Skidelsky and Des Browne for sharing with me their thoughts on individual chapters. I thank them all for their great generosity in terms of time and expertise. Nick Vaughan and Phil Wales have helped me greatly by checking important statistics.

I have written a lot about my home county of Fife which I represented in Parliament for thirty-two years, and to which, no matter where I travel and how far, I always return. In my account, I have drawn on help from friends from schooldays onwards: Peter and Marilyn Livingstone, Alex Rowley (now Scottish Labour Party deputy leader), David Ross, Neil Crooks, Judy Hamilton, Lesley Laird, Jayne Baxter and Bill Taylor. In my work in Fife I have also drawn on help from Henry McLeish, Lindsay Roy, Lesley Hamilton, Angus Hogg, Bill Livingstone, Helen Martin, Rhona White, Margo Doig, Chloe Hill, Jyoti Bhojani, Rachael Thomas – and from Jim Stark and Allan Crowe, two great local-newspaper editors whose friendship I valued and still do. So much of what I have written is based on memories of Fife friends whose guidance and support over many years helped me but who are no longer now with us: David Stoddart, Jim McIntyre, Alex Falconer, Tom Donald, Bert Gough, Helen Dowie and Jimmy Dyce are all remembered and here in spirit in this book.

Nick Brown first showed me how Parliament works: a welcome, indeed crucial, gift. And I'm grateful for those who helped me by serving successively as my parliamentary private secretary: Don Touhig, John Healey MP, Ian Austin MP, Ann Keen, Anne Snelgrove, Angela Smith, Jon Trickett MP and, most recently, Alison McGovern MP, in whom so many hopes for Labour's future rest. For generous assistance and support over my years in Parliament I'm grateful to Sandy Hunt, Carol Bird, Janet Crook, Angie Forrester, Cathy Koester, Lizzie Sowells, Jane Ashley and John Smythe.

For my time at the Treasury I've drawn on accounts – some private, some public – from Ed Miliband MP, Spencer Livermore, Charlie Whelan, Geoffrey Robinson MP, Damian McBride and Michael Ellam.

For help in my time at No. 10, I'm grateful to all political advisers whose individual contributions cannot be properly reflected simply by naming them, but to whom I am nonetheless forever indebted: Greg Beales, Theo Bertram, Iain Bundred, Nicola Burdett, Konrad Caulkett, Dan Corry, Brendan Cox, Patrick Diamond, Jo Dipple, Michael Dugher, Beth Dupuy, Justin Forsyth, Stuart Hudson, Michael Jacobs, Gavin Kelly, Richard Lloyd, Patrick Loughran, Jennifer Moses, David Muir, Nicola Murphy, Geoffrey Norris, Kristy O'Brien, Will Paxton, Nick Pearce, Lisa Perrin, Kath Raymond, Gila Sacks, Anthony Vigour, Chris Wales, Stewart Wood and John Woodcock. I am also grateful for advice I have received over the years from David Cannadine, Linda Colley, Iain McLean, Colin Kidd, Vernon Bogdanor, Rosaleen Hughes, Roger Harding, Alex Evans, Andrew Balls, Gene Frieda, Michael Klein and Nick Lowles. At the Treasury and Downing Street, there is an unsung army of public servants, for whose hard work and consistent presence I am endlessly grateful, and whom I cannot name: from the most senior civil servants to the vital back room who cover cleaning, catering, secretarial and security duties for service often far beyond the call of duty. Now that they are no longer in Whitehall I have permission to thank by name Leeanne Johnston, Helen Etheridge, Barbara Burke, Lucy Parker, Jonathan Portes and Simon Lewis. I am grateful for the continuing support of the Metropolitan Police and the Fife officers of Police Scotland.

The political support I received at No. 10 was led by Fiona Gordon, Rachel Kinnock, Anna Yearley, Joe Irvin, Clare Moody, Lisa Forsyth, Rachel Maycock, Jonathan Ashworth MP, Balshen Izzet, Oona King and Tom Watson MP. I am grateful to all the many ministers and Labour MPs I served alongside, and to the Labour Party general secretaries during and after my time as PM: Peter Watt, Ray Collins, and now Iain McNicol, and the unstintingly hard-working Labour Party staff and volunteers. I am grateful too for the strong relationship I enjoyed – even when sometimes we disagreed – with my trade union friends. I worked closely with Tony Woodley, Bill Morris, John Hannett, Dave Prentis, Rodney Bickerstaffe, Michael Leahy, Billy Hayes, Frances O'Grady, Derek Simpson, Ken Cameron and many others across the country.

In my work with the United Nations, I've had the support of three UN secretary generals whom I admire greatly: Kofi Annan, Ban Ki-moon and António Guterres; and in my education work I have had the privilege of working with committed philanthropists who have become great friends – Asad Jamal of the Pakistan Children's Foundation, John Sexton, president emeritus New York University, Jim Wolfensohn and Stuart Roden – as well as drawing upon the outstanding leadership in their own areas of expertise of Shaheed Fatima QC, Dr Justin van Fleet, Liesbet Steer, Kevin Watkins, Glenys Kinnock, Marylouise Oates, Professor Iain Begg and Reid Lidow and the great heart surgeon Professor Sir Magdi Yacoub who leads the charity Chain of Hope.

To this day Sarah and I share a phenomenal office team in London who have helped steer this book to completion, and I am grateful to Gil McNeil who leads and coordinates our office, Mary B. Bailey, Alexander Fincham, Erin Mulhatton and Ross Fulton – with additional thanks to David Boutcher and Michael Skrein for legal support, and to Jamie Carroll. I have been fortunate to draw on the expertise of David Robson, Rick Gold, Graeme Milligan, Jane Zuckerman, Brenda Price, Stuart Beveridge and Ronald Stevenson. Jony Ive, now president of the Royal College of Art, and Steve Kelly, have both helped make me a little more technologically literate than I once was.

A book is compiled in stages, and none of it could have been completed without the expertise, patience and friendship of Jonny Geller and Catherine Cho at Curtis Brown, Richard Cable, Stuart Williams, Will Hammond and David Milner at The Bodley Head, and their media team led by Joe Pickering and Christian Lewis.

Ours is a close family who have always been there for each other and over our lives my brothers have sacrificed hugely to support me, as have their families, so I owe a huge debt of gratitude to John, his wife Angela and their children Karen and Jonathan with their young families; and to Andrew, Clare and their now grown-up sons Alexander and Patrick.

Sarah's parents Pauline and Patrick and her many brothers with their families have always been supportive of me beyond any call of family duty. Our children have grown up with Melanie Darby and now Vicky Taylor caring expertly for them when Sarah and I have been busy in our public duties, and we really could not have done anything without them.

Sarah has always supported me and I can never thank her enough for her love and enduring friendship. Over several months our children, John and Fraser, would have preferred me to be playing football or computer games with them. By way of an apology, I am dedicating to them – with deep love – a book which took me away from them for a whole precious summer.

Next year, boys, no book, and much more time with the two of you.

INDEX